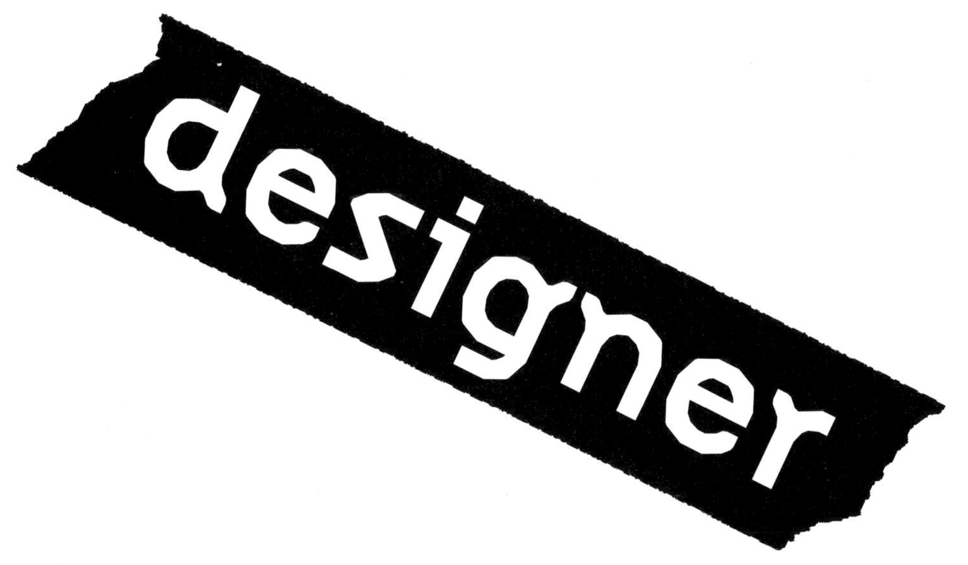

designerposters

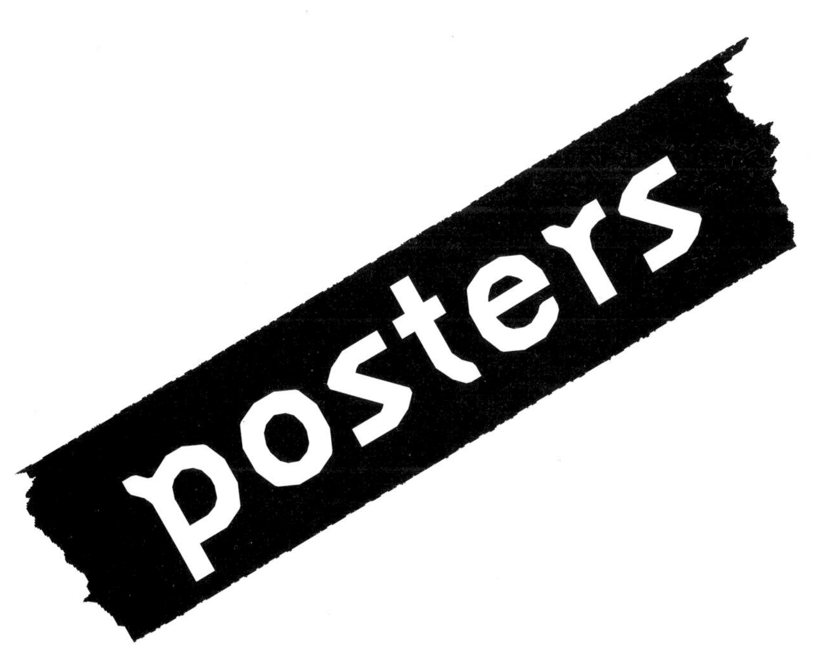

First published in the United States of America by:
Rockport Publishers, Inc.
146 Granite Street
Rockport, Massachusetts 01966-1299
Telephone: (508) 546-9590
Fax: (508) 546-7141

Distributed to the book trade and art trade
in the United States by:
North Light, an imprint of
F & W Publications
1507 Dana Avenue
Cincinnati, Ohio 45207
Telephone: (513) 531-2222

Other Distribution by:
Rockport Publishers
Rockport, Massachusetts 01966-1299

ISBN 1-56496-247-4

10 9 8 7 6 5 4 3 2 1

Art Director: Lynne Havighurst
Designer: Minnie Cho Design
Cover Image: Credit on page 51
Assorted Photography: Douglas Cannon Photography

Manufactured in Hong Kong by
Regent Publishing Services Limited

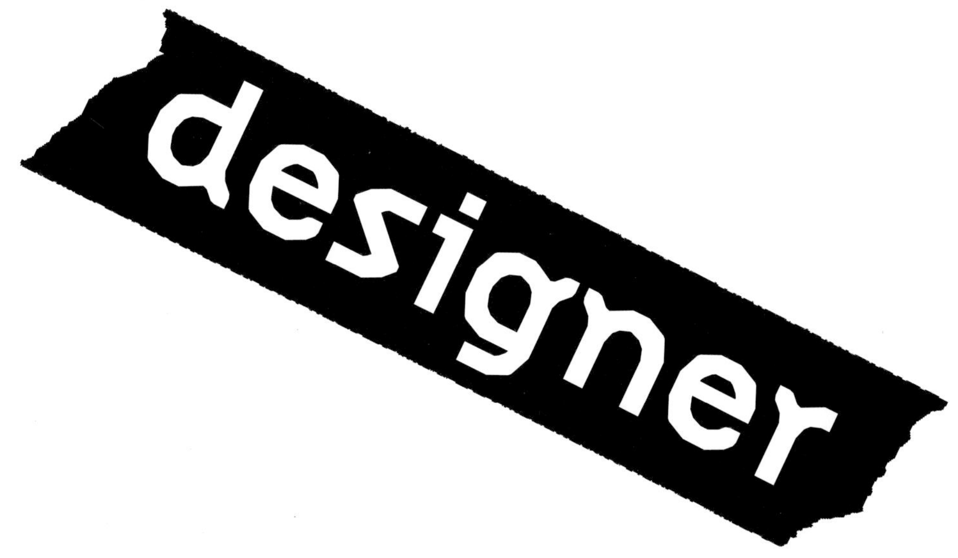

designerposters

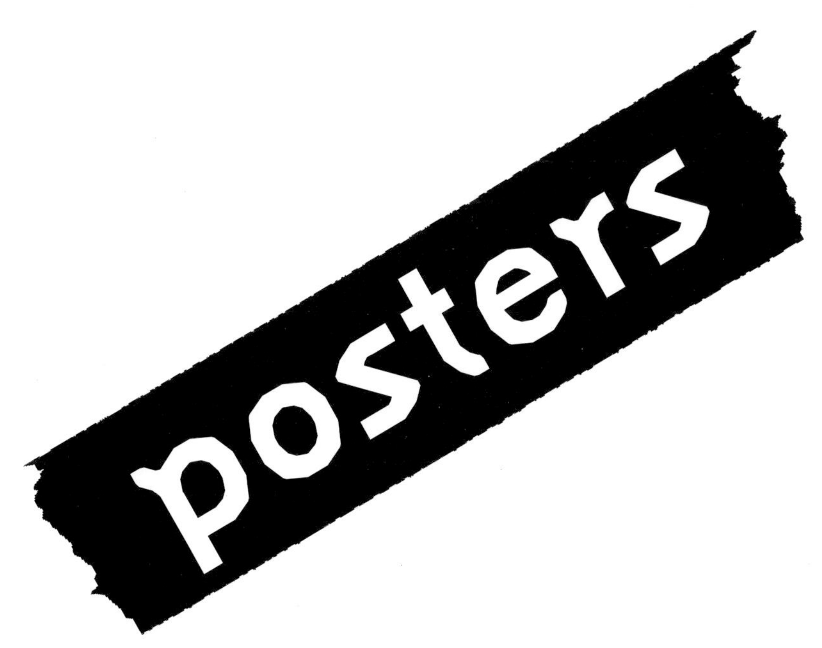

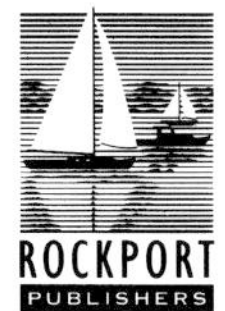

Rockport Publishers, Rockport, Massachusetts

North Light Books, Cincinnati, Ohio

introduction

Once beyond the initial flattery of being asked to write this foreword, I must admit I had to take a very long pause to actually begin to articulate what goes on in my conscious mind when I consider the "poster" medium. In actuality, and I think I can speak for a lot of designers, posters are not something that we're asked to do for our clients with any regularity. So I can't speak from the point of view of someone who turns them out like a press. But certainly the same aesthetic, the same design principles and communication criteria are called upon as for any other design format.

When we do design them, quite often they are an extension of something else. Whether it's an image campaign for a retail center, an exhibition opening or a running event—the posters we generally create are made to work in conjunction with many other media to get the message across. The point is, they don't have to work as hard as they might if they were the sole pipeline of information. They are often image-driven or even commemorative. And I don't think our studio is unique in this situation. The resulting phenomenon is that posters as a medium have gotten away from their original classic intent which, best I can tell, is to get your attention—from a distance. And in the most expedient way possible. After all, posters are meant to be posted in public places such as subways, storefronts and kiosks—where they are seen in passing while on the way to somewhere else. The window of opportunity to communicate is very small.

Reality, however, is that the contemporary poster landscape has evolved a great deal. Posters have become something more than a way to communicate quickly and to inexpensively avoid media placement costs. Their function has become much more diverse than simply being a vehicle for getting across views of underfunded special interests or promoting the next concert coming to town. The poster that once carried some message of dissent on the latest social issue may just as likely show up at your door rolled in a tube announcing a birth or inviting you to a party—a much different use from what inspired the medium originally. And although many "period" posters in retrospect can be considered things of beauty, while still communicating their message in the classic sense, the last decade has seen a proliferation of posters that have been produced that aspire to be <u>just</u> that, a thing of beauty—with no real message at all other than what they convey as image. They are simply decorative objects—something for the living room wall.

There is nothing wrong with making "decorative" posters necessarily. I do understand it. And probably more than once in my career I have succumbed to the temptation. There is simply something very intoxicating and irresistible to the designer, myself included, about seeing your work big. It somehow seems better, or more important. It is, in a way, a vehicle to produce your own fine art, to graphically experiment or explore the latest printing technique. It just dictates a different criteria on which to be judged.

Because the poster is unique in our business in that it has and does cross over in the public's mind as art, the medium has a sort of built in forgiveness factor—it's beautiful so it must be good. I have several old advertising posters framed and hanging in our offices as art that don't say or mean a thing. They just look cool. Again, maybe it's this obsession designers have with scale. The interesting thing to take note of is that in a world filled with advertising messages screaming at you from every direction and every medium, the poster is the one advertising media that almost universally people accept. And to the extreme, steal. Or even hop fences for. Because posters have achieved this level of perceived value, they hang around. Long after that great print ad campaign is in the landfill, the poster will still be on the wall or, at the very least, in the flat file for posterity.

Does this mean that at some point in our future a "Lite Beer" point-of-purchase poster might be considered art? The new retro craze? I doubt it. But who knows what the next hundred years of the poster may bring. Historically, the poster offers a wonderful freeze-frame, shorthand glimpse at our society and the human condition. What is important. What is popular. Where to be. How to dress. How to vote. Who was born. What to see. I assume the trend will continue.

And speaking of what to see. Books like this, to a degree, <u>are</u> a lot of what we see when considering the poster medium. Unless you happen to live in an urban environment with a large pedestrian population, or are walking on a college campus everyday, your exposure to posters is likely limited. Personally, beyond trips to the local video store and the proliferation of photographer, paper and professional design organization mailings, my take on the state of the art of poster design is formulated from graphic design publications. But just because they have been selected for reproduction or that they are beautiful to look at does not necessarily mean they are good "posters". The good ones to me will always be the posters that defy definition—that somehow through juxtaposition of imagery and words (or no words) communicate a quick, clear message in a totally unique fashion—from ten feet away. But what I like, you may not. My Glaser may be your Max. The psychedelic posters of the sixties were illegible to the Haight-Ashbury businessman and my dad. But I never had a problem with them. My, how times have changed, or have they?

—Rex Peteet

Principal
Sibley/Peteet Design
Austin, Texas

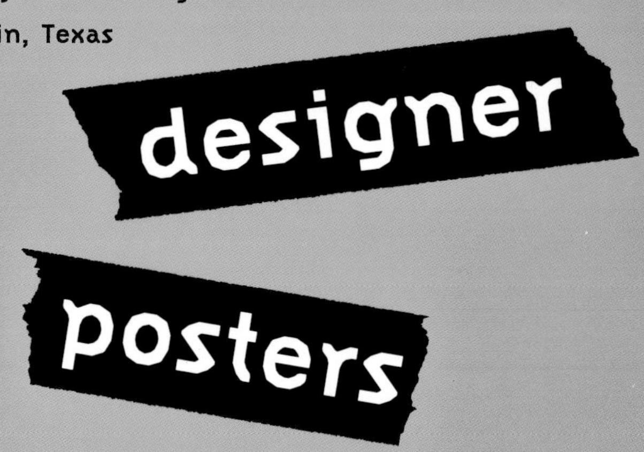

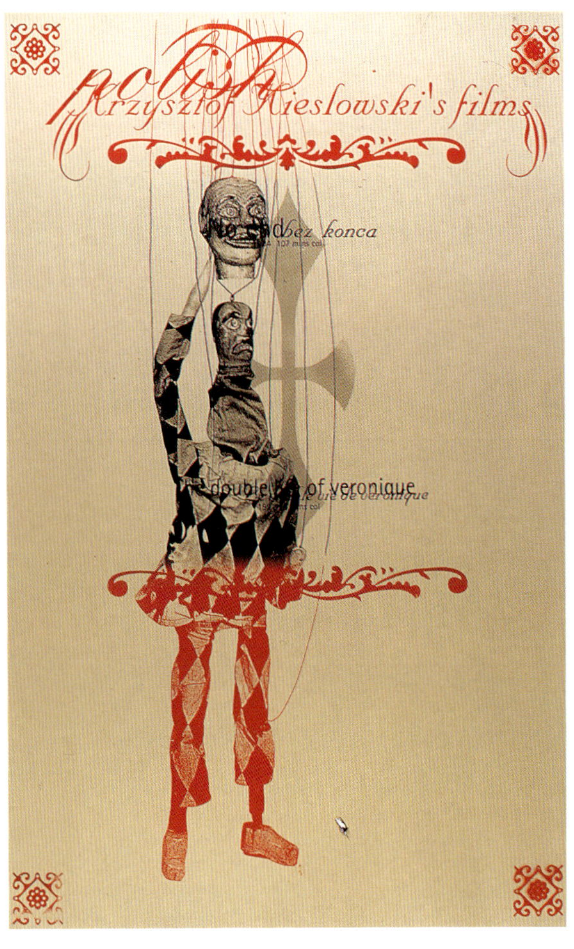

DESIGN FIRM
Margo Chase Design

ALL DESIGN
Margo Chase

PHOTOGRAPHERS
Margo Chase, Merlin Rosenberg

CLIENT
Graphic Communication Society, Oklahoma and Art Directors Club, Tulsa

PURPOSE
Lecture announcement

SIZE
16.25" x 21.5" (41.3cm x 54.6cm)

[right] This lecture announcement employs a literal interpretation of germs imagery: a box of tissue. A Margo Chase Design font, Envision, was used for the type.

[below] The designer used intentionally unsettling imagery from a variety of sources, juxtaposing it with big cut-up type to give the feeling of cage bars blocking the way.

DESIGN FIRM
HMM Communications

ALL DESIGN
Howard M. Montgomery

CLIENT
Cranbrook Academy of Art

PURPOSE
Film series promotion

SIZE
11" x 17"
(27.9cm x 43.2cm)

Designer used a combination of QuarkXPress, montage, and a small Xerox batch run to complete this poster project.

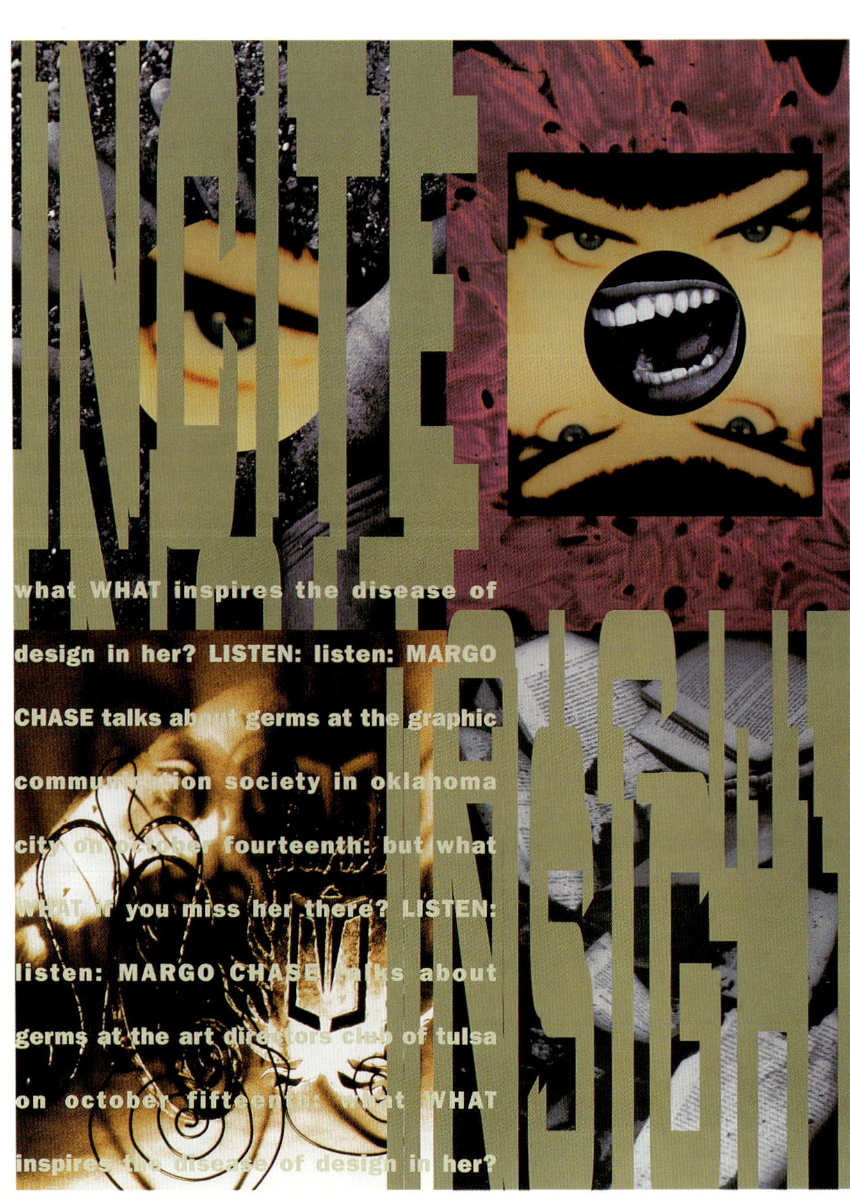

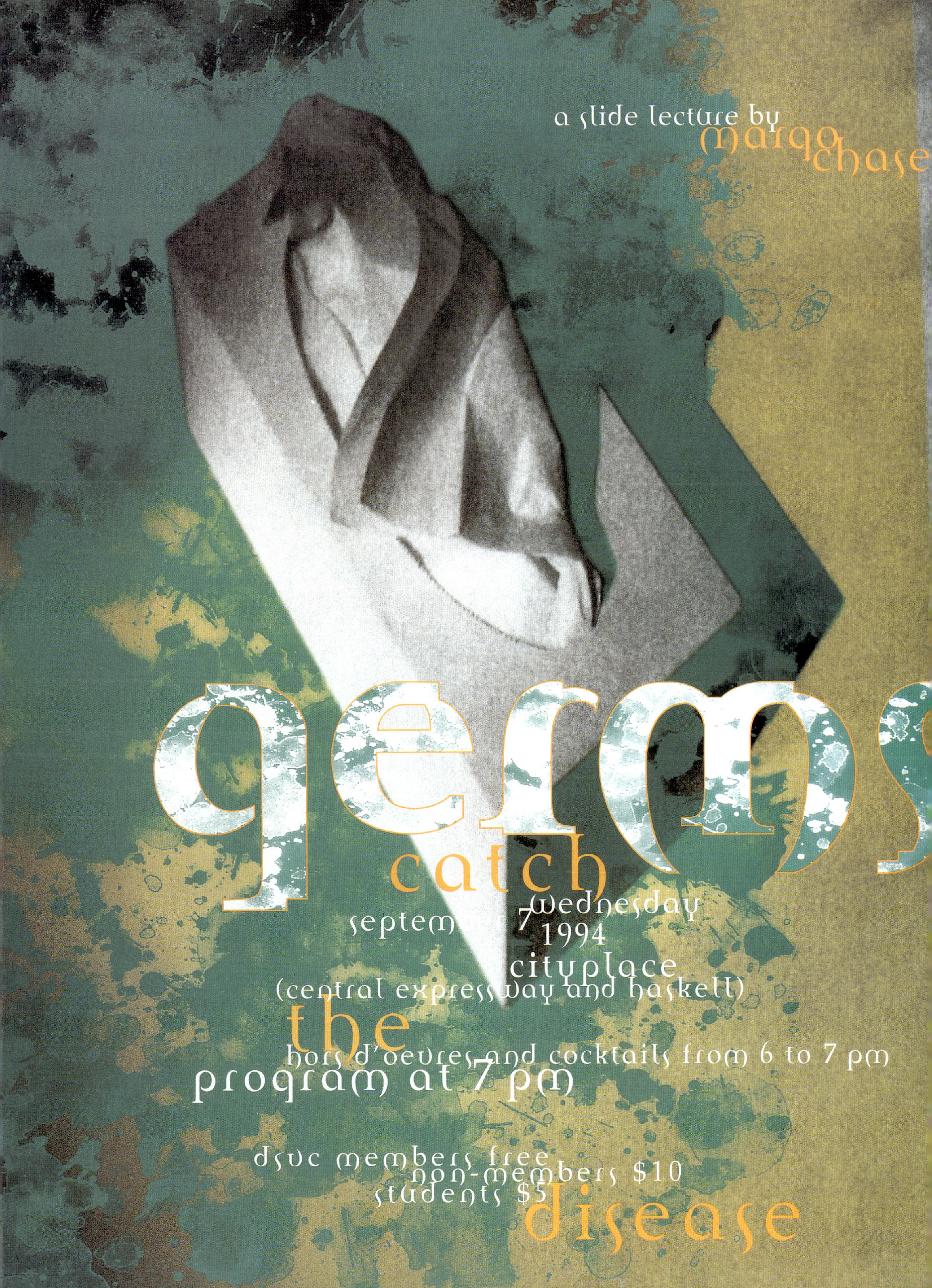
a slide lecture by
margo chase
germs
catch
septem 7 wednesday
1994
cityplace
(central expressway and haskell)
the
hors d'oevres and cocktails from 6 to 7 pm
program at 7 pm
dsvc members free
non-members $10
students $5
disease

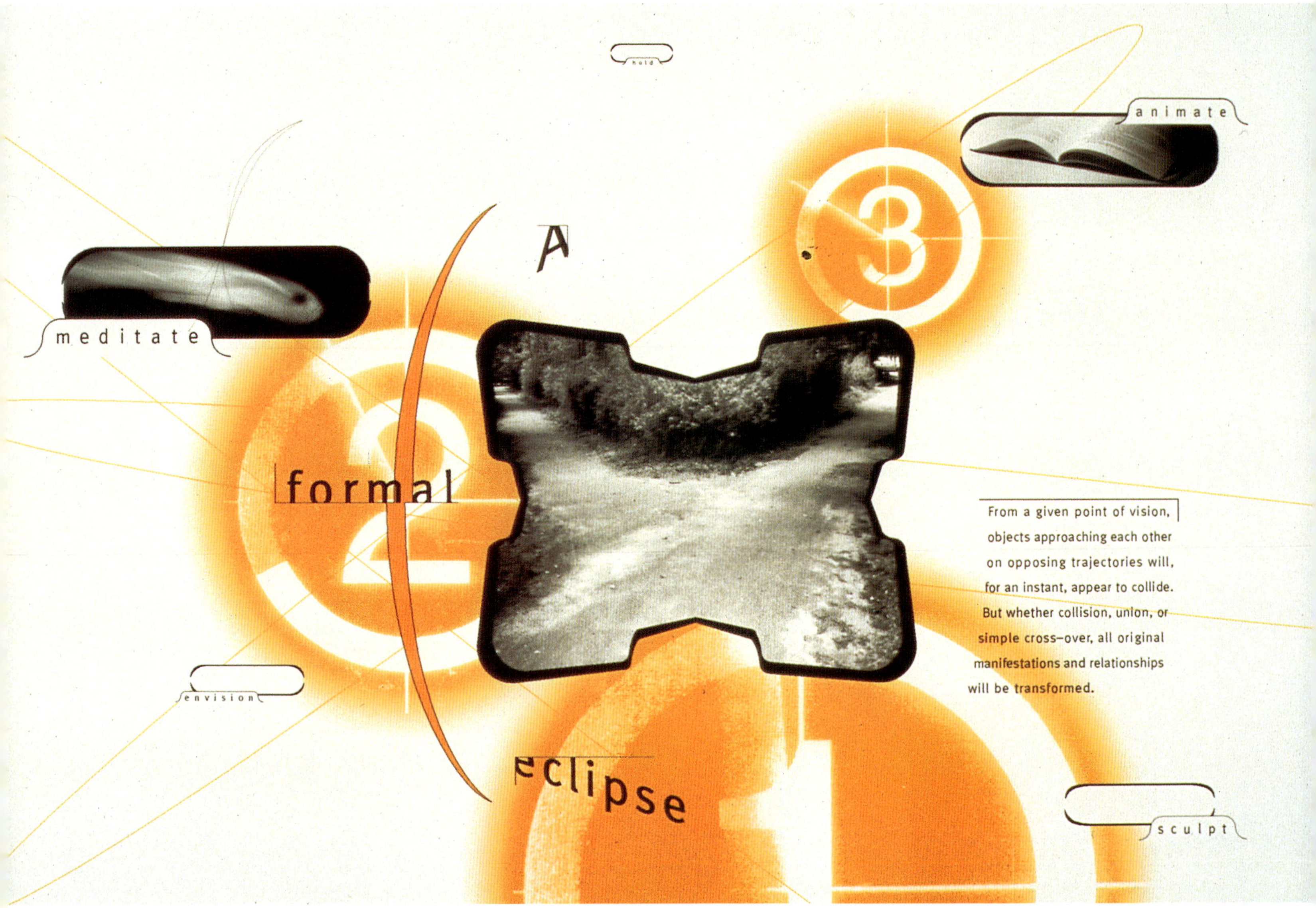

animate

meditate

A

formal

From a given point of vision, objects approaching each other on opposing trajectories will, for an instant, appear to collide. But whether collision, union, or simple cross-over, all original manifestations and relationships will be transformed.

envision

eclipse

sculpt

DESIGN FIRM
Studio Dunbar

ART DIRECTOR
Gert Dunbar

DESIGNER
Jeremy F. Mende

PHOTOGRAPHER
Jeremy F. Mende

CLIENT
Theatre Zeebelt

PURPOSE
Promotion

SIZE
[above and right]
18" x 24"
(43.7cm x 61cm)

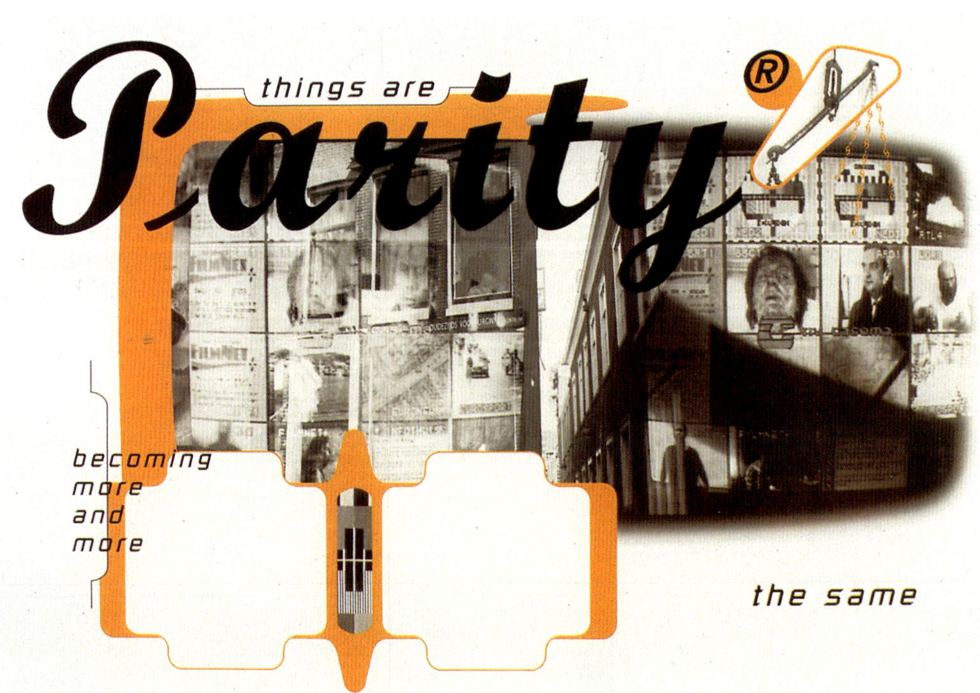

DESIGN FIRM
Watt, Roop & Co.

ART DIRECTOR
Gregory Oznowich

DESIGNERS
Gregory Oznowich, Kurt Roscoe

PHOTOGRAPHER
Martin Reuben Photography, Inc.

CLIENT
The American Institute of Graphic Arts (AIGA), Cleveland Charter

PURPOSE
Event Promotion

SIZE
20.75" x 21.75" (52.7cm x 55.2cm)

[right] This poster was produced in PageMaker 5.0. No special techniques were used, however, special care had to be taken on press since all of the colors used were solid PMS colors trapping against one another.

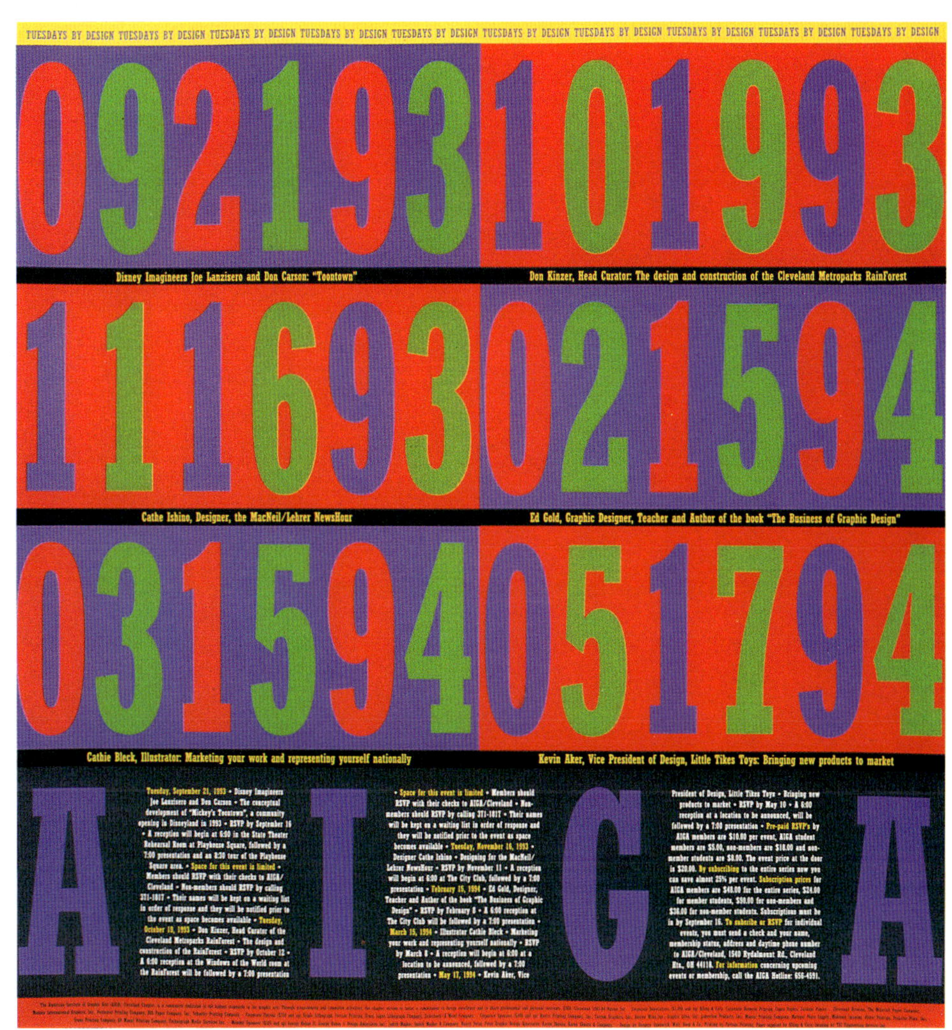

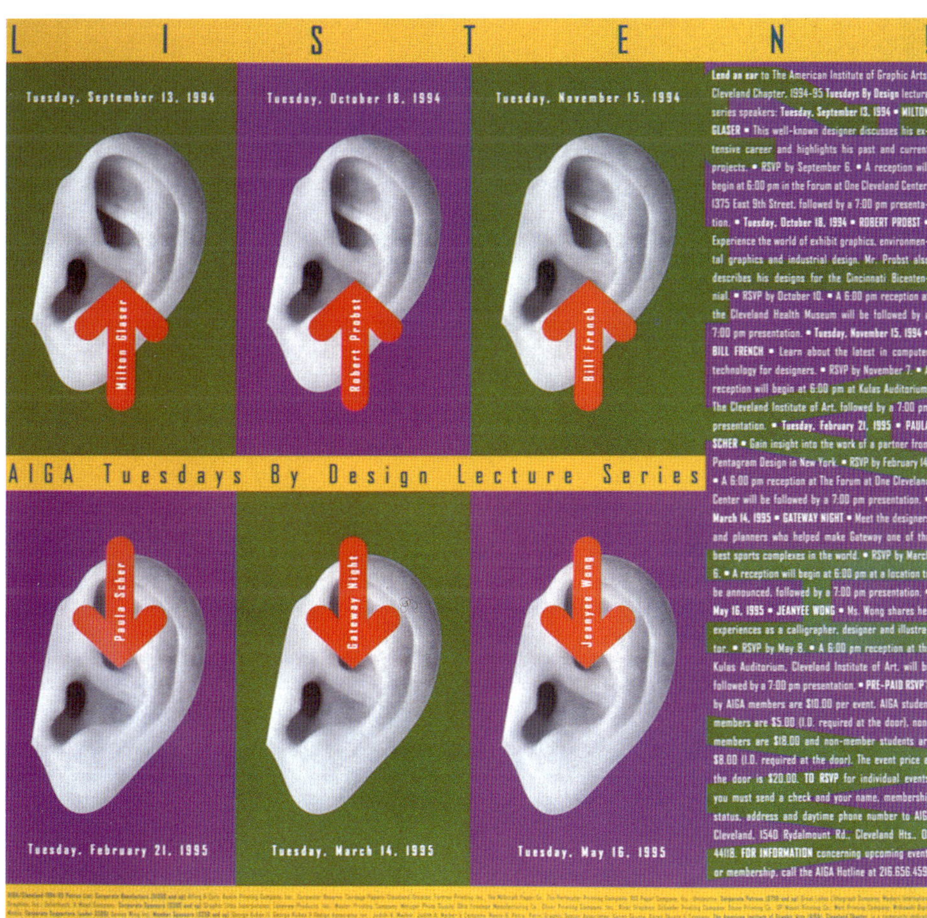

DESIGN FIRM
Watt, Roop & Co.

ART DIRECTOR
Gregory Oznowich

DESIGNERS
Gregory Oznowich, Kurt Roscoe

PHOTOGRAPHER
Martin Reuben Photography, Inc.

CLIENT
The American Institute of Graphic Arts (AIGA), Cleveland Charter

PURPOSE
Event Promotion

SIZE
22" x 21" (55.9cm x 53.3cm)

[left] This poster was produced in PageMaker 5.0. The photos were supplied by the photographer as both high- and low-resolution Adobe Photoshop documents. Designers placed the low-resolution EPS files into Aldus PageMaker for position only, and had the printer drop in the high-resolution versions later.

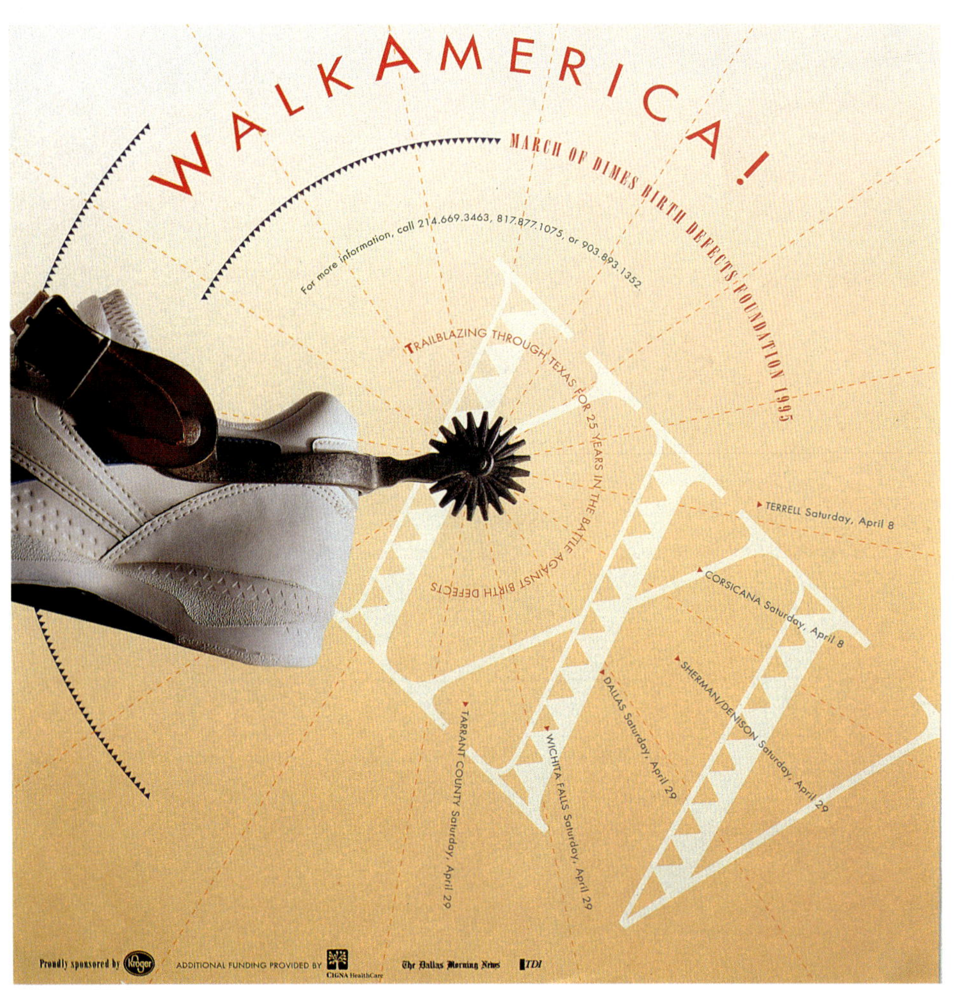

DESIGN FIRM
SullivanPerkins

ART DIRECTOR
Ron Sullivern, Lorraine Charman

DESIGNER
Lorraine Charman

PHOTOGRAPHER
Robb Debenport

COPYWRITER
Christine Lowrance

CLIENT
March of Dimes North Texas Chapter

PURPOSE
WalkAmerica poster

SIZE
19" x 19" (48.3cm x 48.3cm)

The poster combines photography with typesetting and design created in Adobe Illustrator 5.0.

DESIGN FIRM
SullivanPerkins

ART DIRECTOR
Art Garcia

ILLUSTRATOR
Art Garcia

COPYWRITER
Mark Perkins

CLIENT
DSVC

PURPOSE
Promotion

SIZE
23.5" x 25.5" (59.7cm x 59.7cm)

All art was picked up from original art from Art Chantry and composed as a portrait. Base art was printed black with PMS colors as background solids.

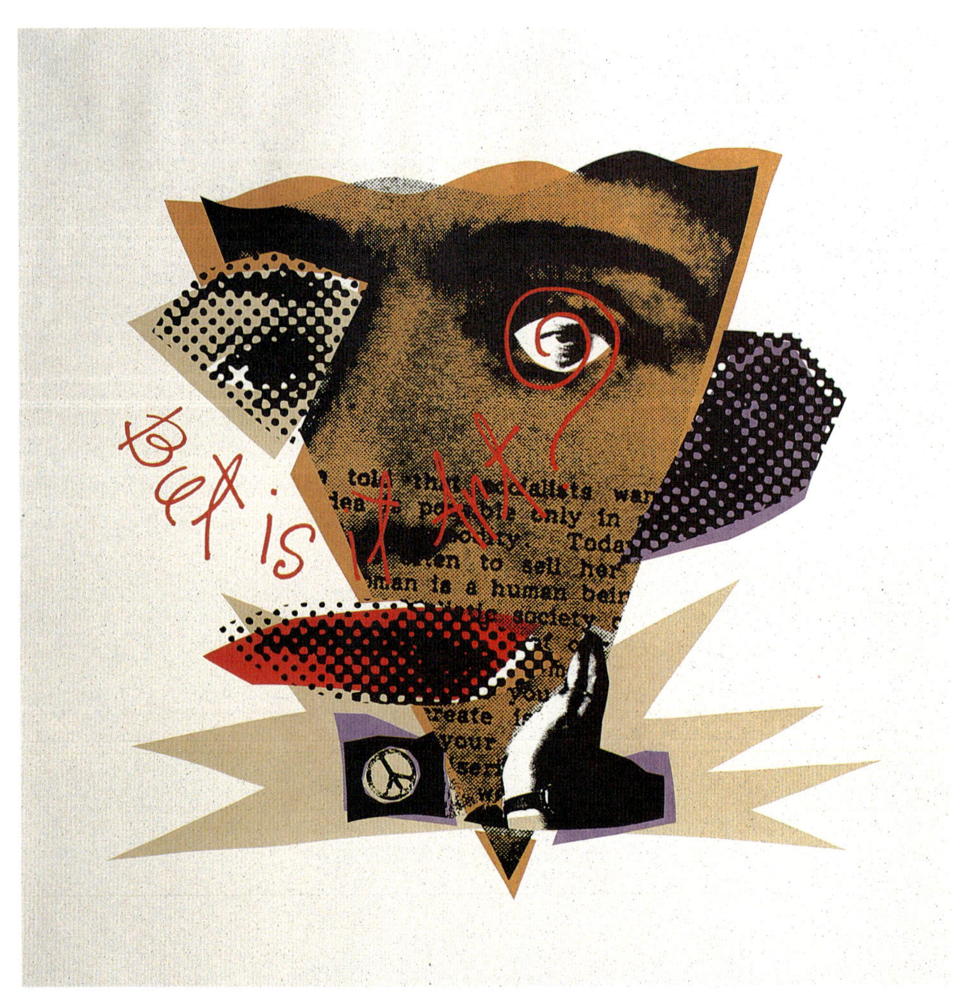

DESIGN FIRM

SullivanPerkins

ART DIRECTOR

Art Garcia

DESIGNER

Art Garcia

ILLUSTRATOR

Art Garcia

COPYWRITER

Mark Perkins

CLIENT

Friends of the Dallas Public Library

PURPOSE

Library poster

SIZE

14.5 x 25

(36.8cm x 63.5cm)

[below]

The original line art was scanned and bitmapped and used as a holiday line to trap other colors. This poster ran on a 2-color press.

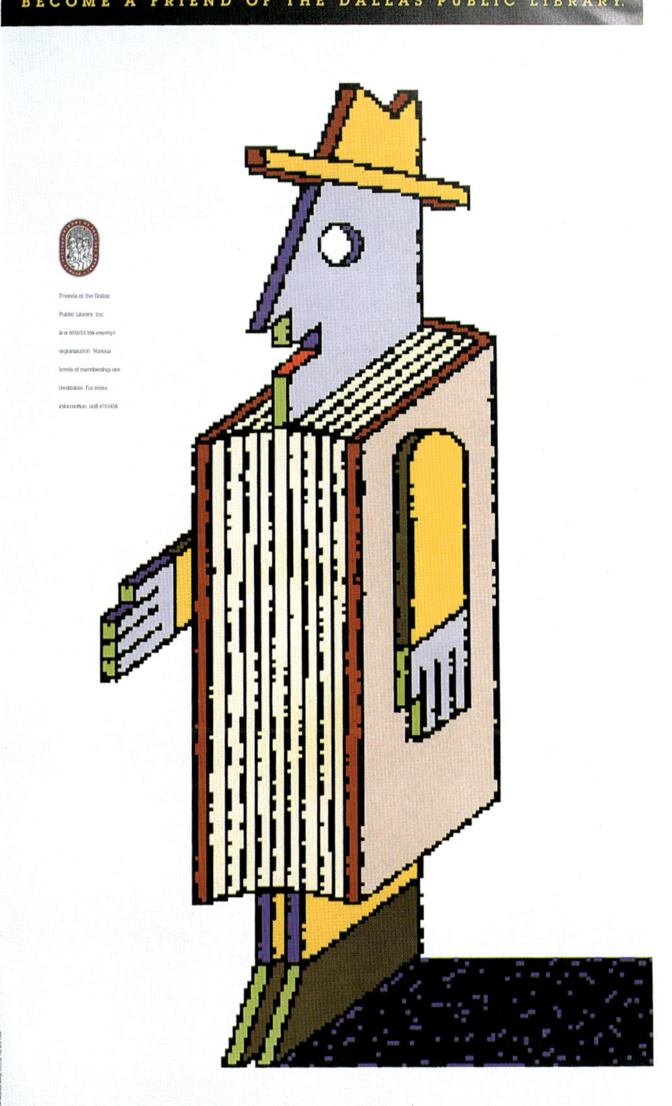

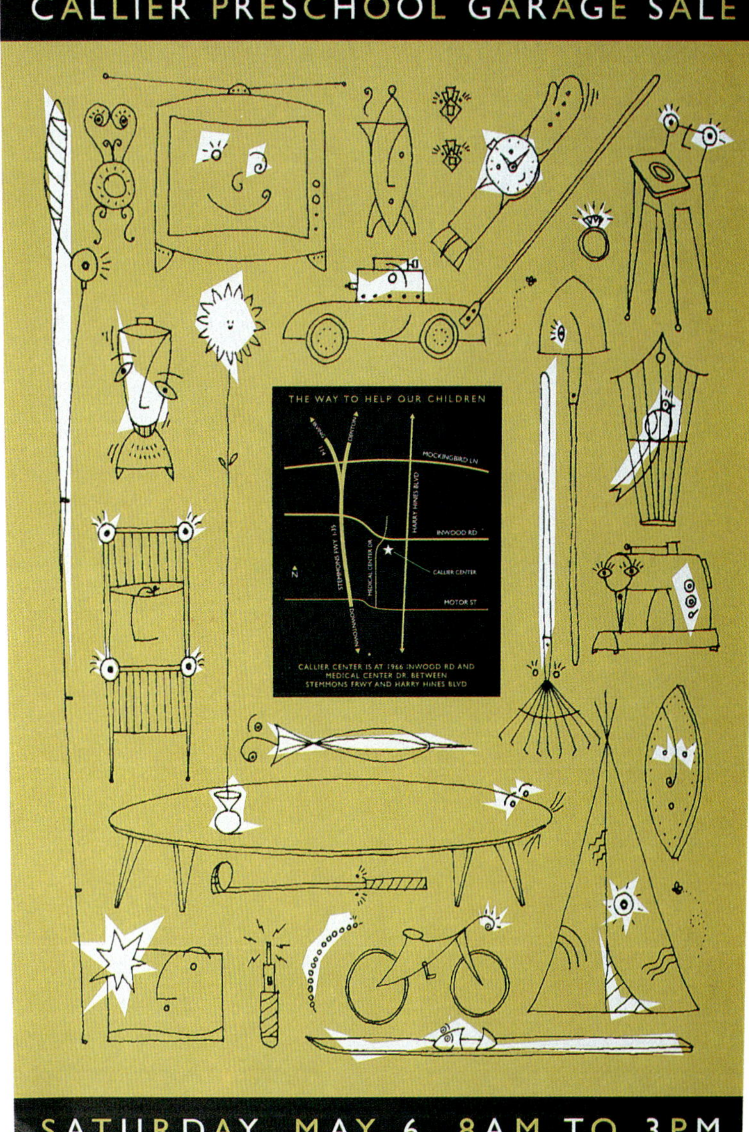

DESIGN FIRM

SullivanPerkins

ART DIRECTOR

Art Garcia

DESIGNER

Art Garcia

COPYWRITER

Michael Langley

CLIENT

Callier Center

PURPOSE

Garage sale promotion

SIZE

11" x 17"

(27.9cm x 43.2cm)

[above]

Line art illustration was scanned and bitmapped. Two PMS colors were used over 90 percent of the image area to make the white appear to be a second color.

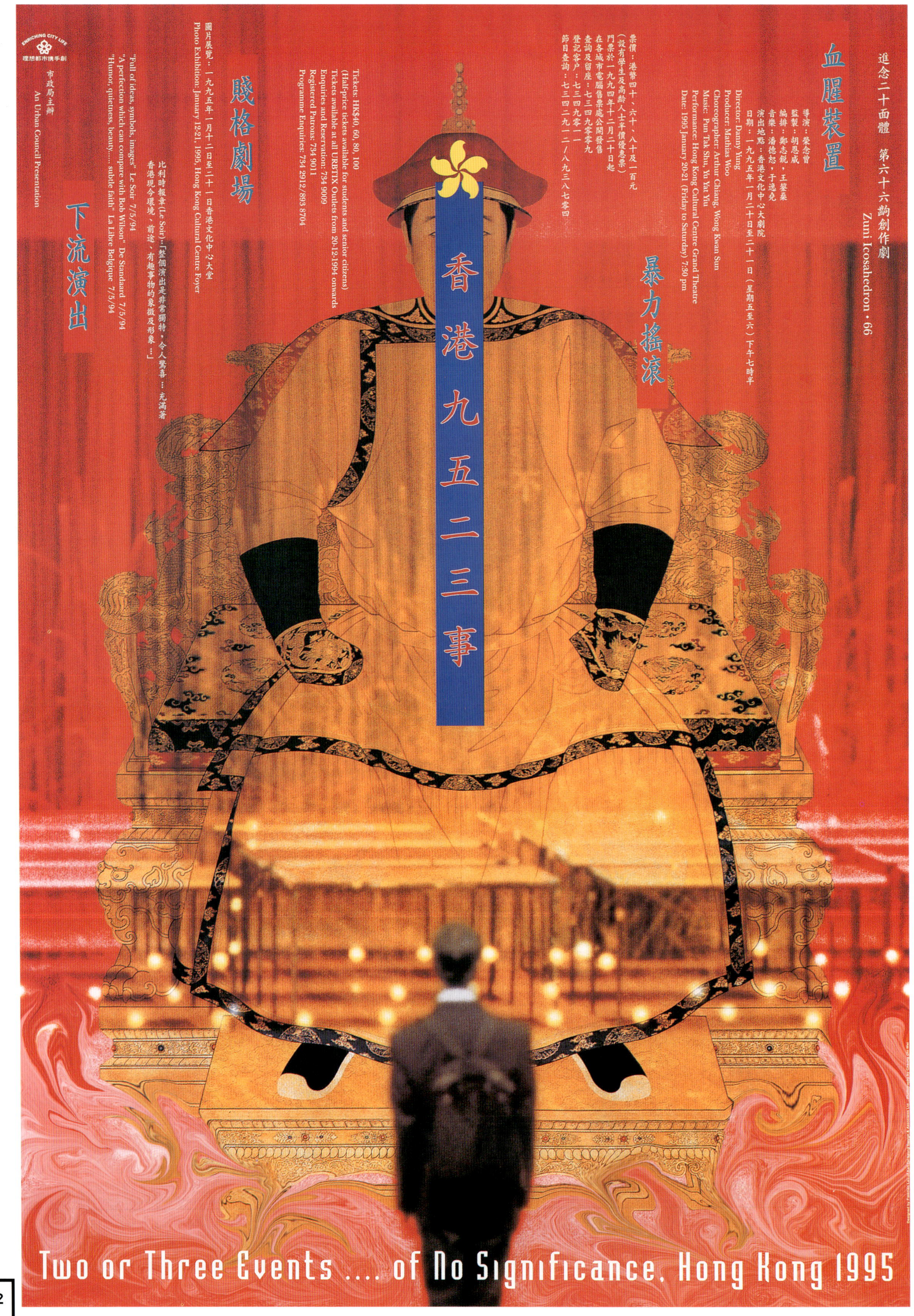

進念二十面體 第六十六齣創作劇
Zuni Icosahedron · 66
血腥裝置
導演：榮念曾
監製：胡恩威
編排：鄭志銳，王鋆燊
音樂：潘德恕，于逸堯
演出地點：香港文化中心大劇院
日期：一九九五年一月二十日至二十一日（星期五至六）下午七時半
Director: Danny Yung
Producer: Mathias Woo
Choreographer: Arthur Chiang, Wong Kwan Sun
Music: Pun Tak Shu, Yu Yat Yiu
Performance: Hong Kong Cultural Centre Grand Theatre
Date: 1995 January 20-21 (Friday to Saturday) 7:30 pm
暴力搖滾
票價：港幣四十、六十、八十及一百元
（設有學生及高齡人士半價優惠票）
門票於一九九四年十二月二十日起
在各城市電腦售票處公開發售
查詢及留座：七三四九零零九
登記客户：七三四九零一一
節目查詢：七三四二九一二/八九三八七零四
Tickets: HK$40, 60, 80, 100
(Half-price tickets available for students and senior citizens)
Tickets available at all URBTIX Outlets from 20-12-1994 onwards
Enquiries and Reservation: 734 9009
Registered Patrons: 734 9011
Programme Enquiries: 734 2912/893 8704
香港九五二三事
賤格劇場
圖片展覽：一九九五年一月十二日至二十一日香港文化中心大堂
Photo Exhibition: January 12-21, 1995, Hong Kong Cultural Centre Foyer
比利時報章(Le Soir)：「整個演出是非常獨特，令人驚喜…充滿著香港現今環境、前途、有趣事物的象徵及形象…」
"Full of ideas, symbols, images" Le Soir 7/5/94
"A perfection which can compare with Bob Wilson" De Standaard 7/5/94
"Humor, quietness, beauty..... subtle faith" La Libre Belgique 7/5/94
下流演出
ENRICHING CITY LIFE
理想都市携手創
市政局主辦
An Urban Council Presentation
Two or Three Events .... of No Significance, Hong Kong 1995

DESIGN FIRM
Kan Tai-keung Design & Associates Ltd.

ART DIRECTOR
Freeman Lau Siu Hong

DESIGNERS
Freeman Lau Siu Hong, Veronica Cheung Lai Sheung

PHOTOGRAPHER
Cheung Chi Wai

CLIENT
Zuni Icosahedron

PURPOSE
Drama promotion

[facing page]
This poster promotes a drama about the political crisis that the Hong Kong will face in 1997. The person standing in front represents a Hong Kong citizen. He fearfully and helplessly faces the ghost, visualized as an ancient Chinese emperor, which symbolizes the totalitarianism.

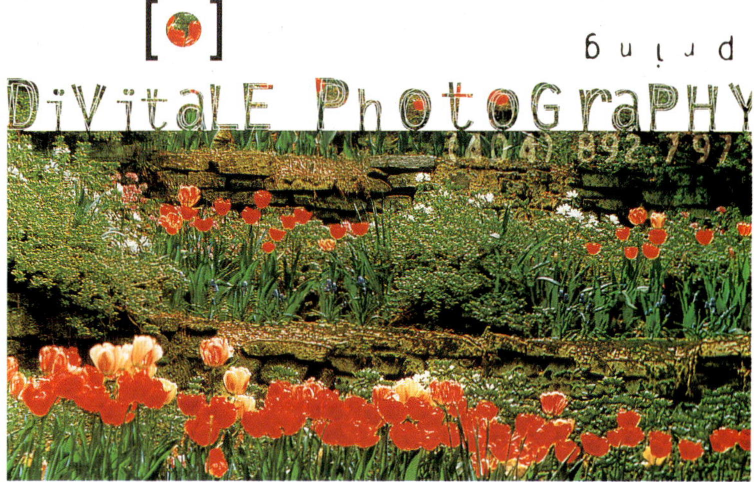

DESIGN FIRM
Fuse

ART DIRECTOR
Rich Godfrey

DESIGNER
Rich Godrey

ILLUSTRATOR
Jim DiVitale

PHOTOGRAPHER
DiVitale Photography

DIGITAL MANIPULATOR
Jim DiVitale

CLIENT
DiVitale Photography

PURPOSE
Self-promotion

SIZE
[left] 10" x 14" (25.4cm x 35.6cm)
[above] 16" x 20" (40.64cm x 50.8cm)

[above] Designers constructed an interesting layout with type around an exciting photograph. Original typography fonts created in Altsys Fontographer and Adobe Illustrator were output to lino. The special effects shown in the image were achieved by the photographer, using traditional darkroom techniques.

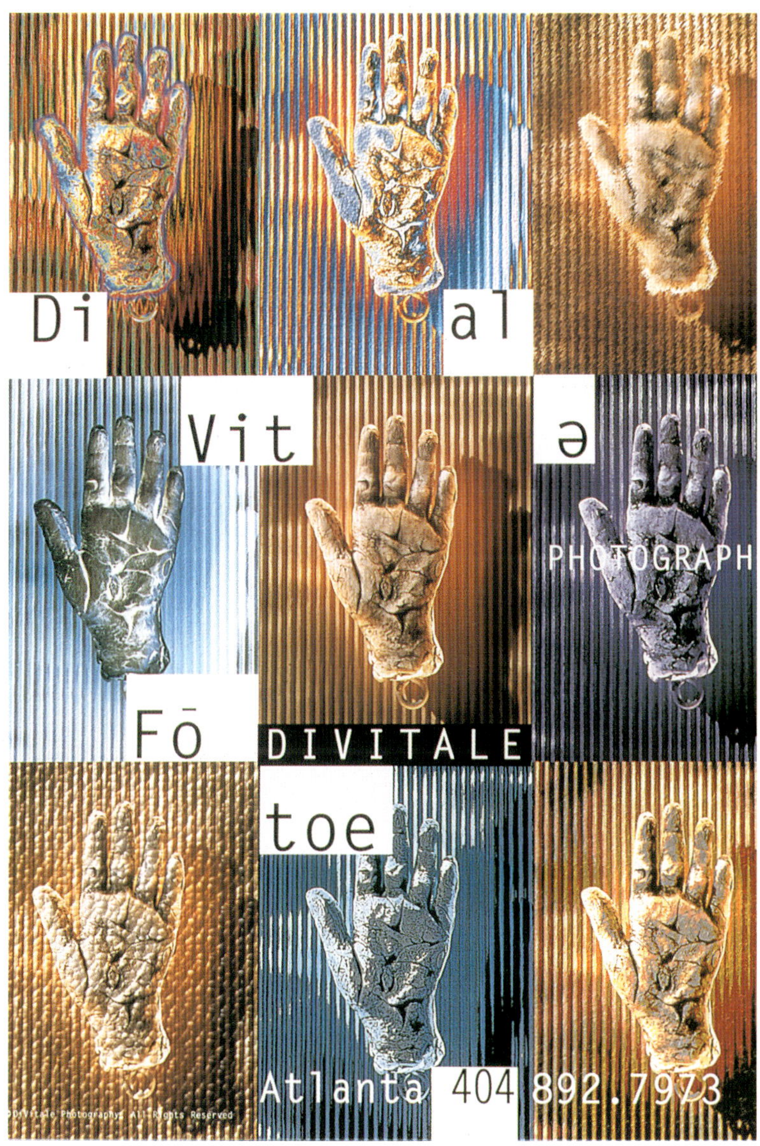

[left] The designer used Altsys Fontographer to create original type which had to work through a repetitive motif and multiple colors without overshadowing the image. The advertising message was delivered through the type and layout without taking away from the visual impact of the image. The image itself was created on the computer with Adobe Photoshop, Aldus Gallery Effects, Kai's Power Tools, and Fractal Design Painter.

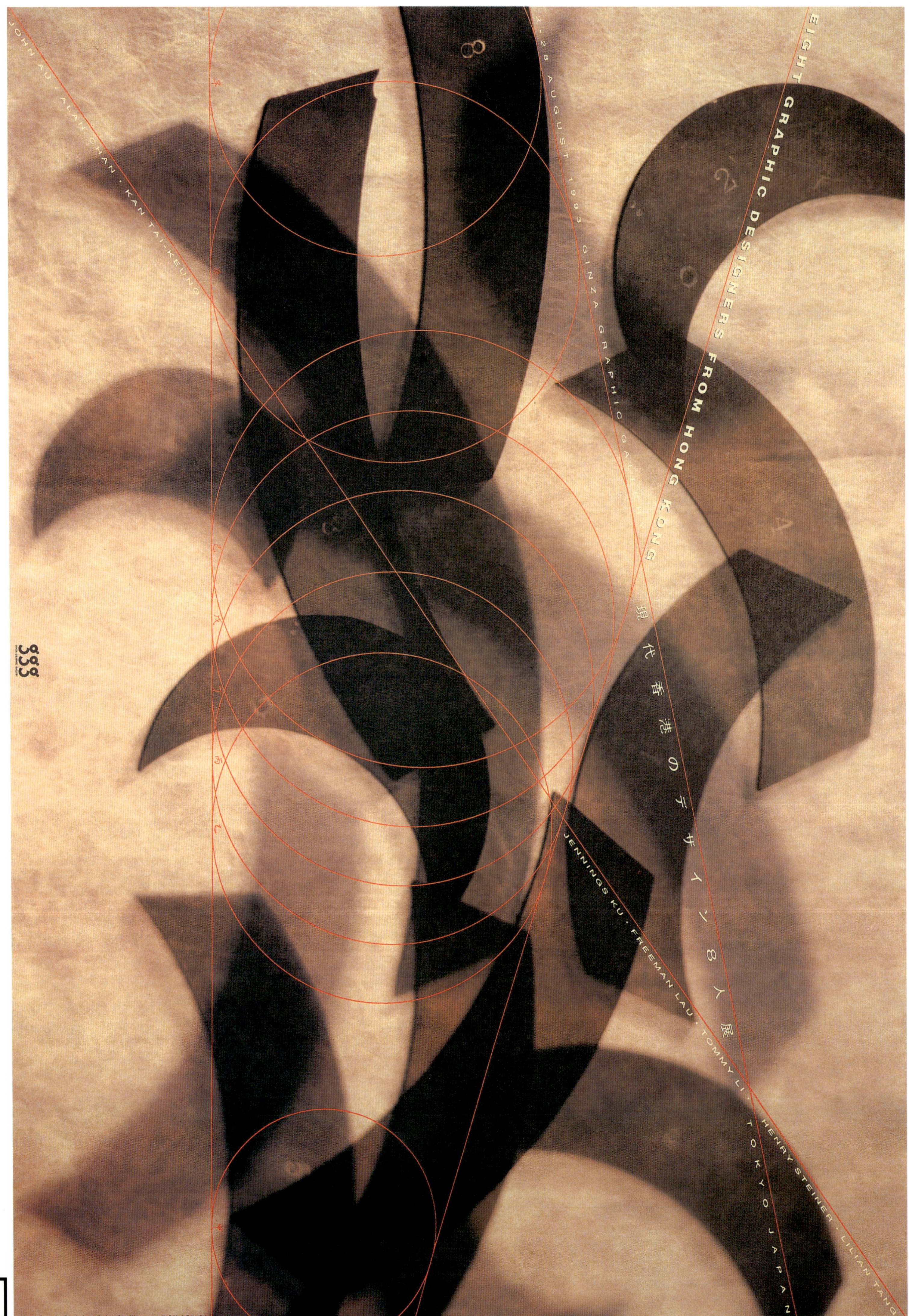
EIGHT GRAPHIC DESIGNERS FROM HONG KONG
現代香港のデザイン8人展
JOHN AU · ALAN CHAN · KAN TAI-KEUNG
2-28 AUGUST 1993 GINZA GRAPHIC GA
JENNINGS KU · FREEMAN LAU · TOMMY LI · HENRY STEINER · LILIAN TANG
TOKYO JAPAN
Designed by Freeman Lau. Printed on Lorenzo Parchment Ochre 220gsm, sponsored by Polytrade Corporation.

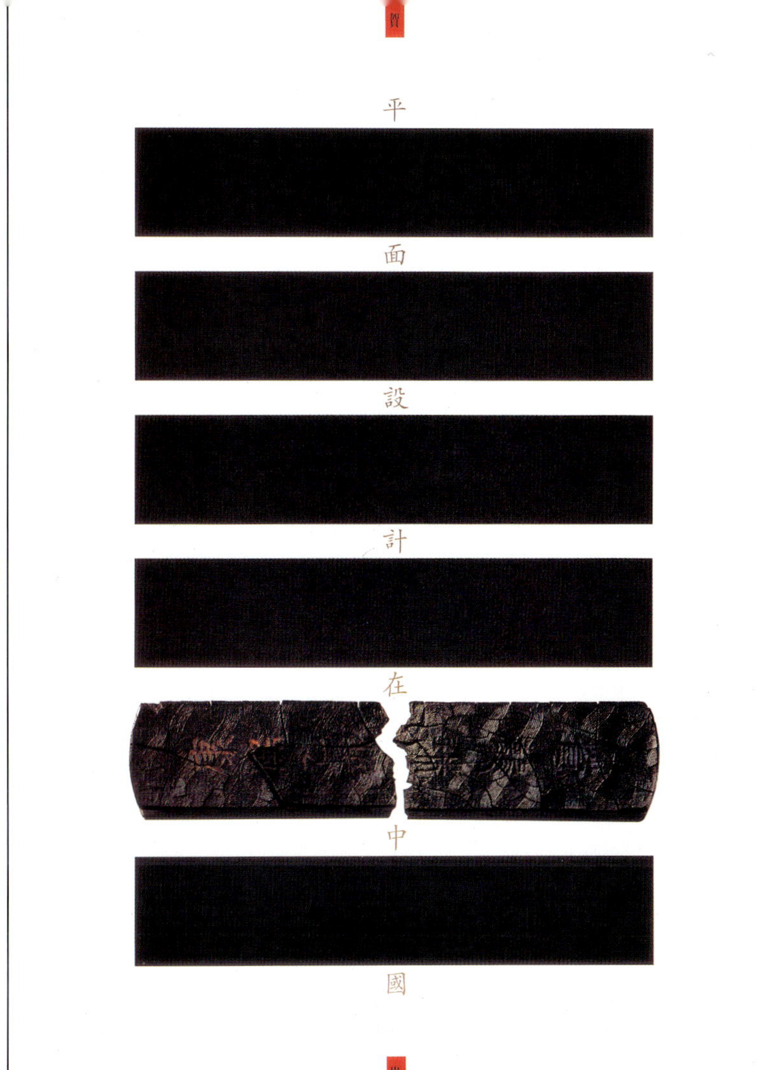

DESIGN FIRM
Kan Tai-keung Design & Associates Ltd.

ART DIRECTOR
Freeman Lau Siu Hong

DESIGNER
Kan Tai-keung

PHOTOGRAPHER
C K Wong

CLIENT
Kan Tai-keung Design & Associates Ltd.

PURPOSE
Self-promotion

SIZE
27.25" x 39"
(69.2cm x 99.1cm)

In this image, an ink stone is differentiated from an array of other black bars by its broken form. It embodies an idea of releasing oneself from the fixed rule and bravely establishes a new vision in aesthetics.

DESIGN FIRM
Kan Tai-keung Design & Associates Ltd.

ART DIRECTOR
Freeman Lau Siu Hong

DESIGNERS
Freeman Lau Siu Hong, Veronica Cheung Lai Sheung

PHOTOGRAPHER
C K Wong

CLIENT
GGG Gallery

PURPOSE
Self-promotion

[facing page]
The circle is a symbol of perfection. This poster reveals the shadows of the 9th Century European French curves for drawing circles which are placed casually at the background. It demonstrates the more liberal and open-minded nature of the Western aesthetics.

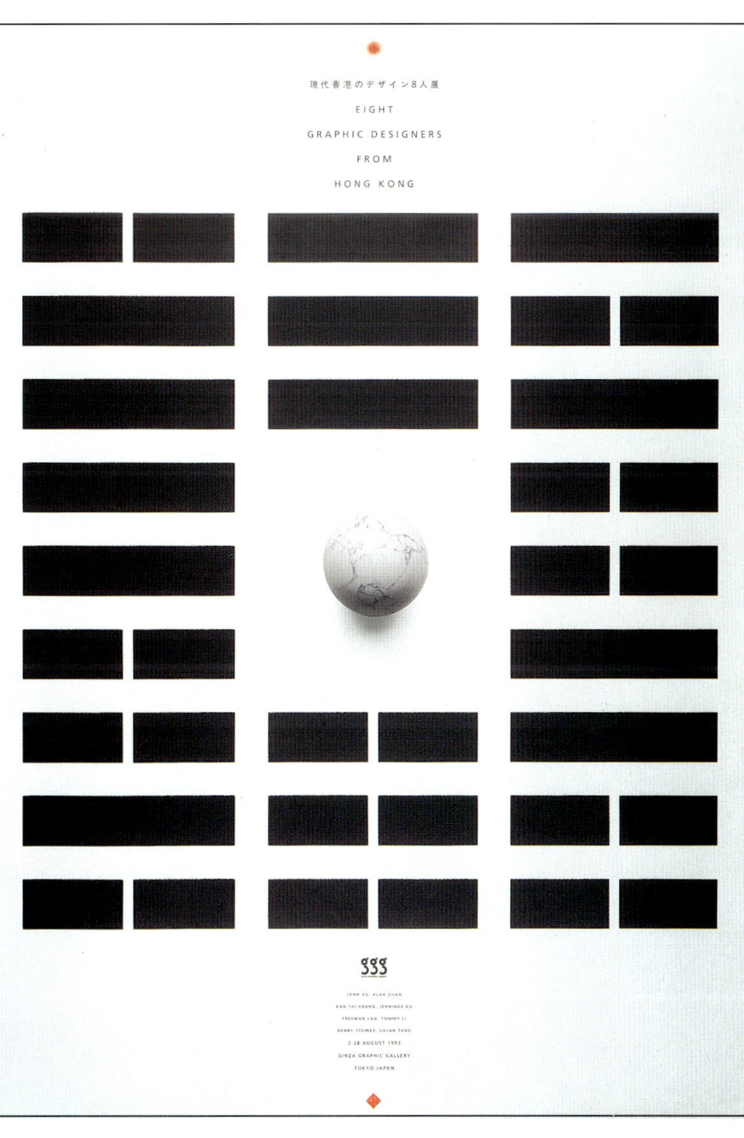

DESIGN FIRM
Kan Tai-keung Design & Associates Ltd.

ART DIRECTOR
Kan Tai-keung

DESIGNER
Kan Tai-keung

PHOTOGRAPHER
C K Wong

CLIENT
GGG Gallery

PURPOSE
Self-promotion

SIZE
33" x 23.25"
(83.8cm x 59.1cm)

This poster is inspired by the eight trigrams, a symbolic pattern of lines discovered by an ancient Chinese mythical emperor - Fu Hsi.

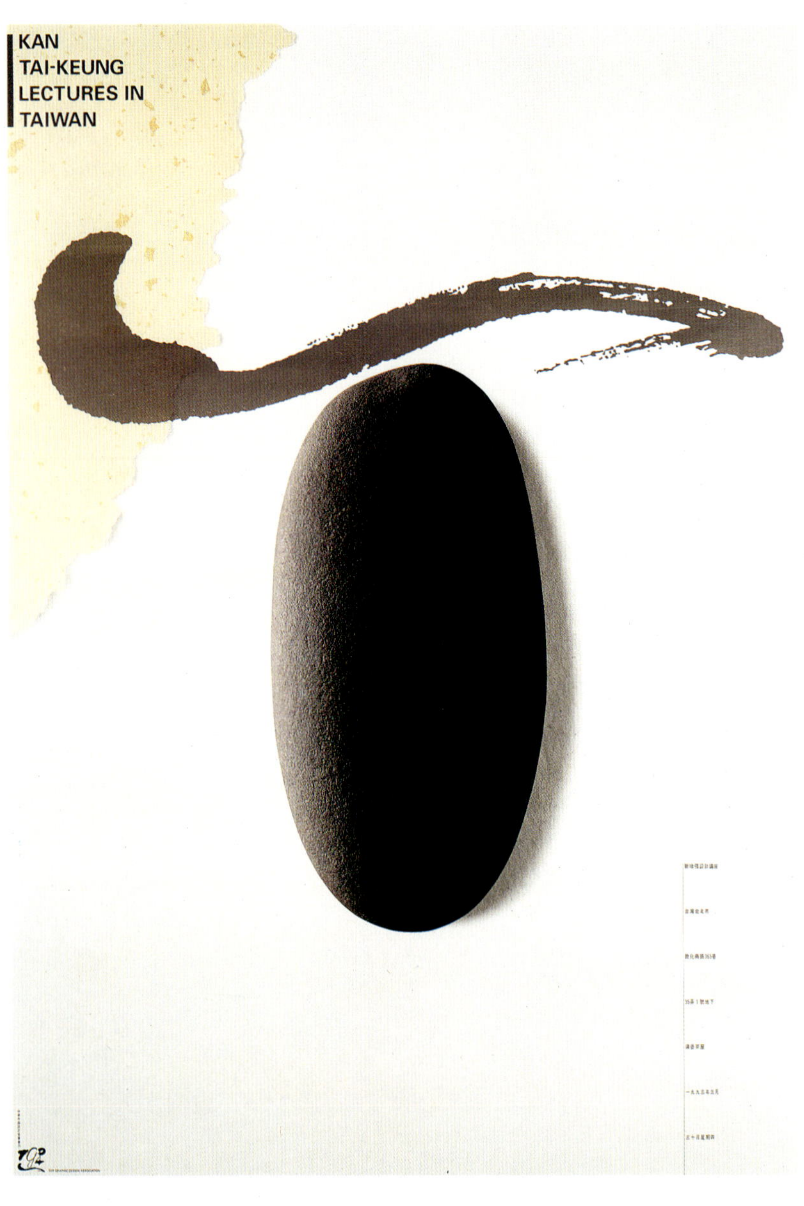

DESIGN FIRM
Kan Tai-keung Design
& Associates Ltd.

ART DIRECTOR
Freeman Lau Siu Hong

DESIGNERS
Freeman Lau Siu Hong,
Veronica Cheung Lai Sheung

CLIENT
Kan Tai-keung Design
& Associates Ltd.

PURPOSE
Self-promotion

[below and facing page]
These posters were designed for an invitational show in Taiwan. Every Chinese character has its own meaning. The designer breaks down several characters and reorganizes them to make a new character with a new meaning.

DESIGN FIRM
Kan Tai-keung Design
& Associates Ltd.

ART DIRECTOR
Kan Tai-keung Design
& Associates Ltd.

DESIGNER
Kan Tai-keung Design
& Associates Ltd.

PURPOSE
Self-Promotion

The ink stone and the pale yellow paper represent Taiwan and Mainland China respectively. The brush strokes resemble the letter "T" and the first character of a Taiwan Chinese name. The stone also suggests the meaning of educational exchange, for there is a Chinese saying, "Even the stone of another mountain has something for you to learn."

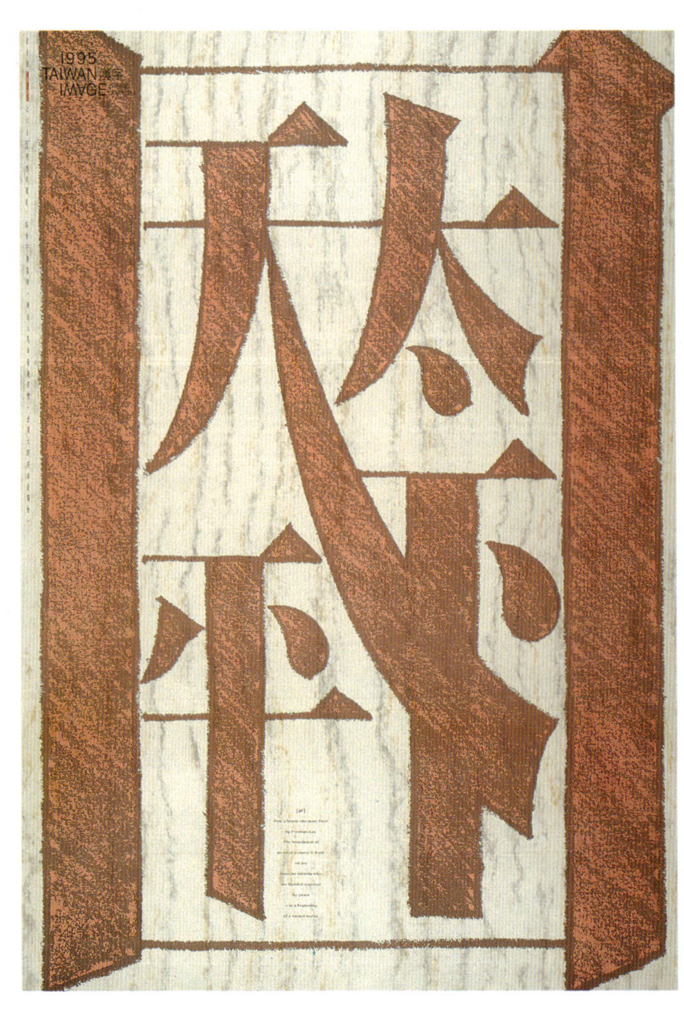

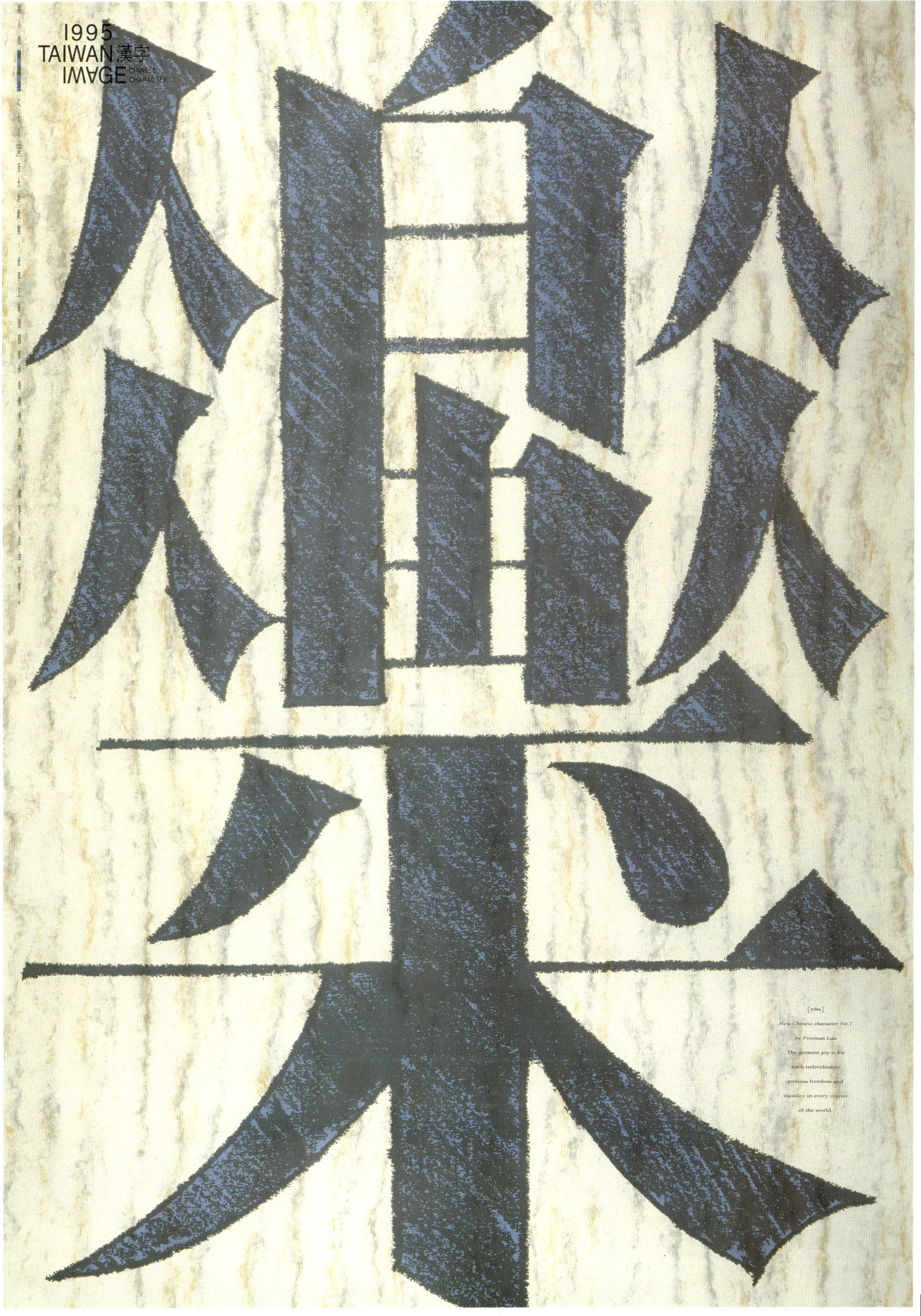
1995
TAIWAN 漢字
IMAGE CHINESE CHARACTER
劉小康新漢字之七 至大的歡樂：世界上每個國家和每個角落的人，都享有自由平等。
[yōu]
New Chinese character No.7
by Freeman Lau
The greatest joy is for each individual to possess freedom and equality in every corner of the world.

DESIGN FIRM
Kan Tai-keung Design & Associates Ltd.

ART DIRECTORS
Kan Tai-keung, Eddy Yu Chi Kong

DESIGNERS
Kan Tai-keung, Eddy Yu Chi Kong

COMPUTER ILLUSTRATOR
Benson Kwun Tin-Yau

PHOTOGRAPHER
C K Wong

CLIENT
Hong Kong Trade Development Council

PURPOSE
Clock promotion

The design of the posters is based on the idea of oriental philosophical thinking to promote an utterly modern product.

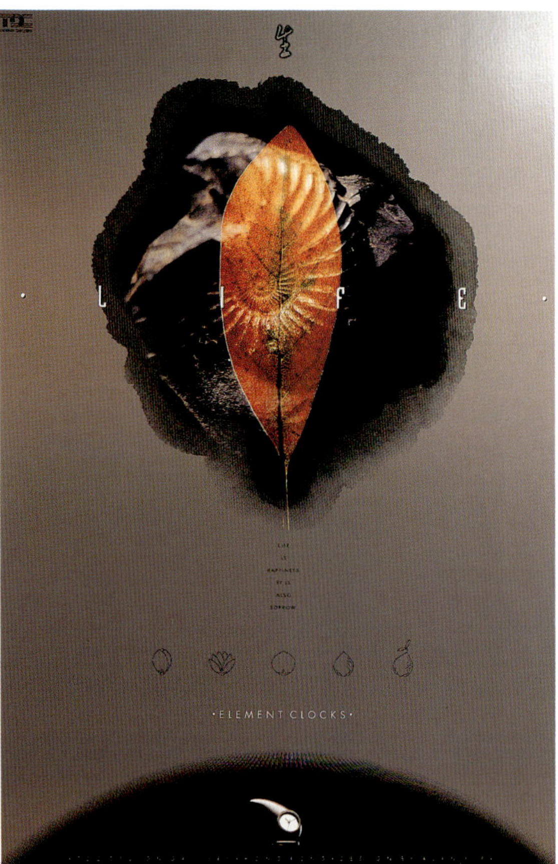

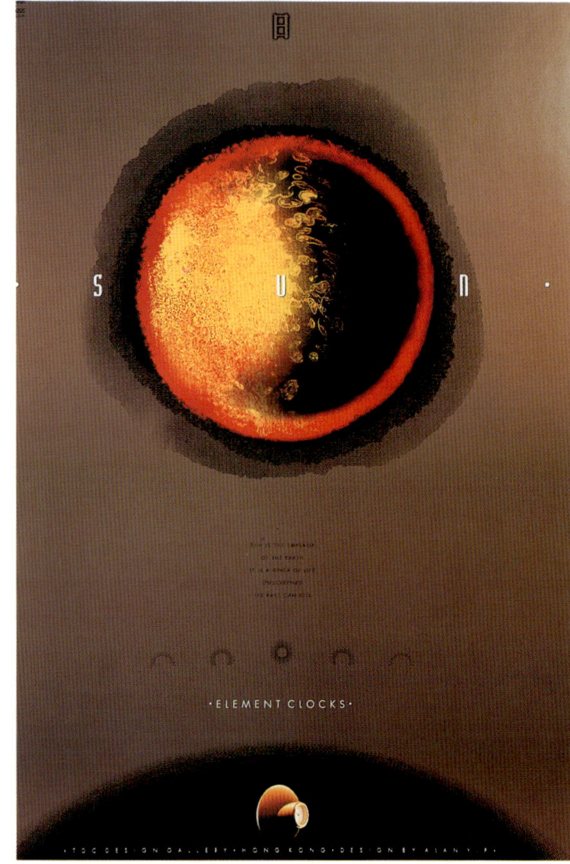

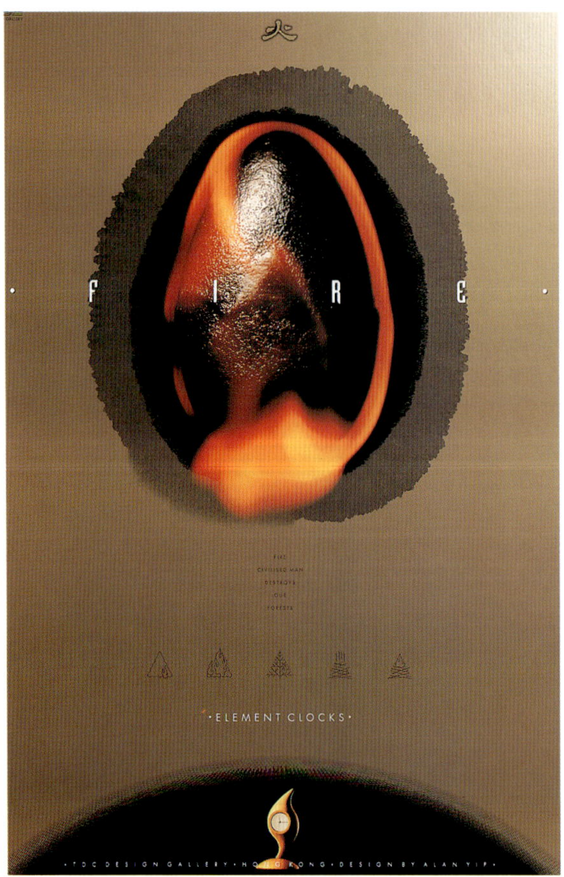

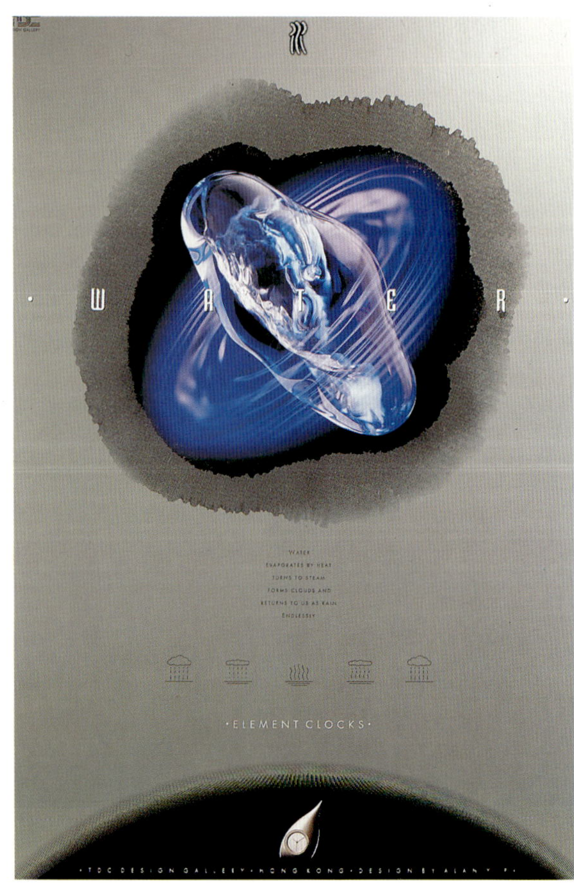

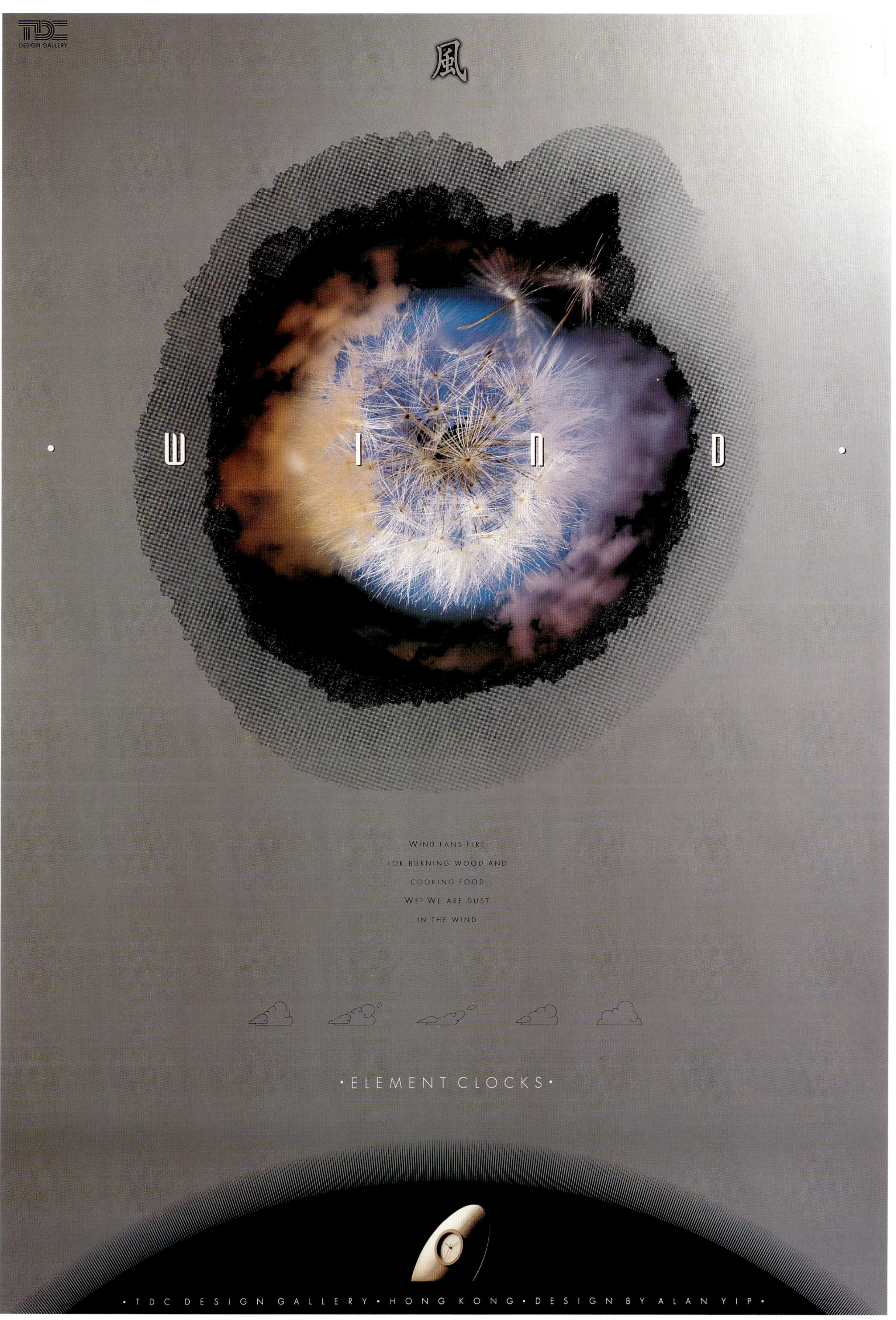
TDC
DESIGN GALLERY
風
W I N D
WIND FANS FIRE
FOR BURNING WOOD AND
COOKING FOOD
WE? WE ARE DUST
IN THE WIND
•ELEMENT CLOCKS•
• TDC DESIGN GALLERY • HONG KONG • DESIGN BY ALAN YIP •

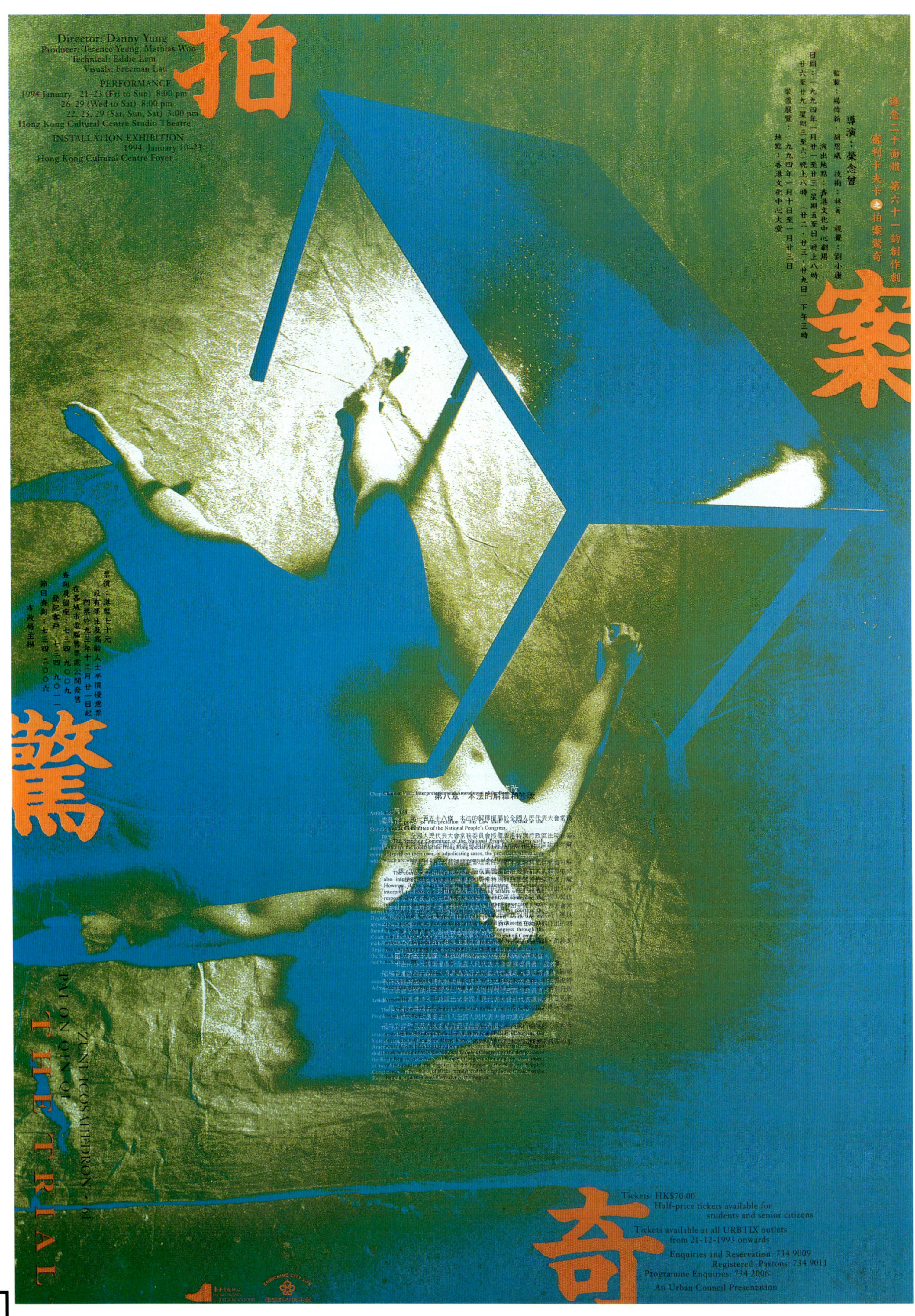
拍
案
驚
奇
Director: Danny Yung
Producer: Terence Yeung, Mathias Woo
Technical: Eddie Lam
Visuals: Freeman Lau
PERFORMANCE
1994 January 21–23 (Fri to Sun) 8:00 pm
26–29 (Wed to Sat) 8:00 pm
22, 23, 29 (Sat, Sun, Sat) 3:00 pm
Hong Kong Cultural Centre Studio Theatre
INSTALLATION EXHIBITION
1994 January 10–23
Hong Kong Cultural Centre Foyer
進念二十面體 第六十一齣創作劇
審判卡夫卡之拍案驚奇
導演：榮念曾
監製：楊偉新，胡恩威 技術：林菁 視覺：劉小康
演出地點：香港文化中心劇場
日期：一九九四年一月廿一至廿三(星期五至日)晚上八時
廿六至廿九(星期三至六)晚上八時 (廿二，廿三，廿九日)下午三時
裝置展覽：一九九四年一月十日至一月廿三日
地點：香港文化中心大堂
票價：港幣七十元
設有學生及高齡人士半價優惠票
門票於九三年十二月廿一日起
在各城市電腦售票處公開發售
查詢及留座：七三四 九〇〇九
登記客戶：七三四 九〇一一
節目查詢：七三四 二〇〇六
市政局主辦
ZUNI ICOSAHEDRON • 61
PAI ON QIN QI
THE TRIAL
第八章 本法的解釋和修改
Tickets: HK$70.00
Half-price tickets available for
students and senior citizens
Tickets available at all URBTIX outlets
from 21-12-1993 onwards
Enquiries and Reservation: 734 9009
Registered Patrons: 734 9011
Programme Enquiries: 734 2006
An Urban Council Presentation

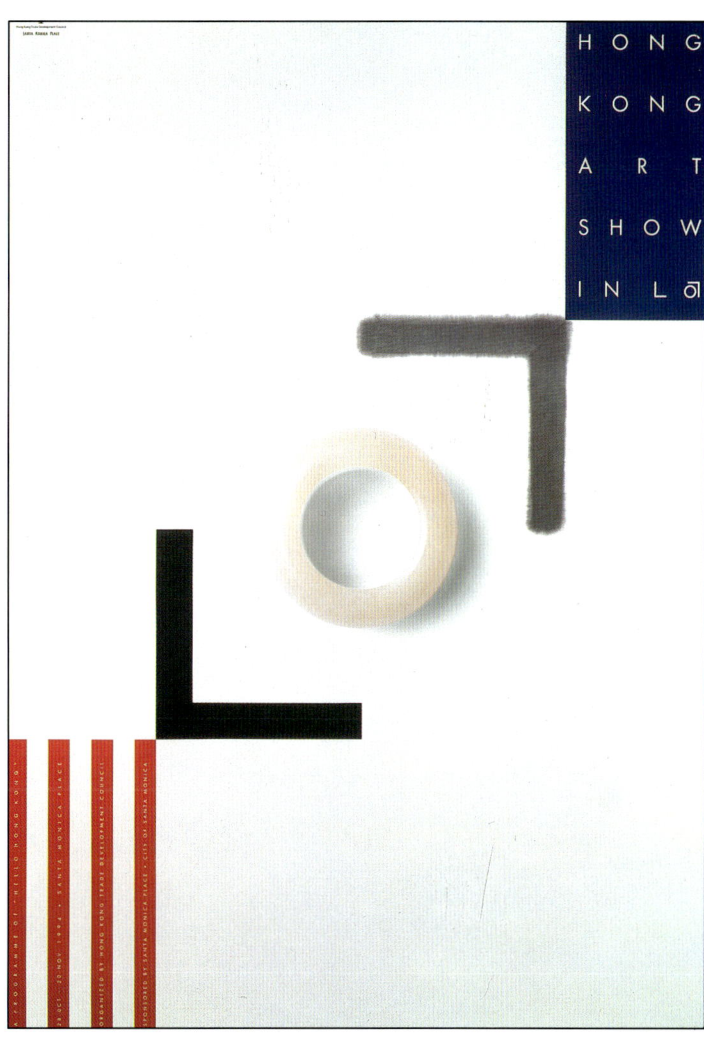

DESIGN FIRM
Kan Tai-keung Design & Associates Ltd.

ART DIRECTOR
Kan Tai-keung

DESIGNER
Kan Tai-keung

PHOTOGRAPHER
C K Wong

CLIENT
Hong Kong Trade Development Council

PURPOSE
Self-promotion

SIZE
27.25" x 39" (69.2cm x 99.1cm)

Designers placed together elements from East and West. The colour strips on the typography are taken from the U.S. national flag to represent the venue of the exhibition.

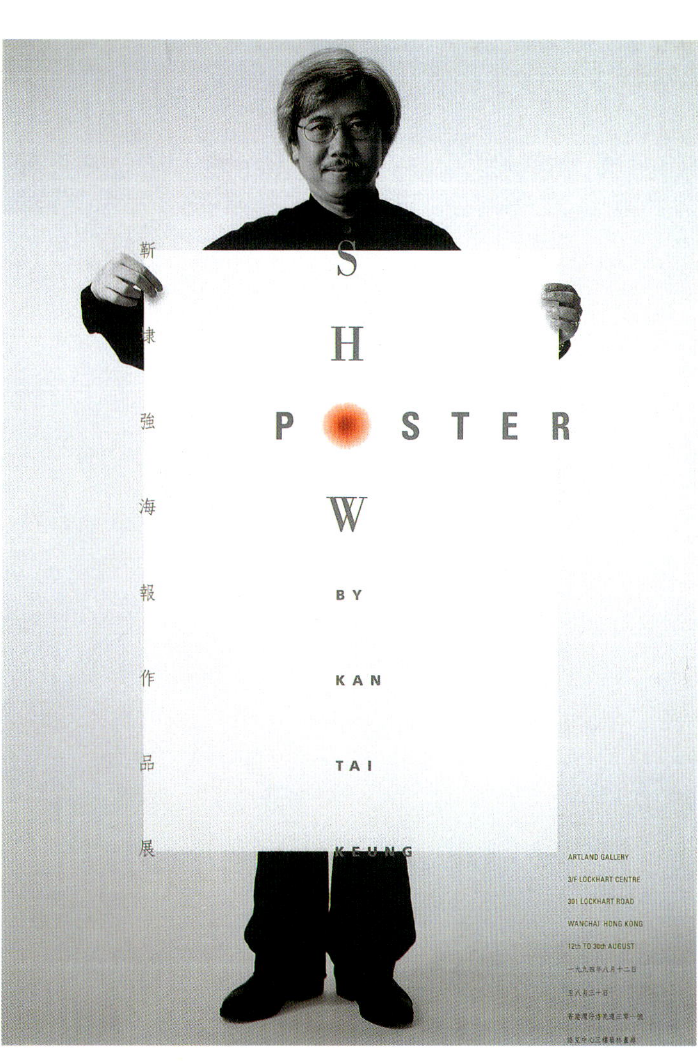

DESIGN FIRM
Kan Tai-keung Design & Associates Ltd.

ART DIRECTOR
Kan Tai-keung

DESIGNER
Kan Tai-keung

PHOTOGRAPHER
C K Wong

CLIENT
Hui's Arts Gallery

PURPOSE
Self-promotion

A photograph of the designer holding a white board with the name of the show in Chinese and English was used for this poster.

DESIGN FIRM
Kan Tai-keung Design & Associates Ltd.

ART DIRECTOR
Freeman Lau Si

DESIGNERS
Freeman Lau Siu Hong, Veronica Cheung Lai Sheung

PHOTOGRAPHER
C K Wong

CLIENT
Zuni Icosahedron

PURPOSE
Drama promotion

[facing page]
This poster was created for an avant-garde drama.

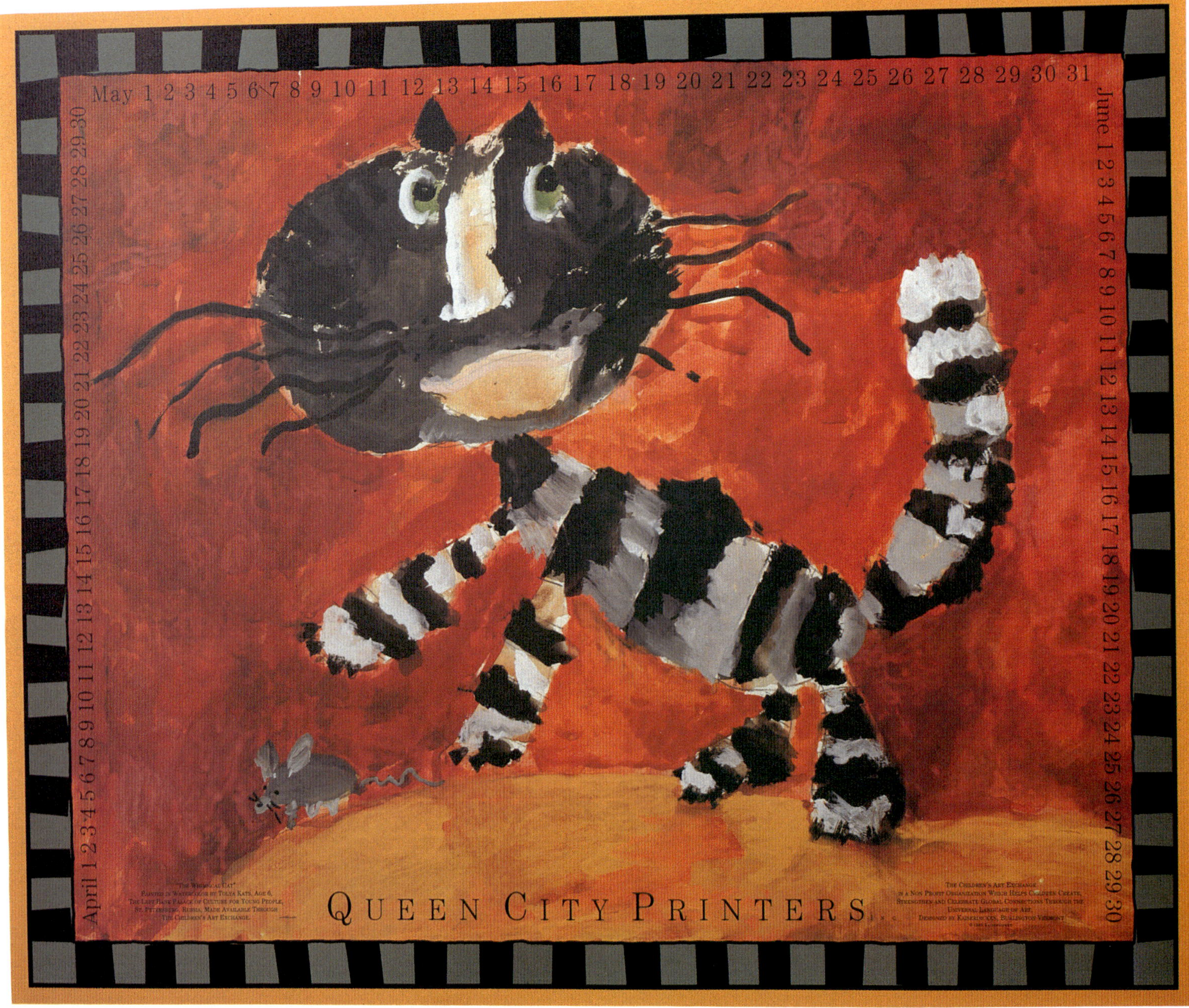

DESIGN FIRM
Kaiserdicken

ART DIRECTOR
Craig Dicken

DESIGNER
Debra Kaiser

ILLUSTRATOR
Tolya Kats

CLIENT
Queen City Printers

PURPOSE
Promotional calendar

SIZE
25.75" x 20.75"
(65.4cm x 52.7cm)

This brilliant painting was done by a 6-year-old from Russia, made available through the Children's Art Exchange—a non-profit organization which "helps children create, strengthen and celebrate global connections through the universal language of art."

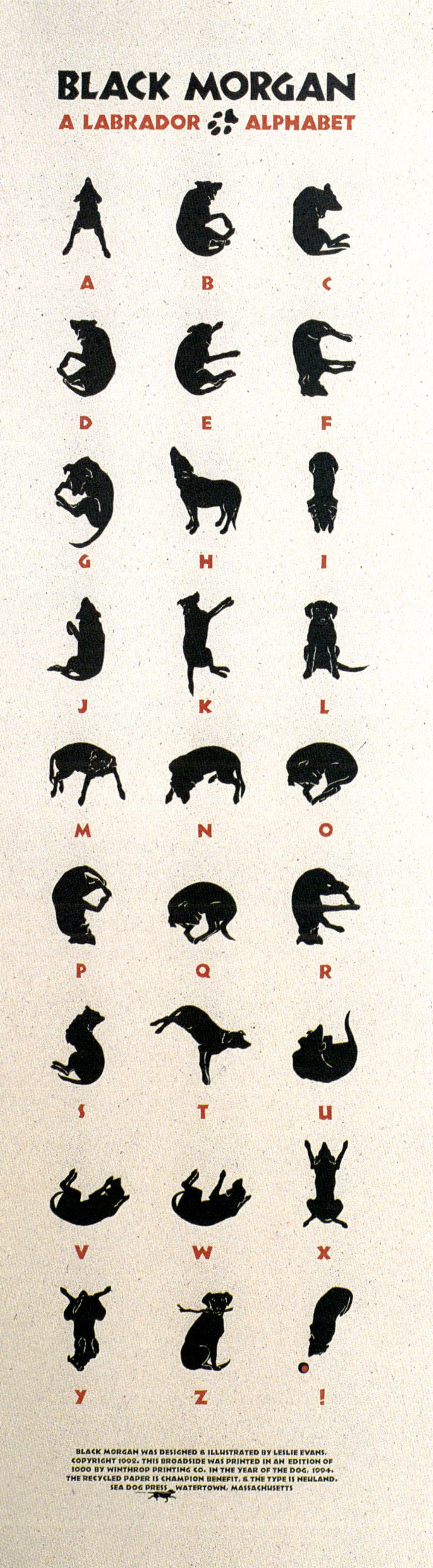

DESIGN FIRM
Sea Dog Press

ALL DESIGN
Leslie Evans

CLIENT
Sea Dog Press

PURPOSE
Self-promotion

SIZE
10" x 32.5"
(25.4cm x 82.6cm)

The original format of this alphabet was a small accordion book done for a class assignment. When a book publishing deal fell through, the designer printed the alphabet as a poster. Illustrations are pen and ink, and type is taken from proofs of Neuland Foundry type.

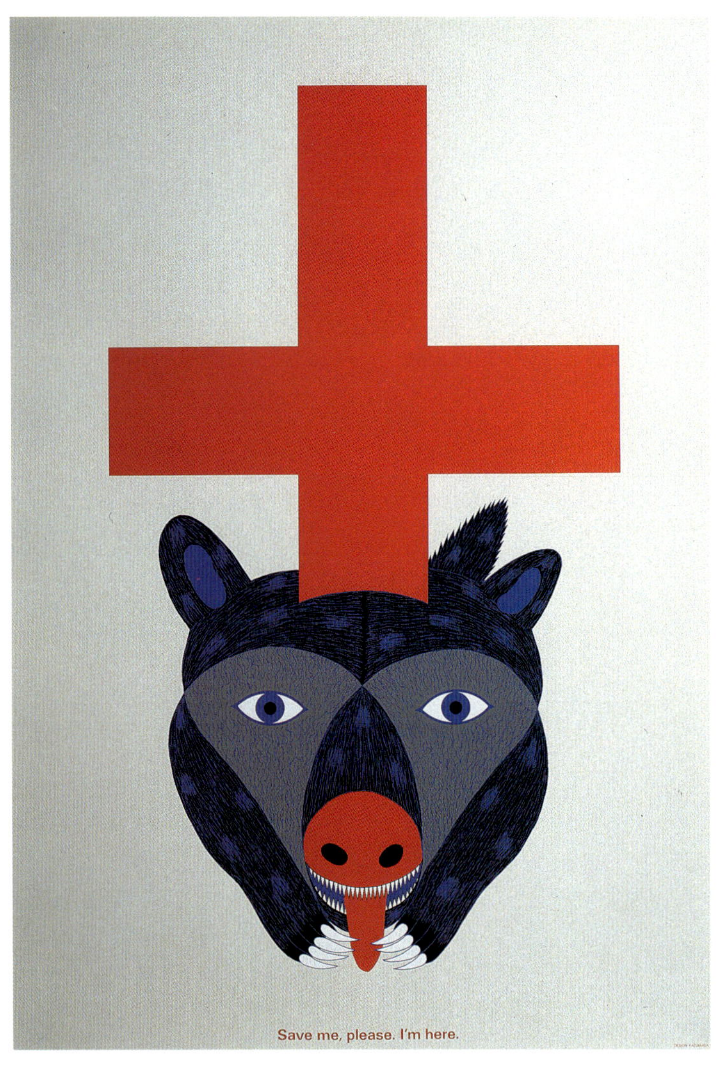

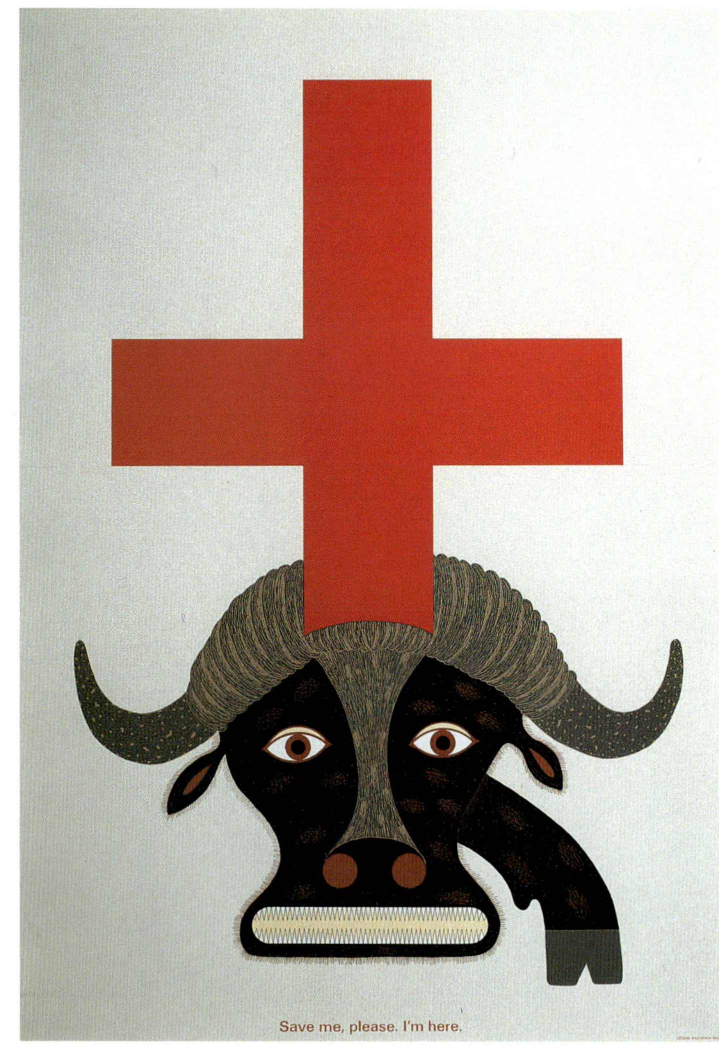

DESIGN FIRM
Nippon Design Center, Inc.

ART DIRECTOR
Kazumasa NAGAI

DESIGNER
Kazumasa NAGAI

CLIENT
Japan Graphic Designers Association

PURPOSE
Exhibition promotion

SIZE
40.5" x 28.5"
(103cm x 72.8cm)

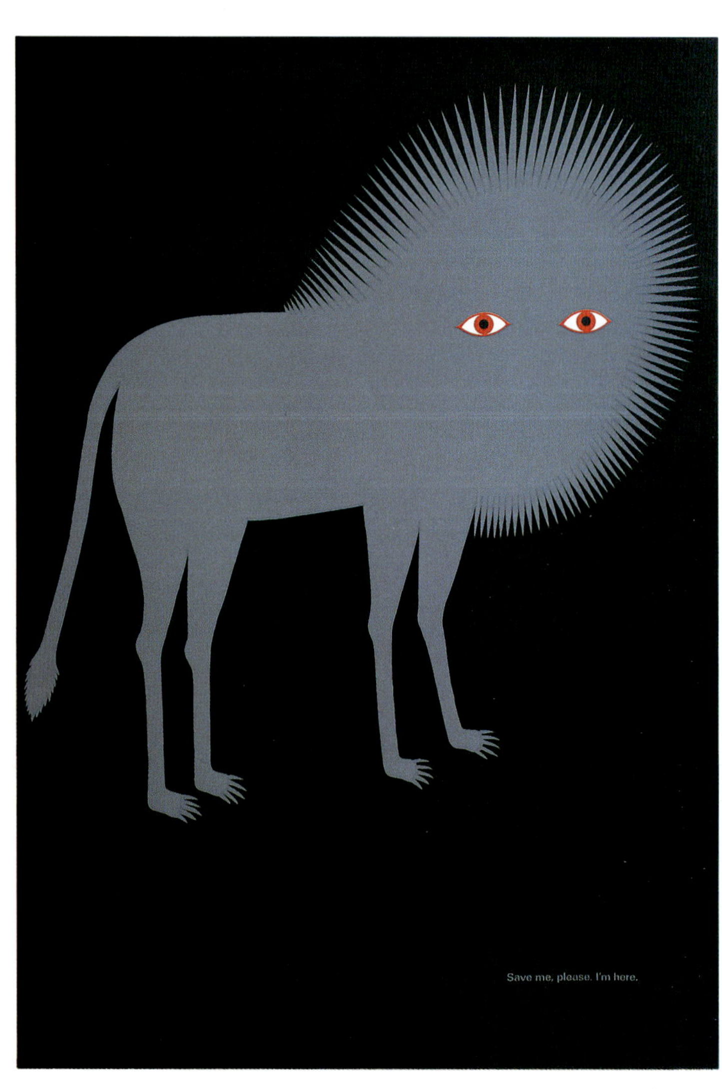

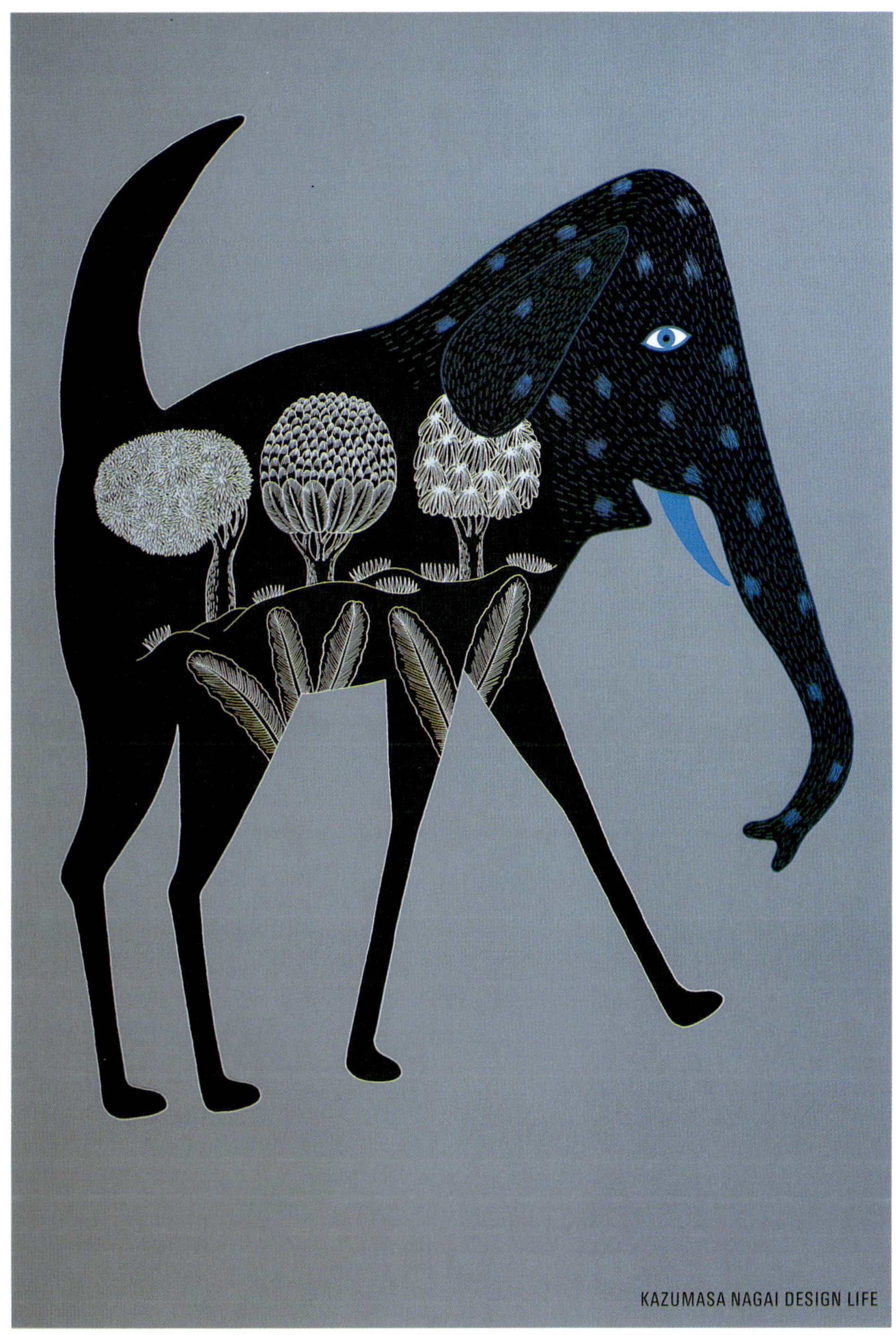

DESIGN FIRM

Nippon Design Center, Inc.

ART DIRECTOR

Kazumasa NAGAI

DESIGNER

Kazumasa NAGAI

CLIENT

Japan Graphic Designers Association

PURPOSE

Exhibition promotion

SIZE

40.5" x 28.5"

(103cm x 72.8cm)

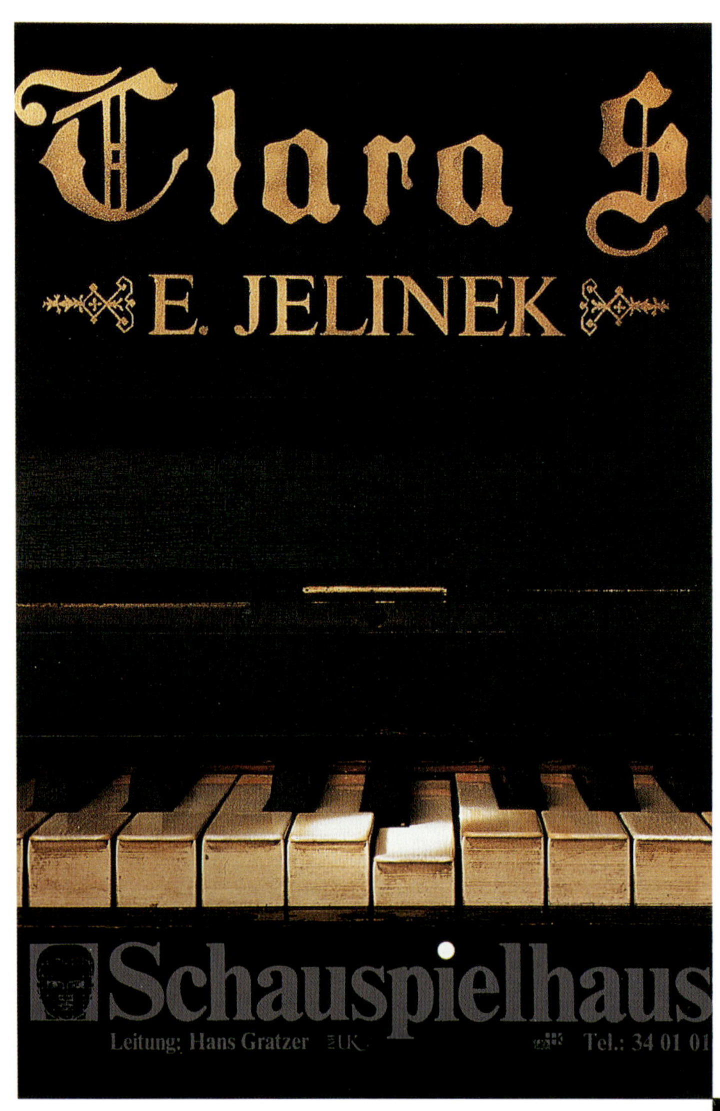

DESIGN FIRM
Gruppe Gut

ART DIRECTOR
Stefan Sagmeister

DESIGNER
Stefan Sagmeister

CLIENT
Schauspiel Haus

PURPOSE
Theater advertisement

SIZE
32.5" x 23"
(82.5cm x 58.4cm)

DESIGN FIRM
Gruppe Gut

ART DIRECTOR
Stefan Sagmeister,
Jurislav Tscharijsky

DESIGNER
Jurislav Tscharijsky

ILLUSTRATOR
Stefan Sagmeister

PHOTOGRAPHER
Jurislav Tscharijsky

CLIENT
Schauspiel Haus

PURPOSE
Theater advertisement

SIZE
32.5" x 23"
(82.6cm x 58.4cm)

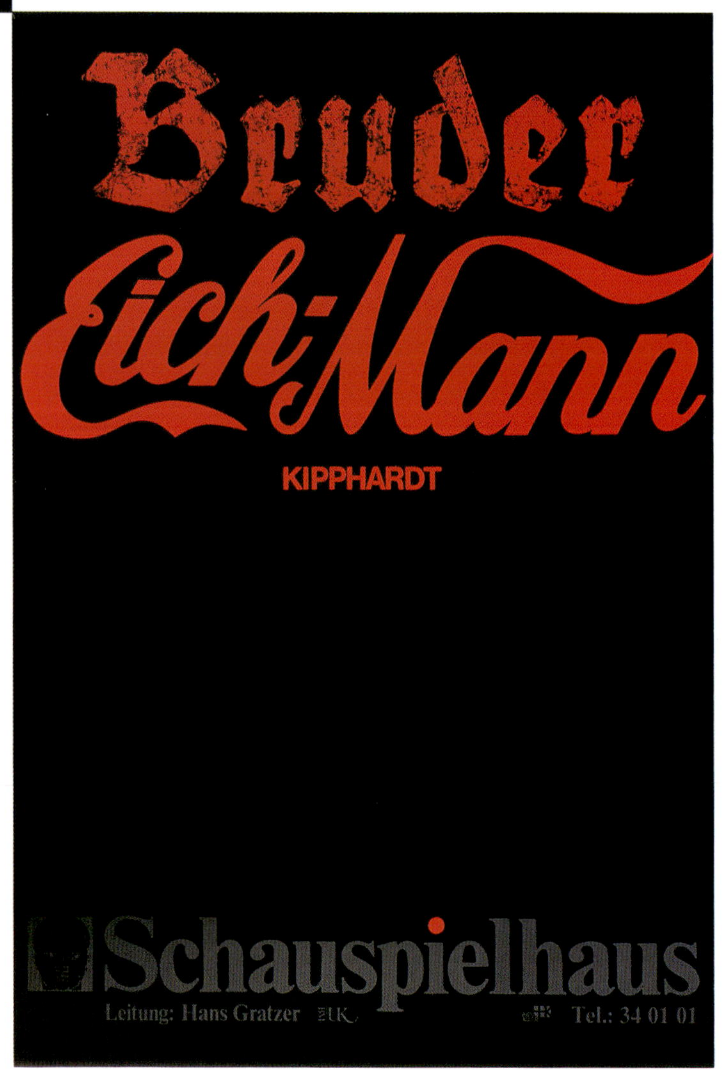

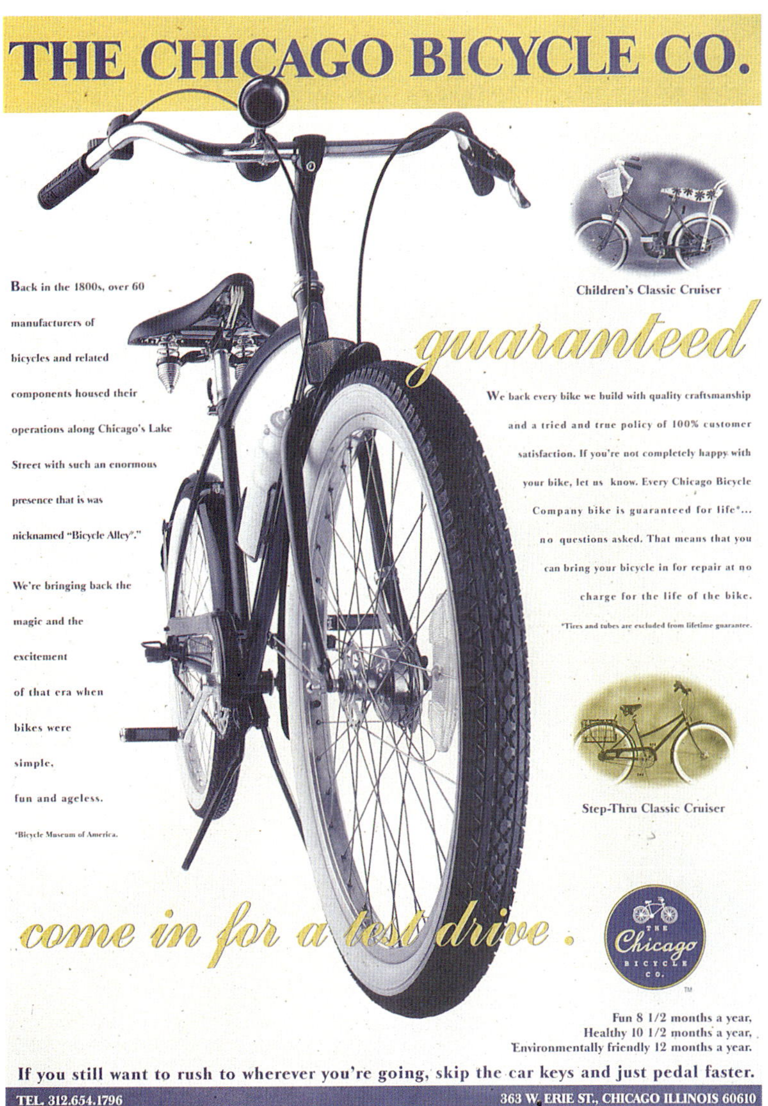

DESIGN FIRM
Maximum Marketing

ART DIRECTOR
Ed Han

DESIGNER
Emilie Cardoso

COPYWRITER
Dana Ross

PHOTOGRAPHER
Dave Rigg Photography, Chicago

CLIENT
The Chicago Bicycle Company

PURPOSE
Promotion

SIZE
14.5" x 20" (36.8cm x 50.8cm)

The designers chose paper, colors, type, and photography that all refer back to a simpler time. The piece first intrigues the viewer with the vignetted photo and words, then reveals itself through a series of questions. Because the client was a young company on a very limited budget, it was necessary for the photography to be multi-functional. The shots were later used in advertising, flyers, and in public relations materials.

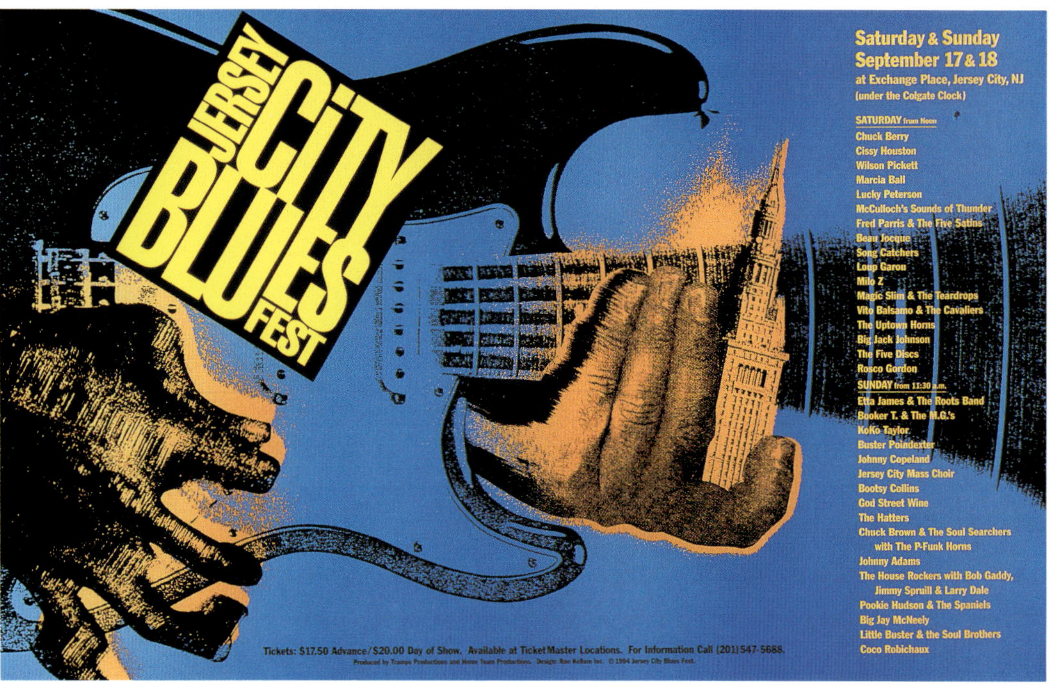

DESIGN FIRM
Ron Kellum, Inc.

ALL DESIGN
Ron Kellum

CLIENT
Tramps Production

PURPOSE
Music festival promotion

SIZE
33" x 21"
(83.8cm x 53.3cm)

Poster was created with the use of Xerox collage with stencils and spray paint.

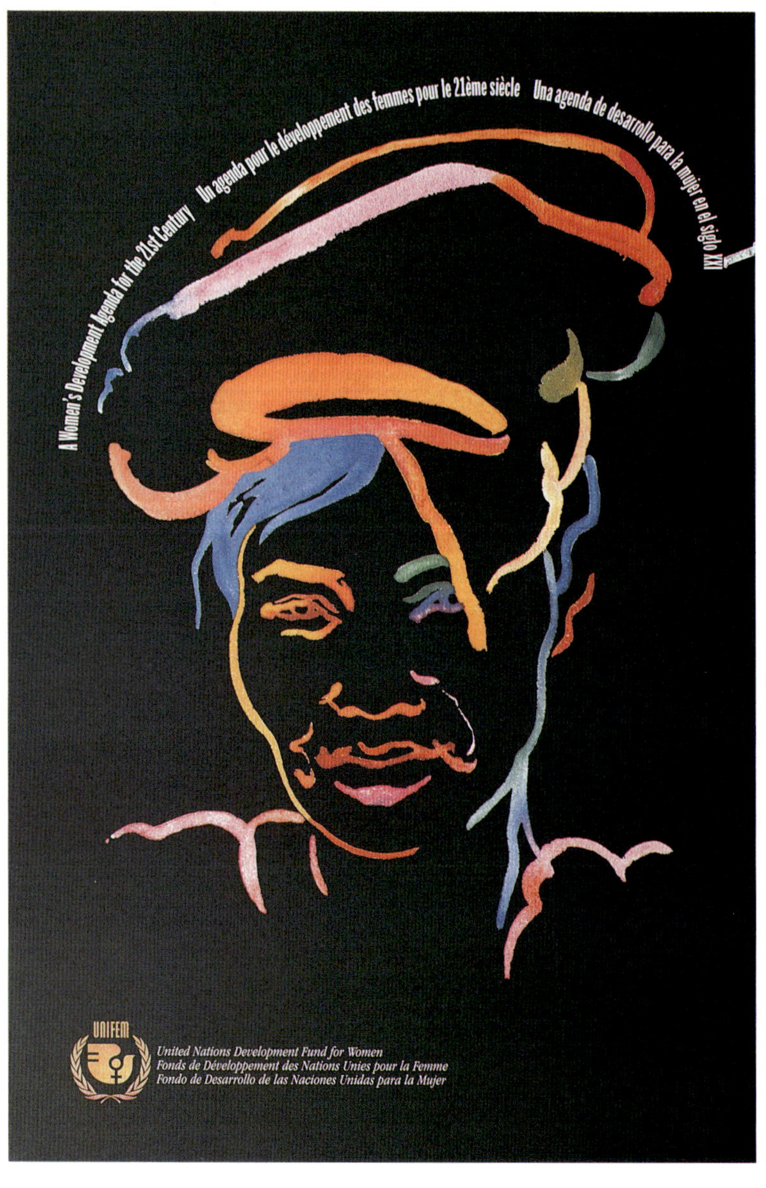

DESIGN FIRM
Emerson, Wajdowicz Studios, Inc.

ART DIRECTOR
Jurek Wajdowicz

DESIGNER
Lisa LaRochelle, Jurek Wajdowicz

ILLUSTRATOR
Jacqui Morgan

CLIENT
UNIFEM

PURPOSE
Conference

SIZE
19" x 28"
(48.3cm x 71.1cm)

DESIGN FIRM
Images

ART DIRECTOR
Walter McCord,
Julius Friedman

DESIGNER
Walter McCord,
Julius Friedman

PHOTOGRAPHER
Craig Guyon

CLIENT
Images

PURPOSE
Self-promotion

SIZE
20" x 30"
(50.8cm x 76.2cm)

[right]

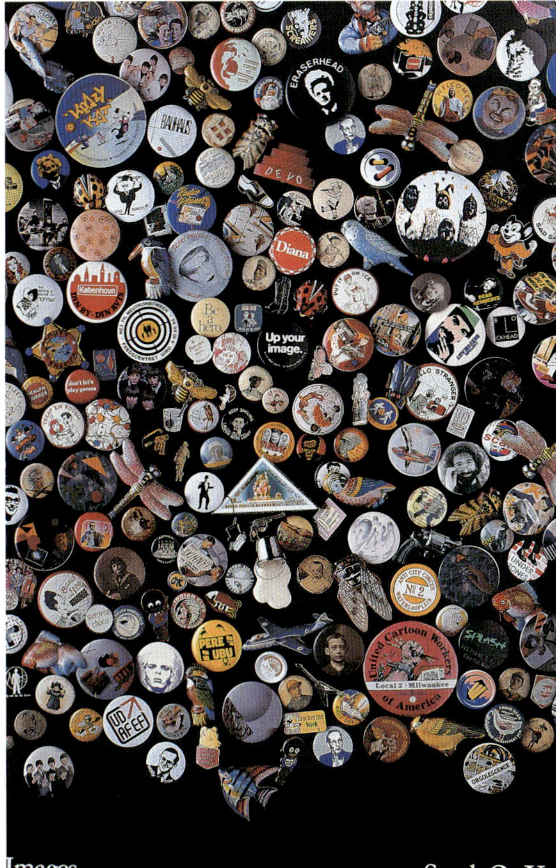

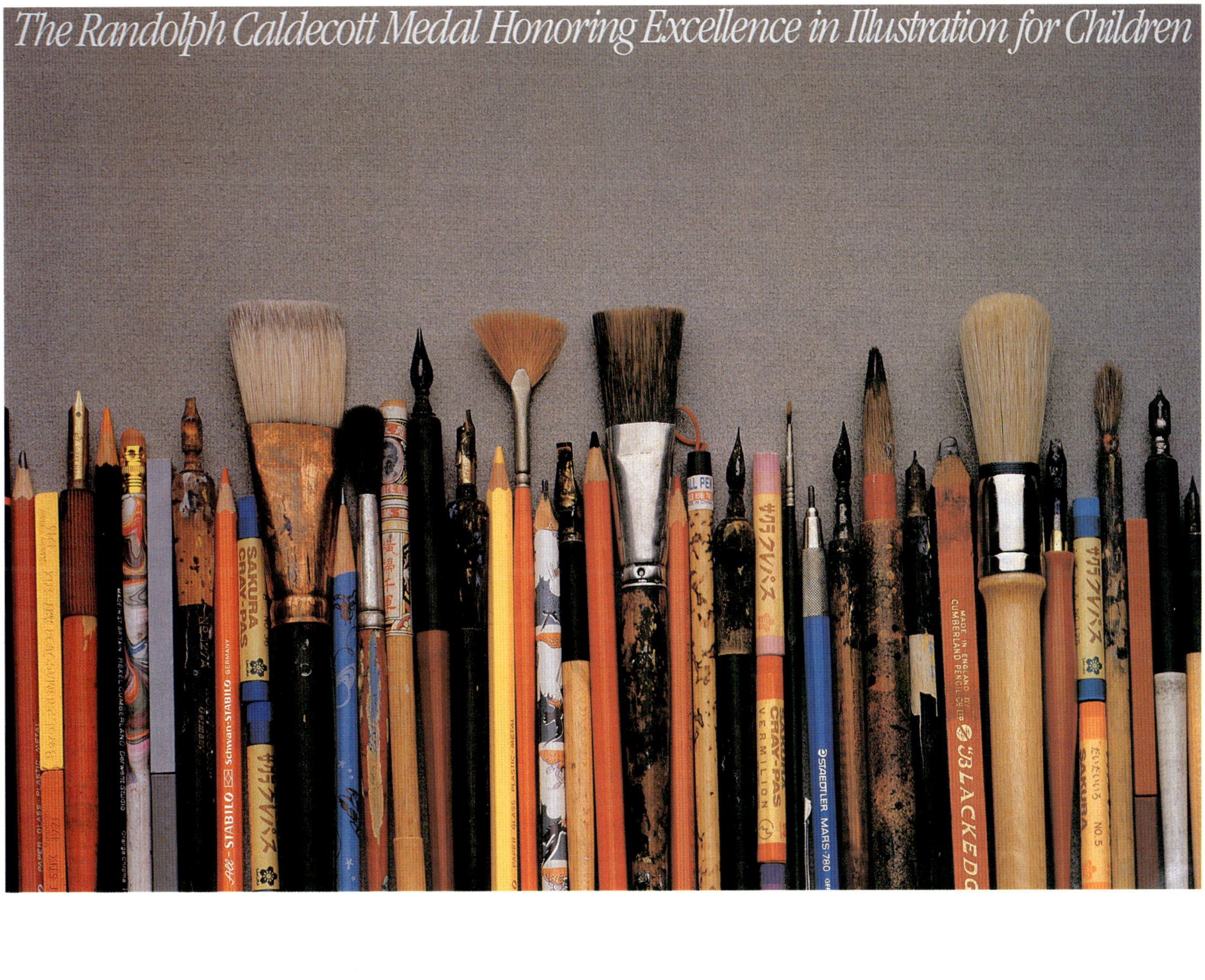

DESIGN FIRM
Images

ART DIRECTOR
Walter McCord,
Julius Friedman

DESIGNER
Walter McCord,
Julius Friedman

PHOTOGRAPHER
Joe Boone

CLIENT
Randolph Caldecott Medal

PURPOSE
Children's literature promotion

SIZE
19.5" x 27"
(49.5cm x 68.6cm)

[below]

The Randolph Caldecott Medal Honoring Excellence in Illustration for Children

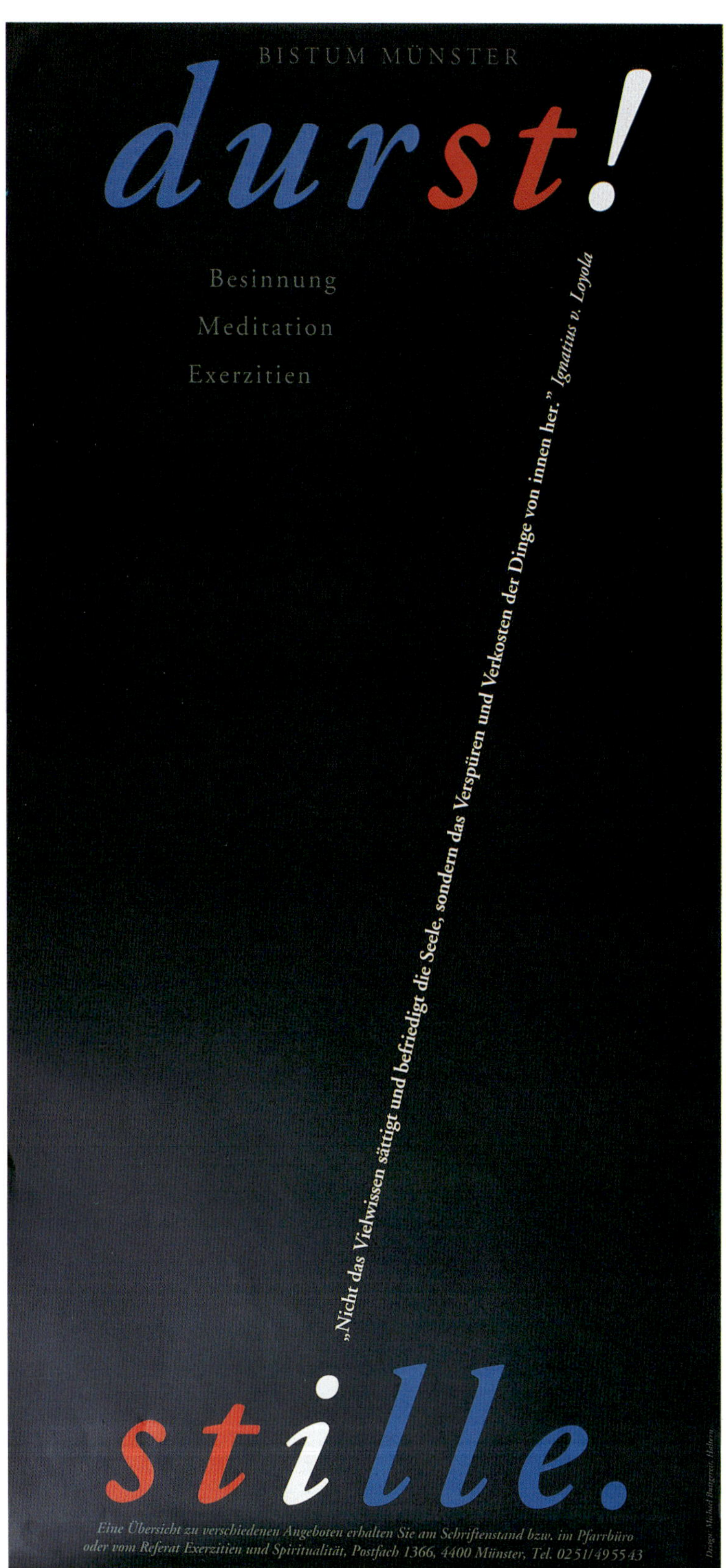

DESIGN FIRM
Buttgereit & Heindenreich

ART DIRECTOR
Michael Buttgereit

DESIGNER
Michael Buttgereit

CLIENT
Bistum Münster

PURPOSE
Invitation to spiritual exercises

SIZE
33" x 15.75" (84cm x 40cm)

Designers used Aldus FreeHand 3.11 to complete this poster.

DESIGN FIRM
Buttgereit & Heindenreich

ART DIRECTOR
Michael Buttgereit & Wolfram Heidenreich

DESIGNER
Michael Buttgereit & Wolfram Heidenreich

CLIENT
Buttgereit & Heidenreich, Kommunikations-design

PURPOSE
Anti-violence and anti-racism poster

Design created with the use of Aldus FreeHand 3.11.

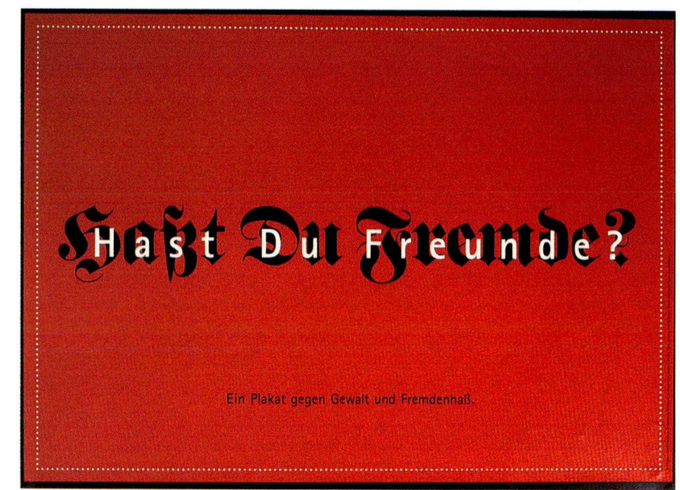

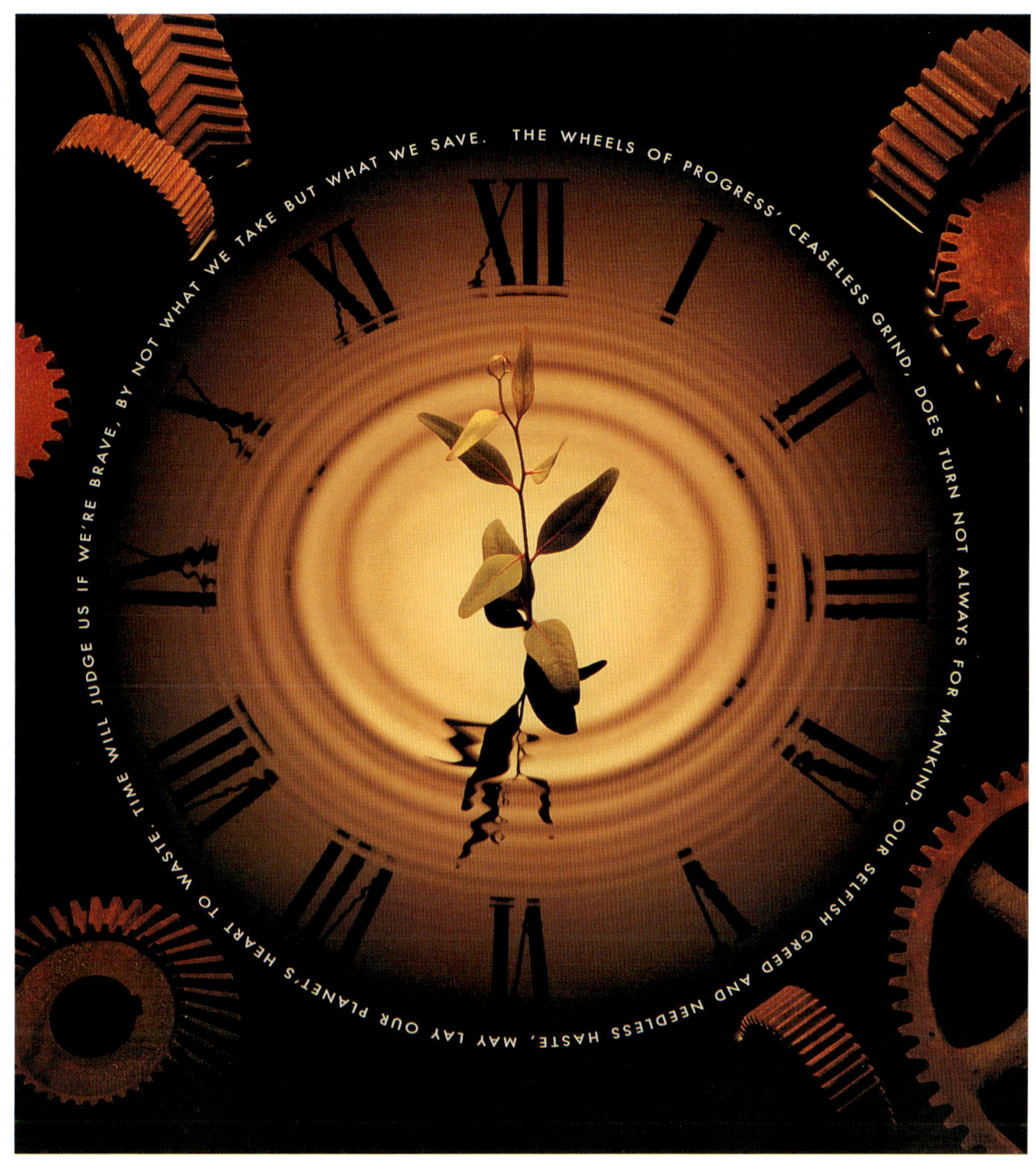

DESIGN FIRM
Watts Graphic Design

ART DIRECTORS
Helen Watts, Peter Watts

DESIGNERS
Helen Watts, Peter Watts

PHOTOGRAPHER
James Vlahogianis

CLIENT
CPI Papers

PURPOSE
Conservation awareness

SIZE
127" x 127" (50cm x 50cm)

The photography for this poster was not retouched.

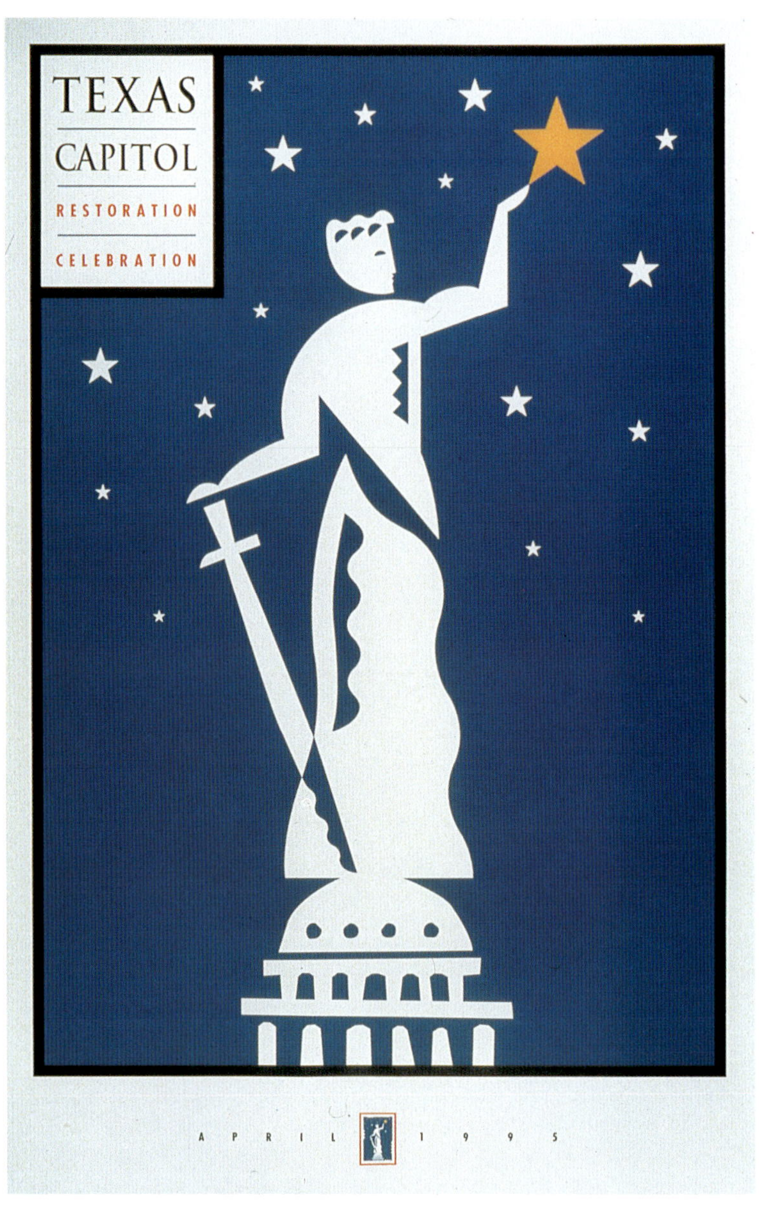

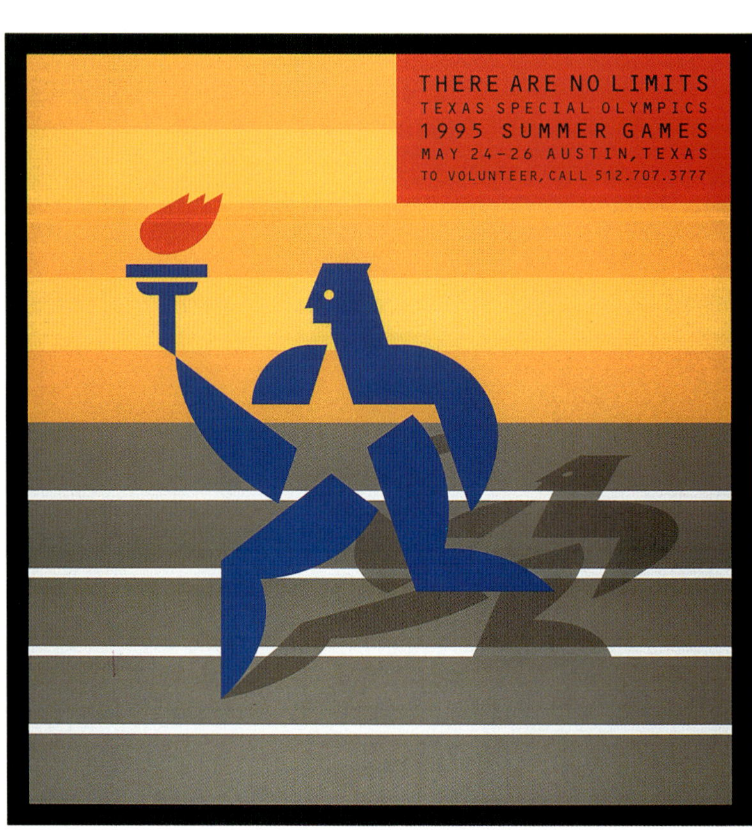

DESIGN FIRM
Sibley/Peteet Design

ART DIRECTOR
Derek Welch

DESIGNERS
Derek Welch, John Evans

ILLUSTRATOR
Derek Welch

CLIENT
Texas Special Olympics

PURPOSE
Summer games promotion

SIZE
24" x 25" (61cm x 63.5cm)

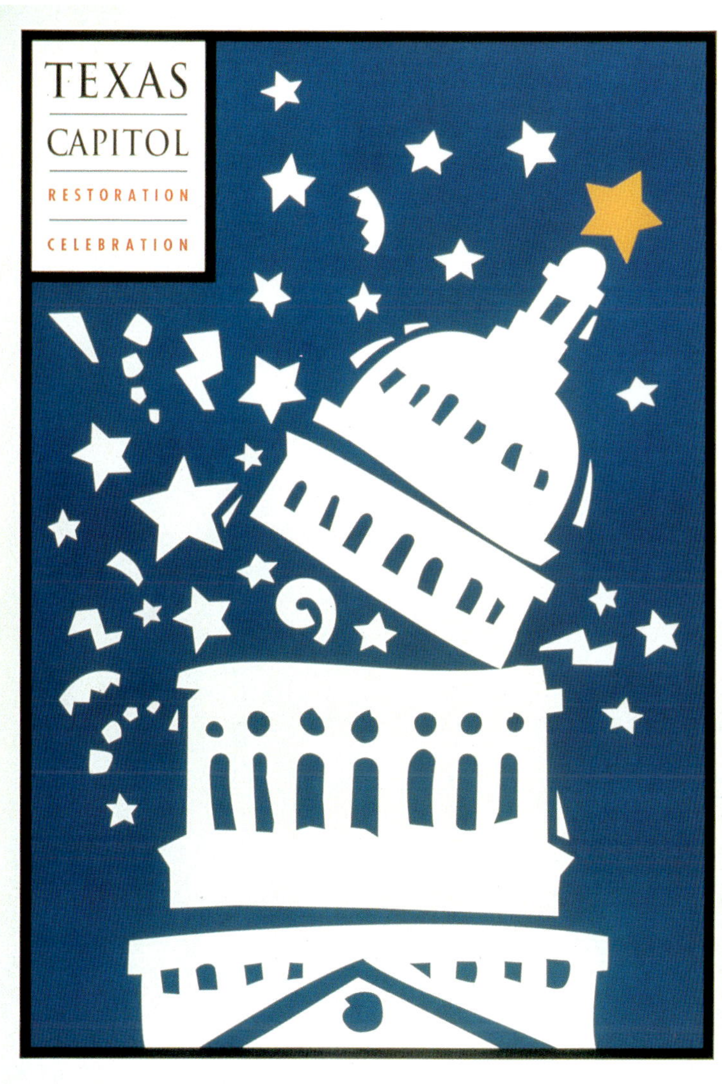

DESIGN FIRM
Sibley/Peteet Design

ART DIRECTOR
Rex Peteet

DESIGNERS
Derek Welch, Rex Peteet, Tom Hough

ILLUSTRATORS
Derek Welch, Rex Peteet, Tom Hough

CLIENT
Texas State Preservation Board

PURPOSE
Opening celebration of renovated capitol

SIZE
24" x 37" (61cm x 94cm)

[left and facing page]

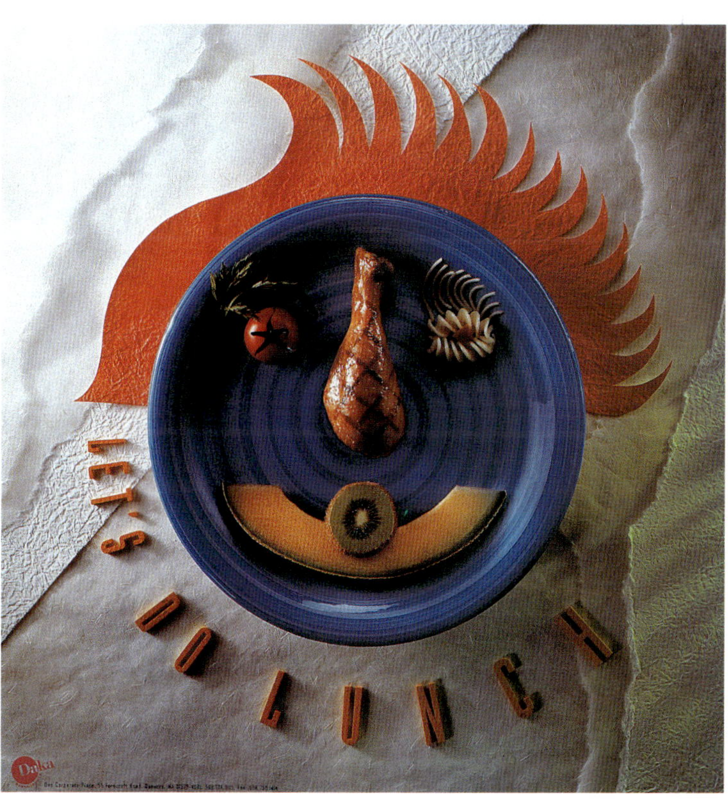

DESIGN FIRM
SullivanPerkins

ART DIRECTOR
Art Garcia

DESIGNER
Art Garcia

PHOTOGRAPHER
Robb Debenport

COPYWRITERS
Mark Perkins, Davy Woodruff

CLIENT
Daka (Van Saxon & Associates)

PURPOSE
Promotion

SIZE
23" x 23.25" (58.4cm x 59.1cm)

All typography was shot as part of the photograph to give a dimension that could not be achieved mechanically.

DESIGN FIRM
Trend Design Ltd.

ART DIRECTOR
Frankie Cheung

DESIGNER
Frankie Cheung

PHOTOGRAPHER
Kenneth Yeung

CLIENT
Urban Council, Hong Kong

PURPOSE
1950s dramatic film promotion

SIZE
28" x 18" (71 cm x 46 cm)

A traditional ladies' handkerchief commonly carried by ladies of the period was used as the main visual, echoing the theme "Time for Tears" — a parade of famous sad movies by three famous directors.

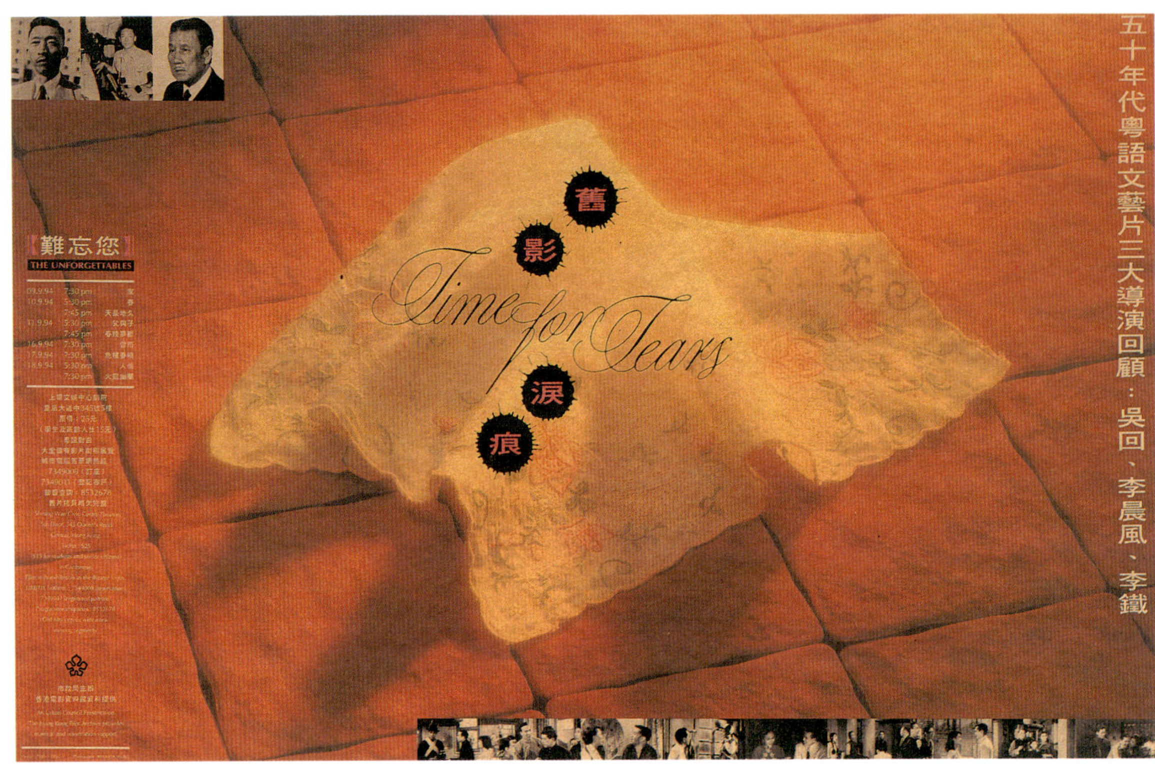

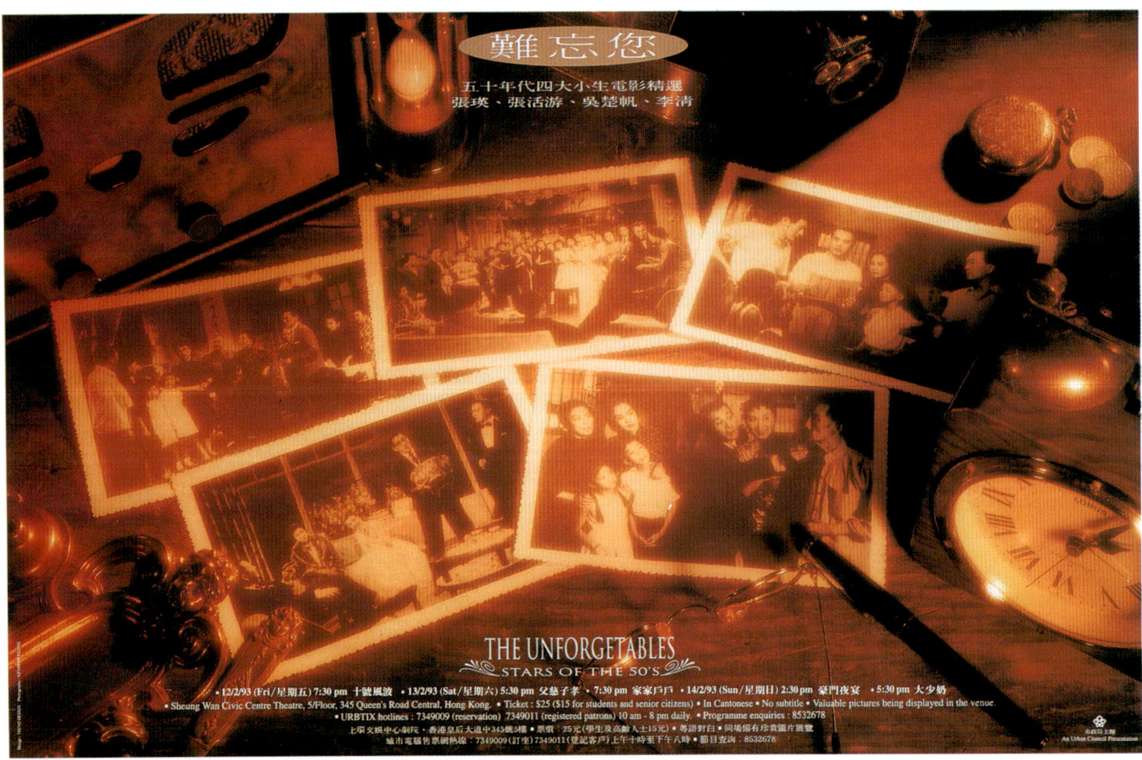

DESIGN FIRM
Trend Design Ltd.

ART DIRECTOR
Frankie Cheung

DESIGNER
Frankie Cheung

PHOTOGRAPHER
Kenneth Yeung

CLIENT
Urban Council, Hong Kong

PURPOSE
1950s dramatic film promotion

SIZE
20" x 30" (50.8cm x 76.2cm)

Images were retrieved from original black and white films and reproduced into black and white prints with the 1950s border. Props were used, including coins of the same period, to deliver the 1950s mood.

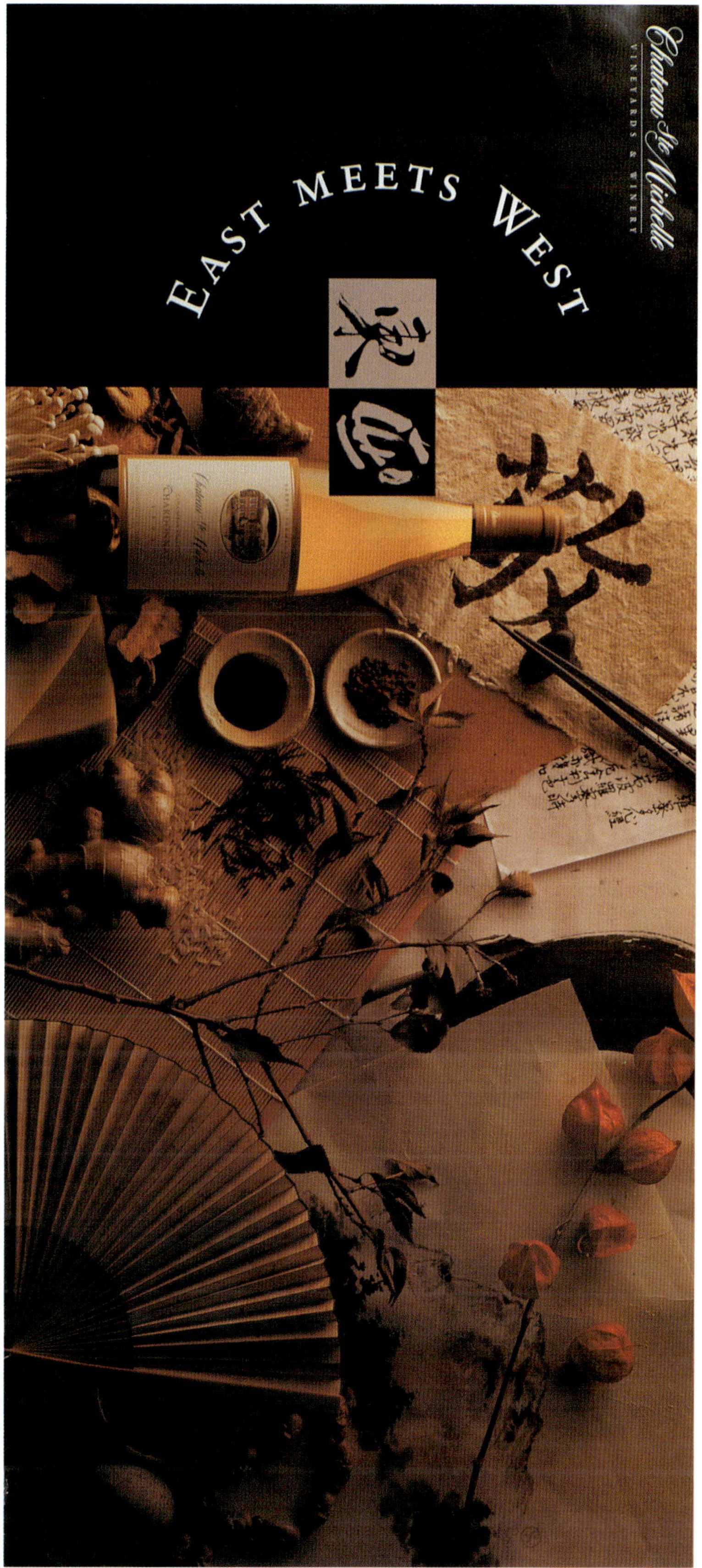

DESIGN FIRM
Studio M D

ART DIRECTORS
Peter Houghton,
Stimson Lane

DESIGNER
Randy Lim

PHOTOGRAPHER
Kevin Latona,
Kevin Latona Photography

CLIENT
Stimson Lane

PURPOSE
Promotion

SIZE
39" x 17.5"
(73.7cm x 44.5cm)

DESIGN FIRM
Vaughn Wedeen Creative, Inc.

ART DIRECTOR
Steve Wedeen

DESIGNERS
Steve Wedeen, Lucy Hitchcock, Dan Flynn

ILLUSTRATOR
Vivian Harder

CLIENT
US West Foundation

PURPOSE
Internal sales promotion

SIZE
24" x 36" (61cm x 91.4cm)

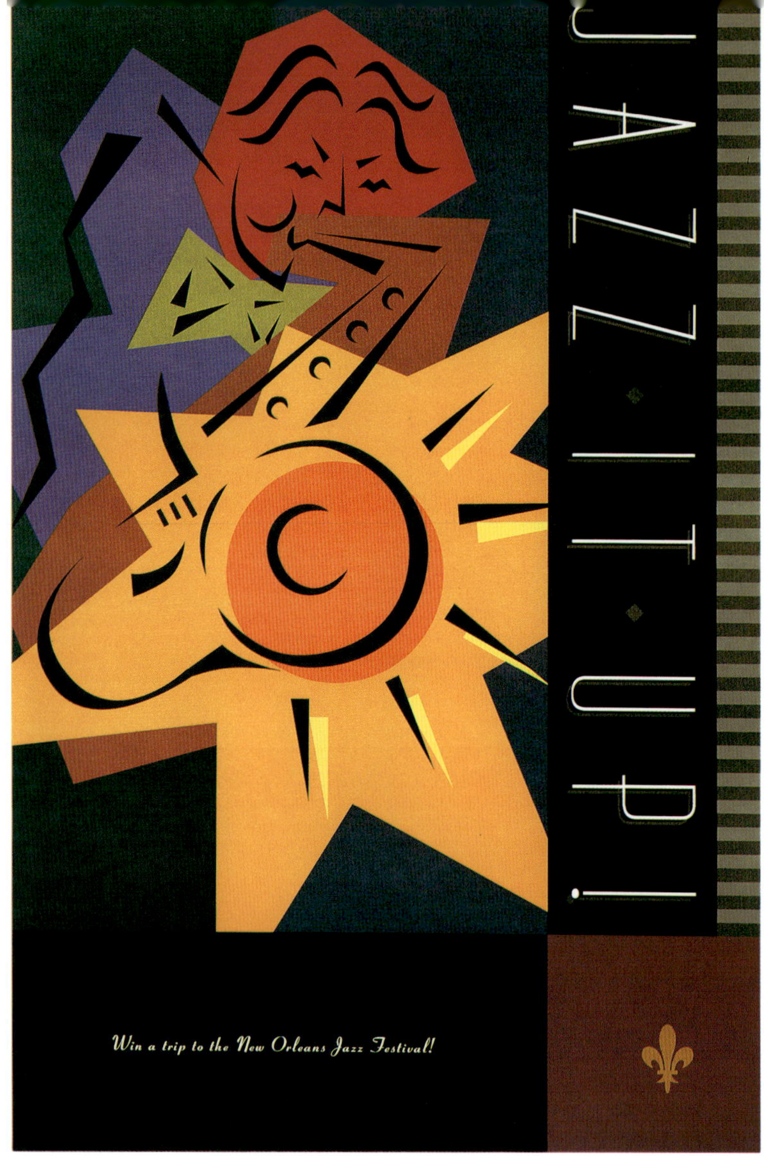

DESIGN FIRM
Vaughn Wedeen Creative, Inc.

ART DIRECTORS
Rick Vaughn, Steve Wedeen

DESIGNER
Rick Vaughn

ILLUSTRATOR
Rick Vaughn

CLIENT
Vaughn Wedeen Creative, Inc.

PURPOSE
Self-promotion

SIZE
19.5" x 35.5" (49.5cm x 90.2cm)

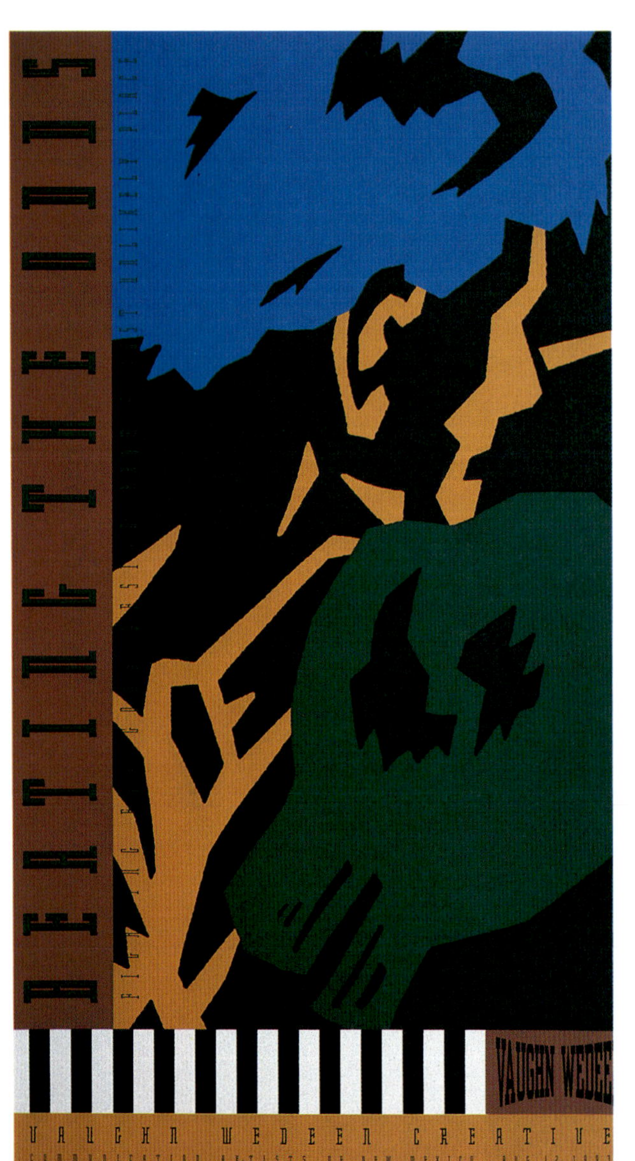

DESIGN FIRM
Vaughn Wedeen Creative, Inc.

ART DIRECTOR
Steve Wedeen

DESIGNERS
Steve Wedeen, Vivian Harder

ILLUSTRATOR
Vivian Harder

CLIENT
Pro-bono

PURPOSE
Commemorative poster

SIZE
15" x 27" (38.1cm x 68.6cm)

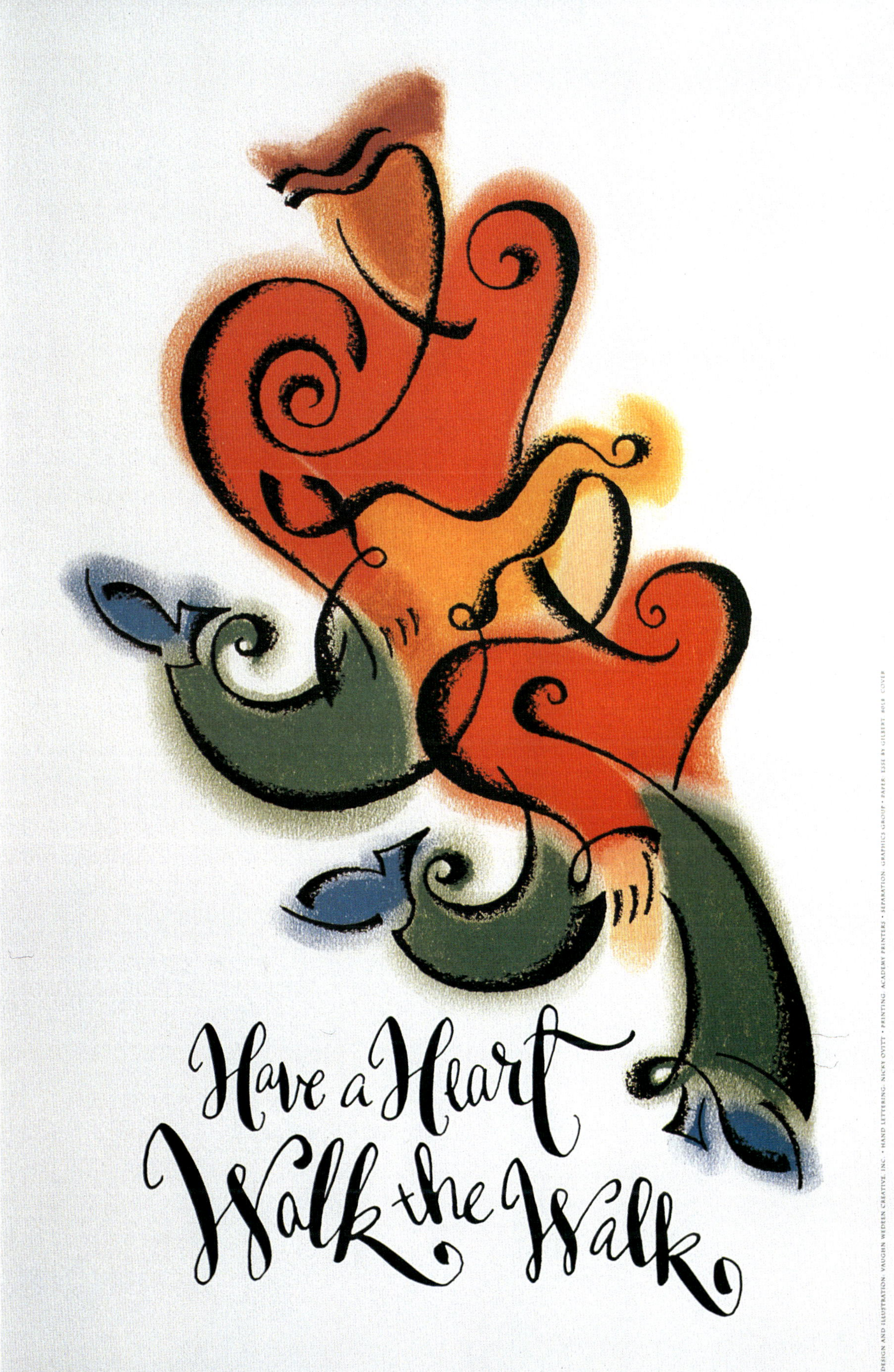
ALBUQUERQUE AIDS WALK 1994
Have a Heart
Walk the Walk
SUNDAY, OCTOBER 23, 1994 TIGUEX PARK

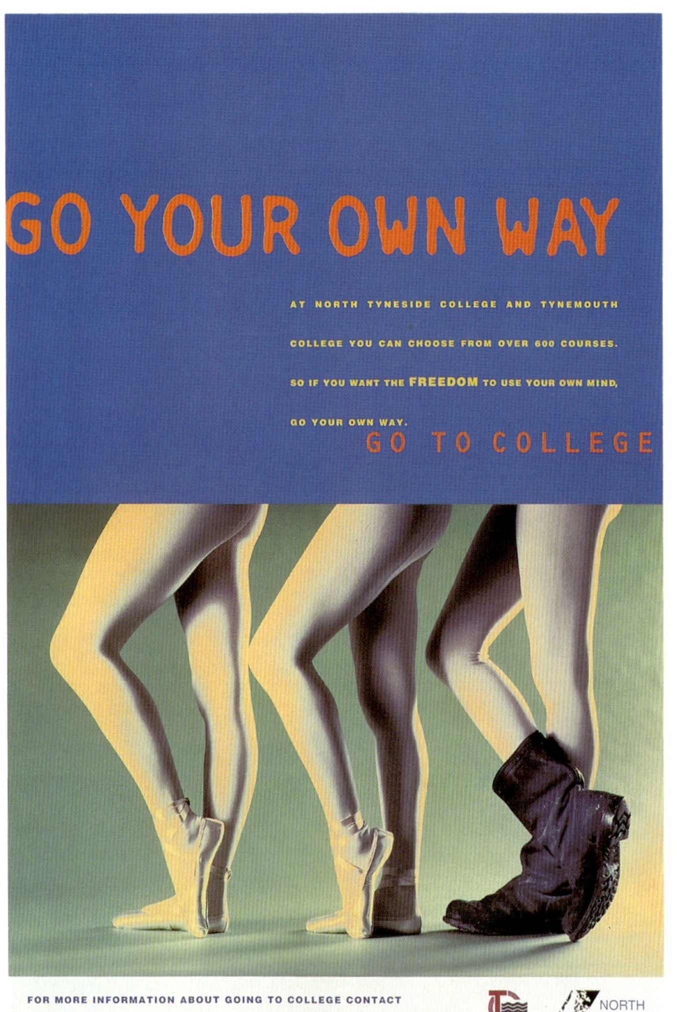

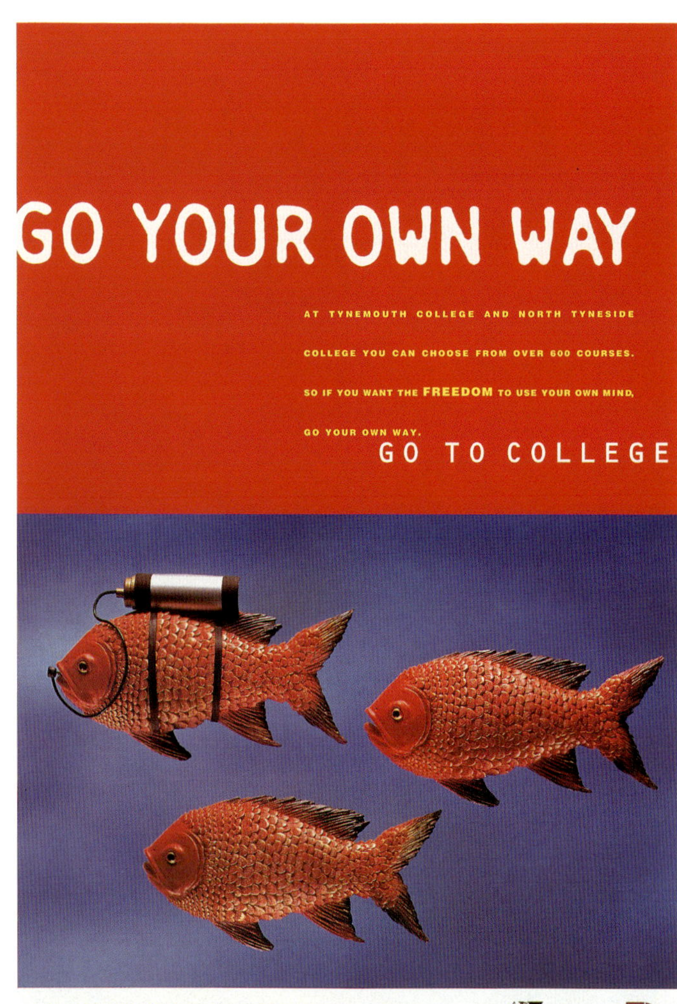

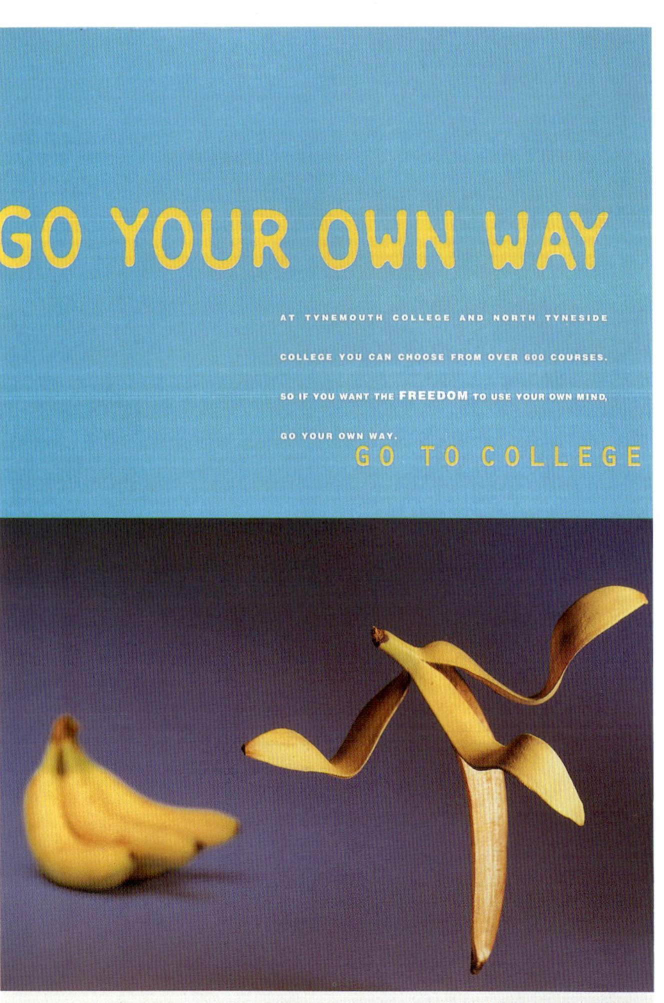

DESIGN FIRM
Yellow M

ART DIRECTORS
Craig Falconer, Lee Manson

DESIGNERS
Craig Falconer, Lee Manson

COPYWRITER
Dawn Coulter

PHOTOGRAPHER
Moy Williams

CLIENT
North Tyneside & Tynemouth College

PURPOSE
College recruitment

SIZE
60" x 40" (152.4cm x 101.6cm)

The fish and frog were modelled in resin and hand-painted. The banana was hand-modelled using an actual banana and hand-painted.

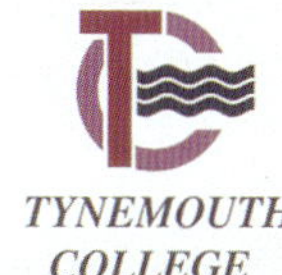
TYNEMOUTH
COLLEGE

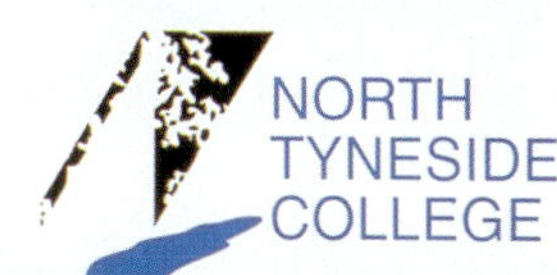
NORTH
TYNESIDE
COLLEGE

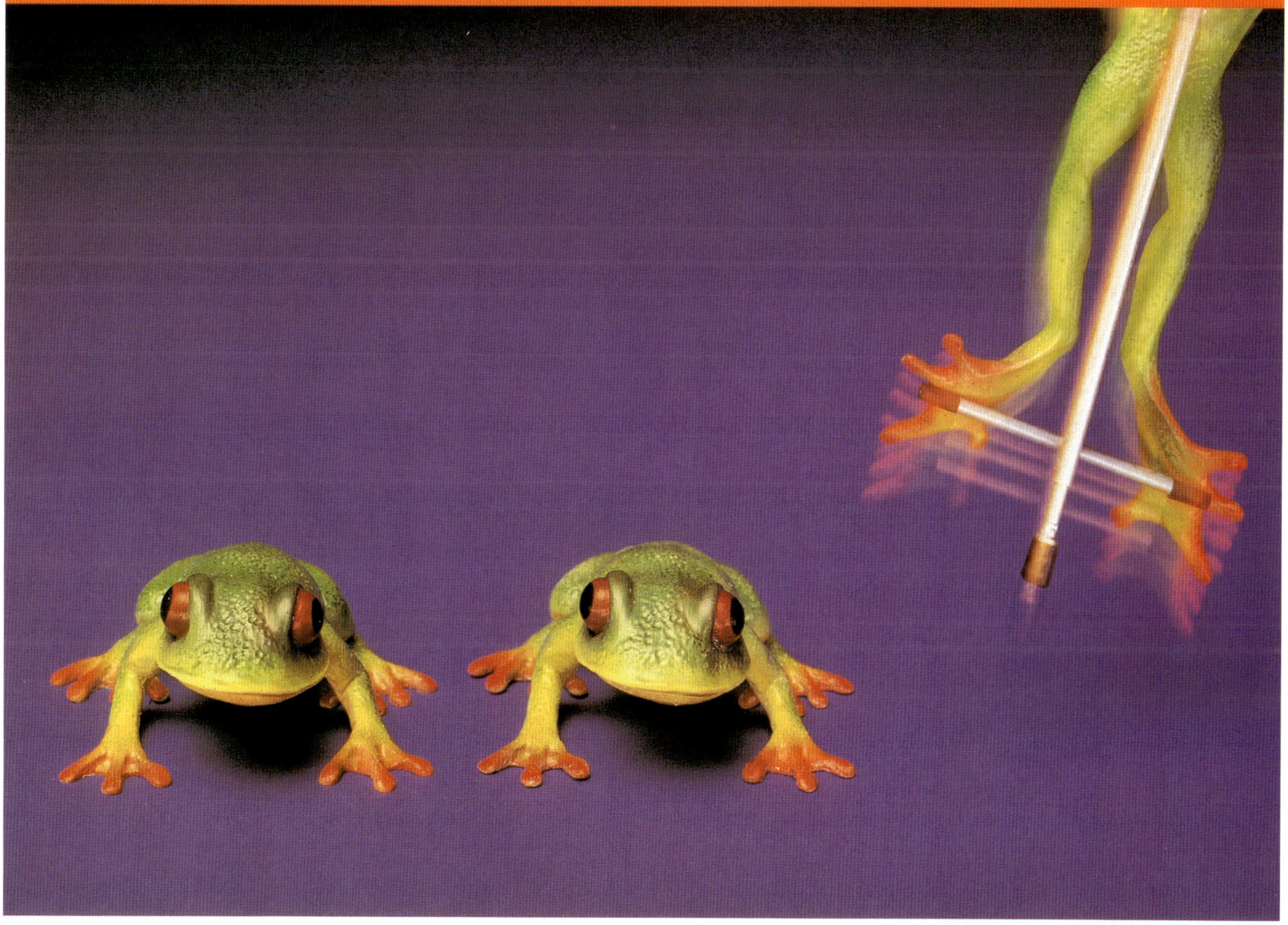

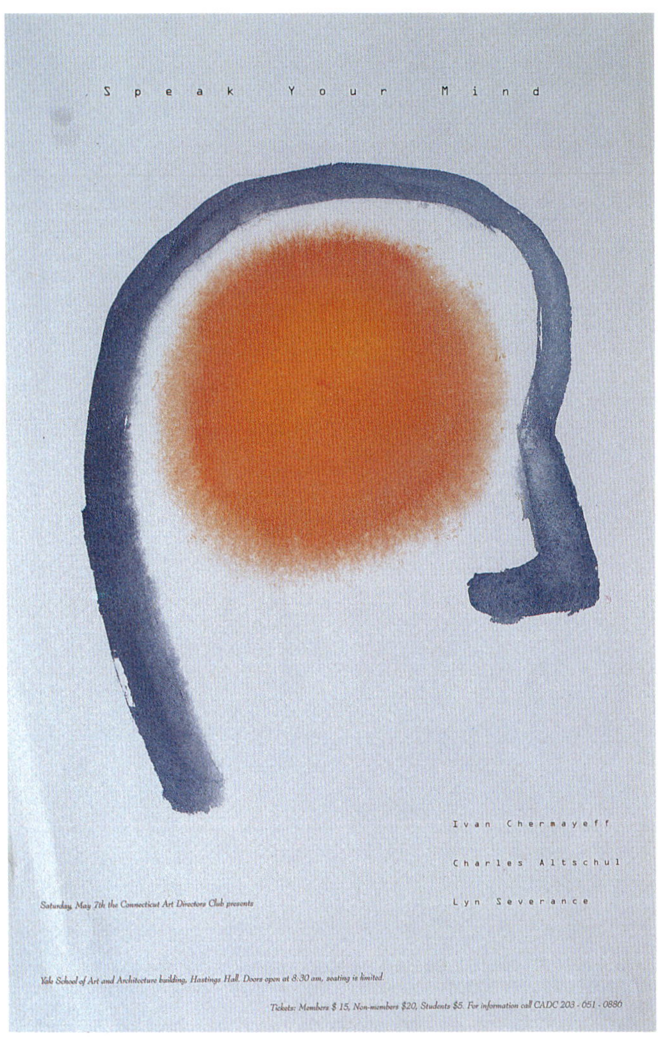

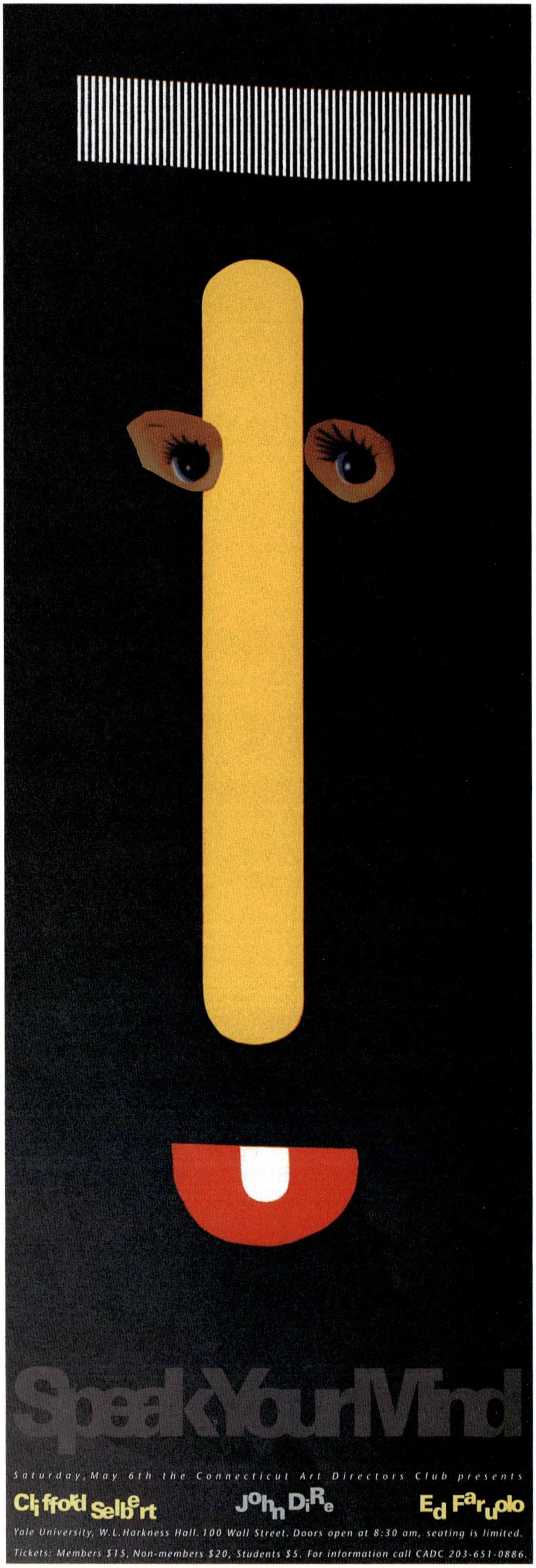

D E S I G N   F I R M

Keiler Design Group

A L L   D E S I G N

Christopher Passehl

C L I E N T

Connecticut Art Directors Club

P U R P O S E

Design event announcement

S I Z E

[right]

7" x 19.5" (17.8cm x 49.5cm)

[above]

11" x 17" (27.9cm x 43.2cm)

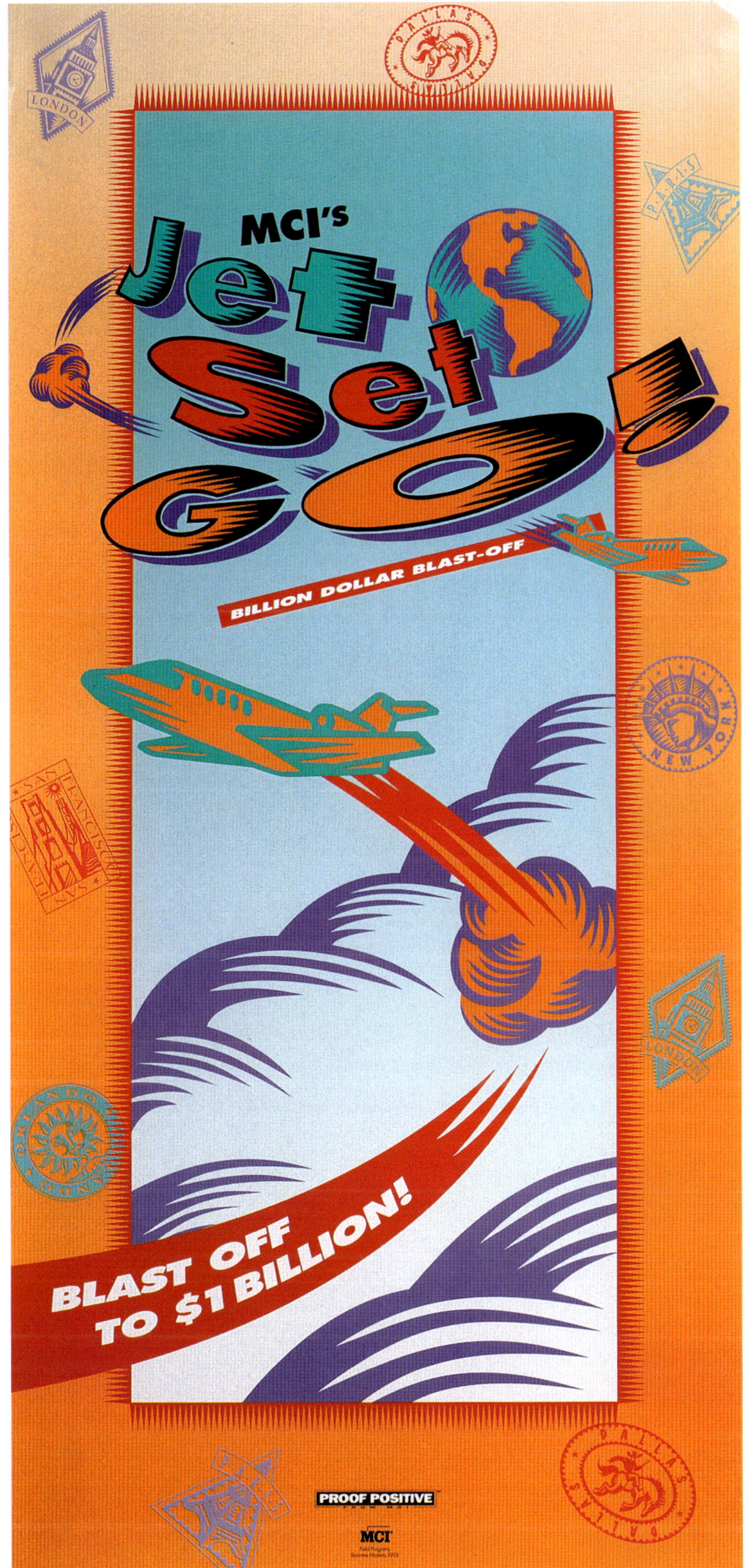

DESIGN FIRM
Group121

ART DIRECTOR
Mark Wilson

DESIGNER
Jay Bernasconi

ILLUSTRATOR
Linda Bleck

CLIENT
MCI

PURPOSE
Promotion for internal sales contest

Poster created with QuarkXPress and Adobe Illustrator.

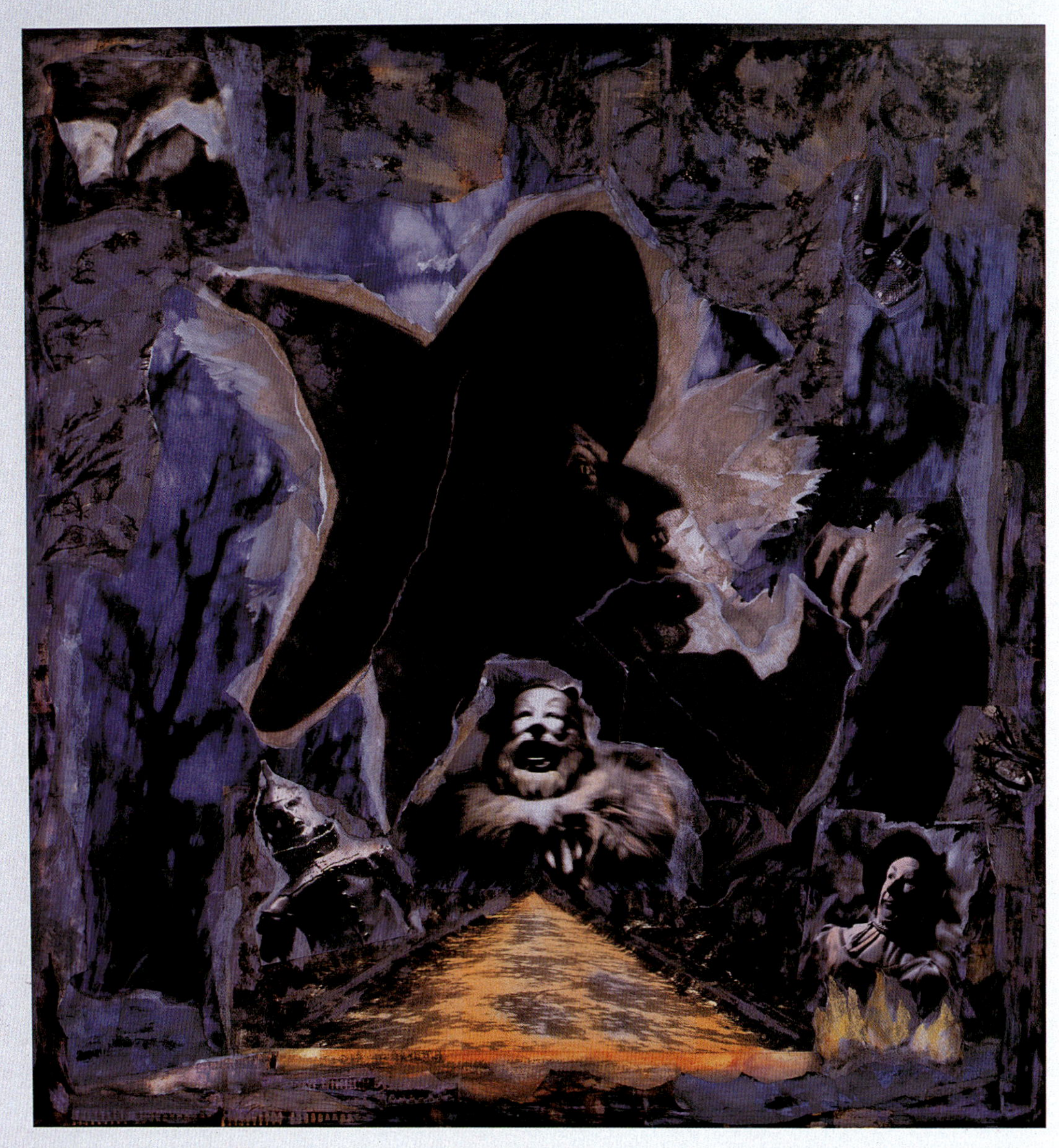

CLASSIC PRODUCTION, UNFORGETTABLE PERFORMANCE.

SPANGLER PRINTERS

PRINTING: SPANGLER PRINTERS DESIGN: MULLER + COMPANY PHOTOGRAPHY: MICHAEL REGNIER KANSAS CITY

DESIGN FIRM

Muller + Company

ART DIRECTOR

Tyler Singer

DESIGNER

Tyler Singer

PHOTOGRAPHER

Michael Regnier

CLIENT

Spangler Printers

PURPOSE

Printer promotion

SIZE

28.5" x 19"

(72.4cm x 48.3cm)

DESIGN FIRM

Towers Perrin

ART DIRECTOR

Kathleen Aiken

DESIGNER

Annette Smaga

CLIENT

Rockford Health Systems

PURPOSE

New benefit program announcement

SIZE

18" x 24" (45.7cm x 61cm)

Photo was worked on in Adobe Photoshop to achieve the soft edges.

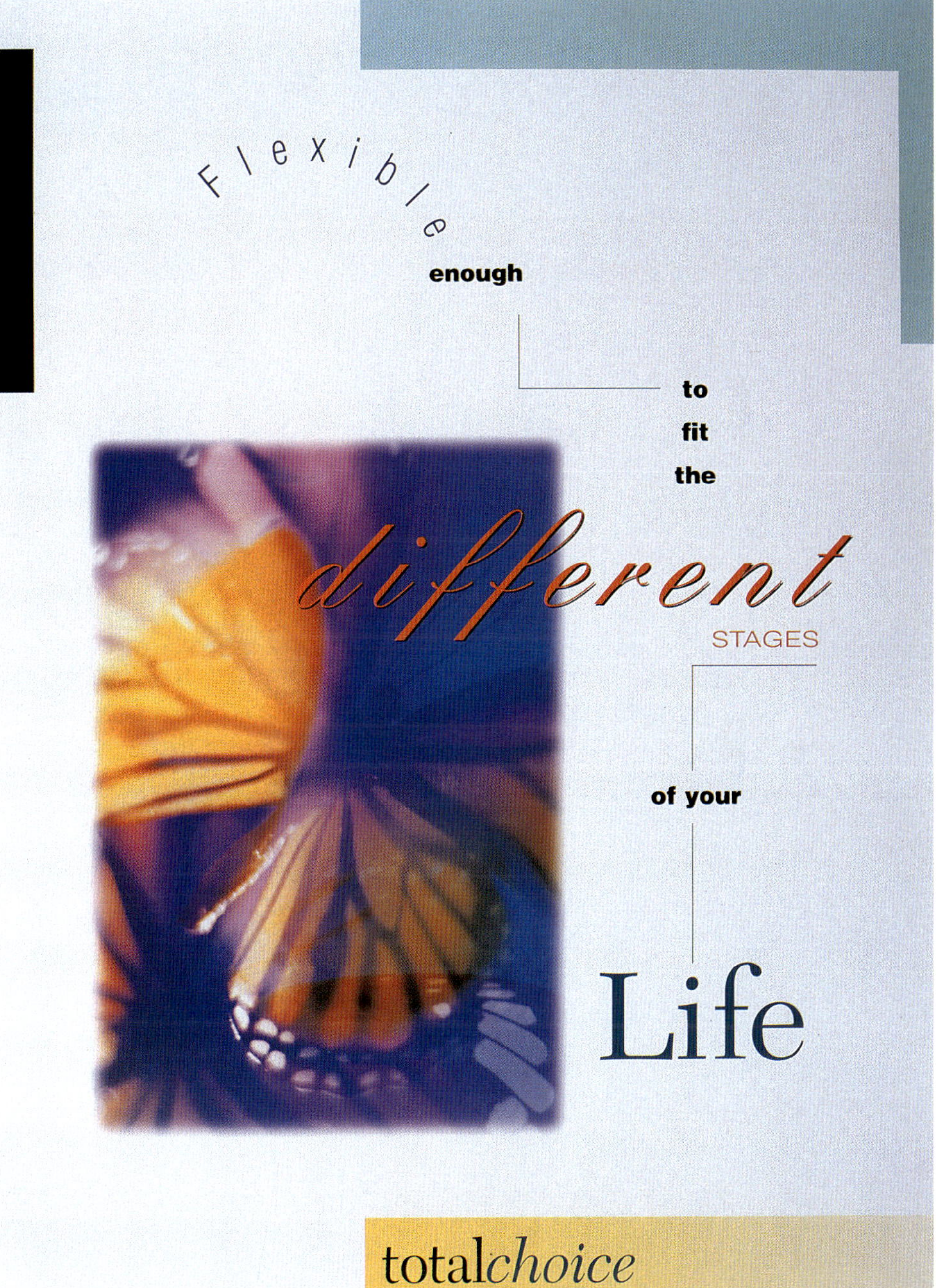

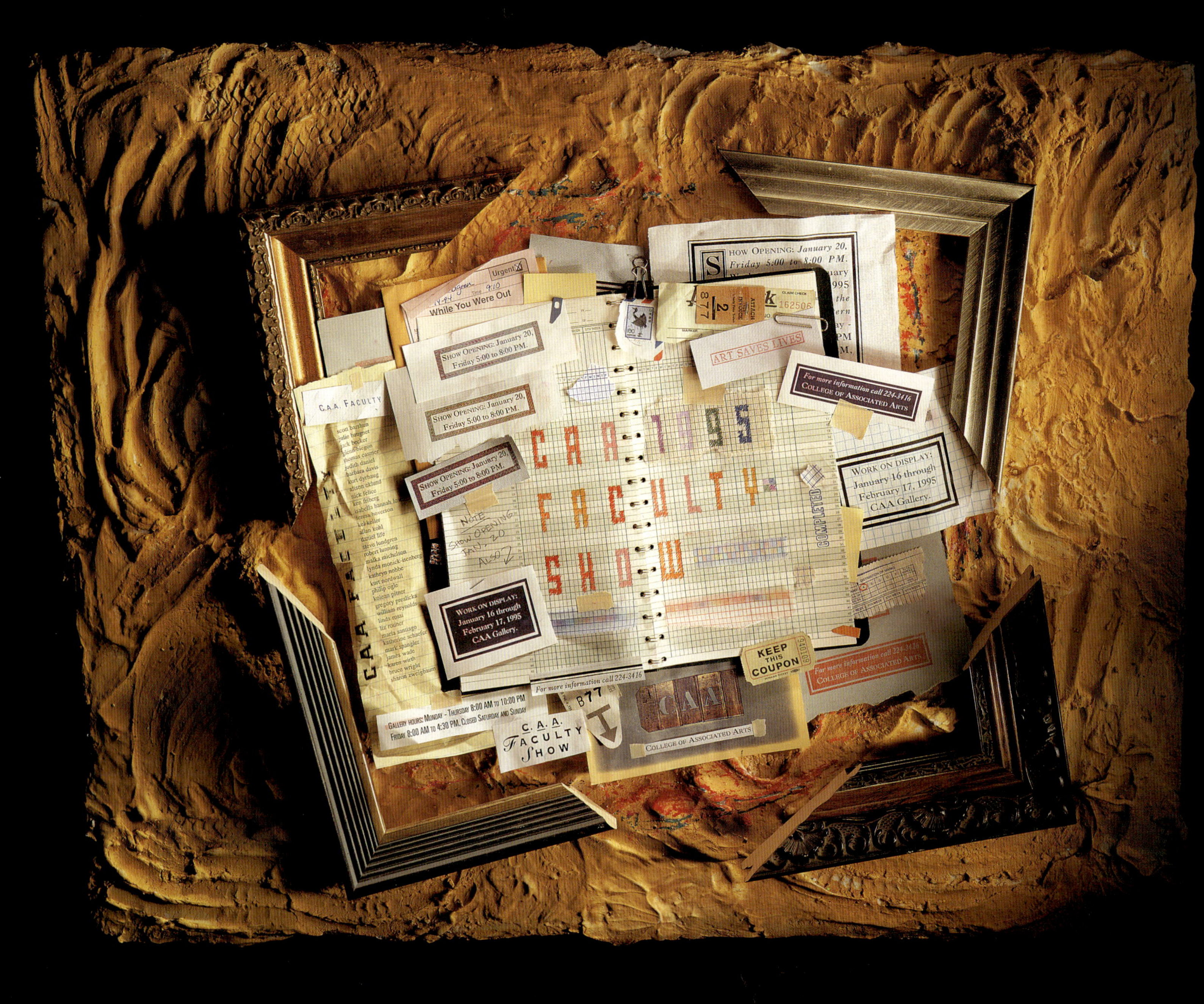

DESIGN FIRM

Steve Lundgren Graphic Design/
Spangler Design Team

ALL DESIGN

Steve Lundgren, Mark Spangler

PHOTOGRAPHER

Gallop Studios

CLIENT

The College of Associated Arts,
St. Paul

PURPOSE

Faculty art show announcement

SIZE

17" x 22" (43.2cm x 55.9cm)

Many things came together to accomplish this poster. Conceptually, the areas of fine arts and communication design both needed to be represented. A teachers grade book collage piece was placed in the center of the poster, surrounded by picture frame corners and a plaster work background.

THE BUCK BUCHANAN SPORTS FESTIVAL

SATURDAY, FEBRUARY 11, 1995, 1-5 P.M. AT THE KANSAS CITY MERCHANDISE MART, 115TH & METCALF

PRESENTED BY: WDAF-TV

Where can you meet and talk to over 90 sports celebrities, get autographs and bid for memorabilia in a huge collector's auction? At the 7th Annual Buck Buchanan Sports Festival & Auction to benefit Special Olympics. Tickets are available for $5 through TicketMaster or at the door the day of the event. For more information call 236-9290.

BUCK BUCHANAN SPORTS FESTIVAL

PREMIER BANK IV SPONSOR

D E S I G N F I R M

David Shultz

A R T D I R E C T O R

David Shultz

D E S I G N E R

David Shultz

C L I E N T

Special Olympics

P U R P O S E

Event promotion

S I Z E

33" x 19"

(83.8cm x 48.26cm)

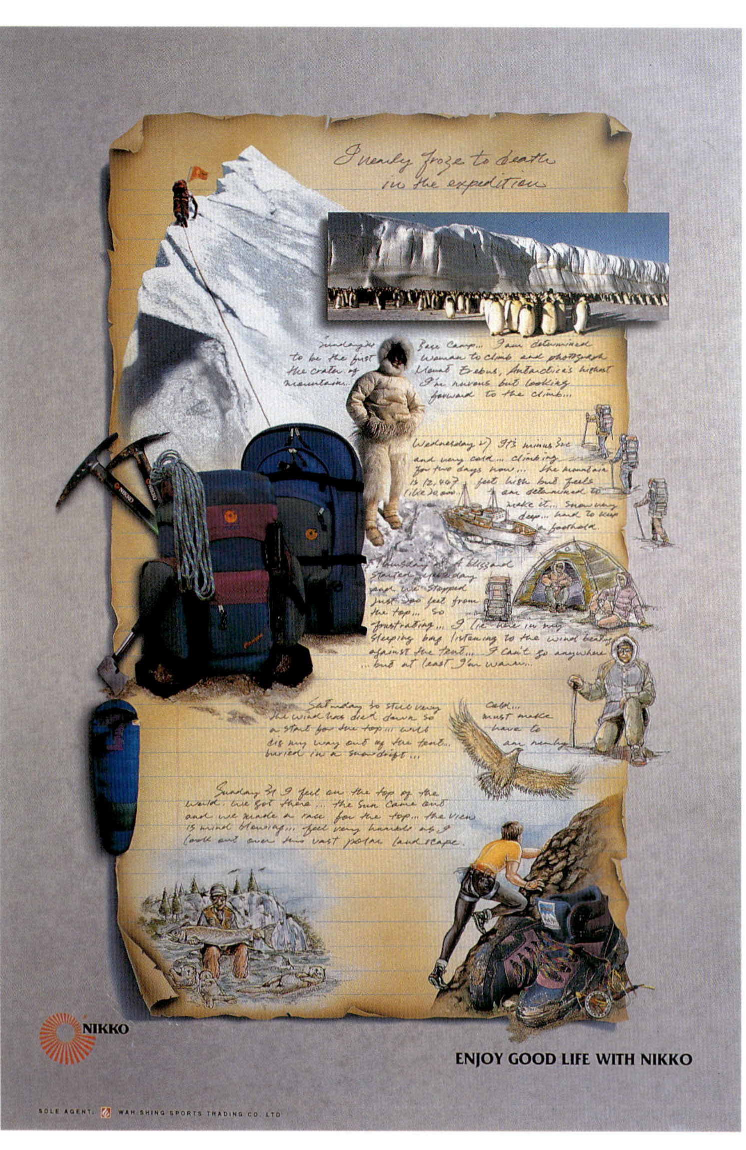

DESIGN FIRM
Masterline Communications, Ltd.

ART DIRECTORS
Grand So, Kwong Chi Man

DESIGNER
Kwong Chi Man

ILLUSTRATOR
James Fong

PHOTOGRAPHER
K.K. Wong

CLIENT
Wah Shing Sports Trading Co., Ltd.

PURPOSE
Advertisement

SIZE
20" x 28" (50.8cm x 71.2cm)

Designers used computer retouching to mix and match several photos and illustrations together.

DESIGN FIRM
Grand Design Co.

ART DIRECTORS
Grand So, Kwong Chi Man

DESIGNER
Grand So, Kwong Chi Man

PHOTOGRAPHER
Almond Chu

CLIENT
Sureap Limited

PURPOSE
Public awareness

SIZE
15" x 22"
(38.6cm x 56cm)

[facing page]

DESIGN FIRM
Grand Design Co.

ART DIRECTORS
Grand So, Kwong Chi Man

DESIGNERS
Grand So, Raymond Au, Terry Lam, Kwong Chi Man

CLIENT
Superbowl -
The Art of Eating Congee

PURPOSE
Advertisement

SIZE
15" x 21" (37.7cm x 53.3cm)

[right] This is the first high-class congee shop in Hong Kong. The concept comes from 1950s Hong Kong. It aims to educate Hong Kong people to appreciate congee.

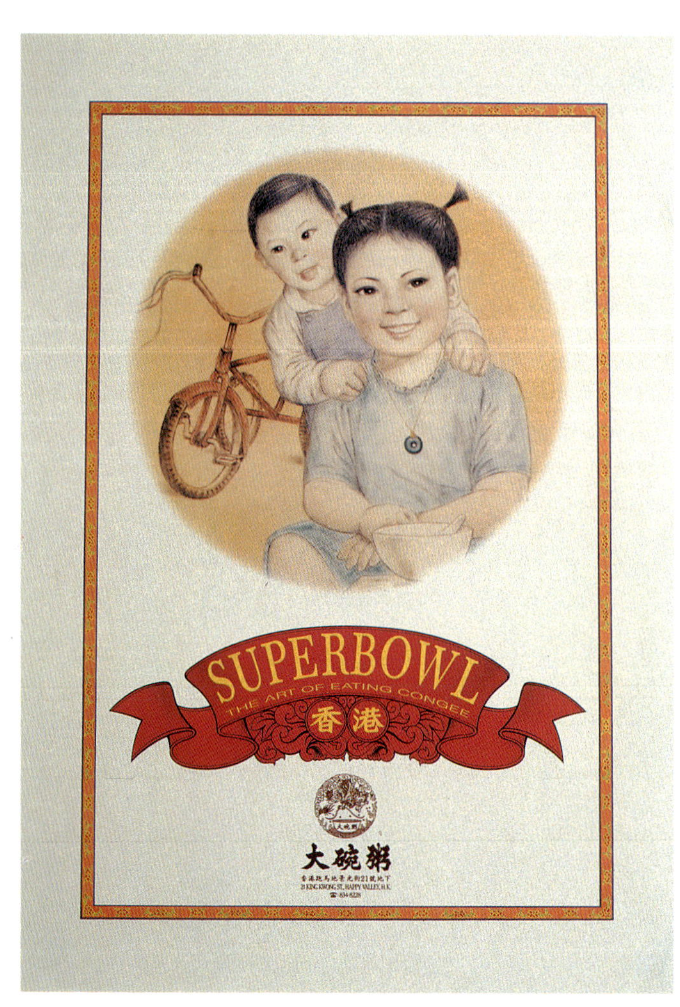

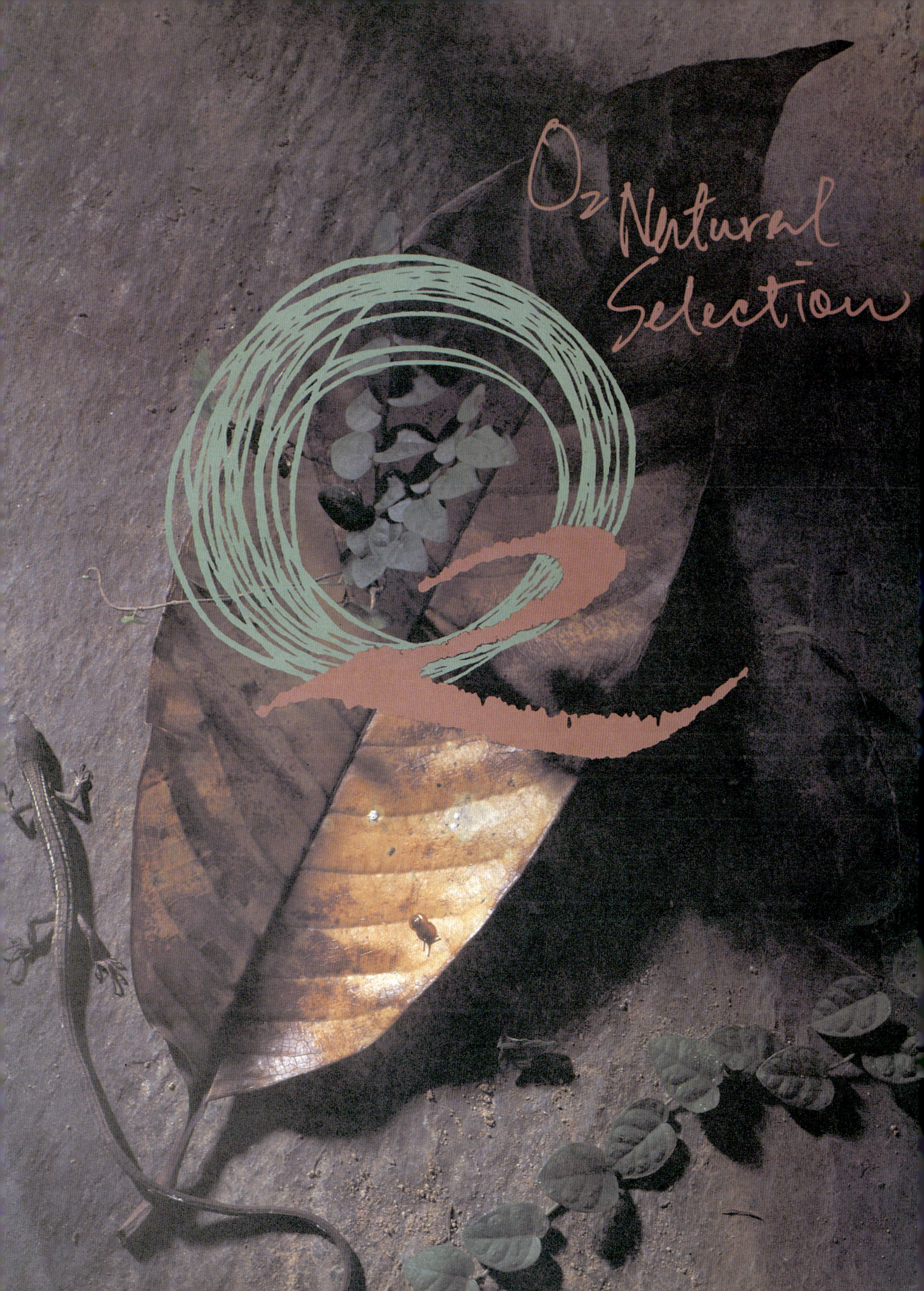
O2 Natural
Selection
2

DESIGN FIRM
Frank Heymann

ALL DESIGN
Frank Heymann

CLIENT
Neves Ensemble
(chamber music)

PURPOSE
Promotion

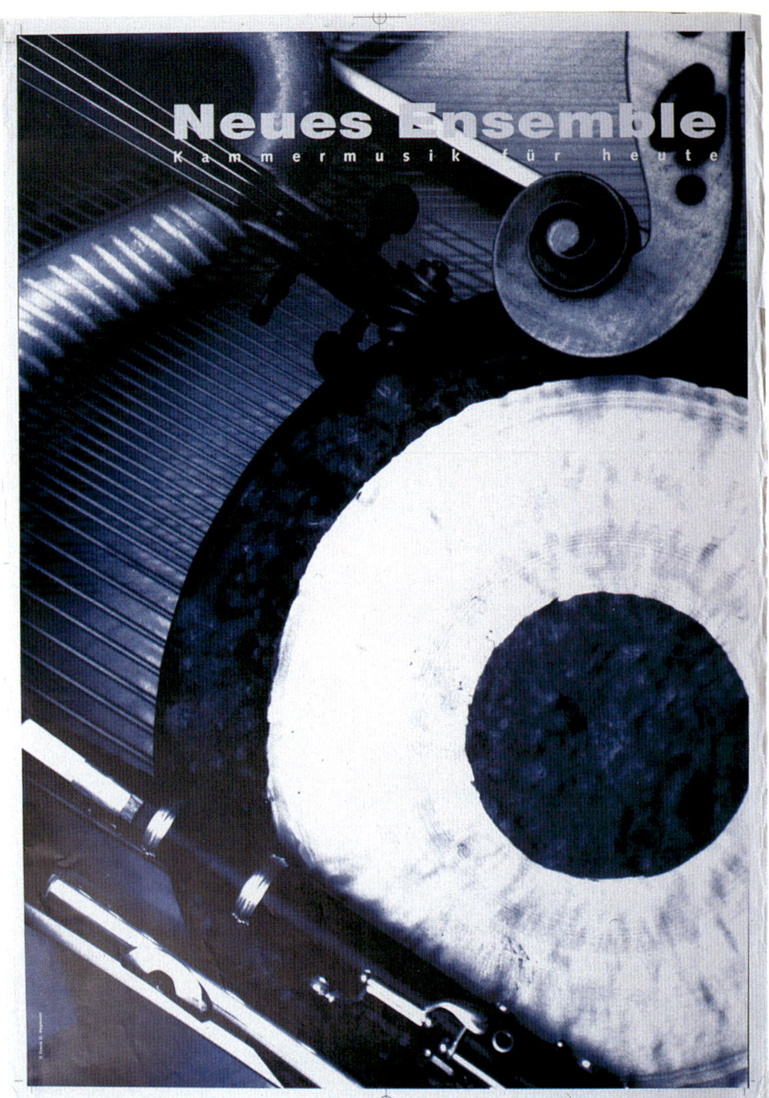

DESIGN FIRM
Design/Art, Inc.

ALL DESIGN
Norman Moore

CLIENT
Design/Art

PURPOSE
Self-promotion

SIZE
24" x 36"
(61cm x 91.4cm)

[facing page]
Desktop scans of photos were manipulated in Adobe Photoshop, while the layout and type were generated in QuarkXPress.

DESIGN FIRM
Frank Heymann

ILLUSTRATORS
Hylnur Hallson,
Frank Heymann

CLIENT
IH Hannover IB Kunst
& Design

PURPOSE
End of World War II
commemoration

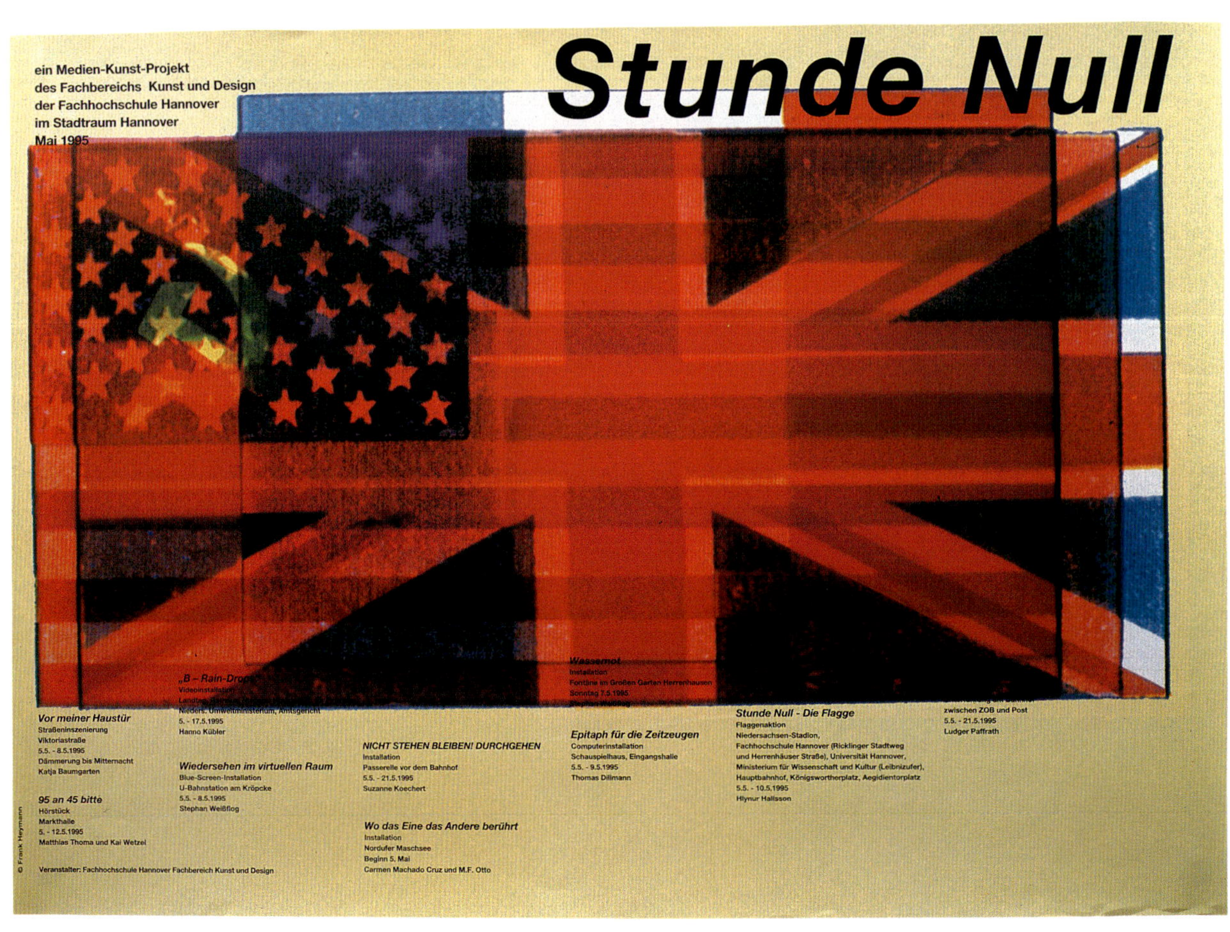

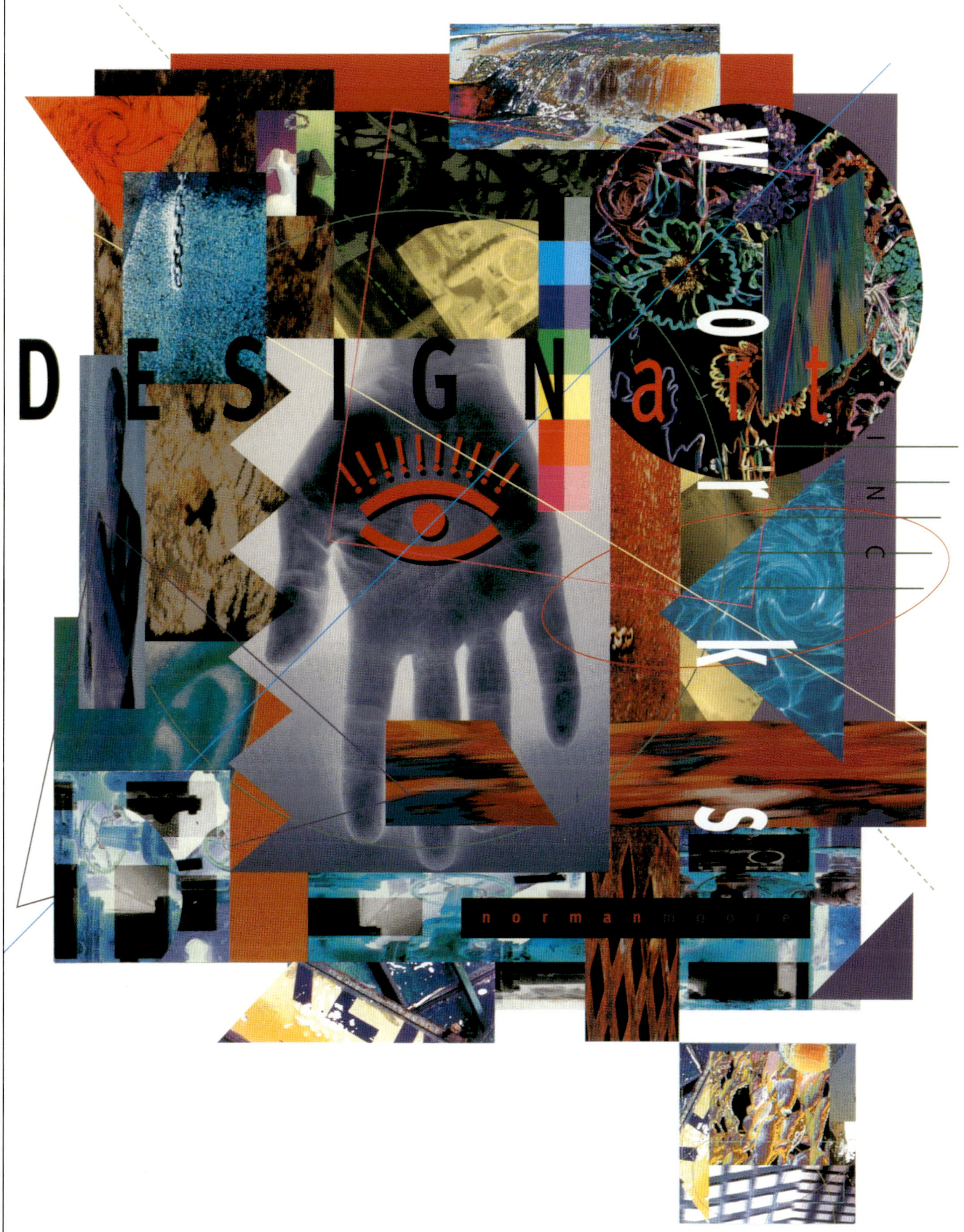

DESIGN art WORKS
INC

norman moore

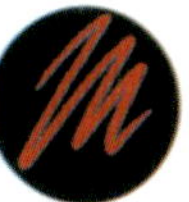

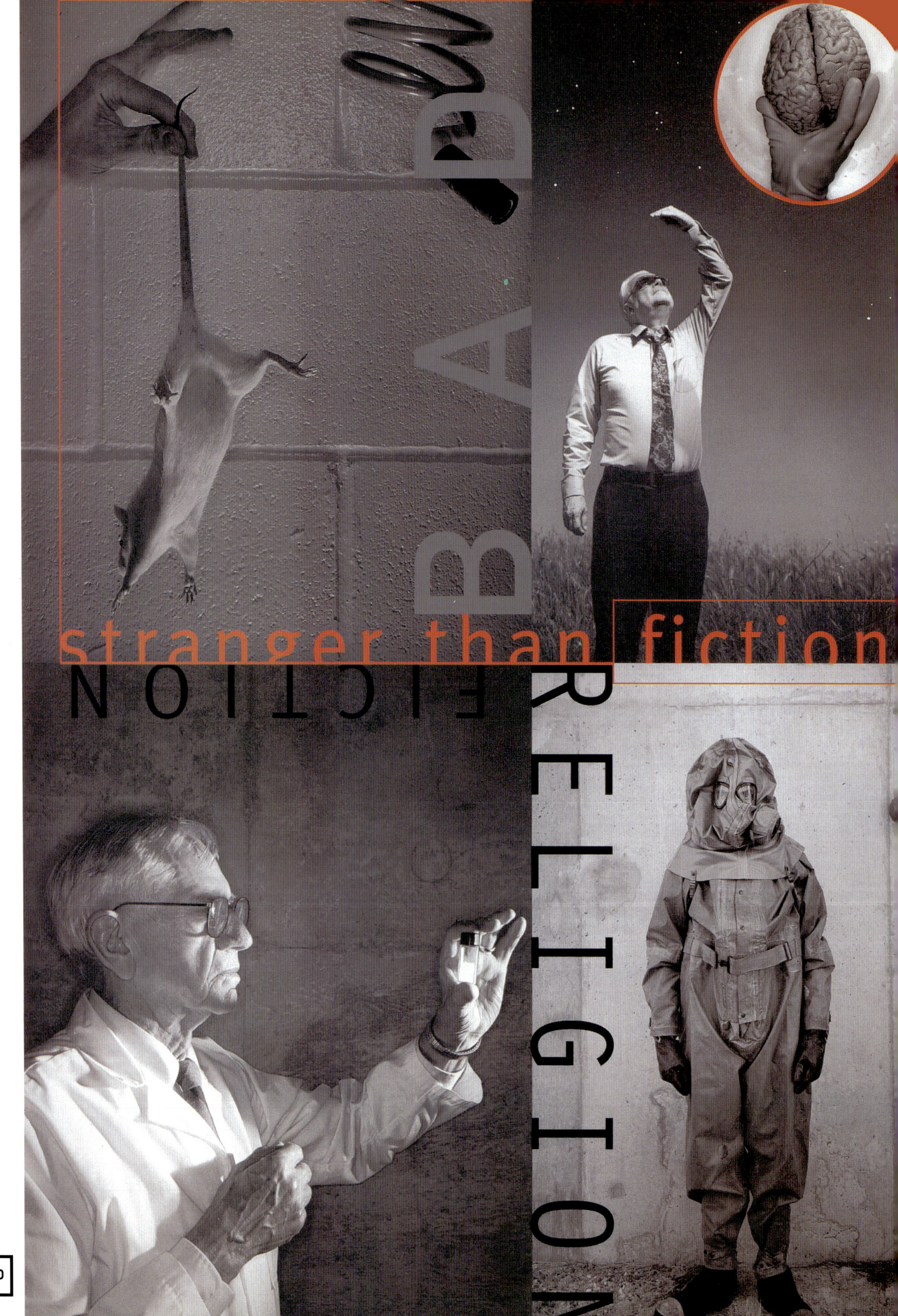

BAD
stranger than fiction
FICTION
RELIGION

DESIGN FIRM
Design/Art, Inc.

ALL DESIGN
Norman Moore

PHOTOGRAPHER
Dan Winters

CLIENT
Atlantic Records

PURPOSE
Record promotion

SIZE
24" x 36"
(61cm x 91.4cm)

[facing page]
High-resolution scans were set up along with and type in QuarkXPress.

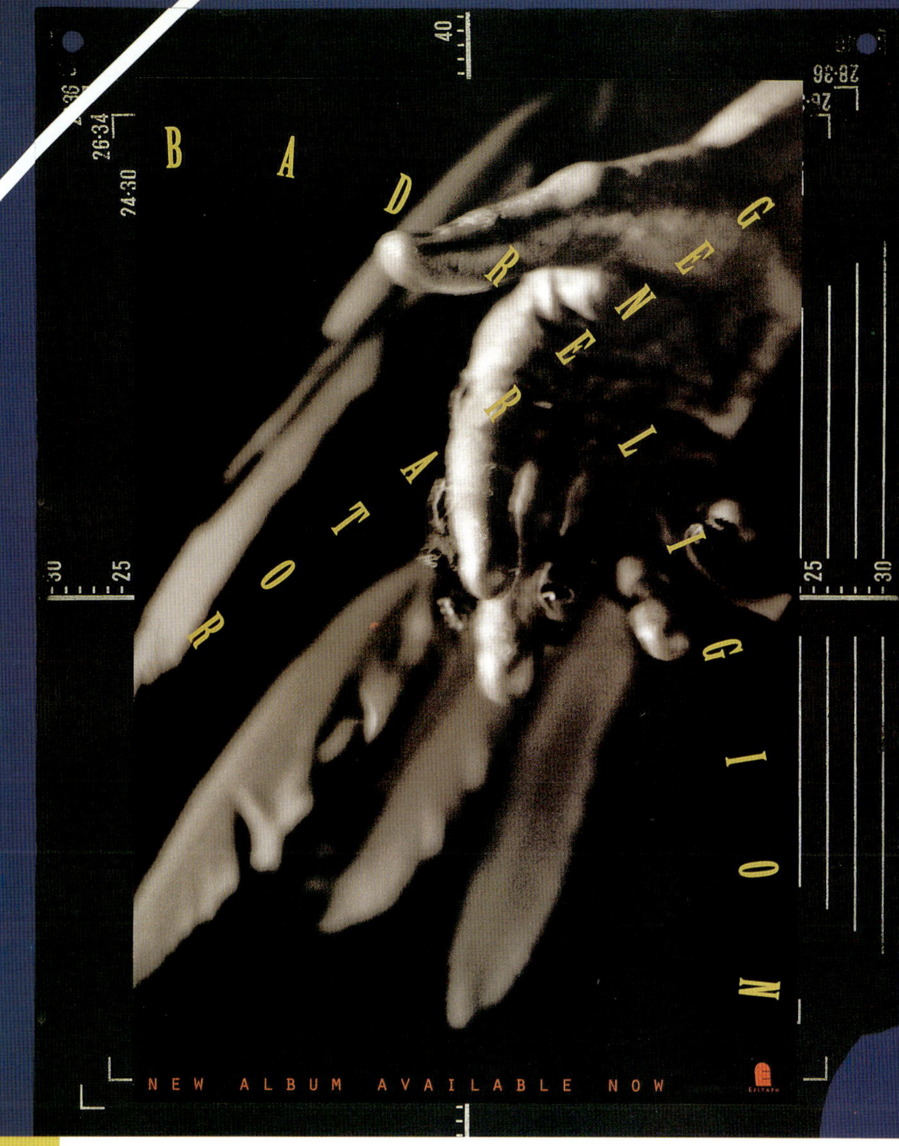

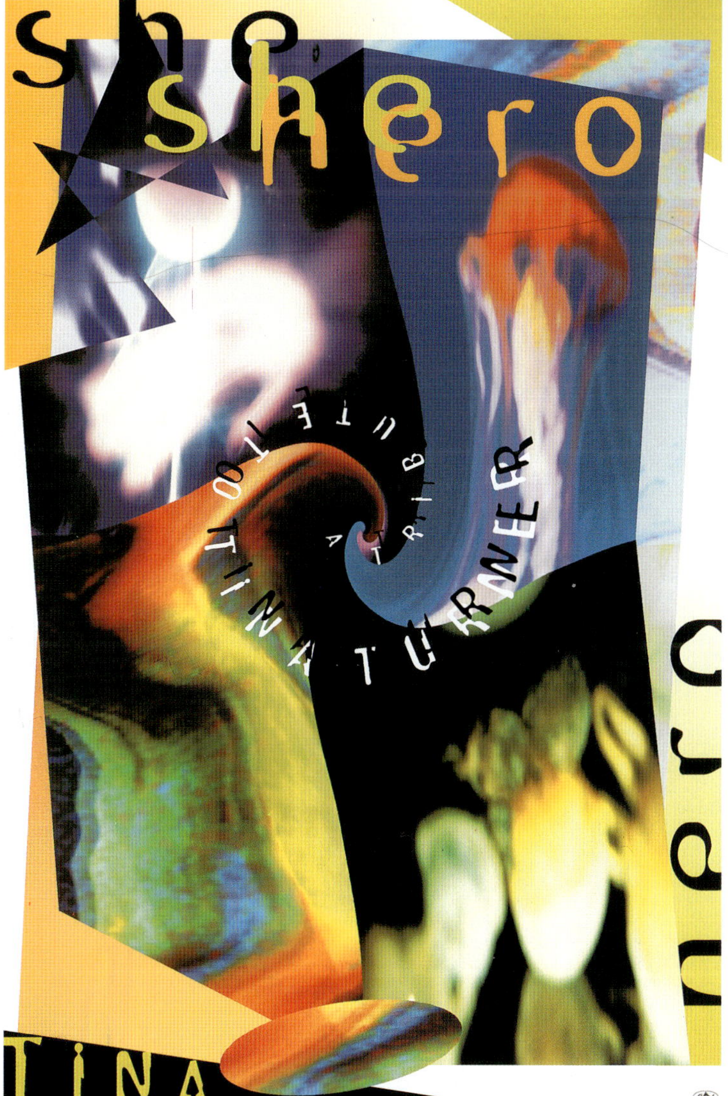

DESIGN FIRM
Design/Art, Inc.

ALL DESIGN
Norman Moore

CLIENT
Capitol Records

PURPOSE
Record promotion

SIZE
24" x 36"
(61cm x 91.4cm)

Desktop scans of photos were manipulated in Adobe Photoshop. Type and layout were completed in QuarkXPress using sketch-pad extension.

DESIGN FIRM
Design/Art, Inc.

ALL DESIGN
Norman Moore

PHOTOGRAPHER
Douglas Brothers

CLIENT
Epitaph Records

PURPOSE
Record promotion

SIZE
24" x 36"
(61cm x 91.4cm)

High-resolution sepia-toned photo lettering was done in Aldus FreeHand 4.0. Layout was completed in QuarkXPress.

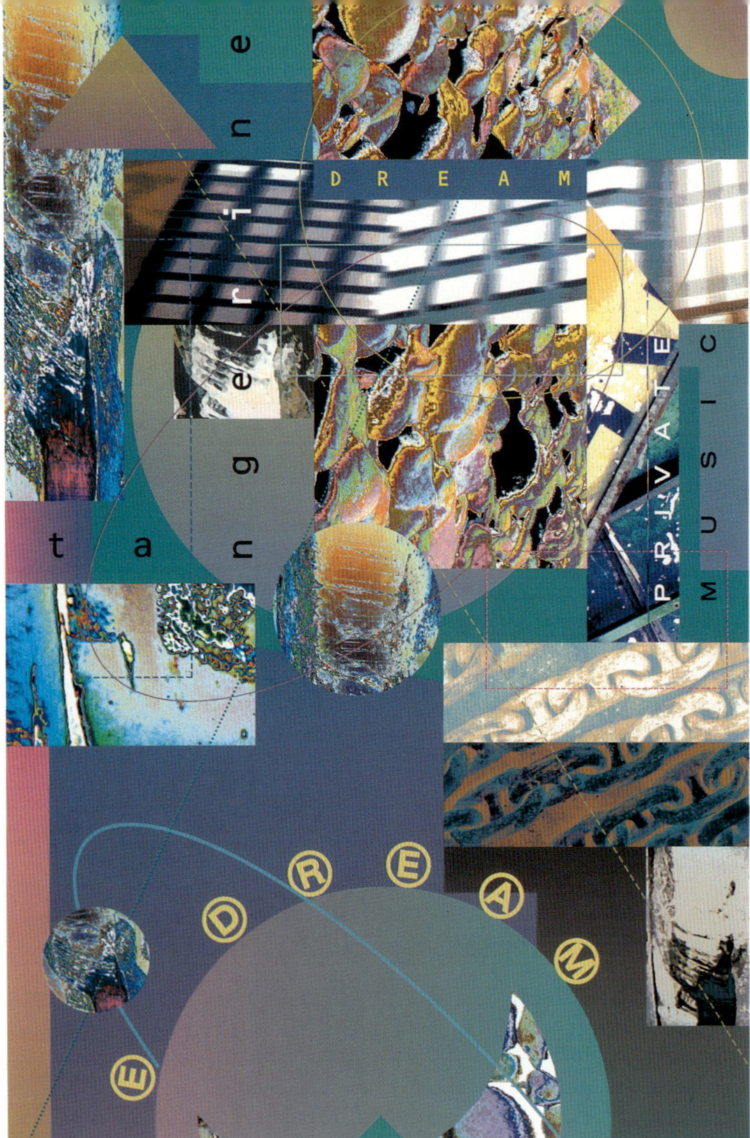

DESIGN FIRM
Design/Art, Inc.

ALL DESIGN
Norman Moore

CLIENT
Private Music

PURPOSE
Record promotion

SIZE
24" x 36"
(61cm x 91.4cm)

Desktop scans of photos were manipulated in Adobe Photoshop.

DESIGN FIRM
Design/Art, Inc.

ALL DESIGN
Norman Moore

CLIENT
Laura Tamburino/
III Sound & Stage

PURPOSE
Art show announcement

SIZE
24" x 36" (61cm x 91.4cm)

[facing page]
A photo of industrial pipes was scanned to a PhotoCD and reversed to a negative and greyscale. The windows were added in Adobe Photoshop, while the type and layout were finished in QuarkXPress.

DESIGN FIRM
Design/Art, Inc.

ALL DESIGN
Norman Moore

CLIENT
Design/Art, Inc.

PURPOSE
Self promotion

SIZE
24" x 36"
(61cm x 91.4cm)

Desktop scans of photographs were manipulated in Adobe Photoshop, while the layout and type were created in QuarkXPress.

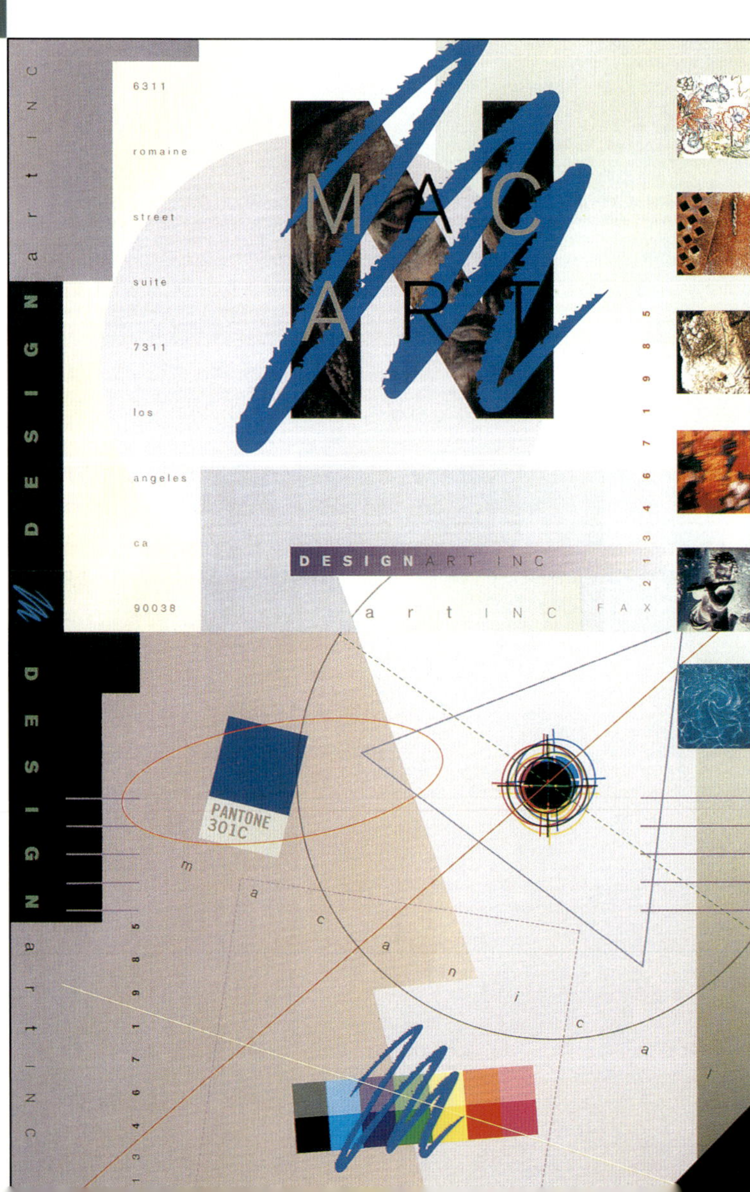

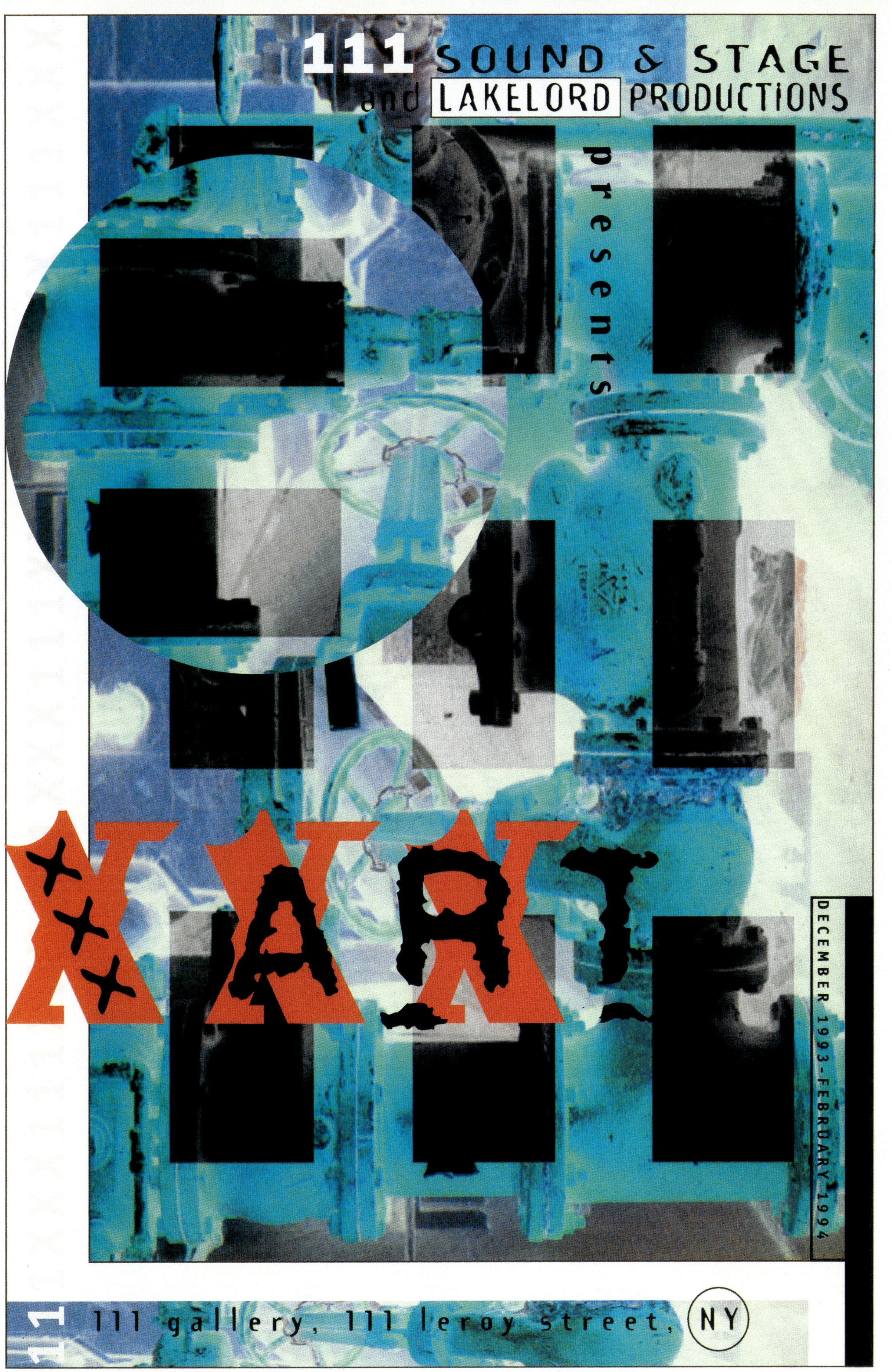
111 SOUND & STAGE
and LAKELORD PRODUCTIONS
presents
XART
DECEMBER 1993-FEBRUARY 1994
111 gallery, 111 leroy street, NY
111

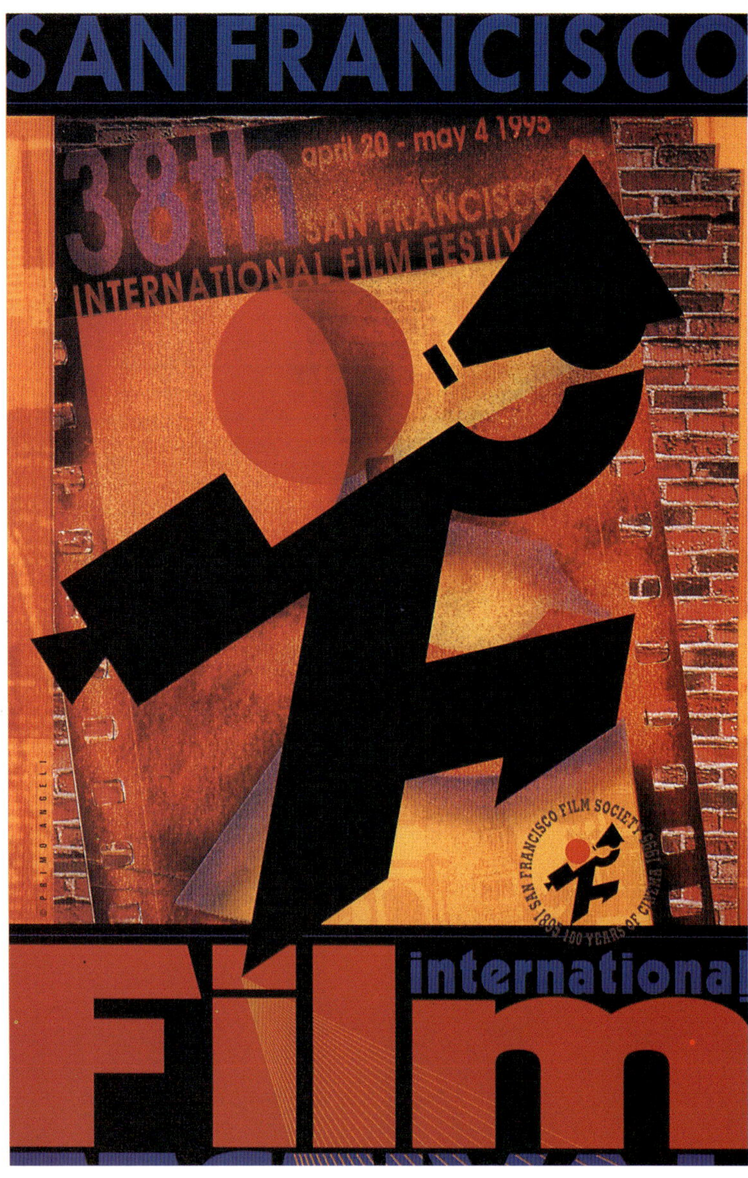

DESIGN FIRM
Primo Angeli, Inc.

ART DIRECTORS
Primo Angeli,
Carlo Pagoda

DESIGNER
Primo Angeli

COMPUTER ILLUSTRATORS
Marcelo De Freitas,
Paul Terrill

CLIENT
San Francisco Film Society

PURPOSE
San Francisco International Film Festival Poster

SIZE
34" x 23"
(86.4cm x 58.4cm)

The poster was created using Adobe Illustrator. The textured look in the collage background was achieved through a unique application of WD-40 directly to the Cal-Comp print-out. The collage was then photographed and re-scanned into the layout and the San Francisco Film Society trademark was superimposed at a diagonal.

DESIGN FIRM
Primo Angeli, Inc.

ART DIRECTOR
Primo Angeli

DESIGNER
Primo Angeli

COMPUTER ILLUSTRATOR
Marcelo De Freitas

PHOTOGRAPHER
June Fouche

CLIENT
Pendleton
(San Francisco)

PURPOSE
Pendleton Mission Dolores Blanket Poster

SIZE
42" x 17.25"
(106.7cm x 43.8cm)

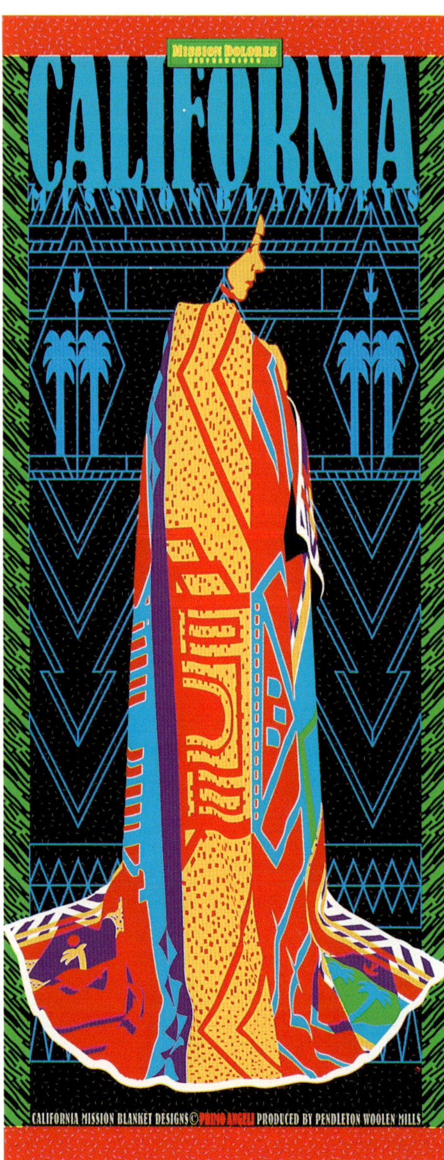

DESIGN FIRM

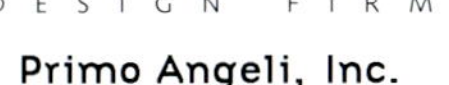

Primo Angeli, Inc.

ART DIRECTOR

Primo Angeli

DESIGNERS

Primo Angeli,
Marcelo De Freitas

COMPUTER ILLUSTRATORS

Marcelo De Freitas,
Nina Dietzel,
Christina Garcia

CLIENT

UN50 Committee

PURPOSE

50th anniversary promotion

SIZE

47" x 23"
(119.4cm x 58.4cm)

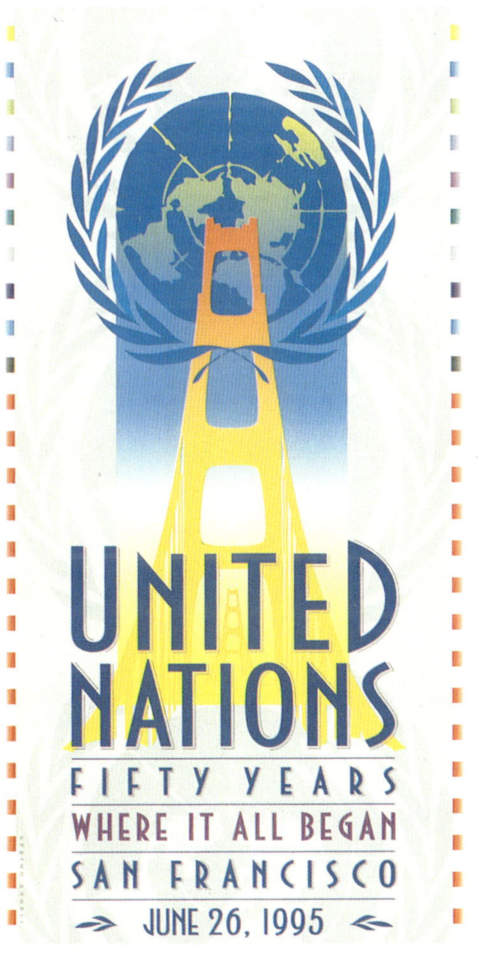

DESIGN FIRM

Sackett Design Associates

ART DIRECTOR

Mark Sackett

DESIGNER

Mark Sackett, Wayne Sakamoto

PHOTOGRAPHER

Pierre Goavec

CLIENT

AR Lithol Pierre Goavec

PURPOSE

Self Promotion

SIZE

4.4" x 15" (11.25 cm x 38 cm)

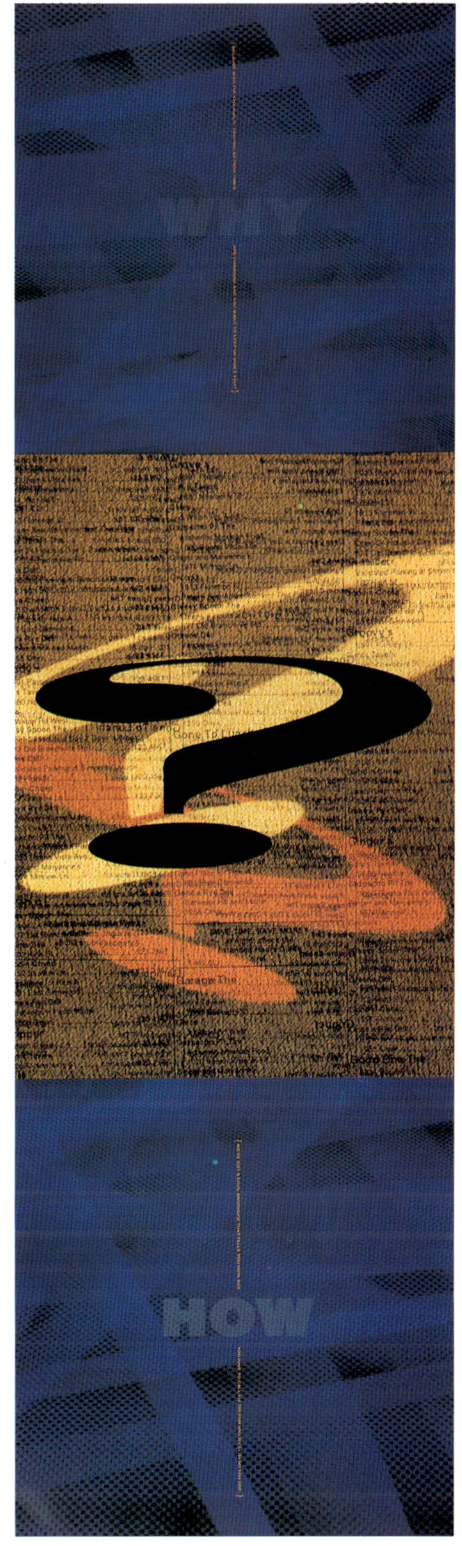

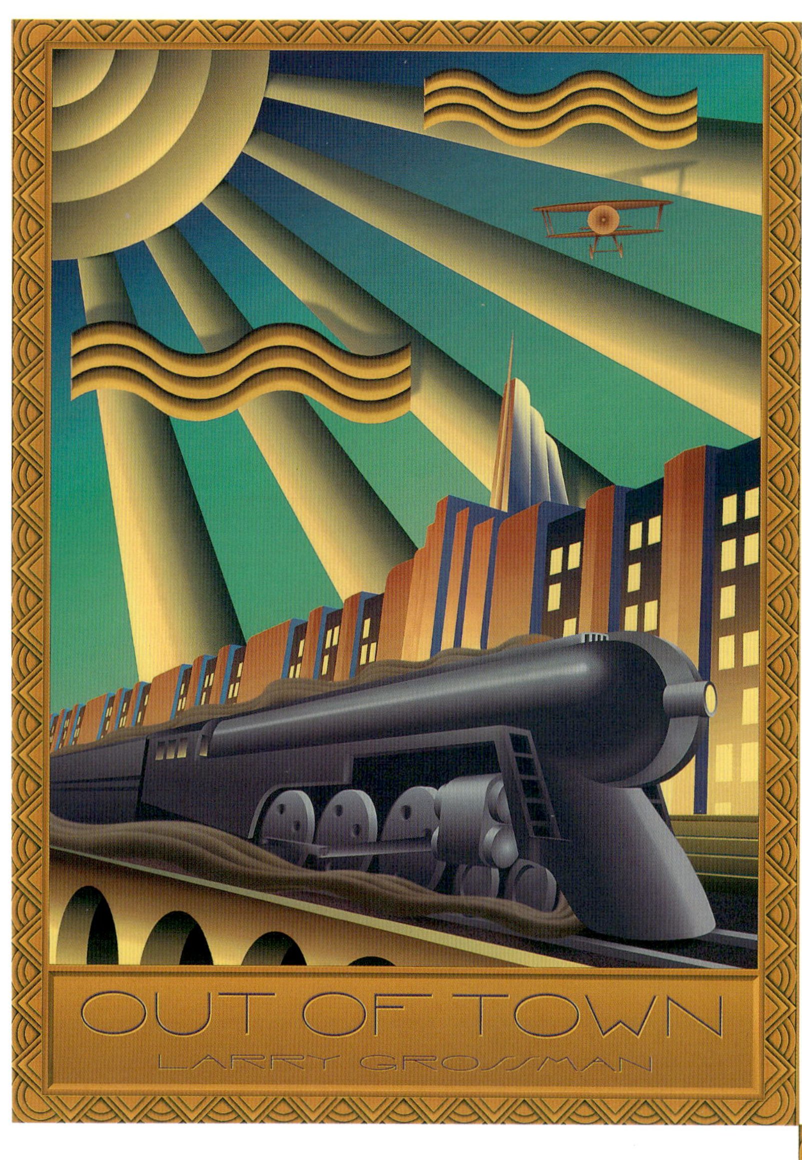

DESIGN FIRM
Larry Grossman

ALL DESIGN
Larry Grossman

CLIENT
Posner Fine Arts

PURPOSE
Gallery retail

Poster created on a 7100 Power Macintosh with Adobe Photoshop software.

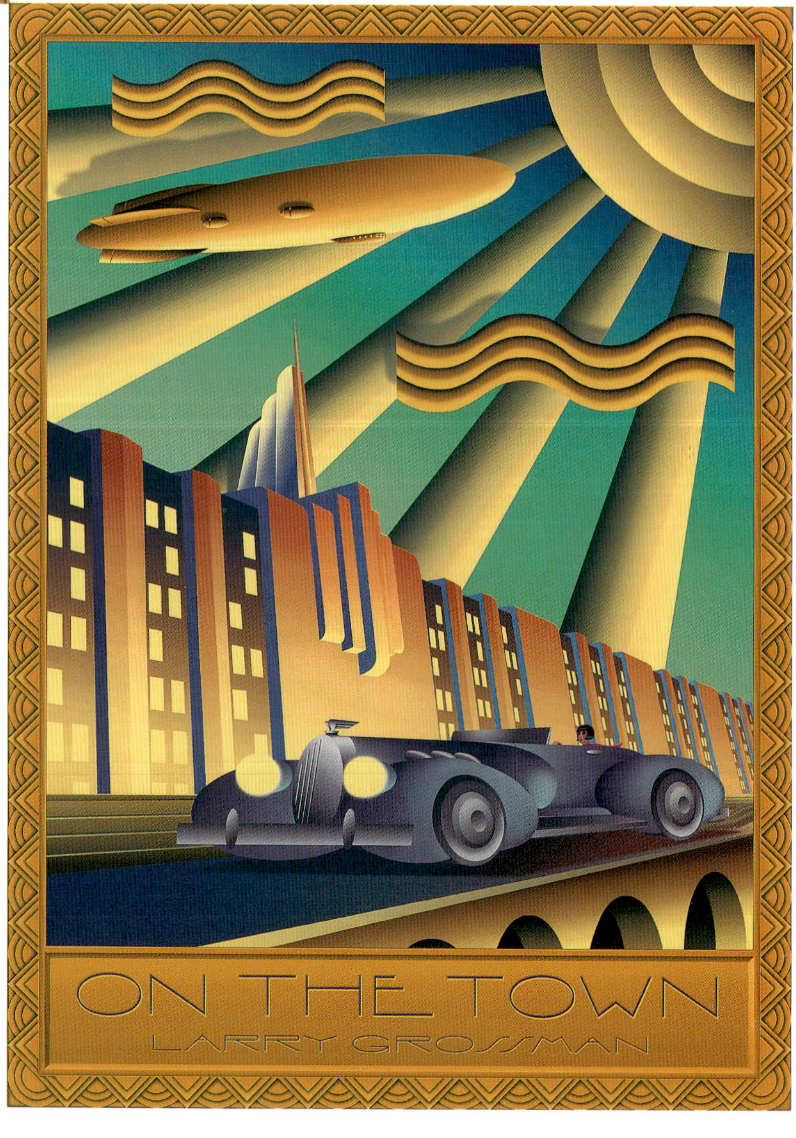

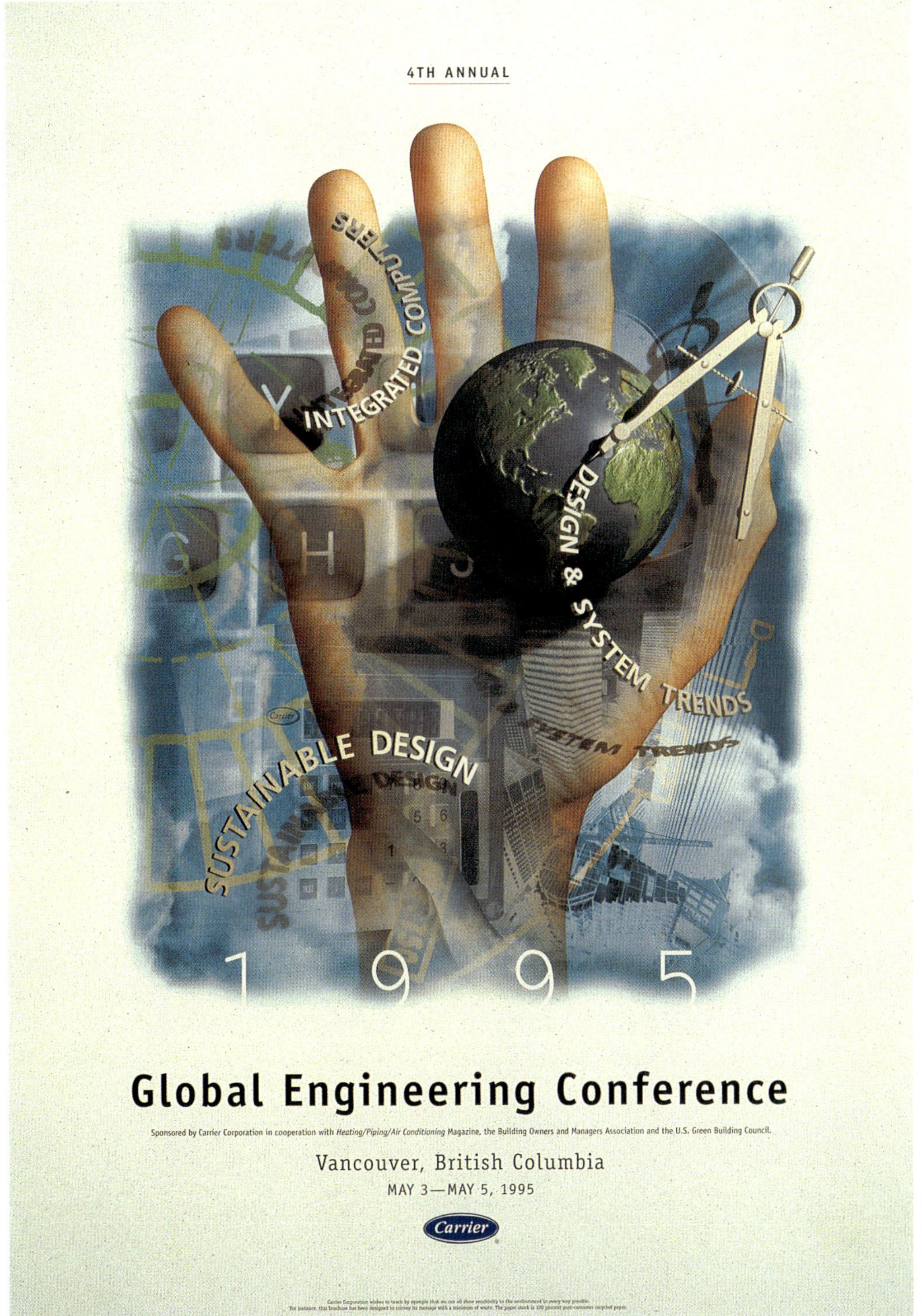

DESIGN FIRM
Jowaisas Design

ART DIRECTOR
Elizabeth Jowaisas

DESIGNER
Elizabeth Jowaisas

ILLUSTRATOR
Heidi Merscher, MC Squared

CLIENT
United Technologies
Carrier Corporation

PURPOSE
Global Engineering conference promotion

SIZE
20" x 28"
(50.8cm x 71.1cm)

Poster produced in QuarkXPress, with illustrations rendered in Adobe Photoshop.

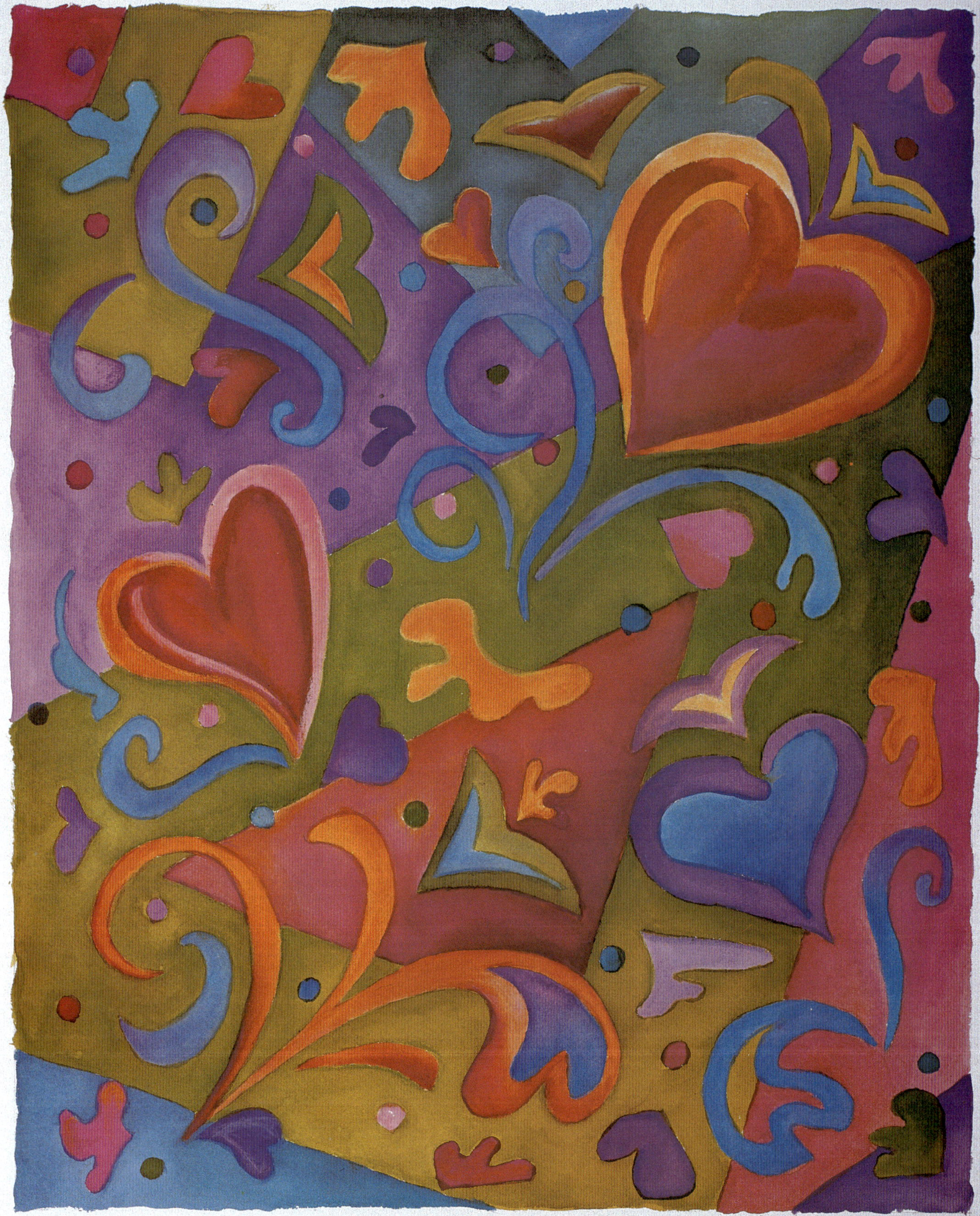

National Nurses Week 1995

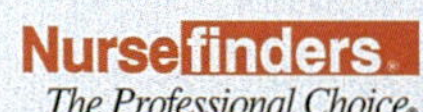

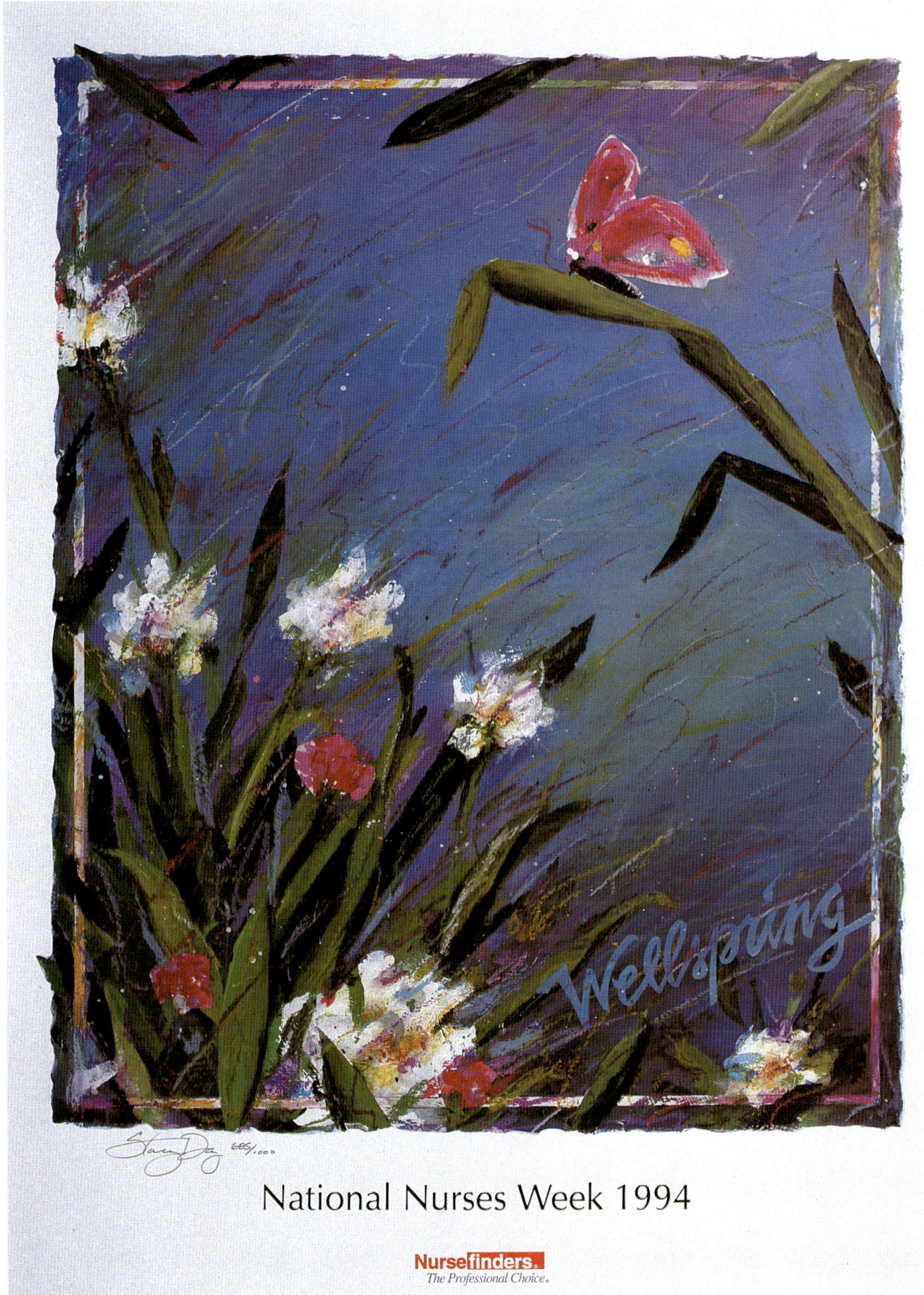

DESIGN FIRM
Duncan Day Advertising

ALL DESIGN
Stacy Day

CLIENT
Nursefinders

PURPOSE
National Nurses Week promotion

SIZE
18" x 24" (45.7cm x 61cm)

[left and facing page]

The illustrations for these posters were hand-drawn.

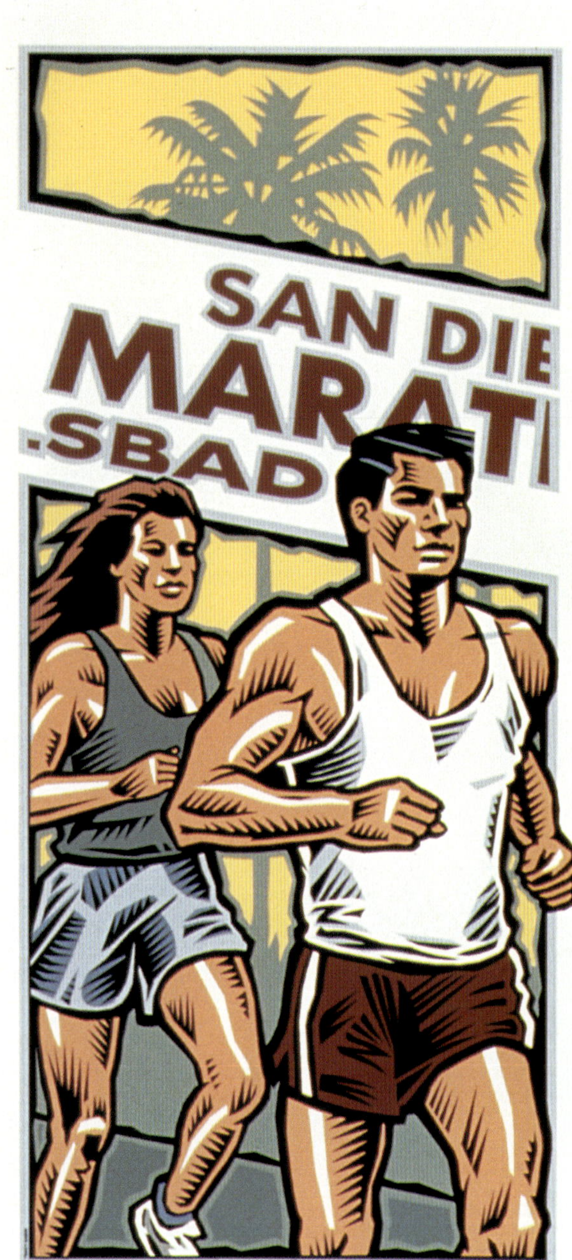

DESIGN FIRM
Tracy Sabin Graphic Design

ART DIRECTOR
Lynn Flannigan

DESIGNER
Tracy Sabin

ILLUSTRATOR
Tracy Sabin

CLIENT
In Motion

PURPOSE
San Diego Marathon promotion

SIZE
12" x 36" (30.5cm x 91.4cm)

Illustration and design for this poster were done in Adobe Illustrator.

DESIGN FIRM
Tracy Sabin Graphic Design

ART DIRECTOR
Tom Morrison and Tom Burke

DESIGNER
Tracy Sabin

ILLUSTRATOR
Tracy Sabin

CLIENT
Morrison & Burke Screen Printers

PURPOSE
Self-promotion calendar

SIZE
28" x 42" (71.1cm x 106.7cm)

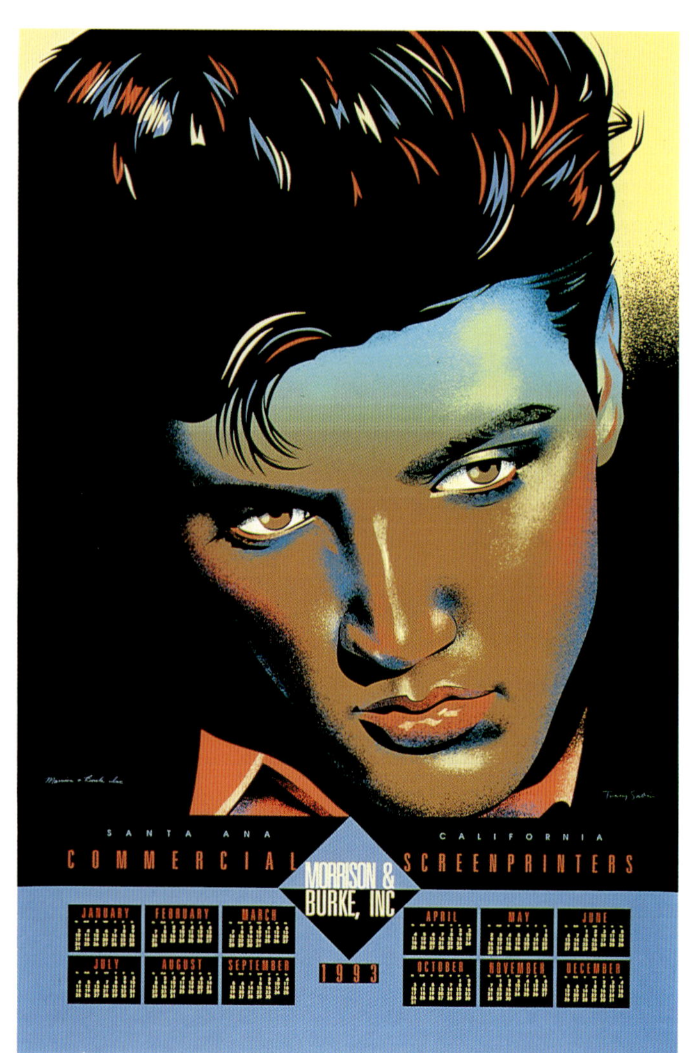

DESIGN FIRM
Tracy Sabin Graphic Design

ART DIRECTOR
Jim Gordon

DESIGNER
Tracy Sabin

ILLUSTRATOR
Tracy Sabin

CLIENT
Gordon Screen Printing

PURPOSE
Self-promotion calendar

SIZE
19" x 34"
(48.3cm x 86.4cm)

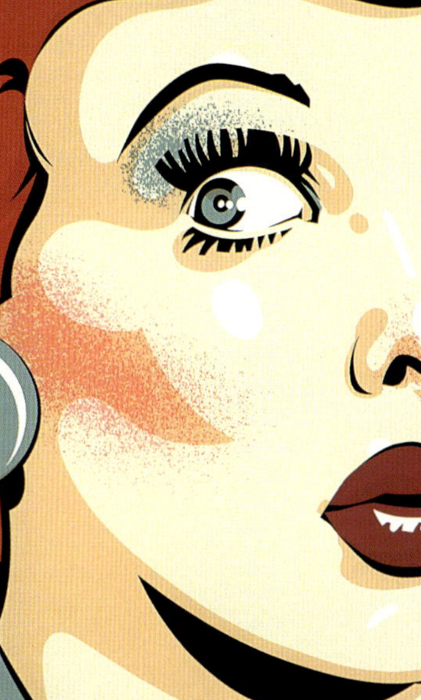

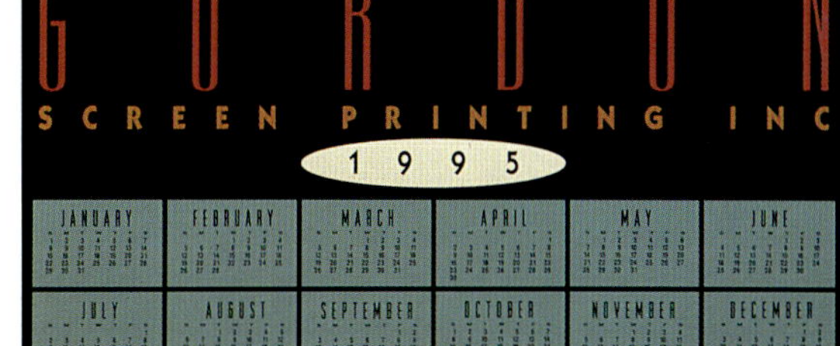

DESIGN FIRM
Yamamoto Moss

ART DIRECTOR
Gregory Pickman

DESIGNER
Gregory Pickman

ILLUSTRATOR
Mercedes McDonald

CLIENT
Twin Cities Marathon

PURPOSE
Race announcement and commemoration

SIZE
22" x 32"
(55.9cm x 81.2cm)

The illustrator used vibrant chalk pastel colors for this race poster.

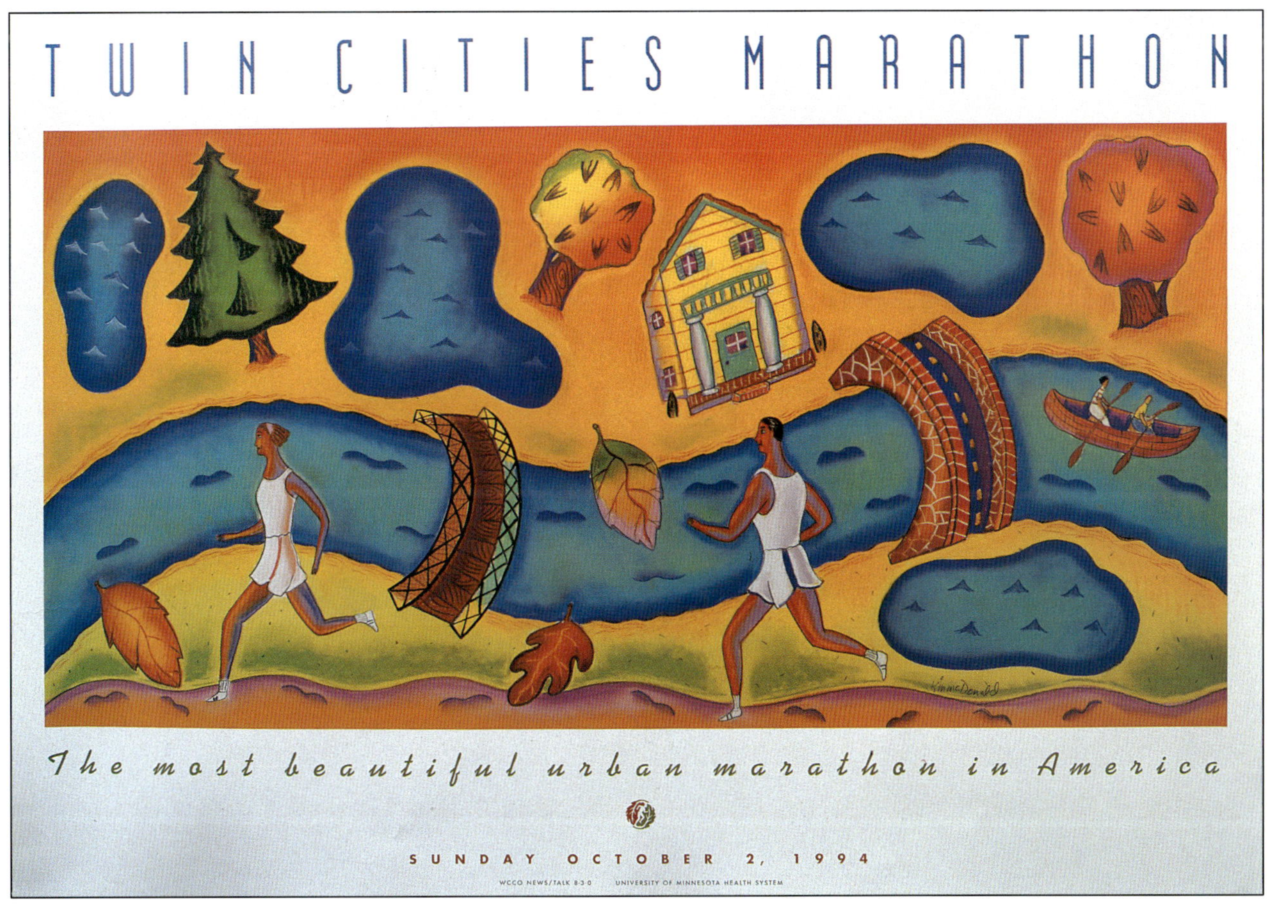

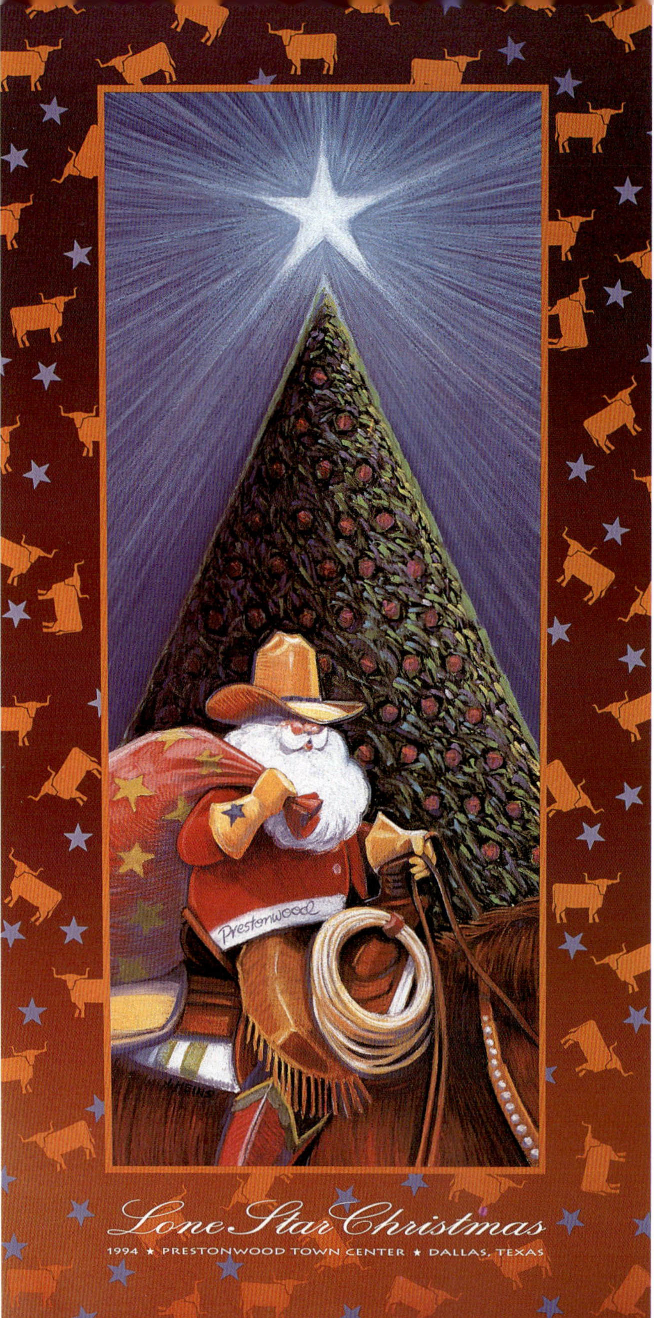

DESIGN FIRM
Heins Creative, Inc.

ART DIRECTORS
Joe Heins, Jim Heins

DESIGNER
Joe Heins

ILLUSTRATOR
Joe Heins

CLIENT
Prestonwood Town Center

PURPOSE
Holiday mall promotion

SIZE
12" x 24" (30.5cm x 61cm)

[left]
Designers used traditional techniques, including hand-illustration with chalk pastels, for this poster design. Three of the nine colors were used in a split-fountain blend created on press.

DESIGN FIRM
Heins Creative, Inc.

ART DIRECTORS
Jim Heins, Joe Heins

DESIGNER
Jim Heins

ILLUSTRATOR
Jim Heins

CLIENT
Diocese of Great Falls-Billings

PURPOSE
Annual fund-raising campaign promotion

SIZE
16" x 24" (40.6cm x 61cm)

[facing page]

DESIGN FIRM
Heins Creative, Inc.

ART DIRECTORS
Jim Heins, Joe Heins

DESIGNER
Jim Heins

ILLUSTRATOR
Jim Heins

CLIENT
Western Heritage Center

PURPOSE
Exhibit promotion

SIZE
17" x 25.5" (43.2cm x 64.8cm)

[right] For this promotion, traditional techniques were used, including hand-illustration with an airbrush and colored pencils.

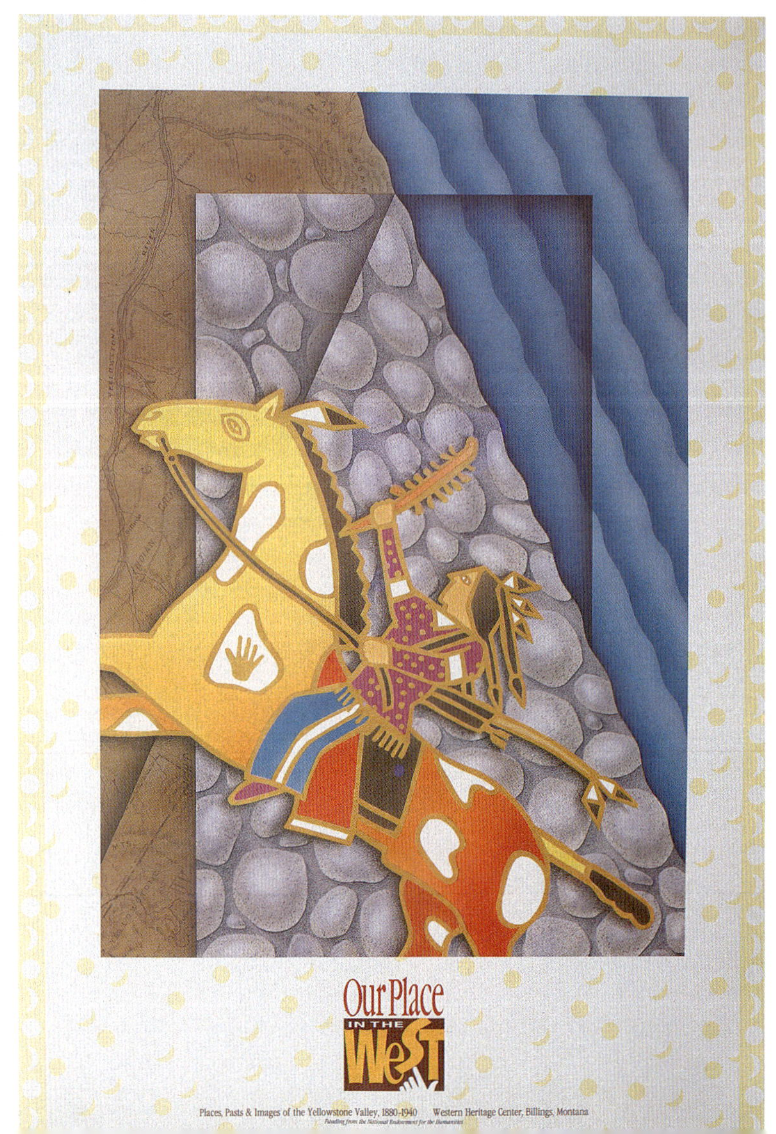

SOW THE SEEDS OF LOVE

MARCH 4 & 5

CARE & SHARE 1995

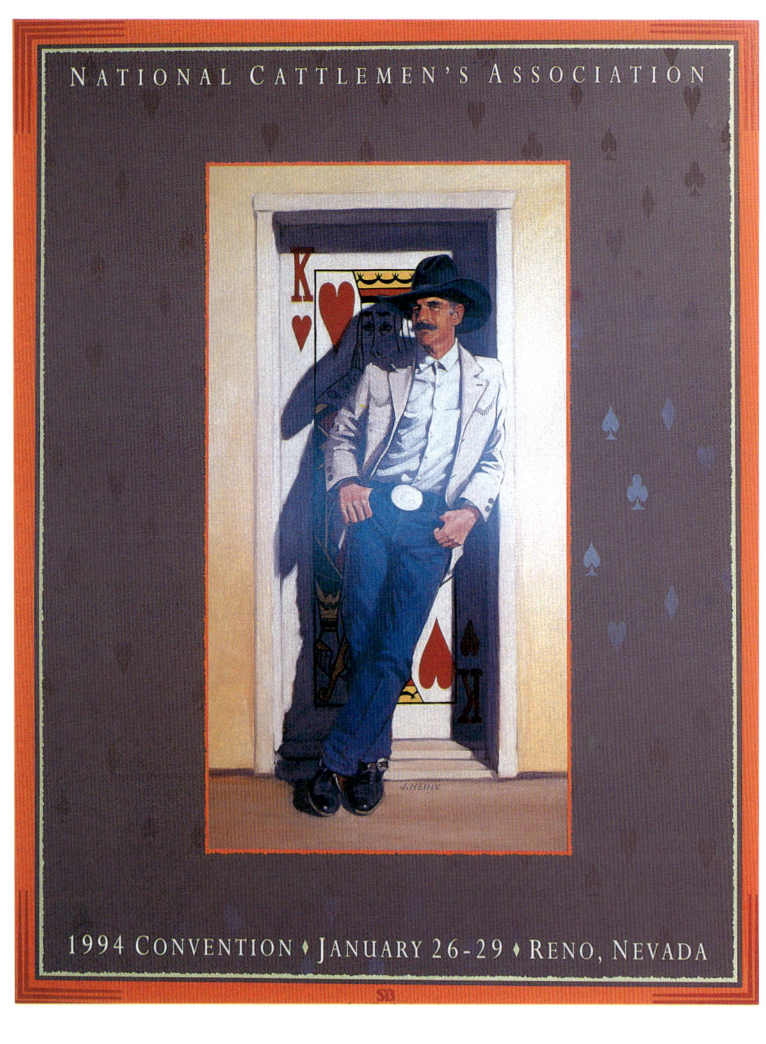

DESIGN FIRM
Dyer Mutchnick Group

ART DIRECTOR
Rod Dyer/Steve Twigger

DESIGNER
Steve Twigger

PHOTOGRAPHER
Steve Twigger

CLIENT
Twentieth Century Fox

PURPOSE
Movie promotion

[facing page]

DESIGN FIRM
Heins Creative, Inc.

ART DIRECTORS
Joe Heins, Jim Heins

DESIGNER
Joe Heins

ILLUSTRATOR
Joe Heins

CLIENT
Smith Kline Beecham Animal Health

PURPOSE
Self-promotion

SIZE
22" x 28" (55.9cm x 71.1cm)

[above and right]

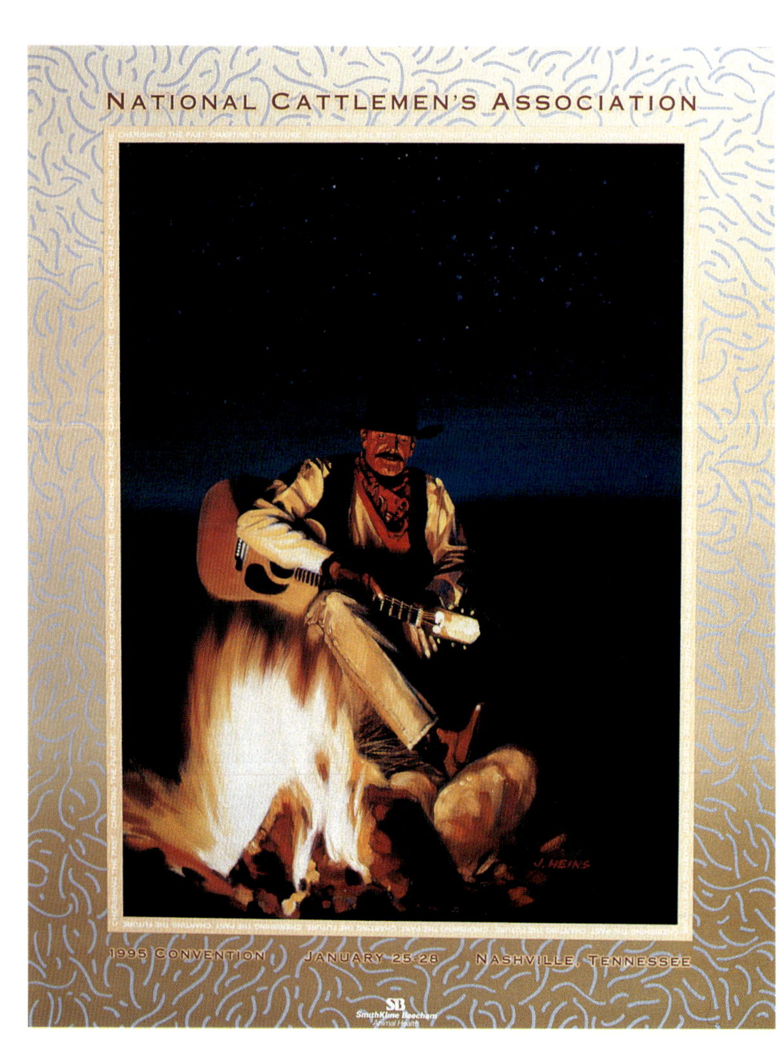

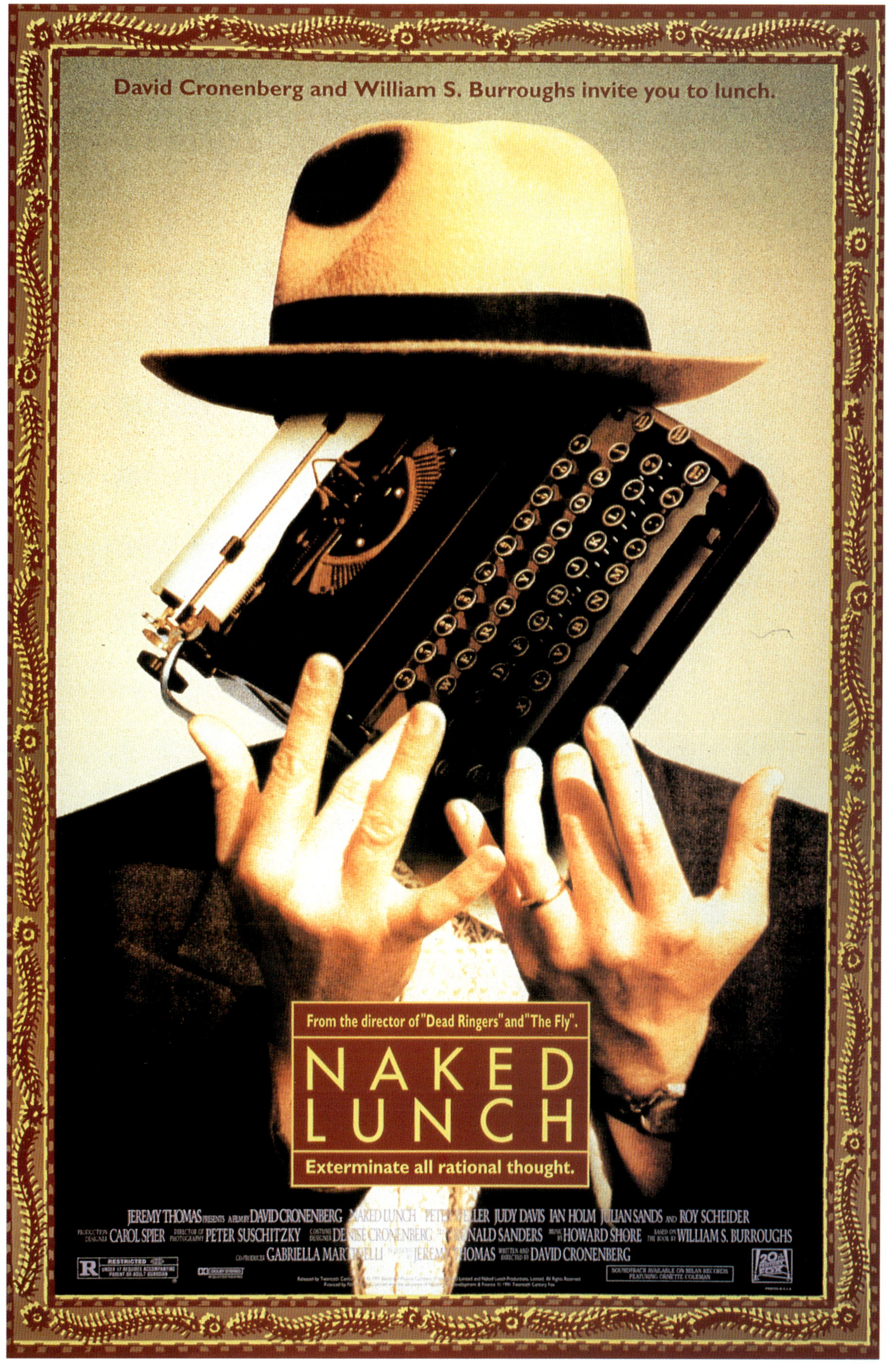
David Cronenberg and William S. Burroughs invite you to lunch.
From the director of "Dead Ringers" and "The Fly".
NAKED LUNCH
Exterminate all rational thought.

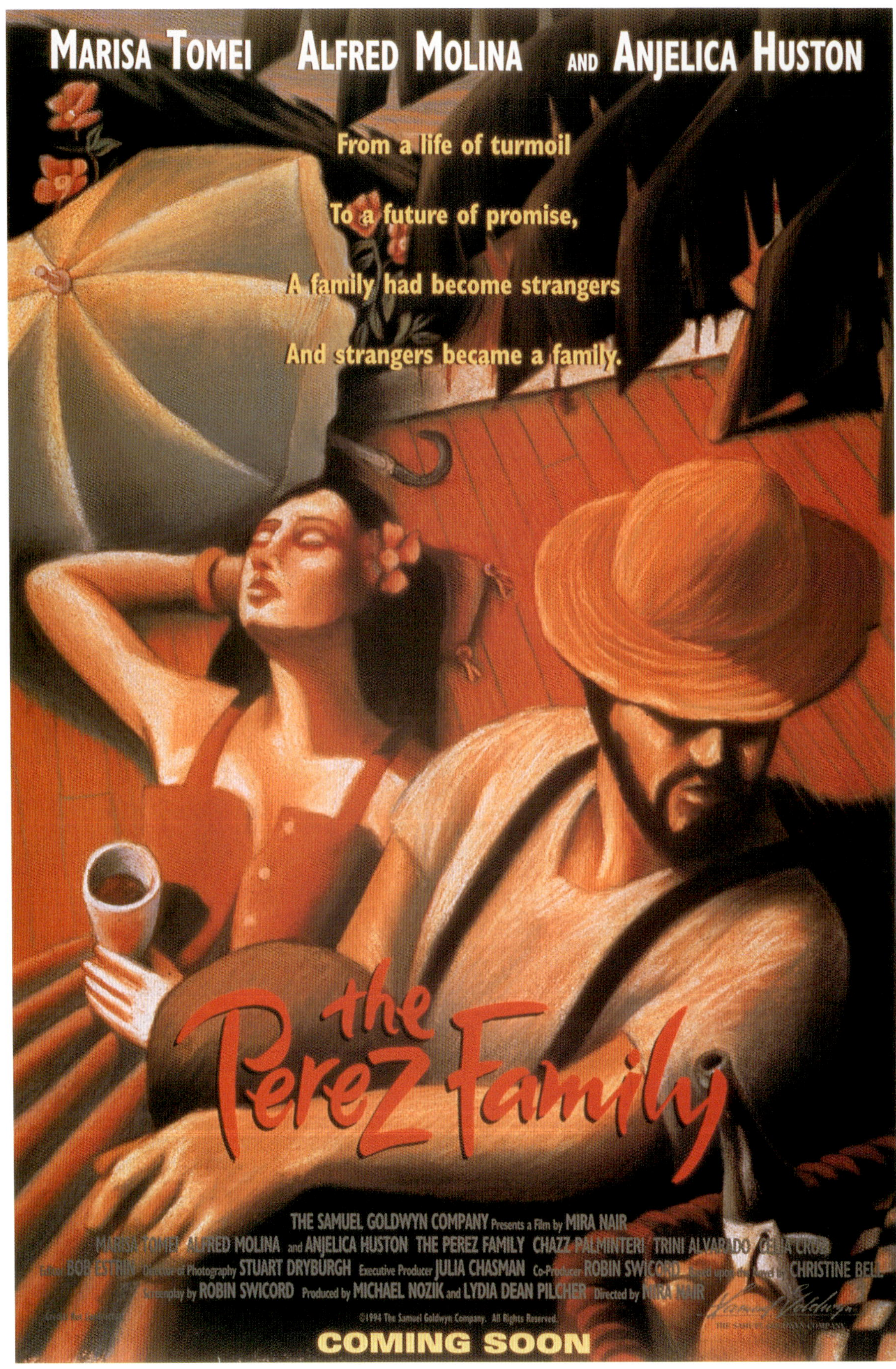
MARISA TOMEI ALFRED MOLINA AND ANJELICA HUSTON
From a life of turmoil
To a future of promise,
A family had become strangers
And strangers became a family.
the Perez Family
THE SAMUEL GOLDWYN COMPANY Presents a Film by MIRA NAIR
MARISA TOMEI ALFRED MOLINA and ANJELICA HUSTON THE PEREZ FAMILY CHAZZ PALMINTERI TRINI ALVARADO CELIA CRUZ
Editor BOB ESTRIN Director of Photography STUART DRYBURGH Executive Producer JULIA CHASMAN Co-Producer ROBIN SWICORD Based upon the Novel by CHRISTINE BELL
Screenplay by ROBIN SWICORD Produced by MICHAEL NOZIK and LYDIA DEAN PILCHER Directed by MIRA NAIR
©1994 The Samuel Goldwyn Company. All Rights Reserved.
COMING SOON

DESIGN FIRM
Dyer Mutchnick Group

ART DIRECTOR
Rod Dyer

DESIGNER
Steve Twigger

CLIENT
Miramax Films

PURPOSE
Movie promotion

SIZE
30" x 40"
(76.2cm x 101.6cm)

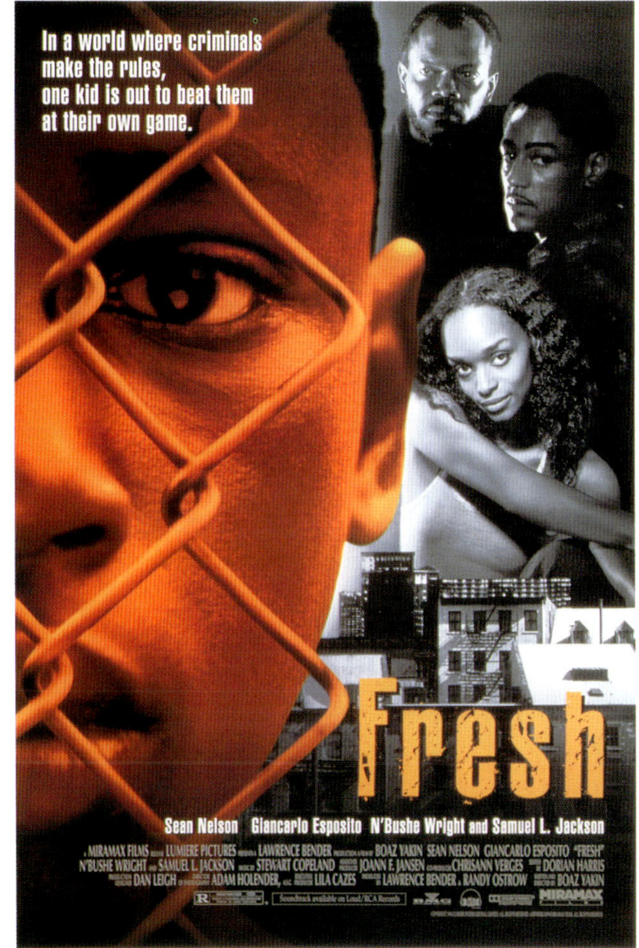

DESIGN FIRM
Dyer Mutchnick Group

ART DIRECTOR
Rod Dyer

DESIGNER
Qris Tamashita

ILLUSTRATOR
Kolea Baker

CLIENT
Samuel Goldwyn

PURPOSE
Movie promotion

SIZE
30" x 40"
(76.2cm x 101.6cm)

[facing page]

DESIGN FIRM
Dyer Mutchnick Group

ART DIRECTOR
Rod Dyer

DESIGNER
Steve Twigger

CLIENT
Columbia Tri Star
Home Video

PURPOSE
Video promotion

SIZE
30" x 40"
(76.2cm x 101.6cm)

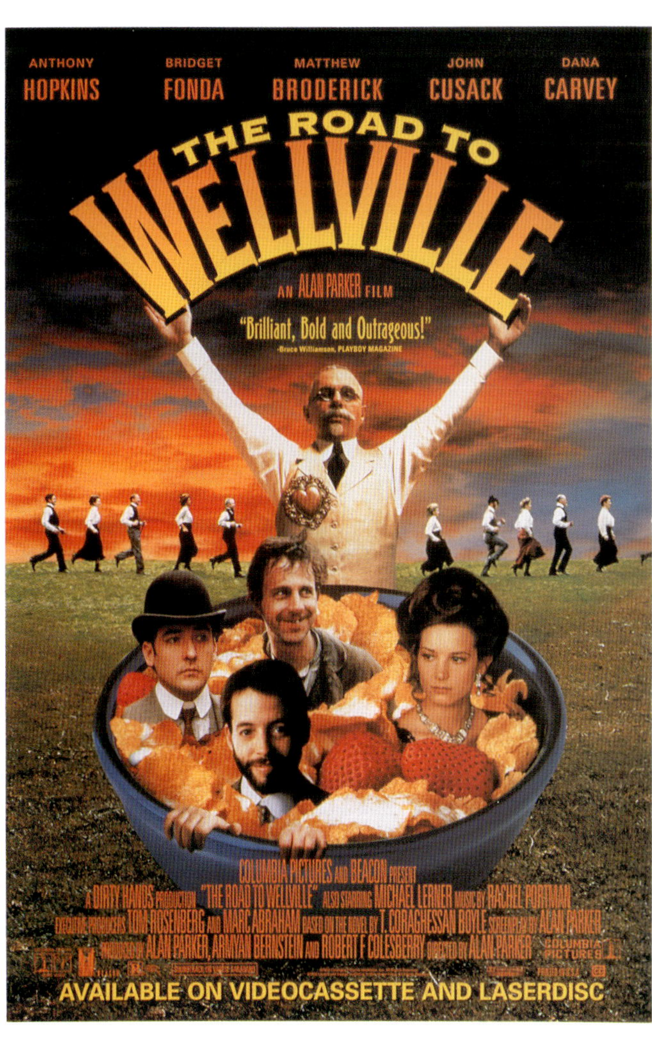

DESIGN FIRM
Dyer Mutchnick Group

ART DIRECTOR
Rod Dyer

DESIGNER
Steve Twigger

CLIENT
Miramax Films

PURPOSE
Movie promotion

SIZE
30" x 40"
(76.2cm x 101.6cm)

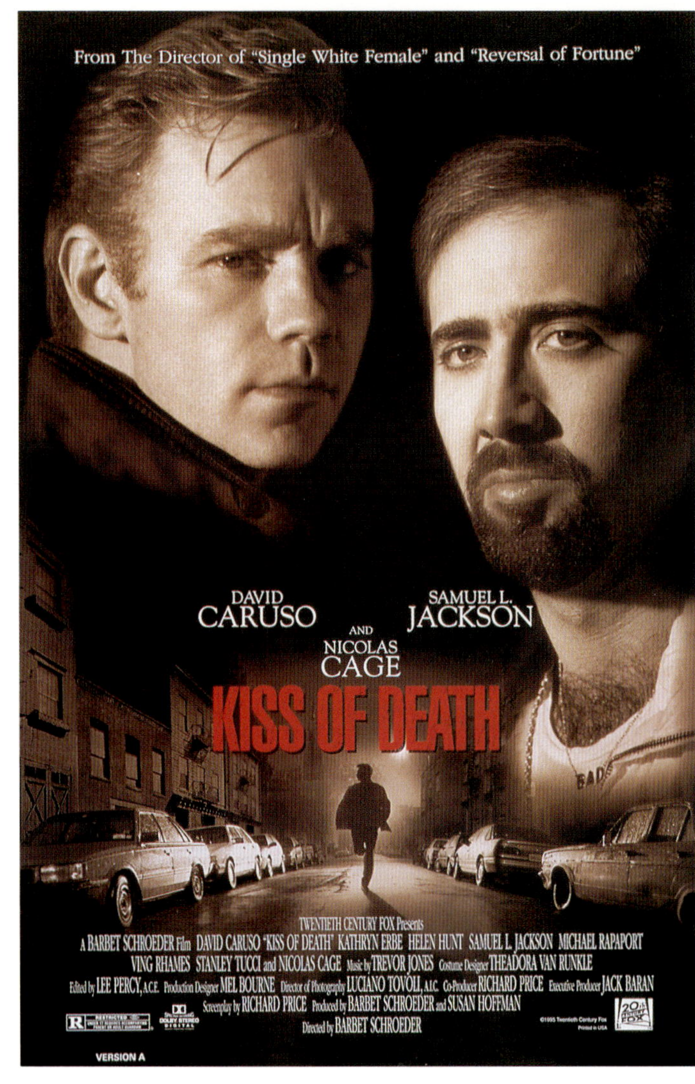

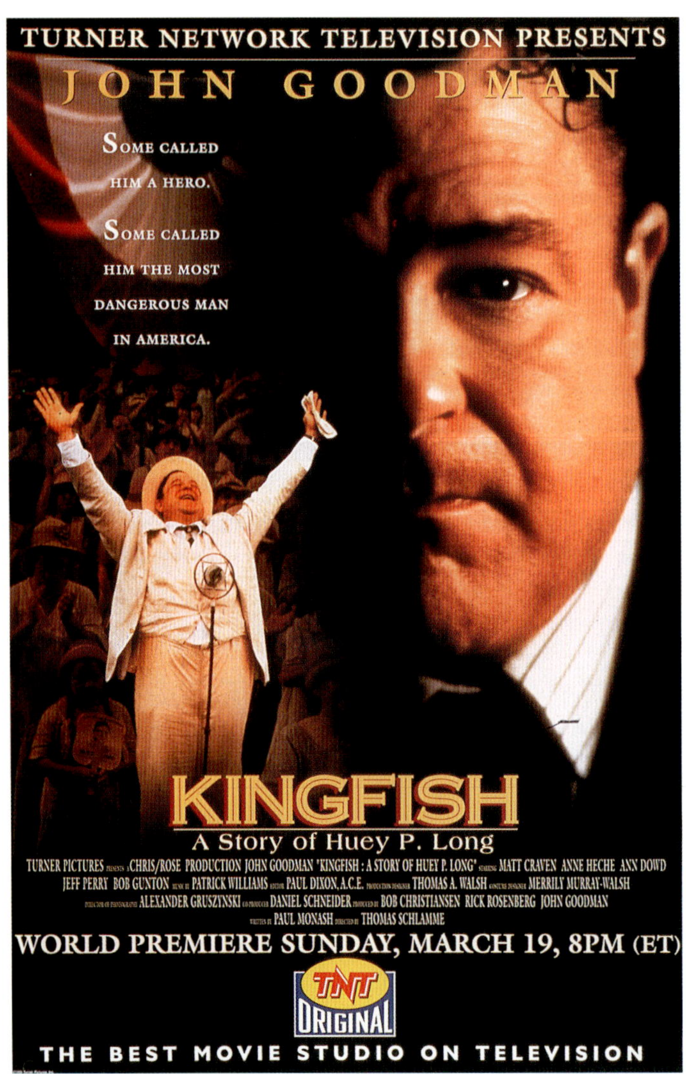

DESIGN FIRM
Dyer Mutchnick Group

ART DIRECTOR
Rod Dyer

DESIGNER
Christopher Cantley

CLIENT
TNT

SIZE
30" x 40"
(76.2cm x 101.6cm)

DESIGN FIRM
Dyer Mutchnick Group

ART DIRECTOR
Rod Dyer

DESIGNER
John Sabel

ILLUSTRATOR
Kamagami/Carroll & Associates

CLIENT
Warner Bros.

PURPOSE
Movie promotion

SIZE
30" x 40"
(76.2cm x 101.6cm)

[facing page]

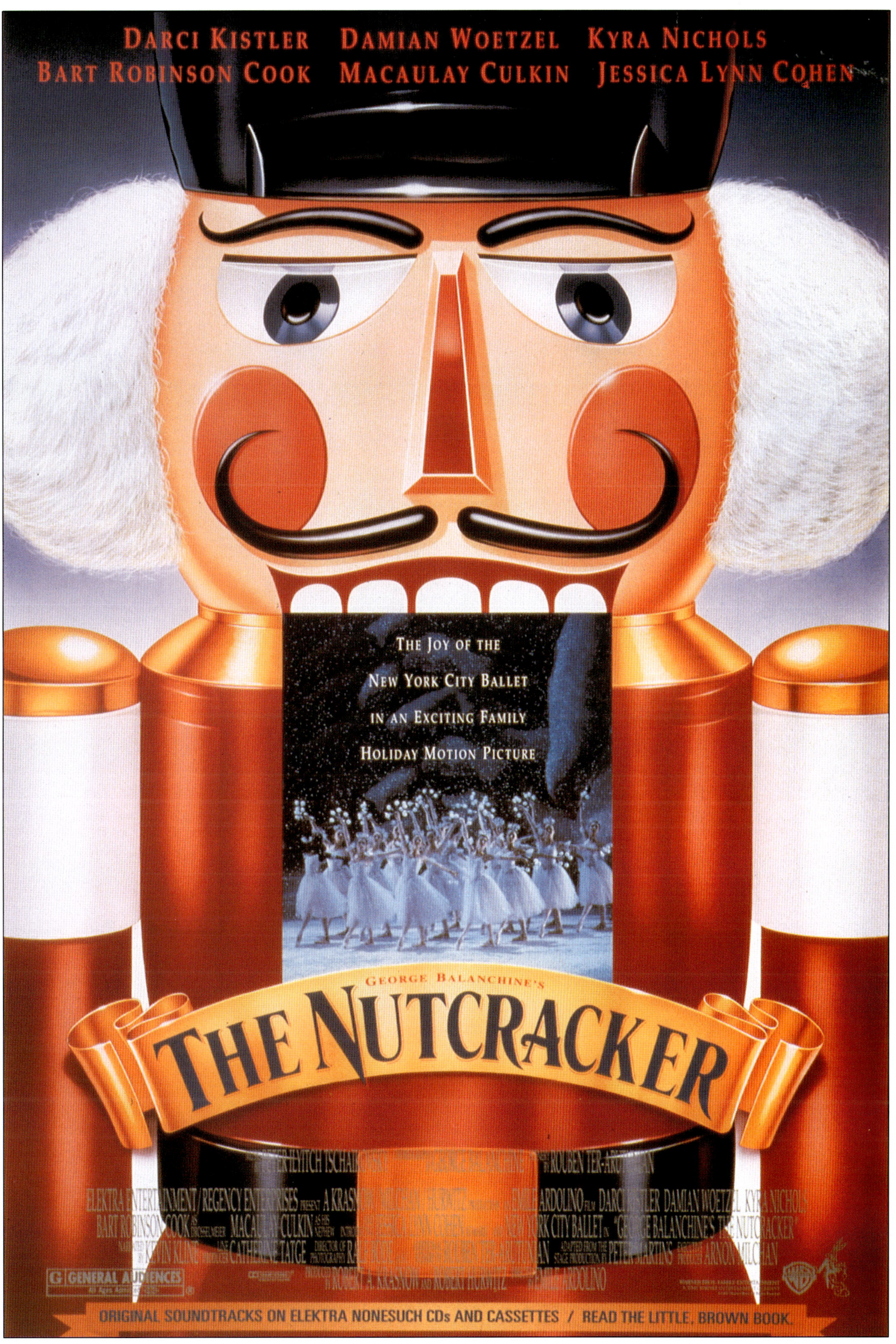

Darci Kistler Damian Woetzel Kyra Nichols
Bart Robinson Cook Macaulay Culkin Jessica Lynn Cohen
The Joy of the
New York City Ballet
in an Exciting Family
Holiday Motion Picture
George Balanchine's
The Nutcracker
G GENERAL AUDIENCES
ORIGINAL SOUNDTRACKS ON ELEKTRA NONESUCH CDs AND CASSETTES / READ THE LITTLE, BROWN BOOK.

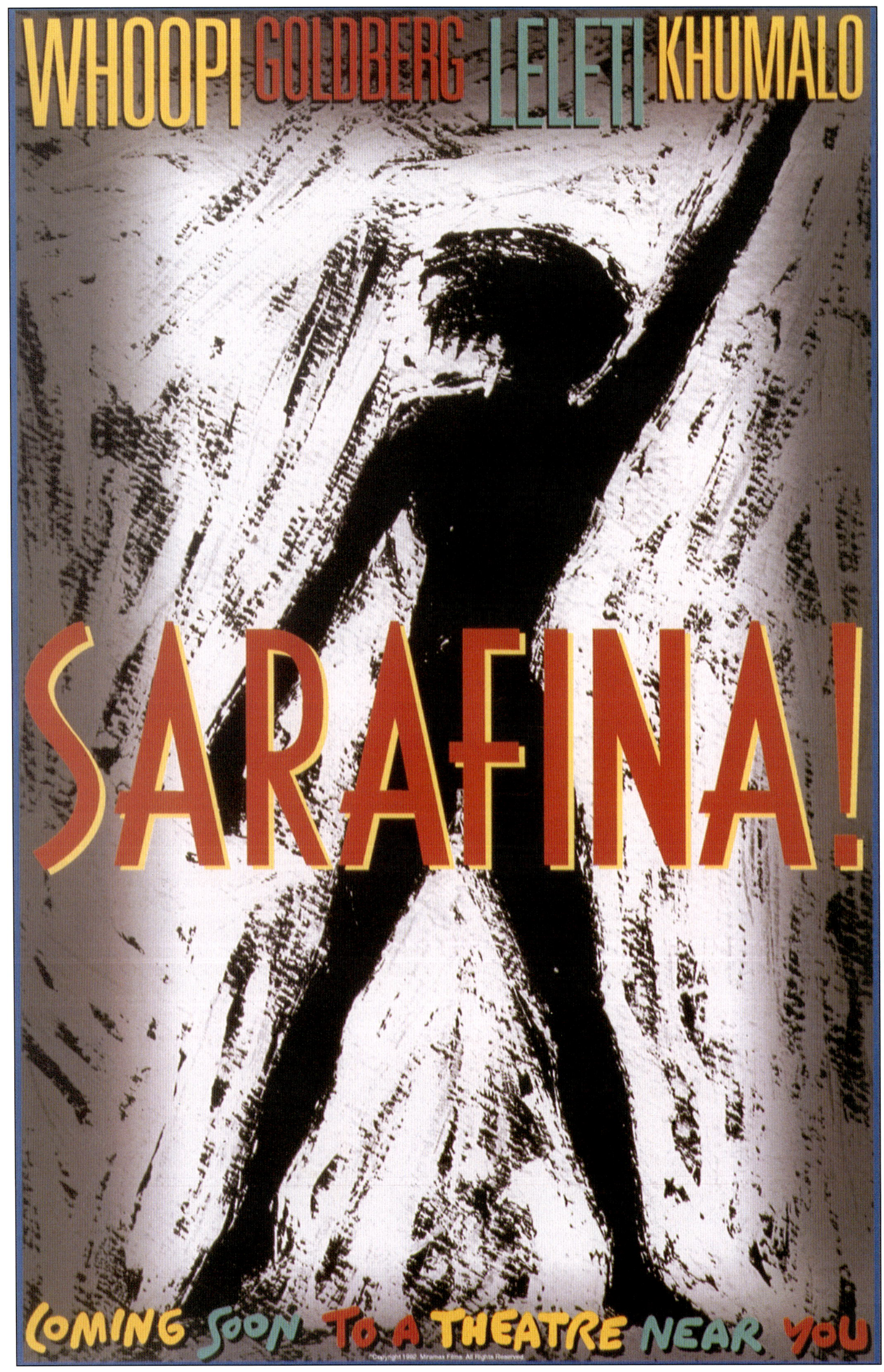
WHOOPI GOLDBERG LELETI KHUMALO
SARAFINA!
COMING SOON TO A THEATRE NEAR YOU
©Copyright 1992 Miramax Films. All Rights Reserved.

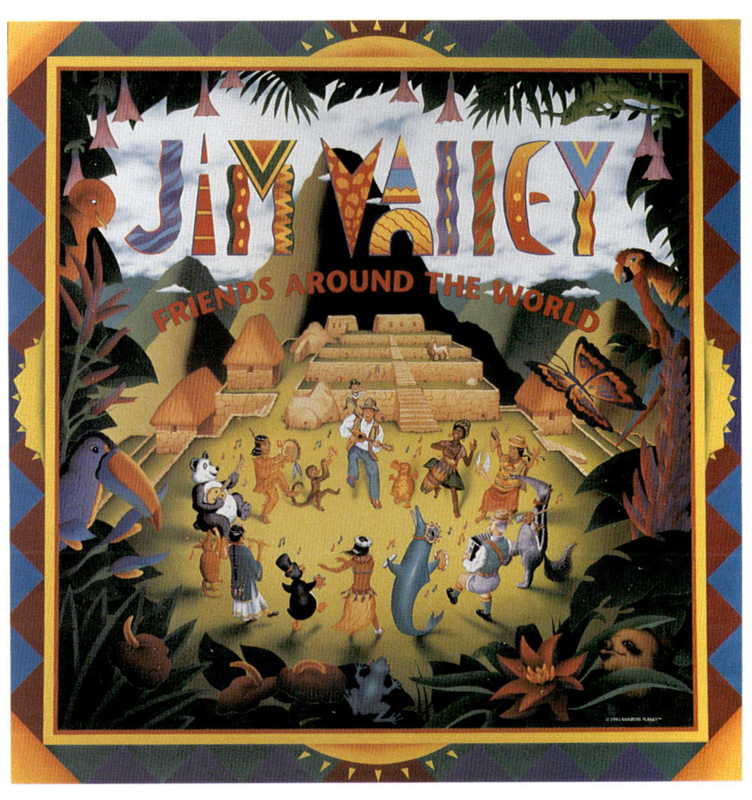

TYPE DESIGN
Stephen Peringer

ILLUSTRATOR
Stephen Peringer

CLIENT
Jim Valley & Rainbow Planet

PURPOSE
"Friends Around The World"
cassette and CD promotion

SIZE
23" x 23" (58.4cm x 58.4cm)

Design completed with the use
of airbrush and acrylic.

DESIGN FIRM
Dyer Mutchnick Group

ART DIRECTOR
Steve Twigger, Rod Dyer

DESIGNER
Steve Twigger

ILLUSTRATOR
Steve Twigger

CLIENT
Miramax

PURPOSE
Movie Teaser Poster

SIZE
27.5" x 42"
(69.9cm x 106.7cm)

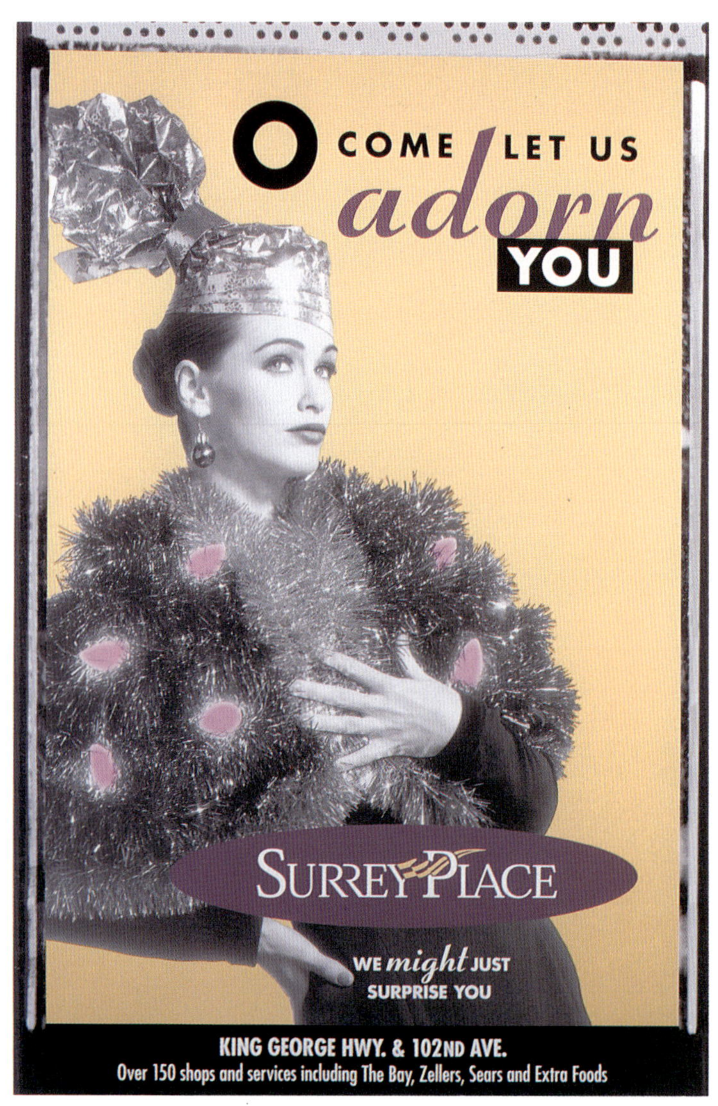

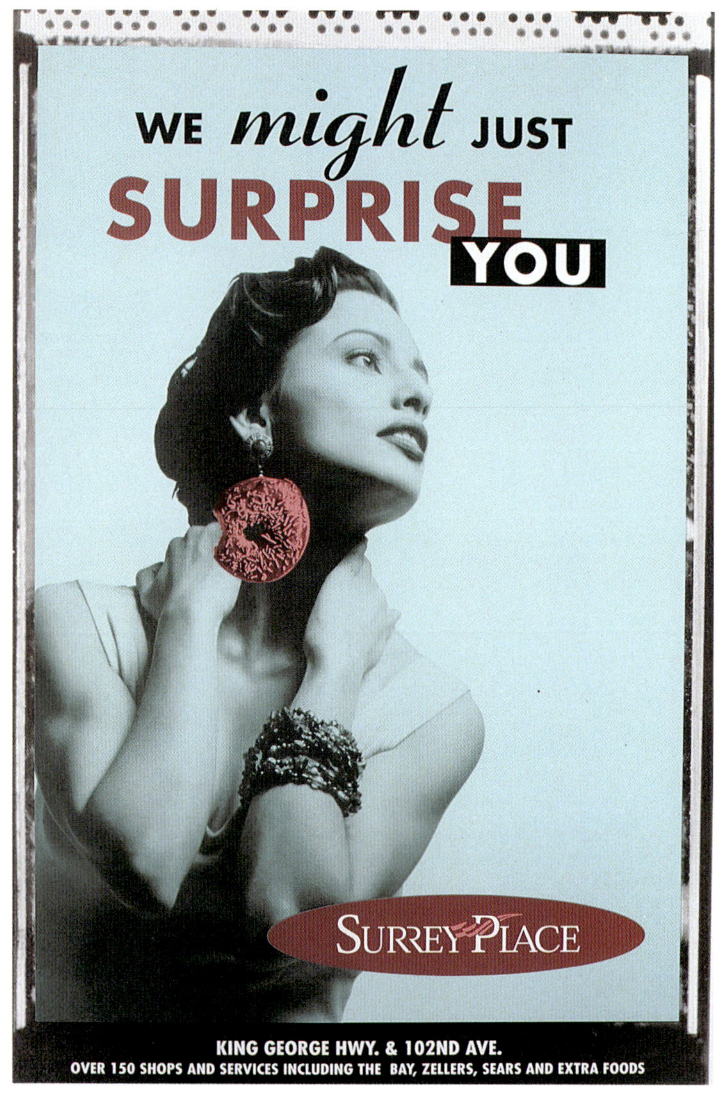

DESIGN FIRM

Suburbia Studios

ART DIRECTORS

Jeremie White,

Nancy Yeasting

DESIGNERS

Jeremie White,

Nancy Yeasting

PHOTOGRAPHER

Jane Weitzel,

Derik Murray Photography

CLIENT

Surrey Place Mall

(Series - 5)

PURPOSE

Mall promotion

SIZE

48" x 72"

(121.9cm x 182.8cm)

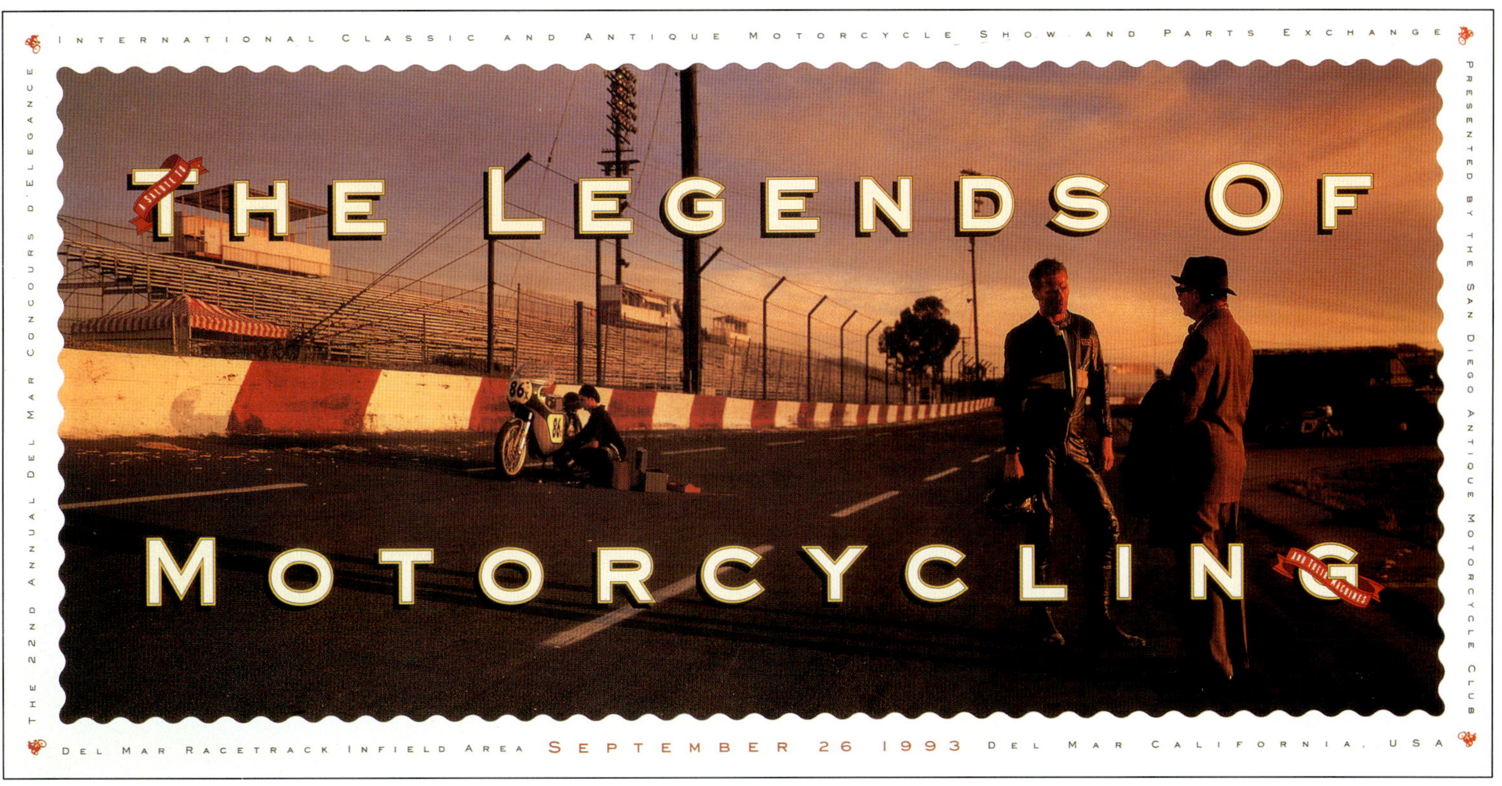

DESIGN FIRM
Mires Design, Inc.

ART DIRECTOR
John Ball

DESIGNERS
John Ball, Miguel Perez

PHOTOGRAPHER
Chris Wimpey

CLIENT
San Diego
Antique Motorcycle Club

PURPOSE
Event advertisement

SIZE
32" x 16"
(81.3cm x 40.6cm)

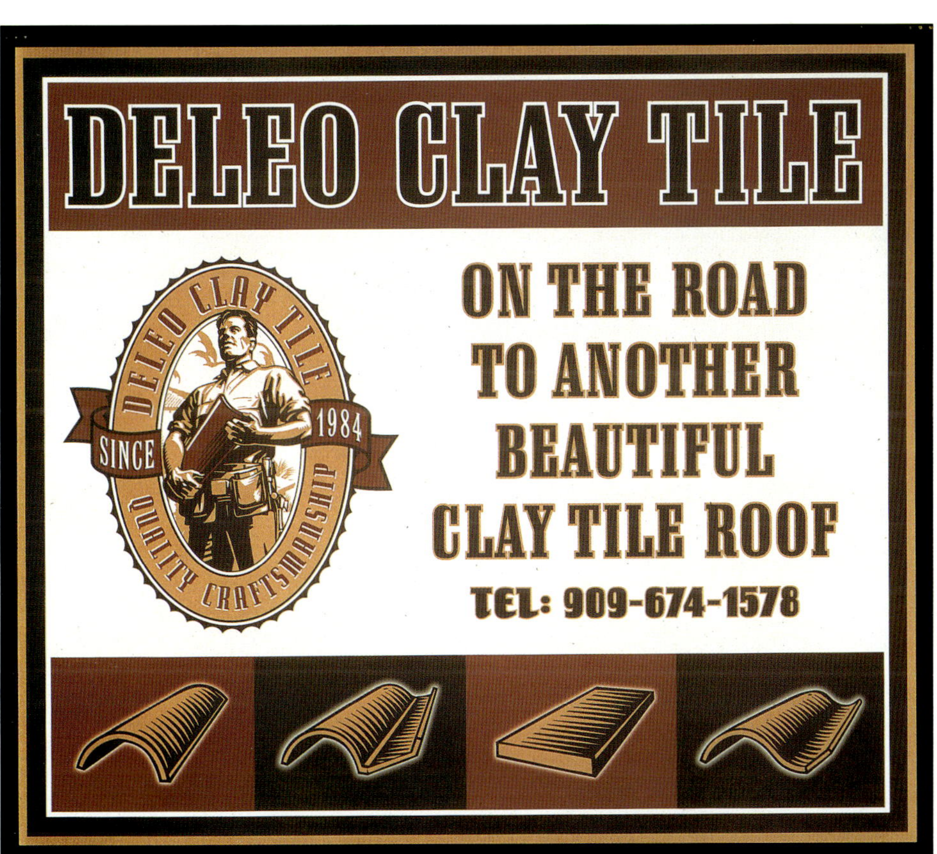

DESIGN FIRM
Mires Design, Inc.

ART DIRECTOR
José Serrano

DESIGNER
José Serrano

ILLUSTRATOR
Nancy Stahl

CLIENT
Deleo Clay Tile Co.

PURPOSE
Advertisement

SIZE
18" x 21"
(45.7cm x 53.3cm)

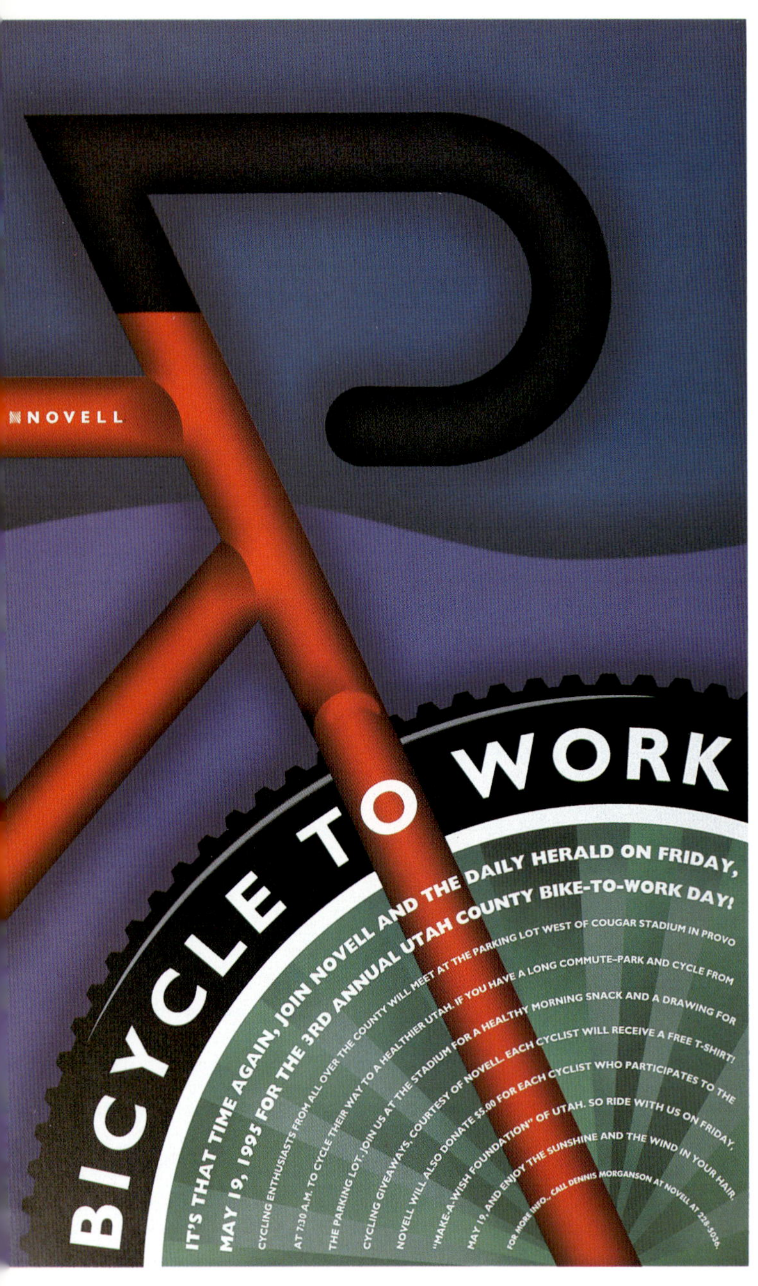

DESIGN FIRM
Richards & Swensen, Inc.

ART DIRECTOR
Michael Richards

DESIGNERS
Michael Richards,
Connie Christensen

ILLUSTRATOR
Connie Christensen

CLIENT
Novell, Inc.

PURPOSE
"Bicycle to Work Day" promotion

SIZE
14" x 22" (35.6cm x 55.9cm)

A rough drawing was scanned and recreated in Adobe Illustrator 5.5 then rasterized into Adobe Photoshop 3.0 where the basic colors were applied. Through Adobe Photoshop's layers and channels the designer applied shadows and light effects to make the colors play off each other. Lastly, the type was merged with the image again in Adobe Illustrator at a one-to-one ratio. Then the file was run out to film for offset printing through Adobe Separator.

DESIGN FIRM
Segura

ART DIRECTOR
Carlos Segura

DESIGNER
Carlos Segura

ILLUSTRATOR
Tony Klassen

CLIENT
[T-26] digital type foundry

PURPOSE
Promotion

SIZE
24" x 36"
(60.9cm x 91.4cm)

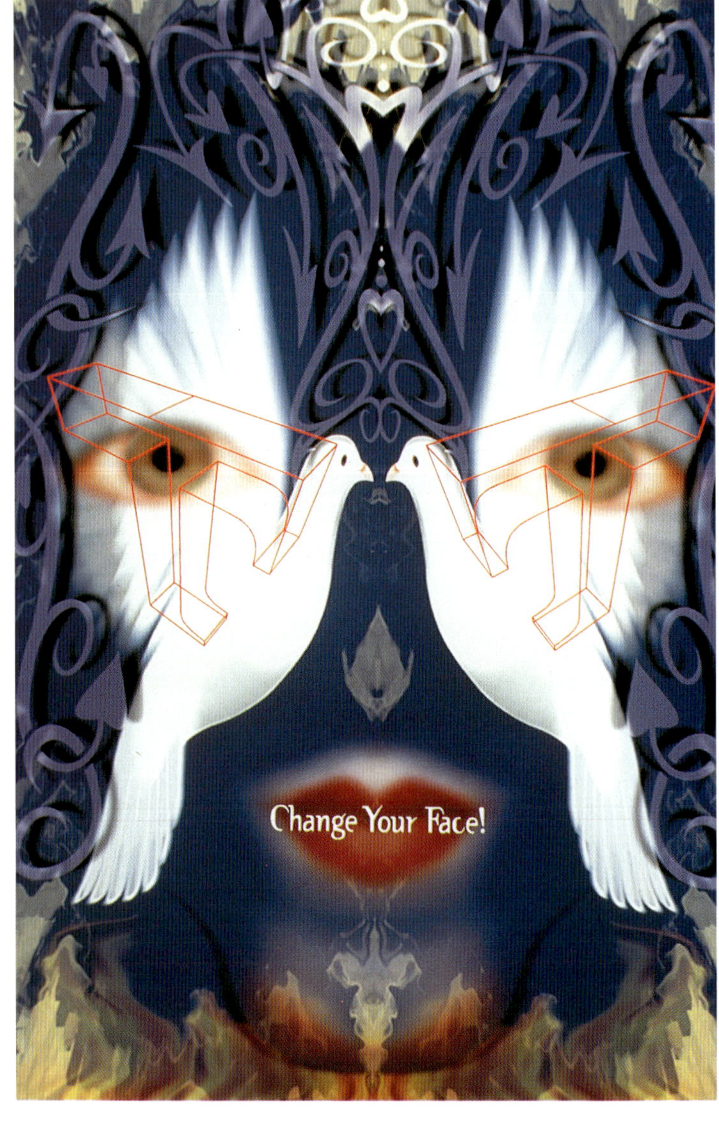

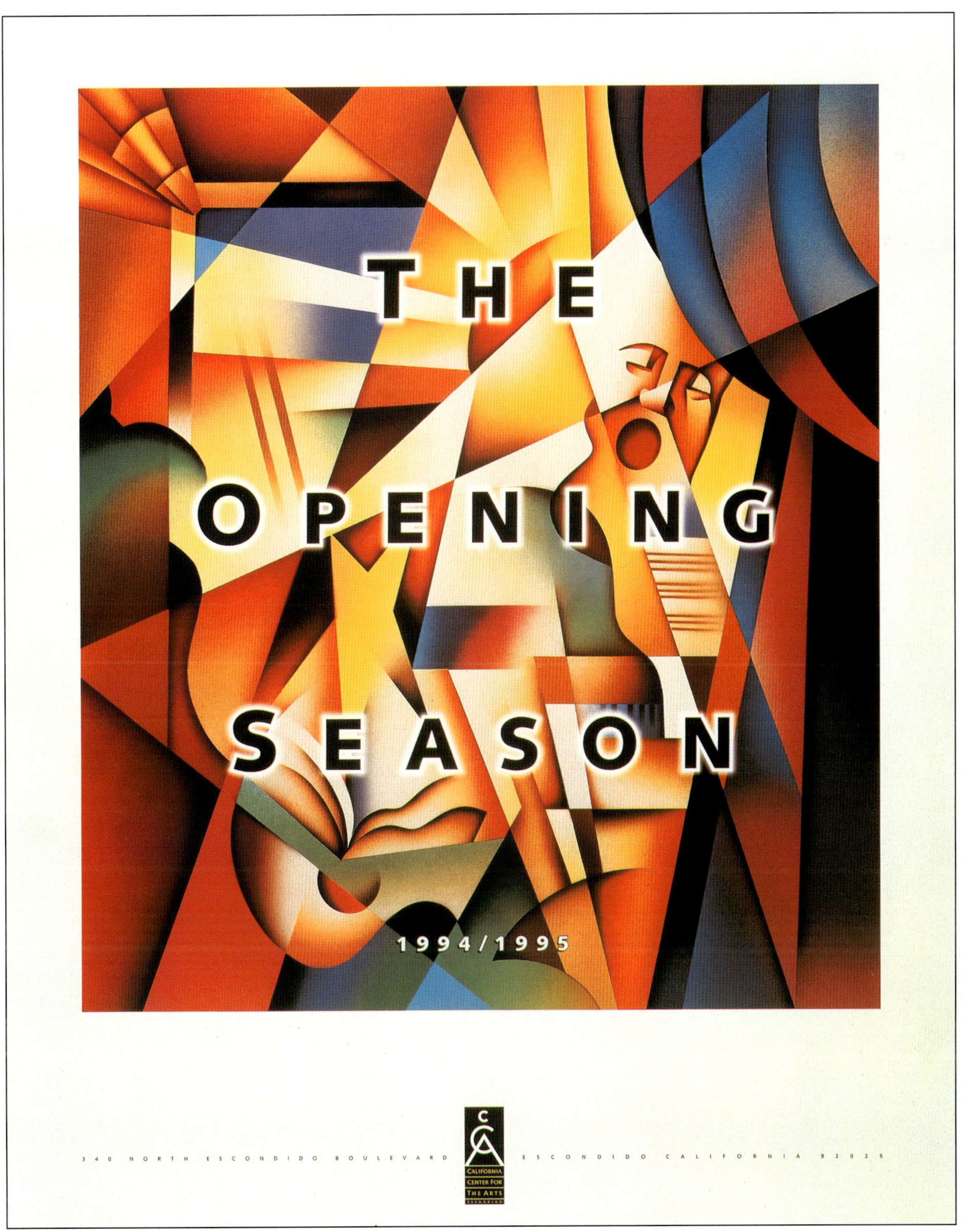

DESIGN FIRM

Mires Design, Inc.

ART DIRECTOR

John Ball

DESIGNER

John Ball

ILLUSTRATOR

John Jinks

CLIENT

California Center for the Arts, Escondido

PURPOSE

promote the opening season of performances

SIZE

25" x 33" (63.5cm x 83.8cm)

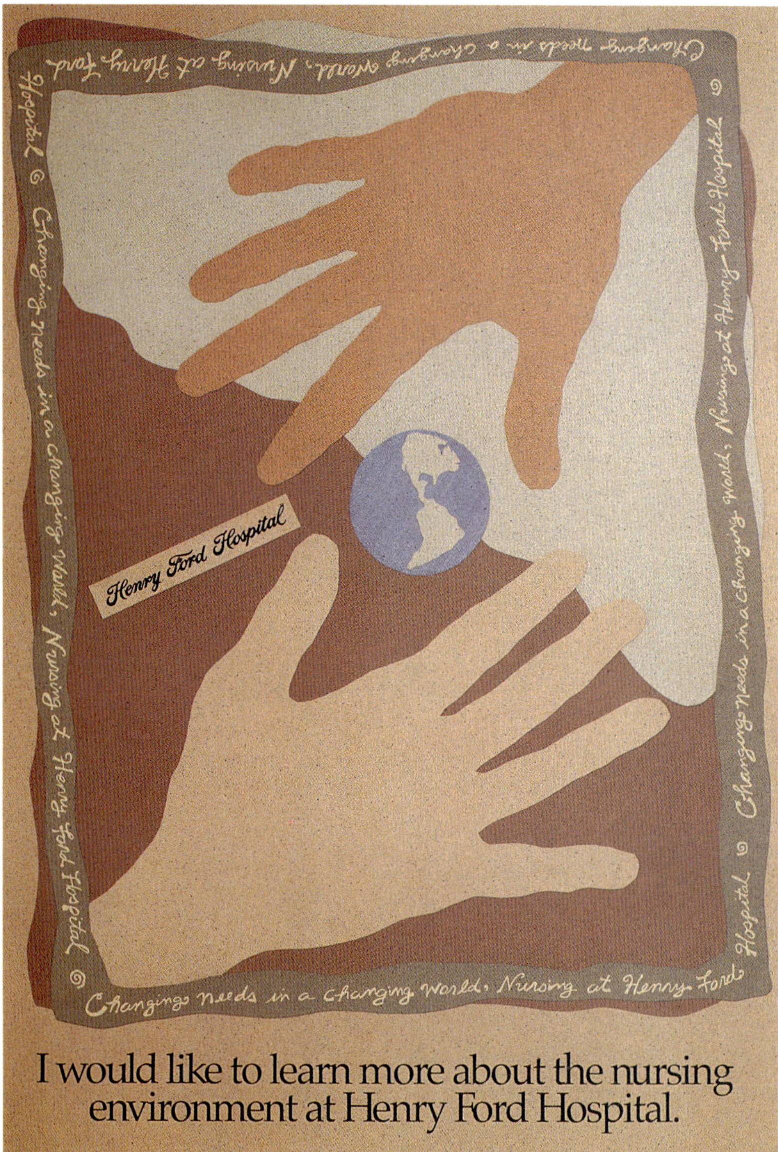

DESIGN FIRM
Noonan Media

ALL DESIGN
Tim Noonan

CLIENT
Henry Ford Hospital

PURPOSE
Nursing employment recruitment

SIZE
12" x 17" (30.5cm x 43.2cm)

The designer created this poster with the use of cut-paper illustration, hand-lettering, and scanned images. A pad of 50 BRC cards was glued to each poster.

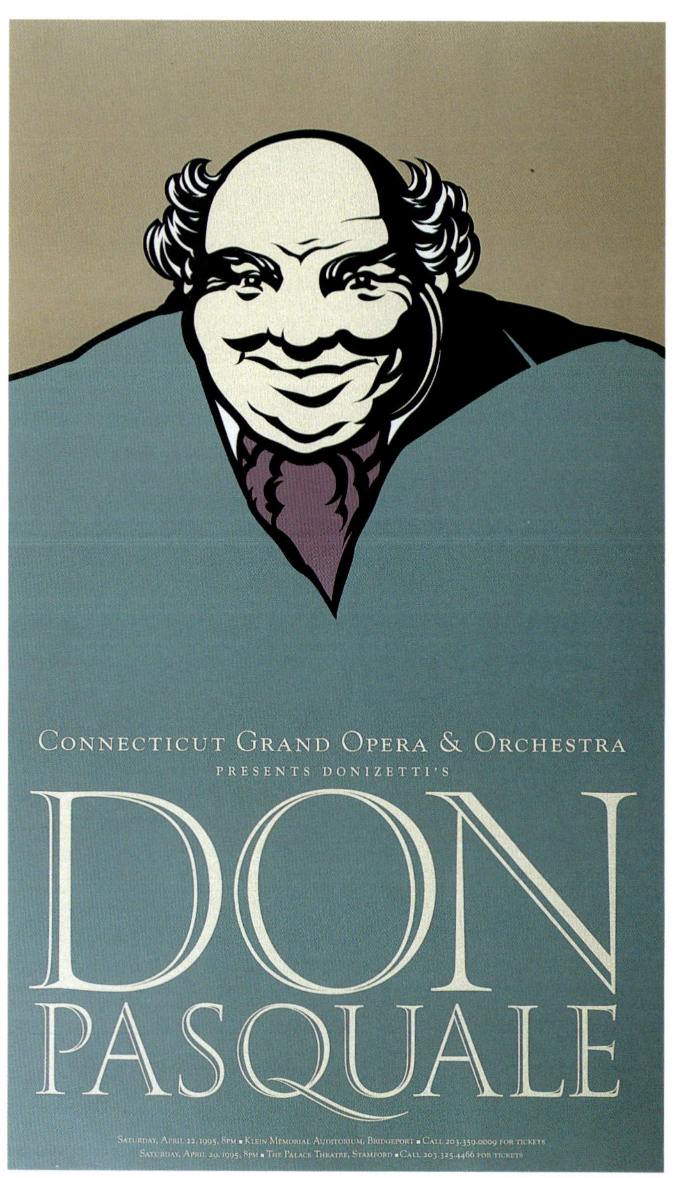

DESIGN FIRM
Tom Fowler, Inc.

ART DIRECTOR
Thomas G. Fowler

DESIGNER
Samuel Toh

ILLUSTRATOR
Samuel Toh

CLIENT
Connecticut Grand Opera & Orchestra

PURPOSE
Opera performance promotion

SIZE
16" x 28" (40.6cm x 71.1cm)

Designers used Adobe Illustrator and hand-tooled typography for this design.

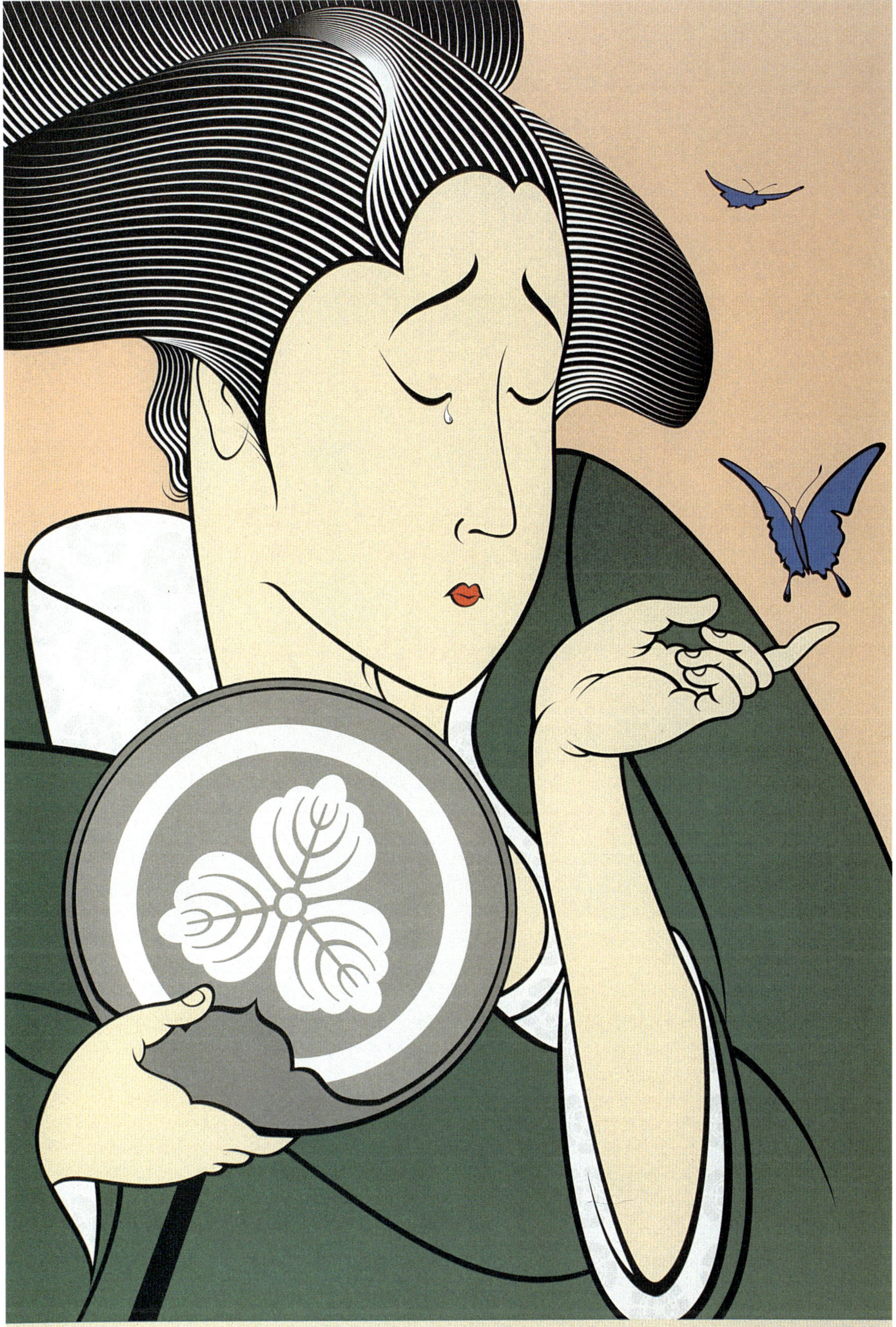

D E S I G N F I R M

Tom Fowler, Inc.

A R T D I R E C T O R

Thomas G. Fowler

D E S I G N E R

Thomas G. Fowler

I L L U S T R A T O R S

Samuel Toh, Thomas G. Fowler

C L I E N T

Connecticut Grand Opera & Orchestra

P U R P O S E

Opera performance promotion

S I Z E

16" x 28" (40.6cm x 71.1cm)

Adobe Illustrator was used for this design. The color palette was influenced by traditional Japanese wood block prints.

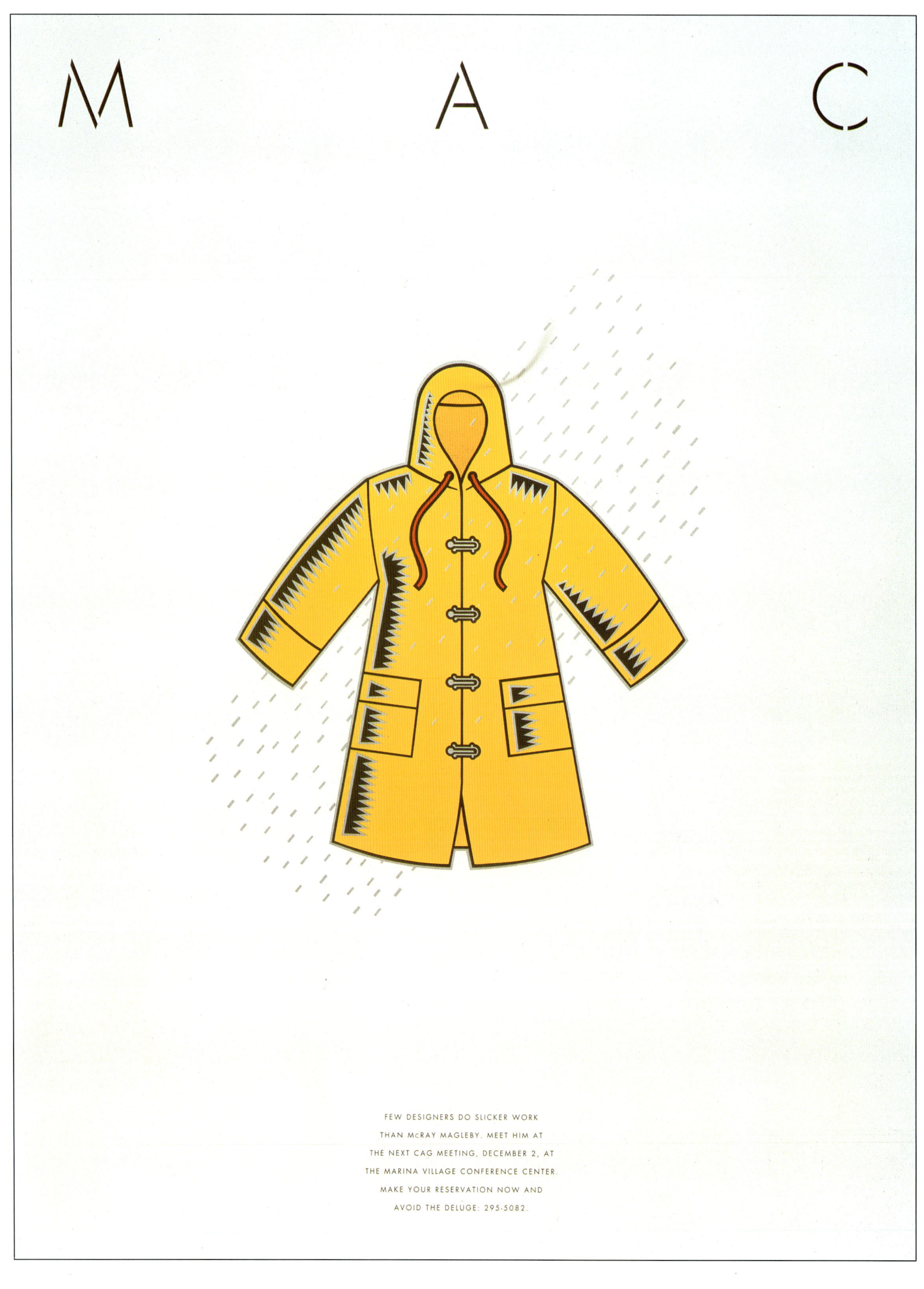
M A C
FEW DESIGNERS DO SLICKER WORK
THAN McRAY MAGLEBY. MEET HIM AT
THE NEXT CAG MEETING, DECEMBER 2, AT
THE MARINA VILLAGE CONFERENCE CENTER.
MAKE YOUR RESERVATION NOW AND
AVOID THE DELUGE: 295-5082.

DESIGN FIRM
Mires Design, Inc.

ART DIRECTOR
John Ball

DESIGNER
John Ball

ILLUSTRATOR
Tracy Sabin

CLIENT
Communicating Arts Group

PURPOSE
Exhibition advertisement

SIZE
24" x 18" (61cm x 45.7cm)

DESIGN FIRM
Walcott-Ayers Group

ART DIRECTOR
Jim Walcott-Ayers

DESIGNER
Meghan Mahler

ILLUSTRATOR
Meghan Mahler

CLIENT
California Resource Recovery Association

PURPOSE
Recycling Conference promotion

SIZE
18" x 27" (45.7cm x 68.6cm)

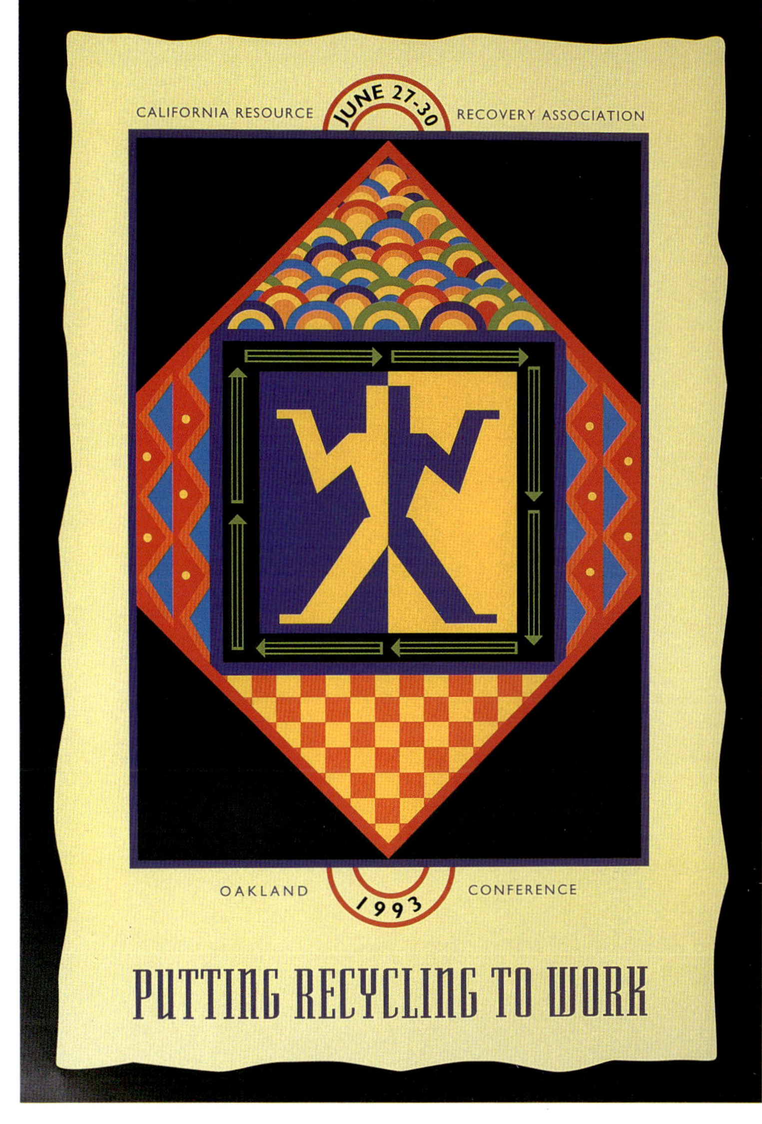

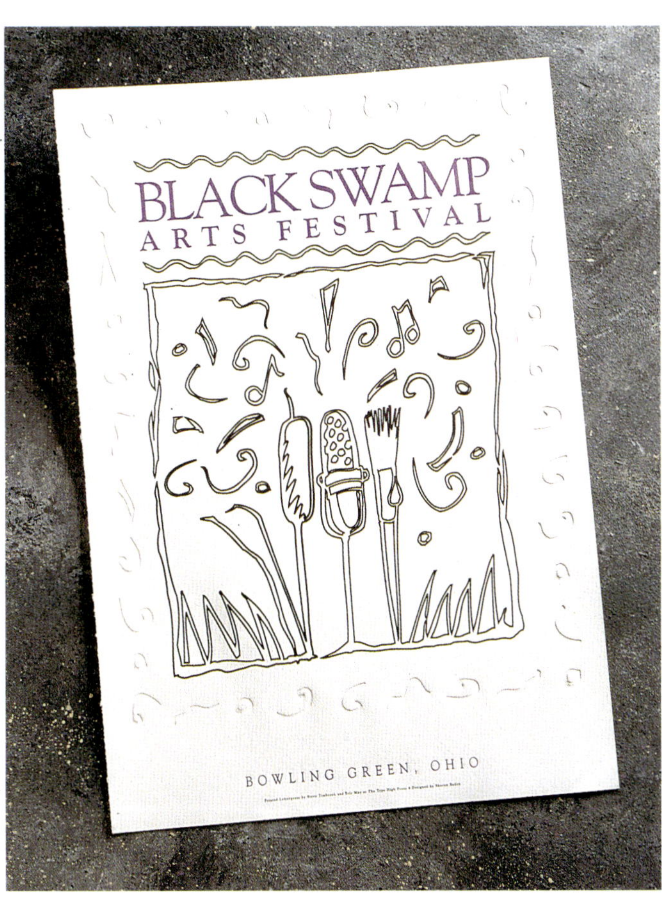

DESIGN FIRM

ART DIRECTOR
Sharon Baden

ALL DESIGN
Sharon Baden

CLIENT
Arts Allied/Black Swamp Arts Festival

PURPOSE
Commemorative poster for arts festival

SIZE
16" x 23" (40.6cm x 58.4cm)

A hand-drawn sketch was finished in Aldus FreeHand. The poster was printed letterpress 3-colors and with one blind impression.

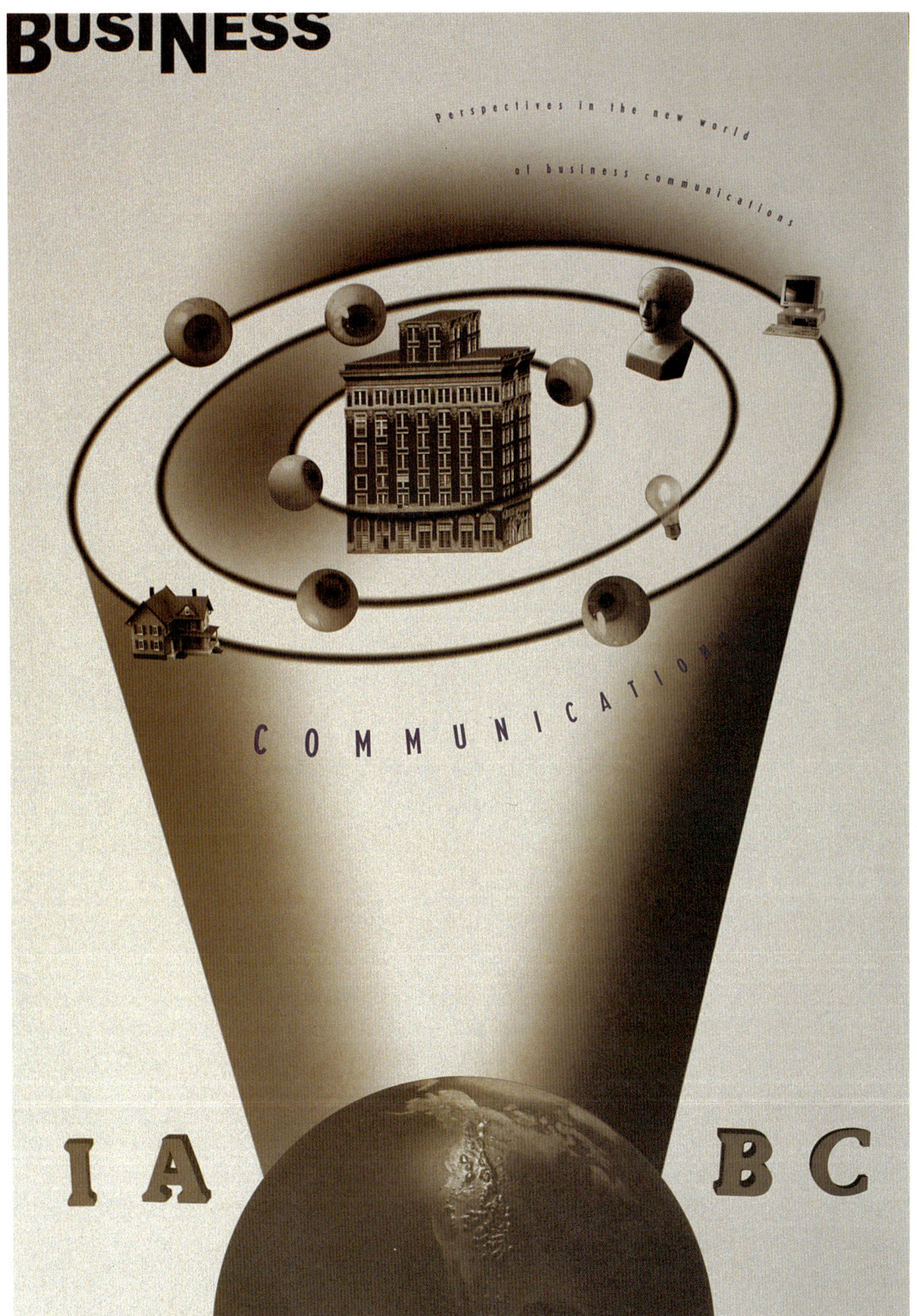

DESIGN FIRM
Peterson & Company

ART DIRECTOR
Scott Ray

DESIGNER
Scott Ray

PHOTOGRAPHER
Eric Pearle

CLIENT
International Association of Business Communicators

PURPOSE
Business seminar announcement

SIZE
18" x 24" (45.7cm x 61cm)

DESIGN FIRM
Peterson & Company

ART DIRECTOR
Scott Ray

DESIGNER
Scott Ray

ILLUSTRATORS
Aletha Repell,
Shayne Eliason

CLIENT
Dallas Press Club

PURPOSE
Katies Award Ceremony announcement

SIZE
35" x 15.5"
(88.9cm x 39.3cm)

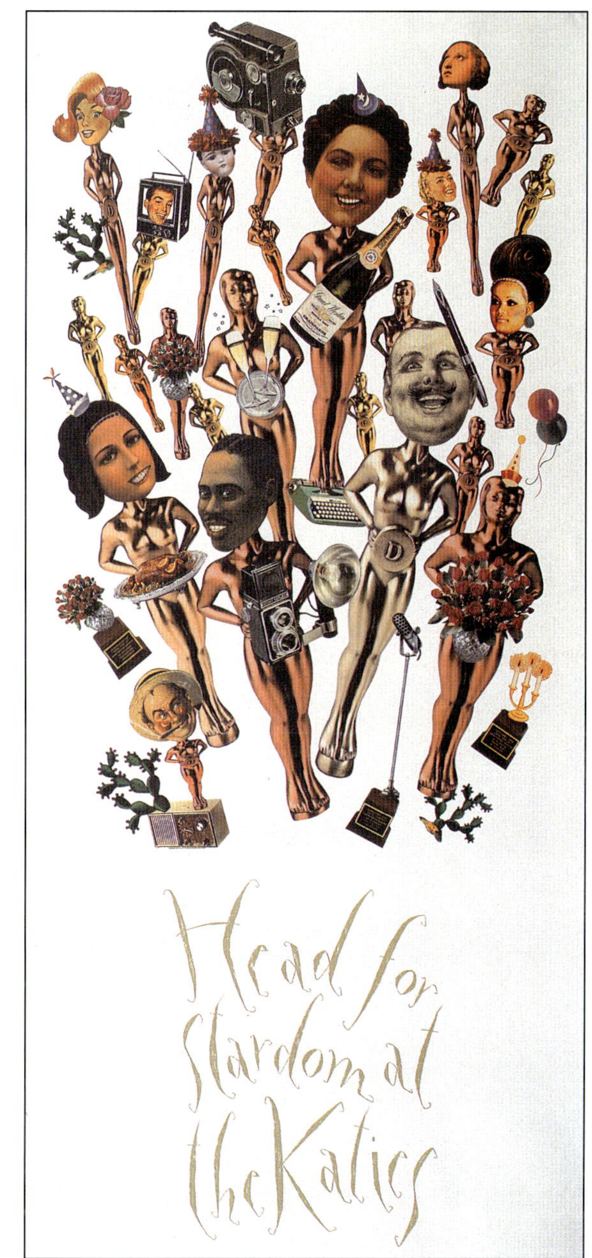

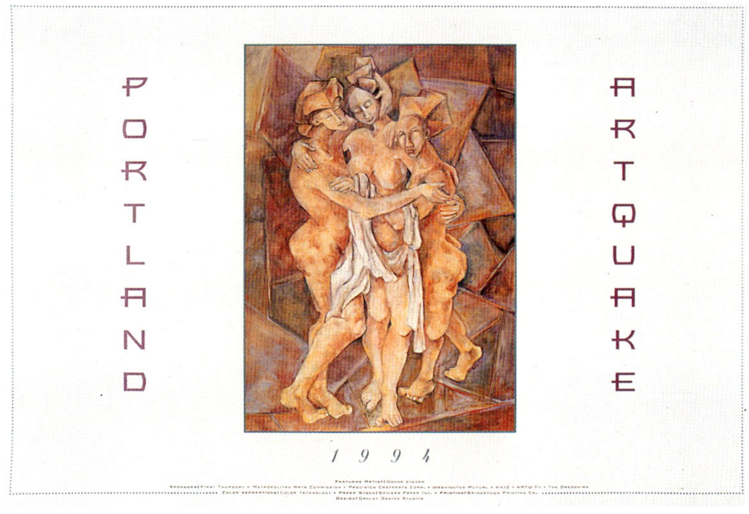

DESIGN FIRM
Oakley Design Studios

ART DIRECTOR
Tim Oakley

DESIGNER
Tim Oakley

ILLUSTRATOR
Donna Steger

CLIENT
Portland Art Quake, Inc.

PURPOSE
Promotion

SIZE
22" x 26" (55.9cm x 66cm)

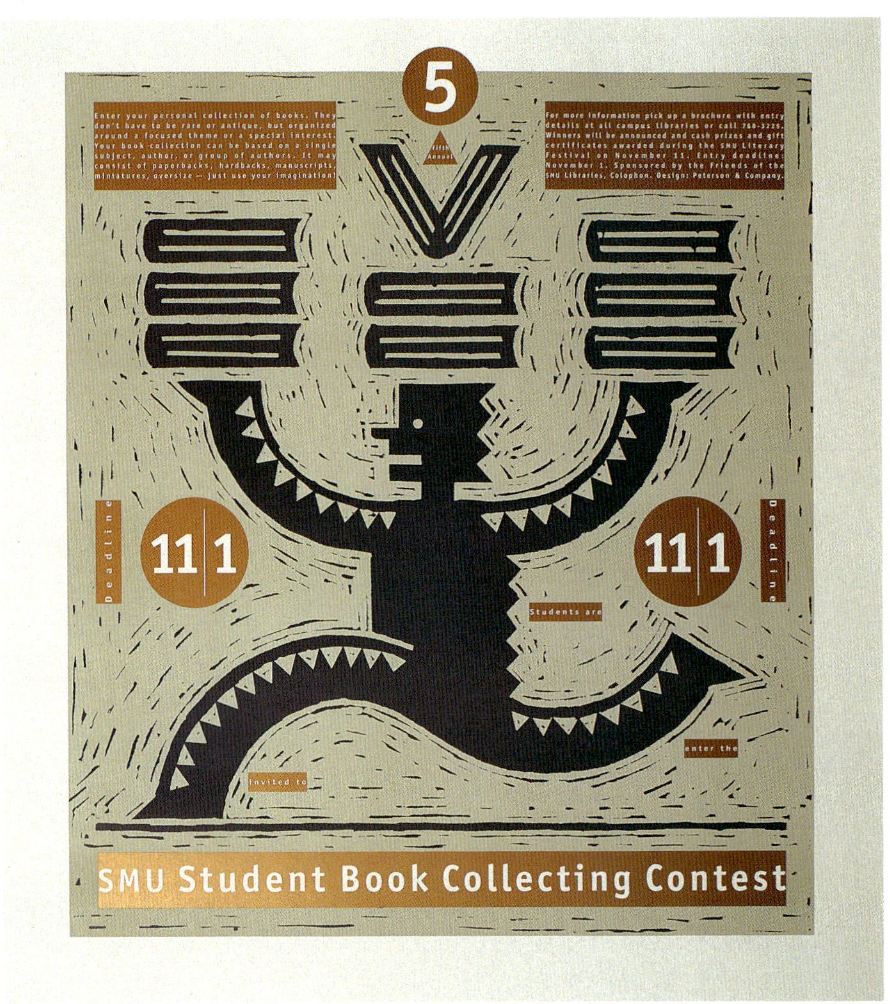

DESIGN FIRM
Peterson & Company

ALL DESIGN
Bryan L. Peterson

CLIENT
Friends of the SMU Library

PURPOSE
Book collecting contest advertisement

SIZE
18" x 24"
(45.7cm x 61cm)

[above and right]

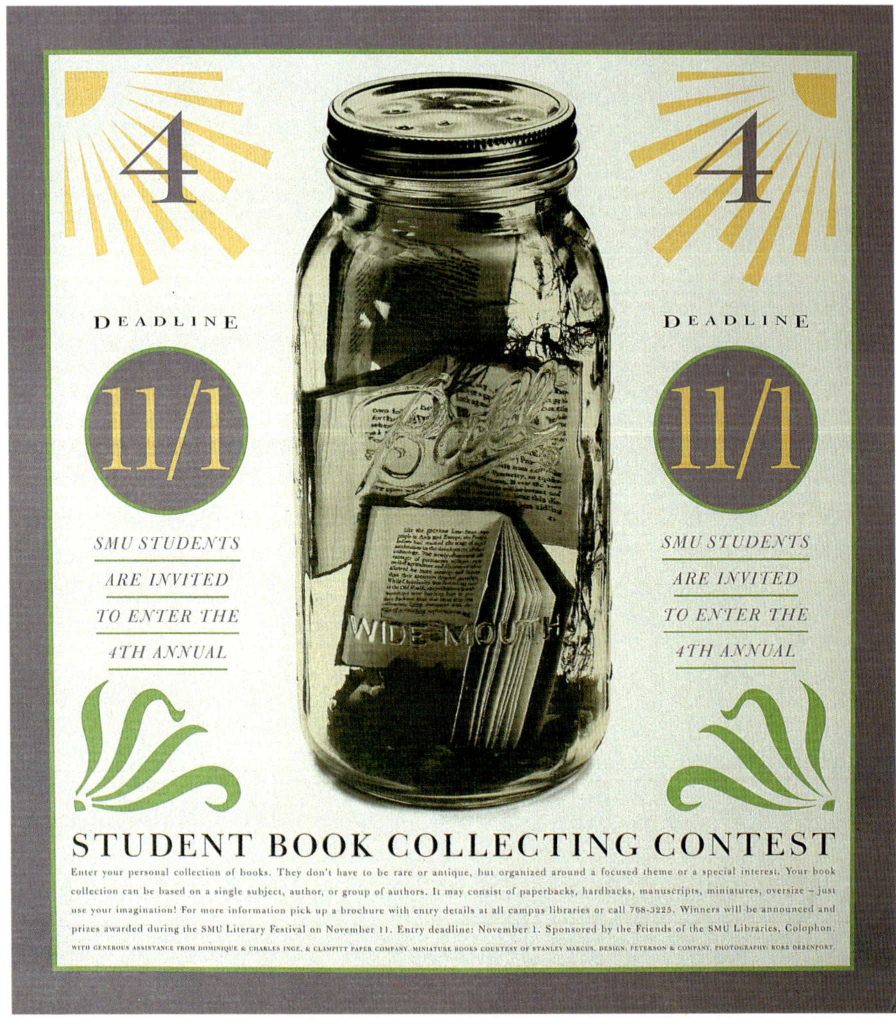

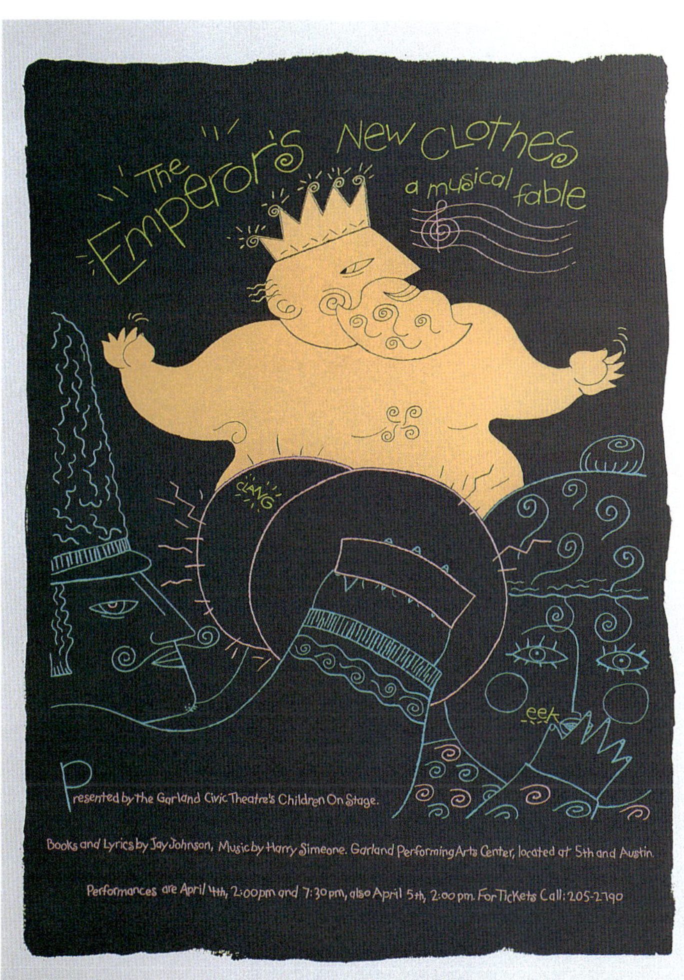

DESIGN FIRM
Peterson & Company

ART DIRECTOR
Scott Ray

DESIGNER
Scott Ray

ILLUSTRATOR
Lynn Rowe Reed

CLIENT
Children's Civic Theater

PURPOSE
Play performance announcement

SIZE
20" x 28"
(50.8cm x 71.1cm)

DESIGN FIRM
Peterson & Company

ART DIRECTOR
Scott Ray

DESIGNER
Scott Ray

ILLUSTRATOR
Bryan L. Peterson

CLIENT
Literary Instruction for Texas

PURPOSE
Awareness poster

SIZE
25" x 39"
(63.5cm x 99cm)

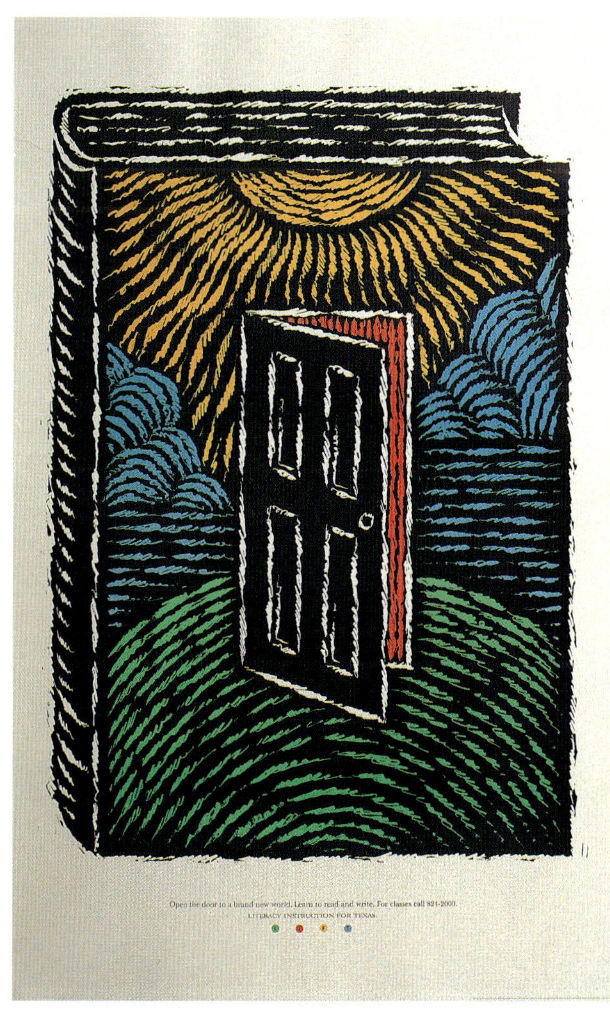

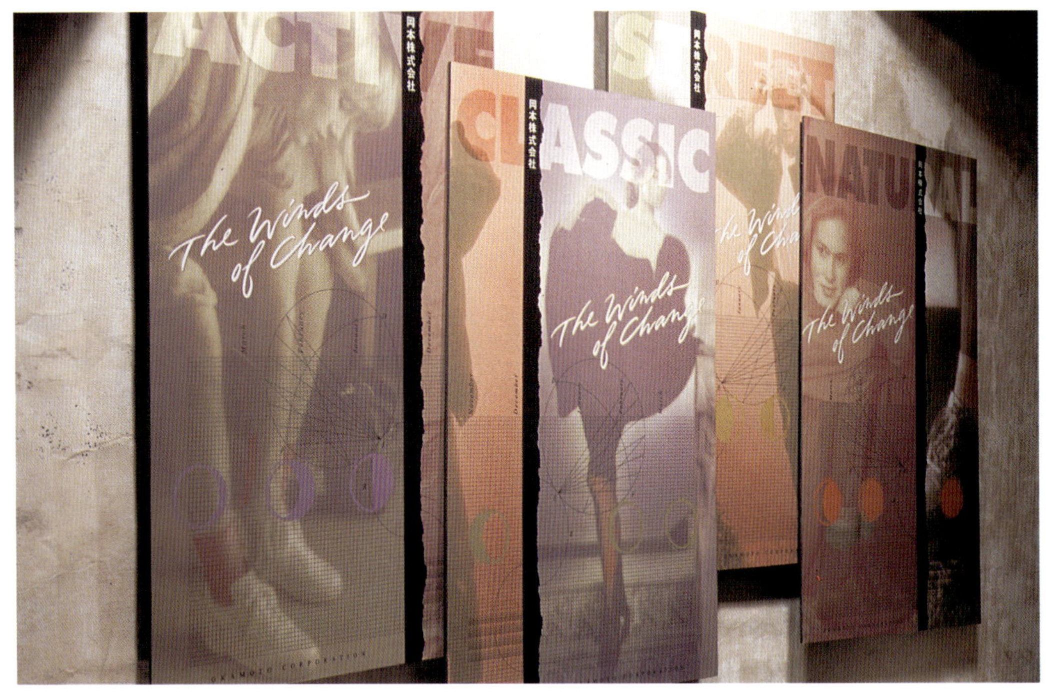

DESIGN FIRM

Hornall Anderson Design Works, Inc.

ART DIRECTOR

John Hornall

DESIGNERS

John Hornall, Julie Lock,
Mary Hermes, Julie Keenan

CLIENT

Okamoto Corporation

PURPOSE

Tenjikai "Ladies Fashion Division"
Show advertisement

SIZE

24" x 36"
(60.9cm x 91.4cm)

Adobe Photoshop and Aldus FreeHand were used by designers to scan and manipulate the color of posters.

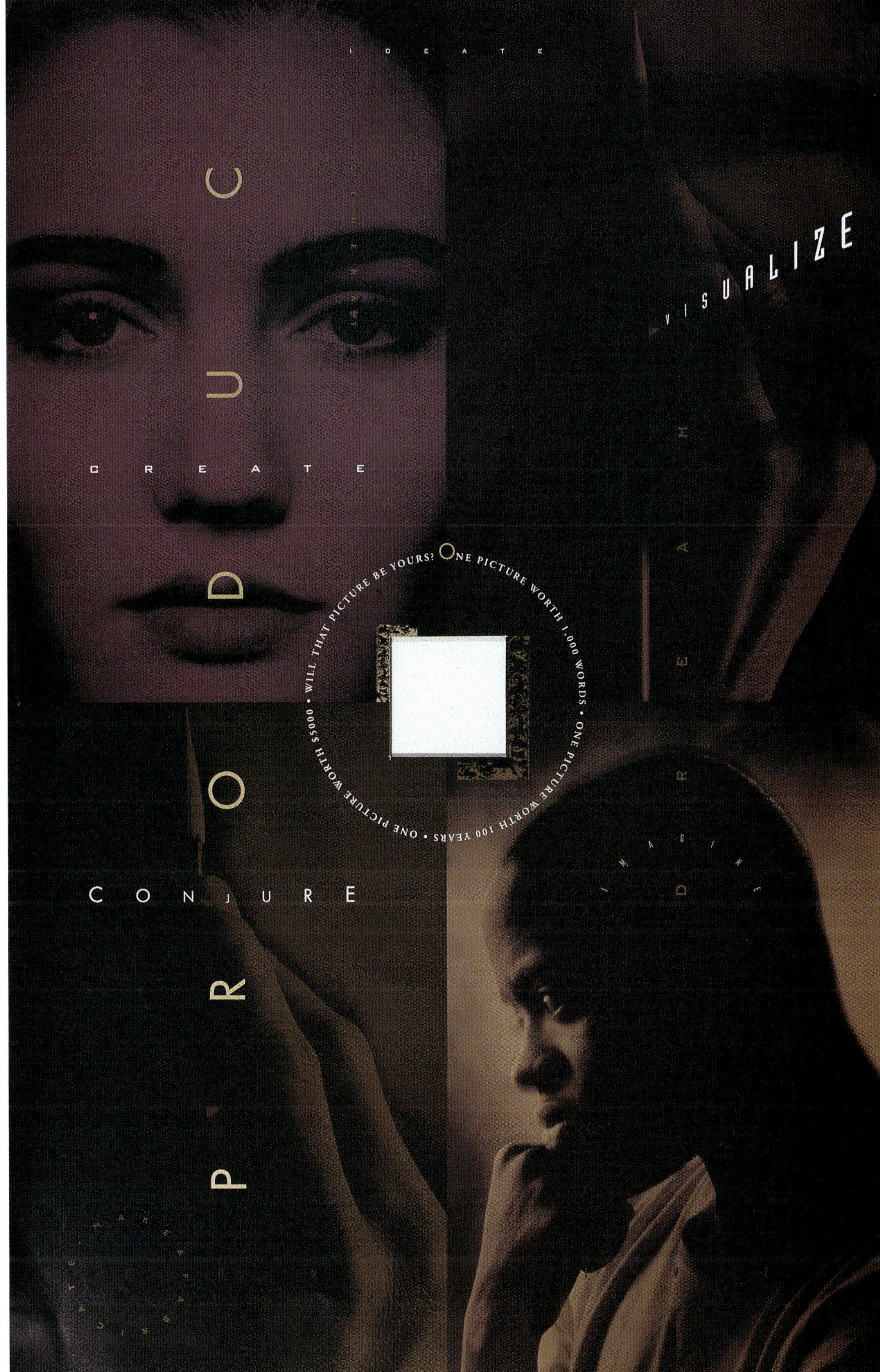

DESIGN FIRM
Greteman Group

ART DIRECTOR
Sonia Greteman

DESIGNERS
Sonia Greteman, James Strange

PHOTOGRAPHER
Ron Berg

CLIENT
Wichita State University

PURPOSE
Fine arts competition promotion

SIZE
13.5" x 21" (34.3cm x 53.3cm)

DESIGN FIRM
Mink Design

ALL DESIGN
Matt Scherer

CLIENT
The Gathering Place

PURPOSE
Awareness poster

SIZE
22" x 28.5"
(55.9cm x 72.4cm)

The illustration was done very small with a pencil and then scanned in and blown-up. Type was added in Adobe Illustrator and just the black plate was played out. Colors were cut by hand out of Rubylith. The lighter gray was printed first, then the blue, and then a reverse of the type.

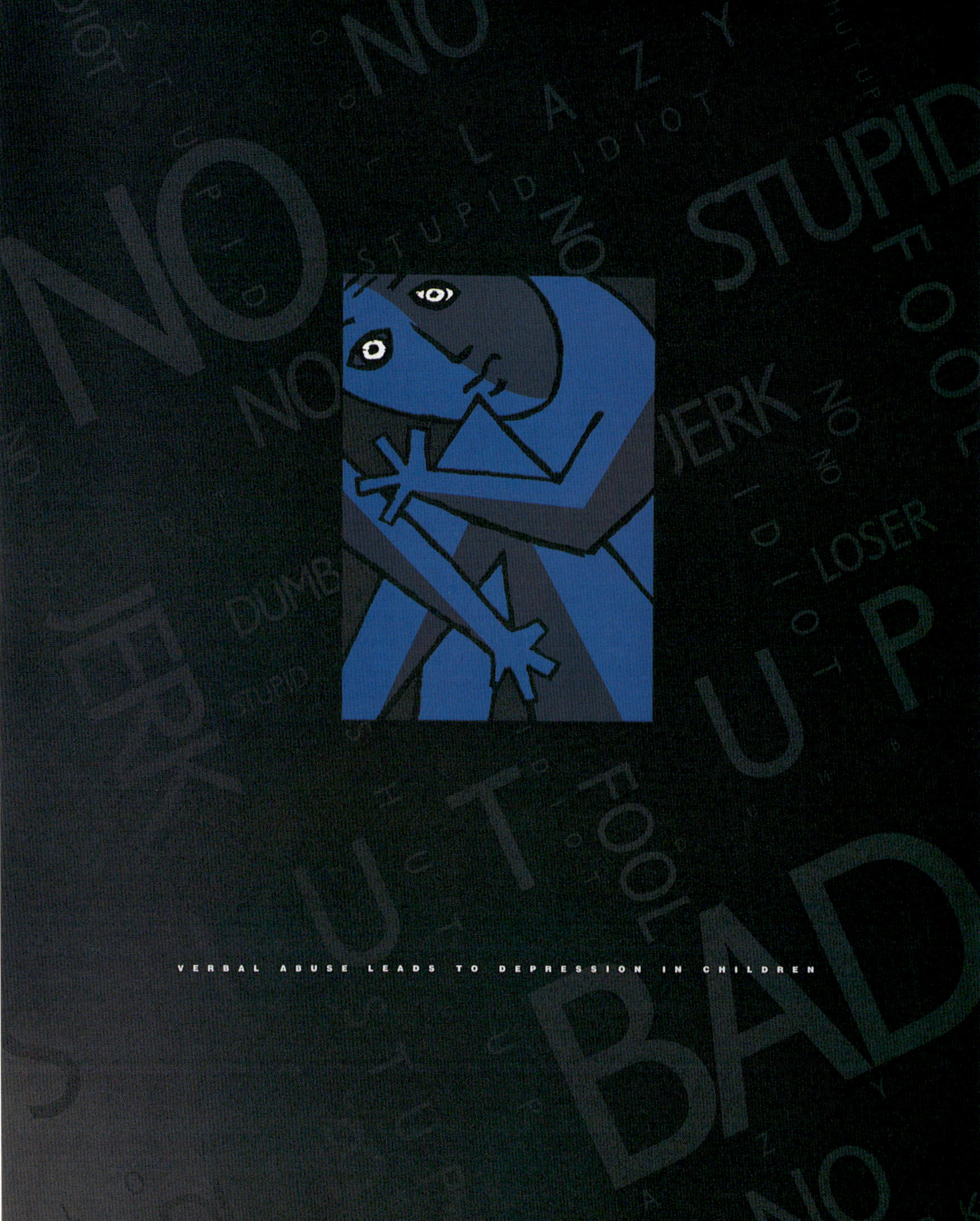

DESIGN FIRM
Ostro Design

ALL DESIGN
Michael Ostro

CLIENT
Special Olympics
World Games

PURPOSE
International event
promotion

SIZE
23.5" x 35"
(59.7cm x 89cm)

Designer used traditional pastel and color pencil illustration.

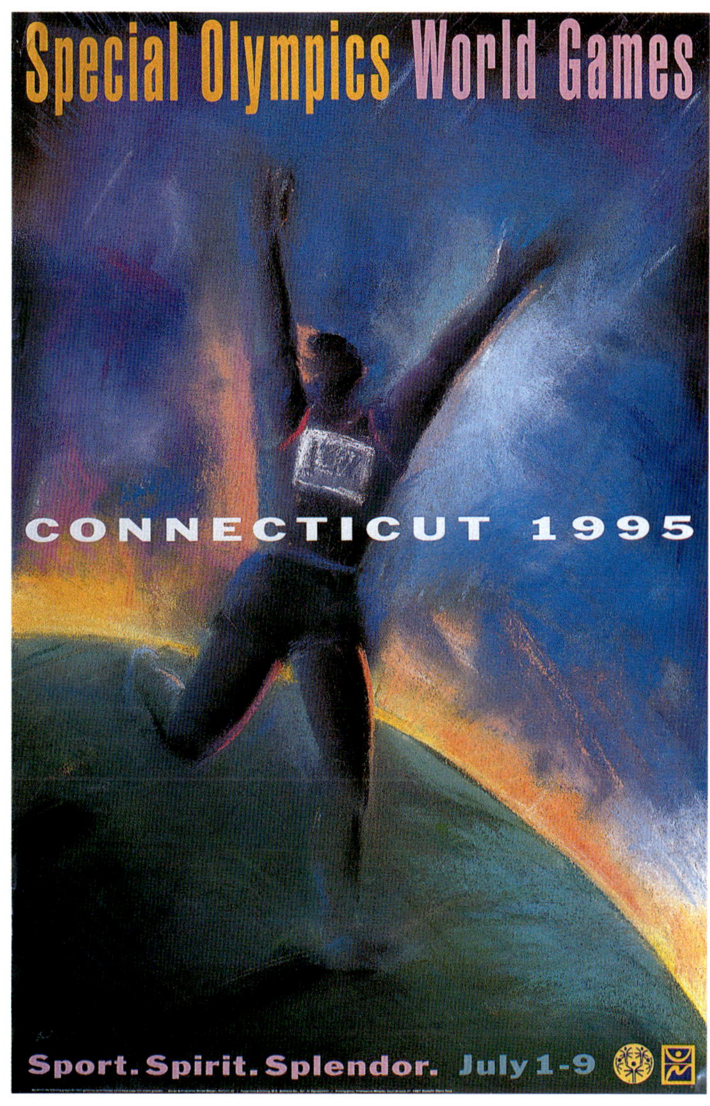

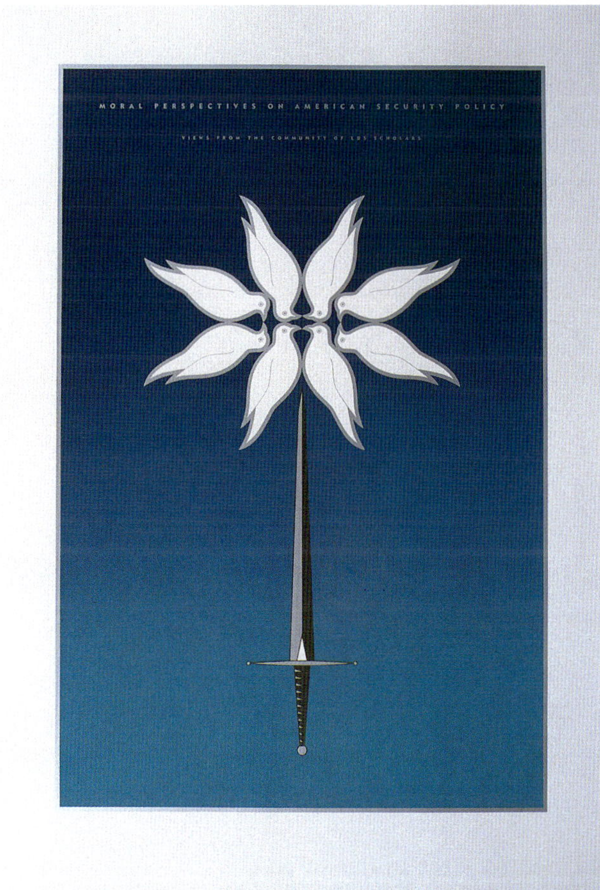

DESIGN FIRM
BYU Graphics

ALL DESIGN
Matt Scherer

CLIENT
Kennedy Center
for International Studies

PURPOSE
Symposium announcement

SIZE
23" x 35" (58.4cm x 88.9cm)

A single bird was drawn by hand and then scanned and traced in Adobe Illustrator. It was then duplicated to achieve the final design. A metallic silver was under-printed under the blue blend and also became the trap lines.

DESIGN FIRM
Joseph Rattan Design

ART DIRECTOR
Joseph Rattan

DESIGNERS
Diana McKnight, Joseph Rattan

ILLUSTRATOR
Diana McKnight

CLIENT
The Dallas Children's Theater

PURPOSE
Concert promotion

SIZE
10" x 35" (25.4cm x 88.9cm)

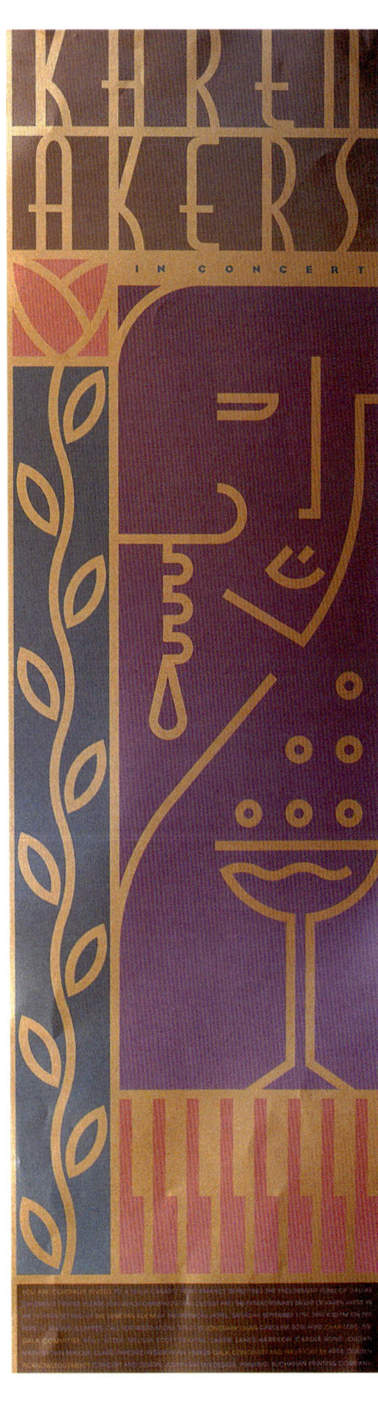

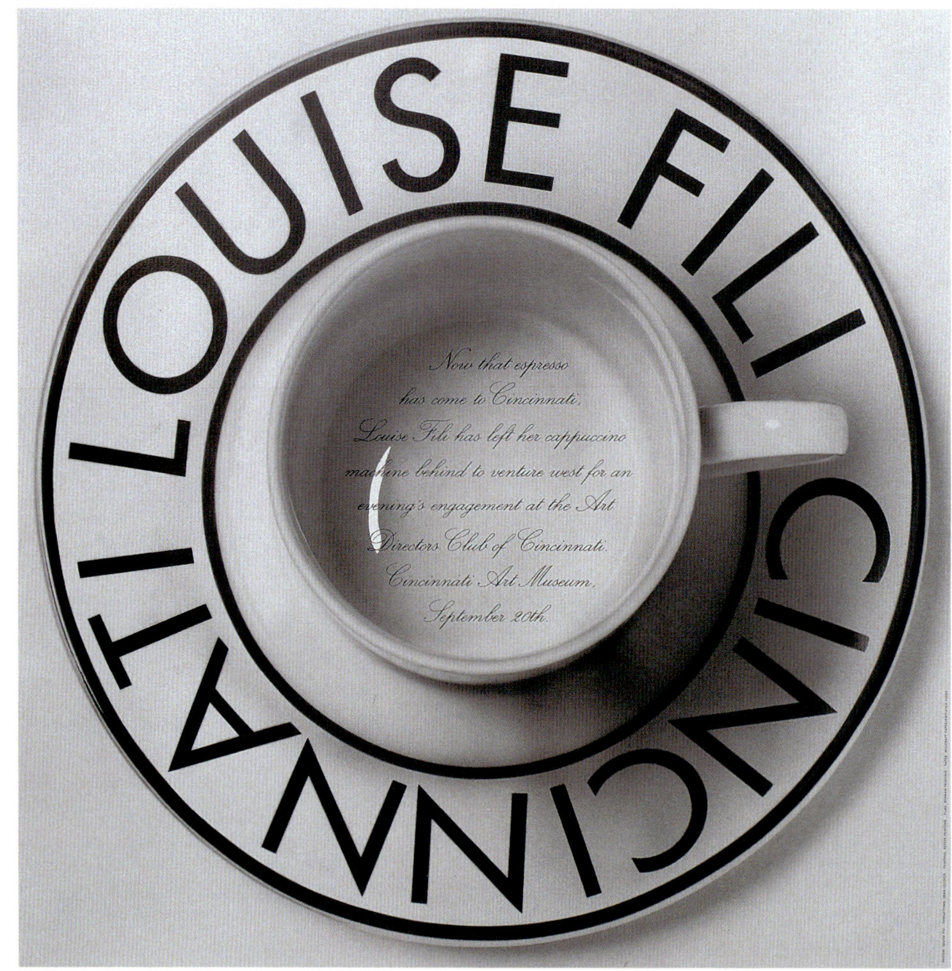

DESIGN FIRM
Louise Fili Ltd.

ART DIRECTOR
Louise Fili

DESIGNER
Louise Fili

RETOUCHER
Ralph Wernli

PHOTOGRAPHER
Ed Spiro

CLIENT
Cincinnati Art Directors Club

PURPOSE
Lecture announcement

SIZE
18.25" x 18.25"
(46.4cm x 46.4cm)

Type was set and hand-applied to the saucer. The cup and saucer were then photographed, printed, and retouched to eliminate cut marks. Type (script) was supplied on disk.

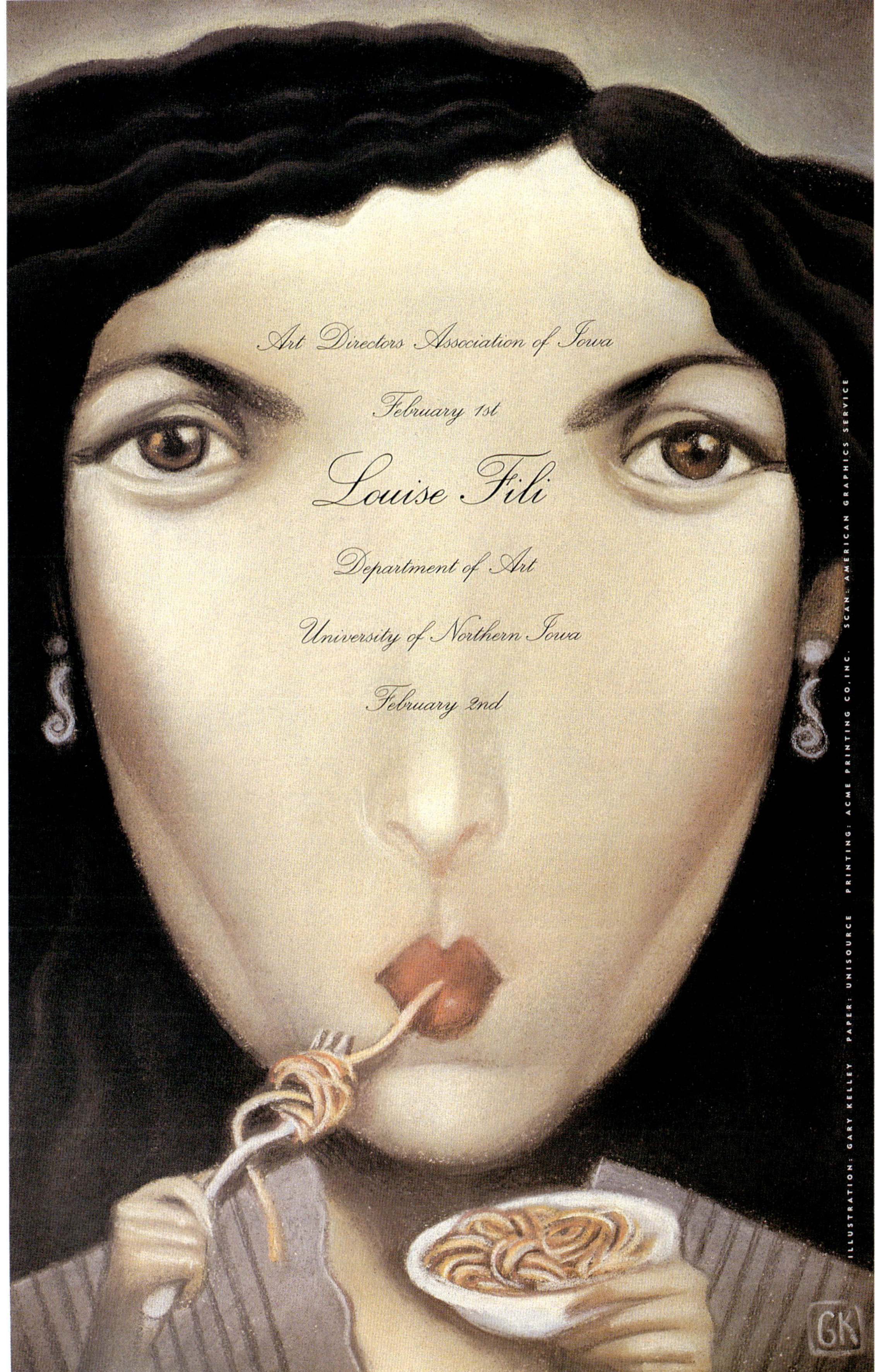

DESIGN FIRM
Louise Fili Ltd.

ART DIRECTOR
Louise Fili

DESIGNER
Louise Fili

ILLUSTRATOR
Gary Kelley

CLIENT
University of Northern Iowa

PURPOSE
Lecture announcement

SIZE
11" x 17"
(27.9cm x 43.2cm)

A pastel illustration was used for this piece along with computer-generated type.

D E S I G N   F I R M
Mires Design, Inc.

A R T   D I R E C T O R
José Serrano

D E S I G N E R
José Serrano

P H O T O G R A P H E R
Carl Vanderschuit

C L I E N T
Deleo Clay Tile Co.

P U R P O S E
Promotion

S I Z E
12" x 16"
(30.5cm x 40.6cm)

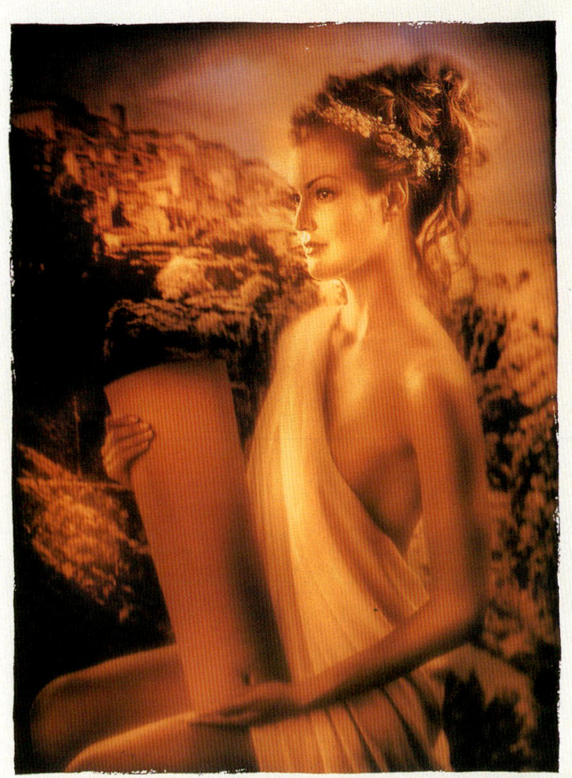

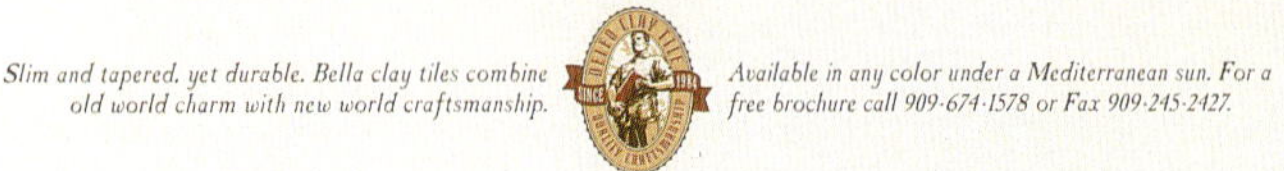

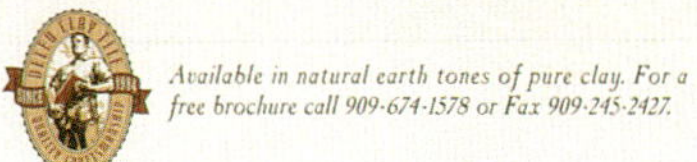

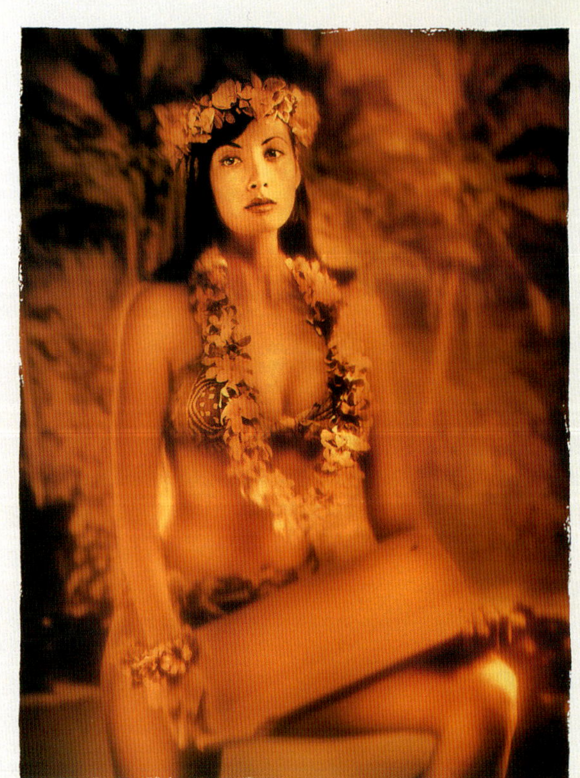

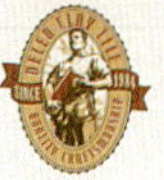

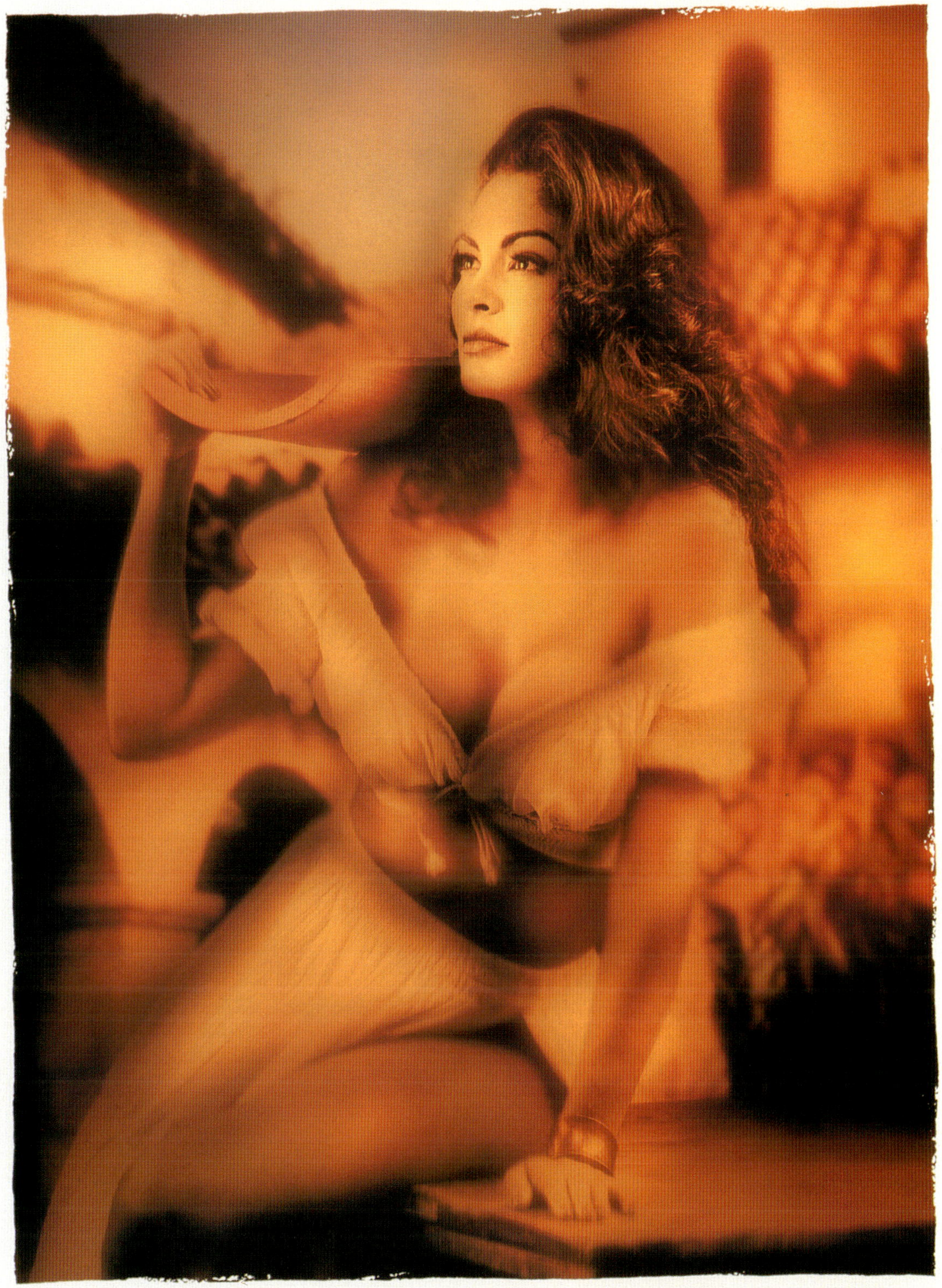

MISSION BELLE

Two-Piece Mission Roofing Tiles from Deleo Clay Tile

These natural clay tiles are as stylish today as when they first graced the historic missions of early California.

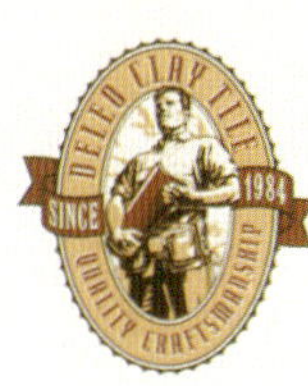

Available in any color including, of course, traditional reds. For a free brochure call 909·674·1578 or Fax 909·245·2427.

DESIGN FIRM
Paul Kaza Associates

ALL DESIGN
Todd Logan

PHOTOGRAPHER
Alan Jakubek

CLIENT
Queen City Printers

PURPOSE
Printer promotional calendar

SIZE
19" x 27"
(48.2cm x 68.5cm)

Designed on Macintosh IIci using QuarkXPress 3.3 and Adobe Illustrator 5.5. The hand-illustration was scanned in and placed.

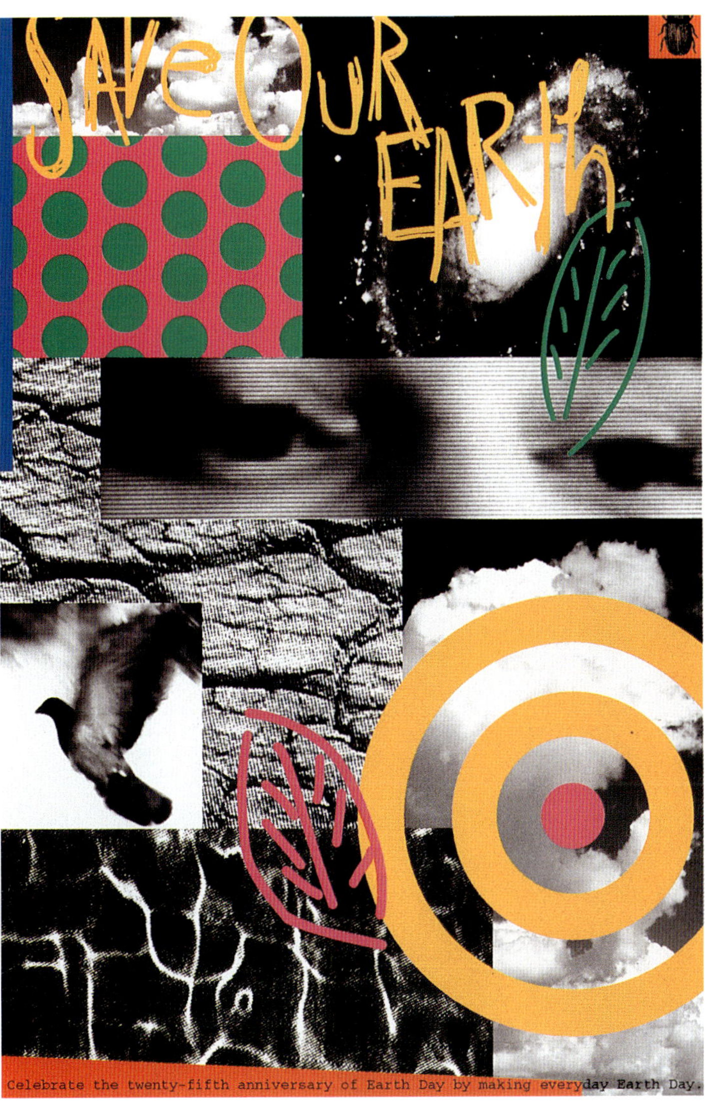

DESIGN FIRM
Morla Design

ART DIRECTOR
Jennifer Morla

DESIGNER
Jennifer Morla, Petra Geiger

ILLUSTRATOR
Jennifer Morla

PHOTOGRAPHER
Holly Stewart

CLIENT
The Pushpin Group

PURPOSE
25th Anniversary of Earth Day promotion

SIZE
60 x 90 cm (152.4cm x 228.6cm)

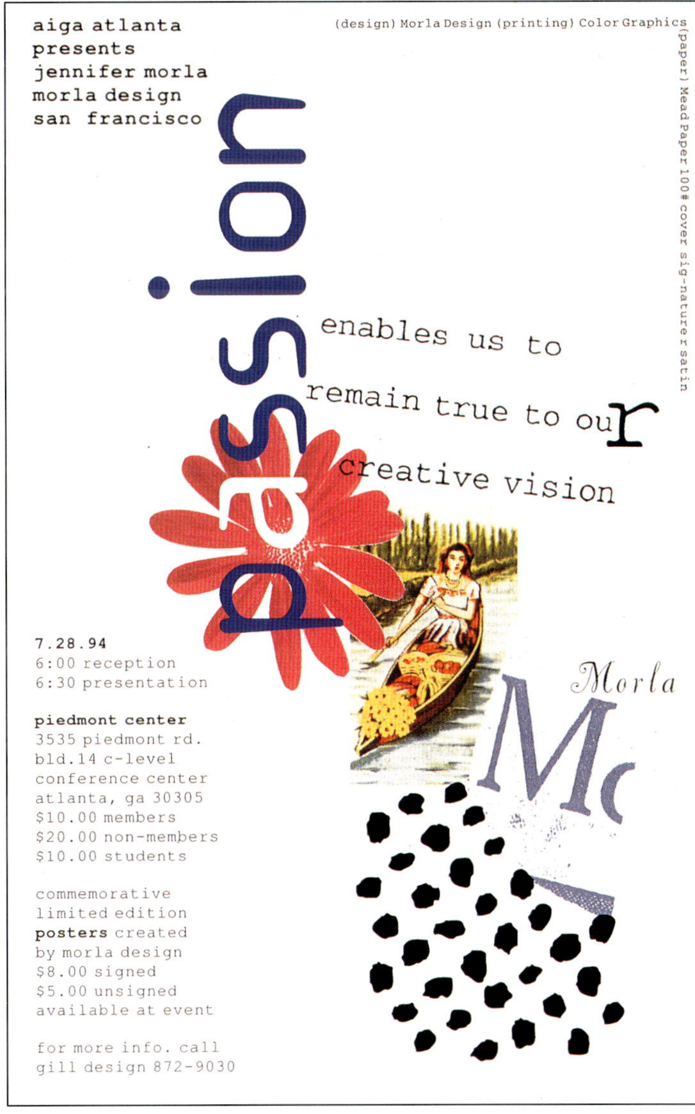

DESIGN FIRM
Morla Design

ART DIRECTOR
Jennifer Morla

DESIGNERS
Jennifer Morla, Petra Geiger

PHOTOGRAPHER
Holly Stewart (Daisy)

CLIENT
Aiga/Atlanta

PURPOSE
Lecture announcement

SIZE
20" x 36" (50.8cm x 91.4cm)

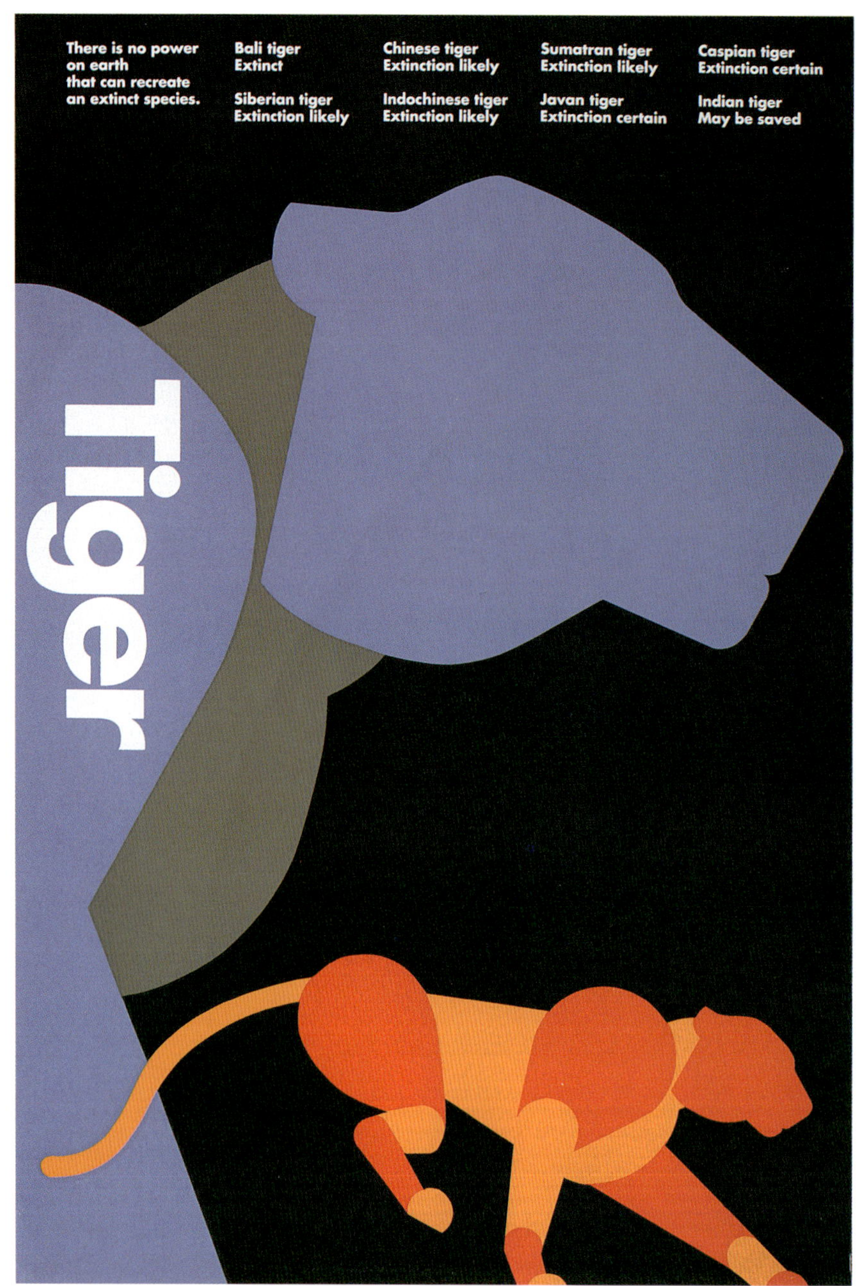

DESIGN FIRM
Ramona Hutko Design

ALL DESIGN
Ramona Hutko

CLIENT
Ramona Hutko Design

PURPOSE
Promotional gift

SIZE
20" x 30"
(50.8cm x 76.2cm)

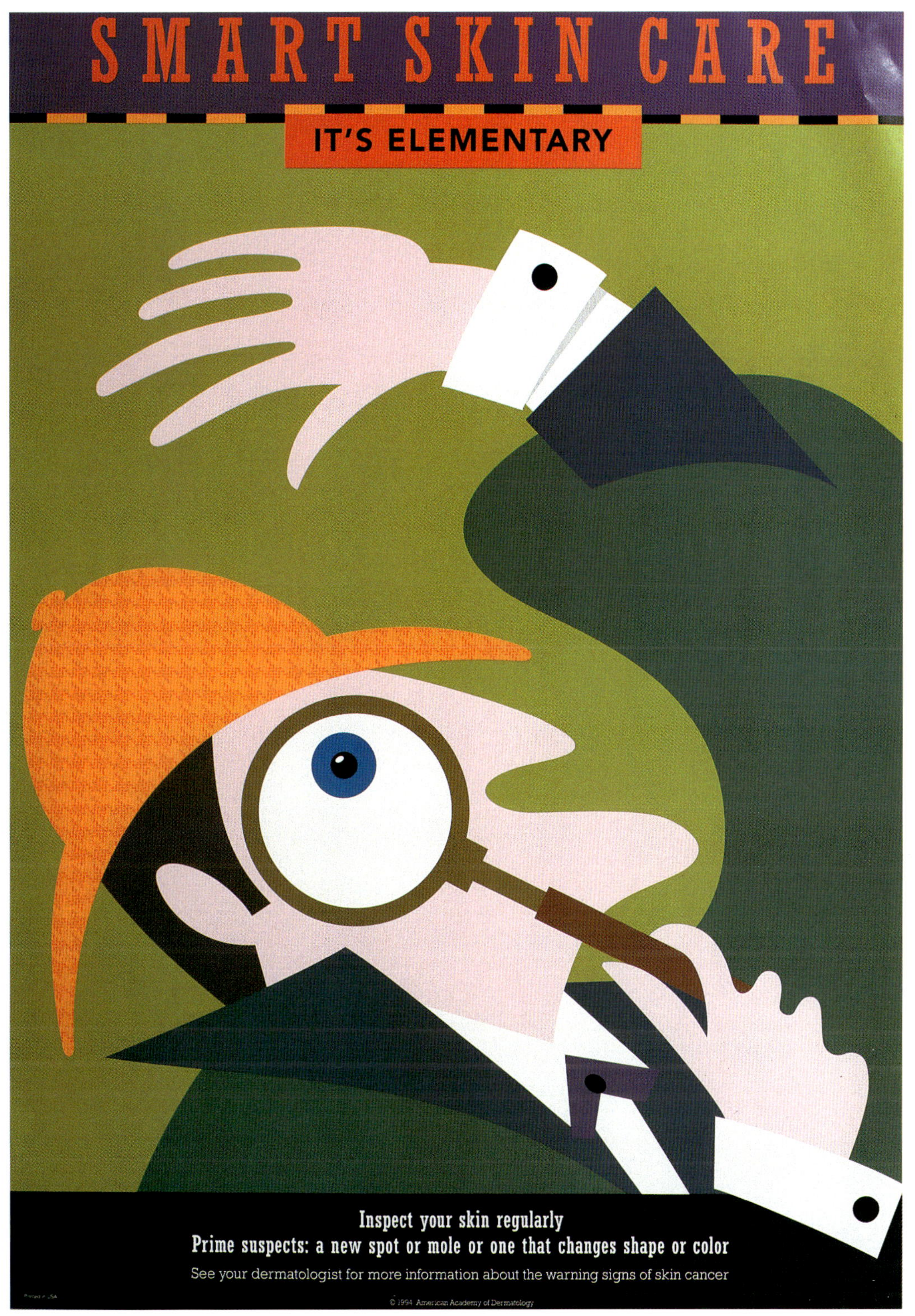

DESIGN FIRM
Hafeman Design Group

ALL DESIGN
Bill Hafeman

CLIENT
American Academy of Dermatology

PURPOSE
Awareness poster

SIZE
19" x 24"
(48.2cm x 61cm)

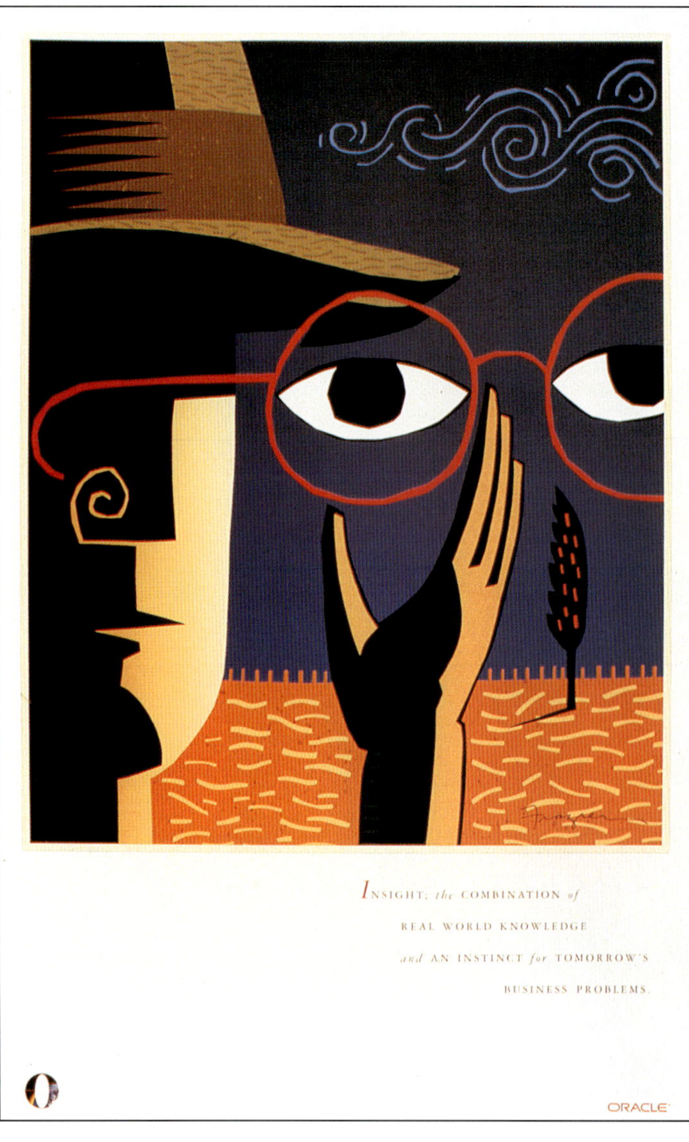

DESIGN FIRM
Frazier Design

ALL DESIGN
Craig Frazier

CLIENT
Oracle Corporation

PURPOSE
Promotion

SIZE
24" x 32"
(61cm x 81.3cm)

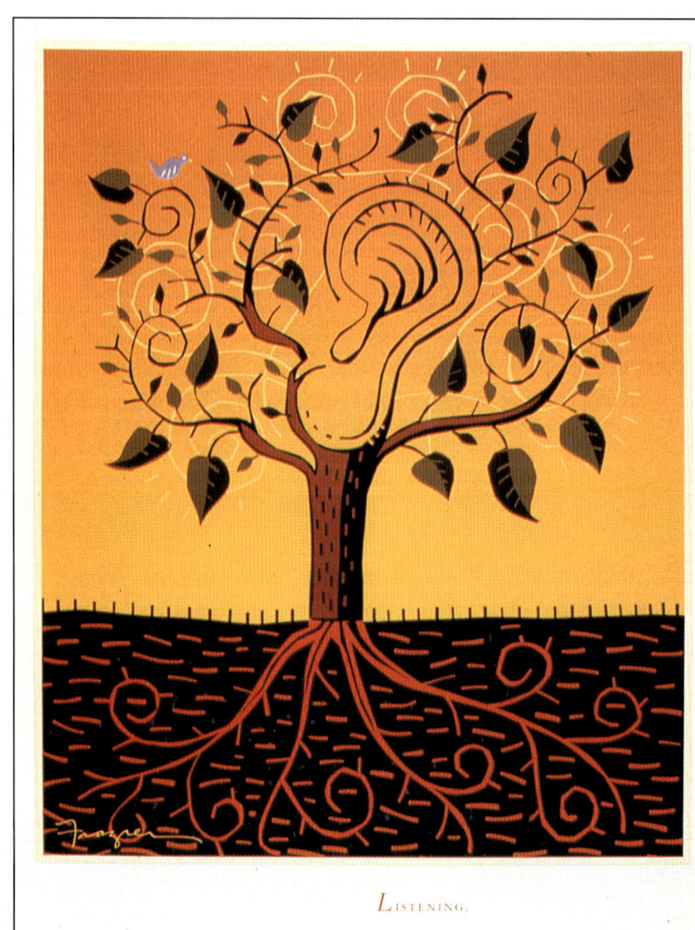

DESIGN FIRM
Frazier Design

ALL DESIGN
Craig Frazier

CLIENT
Oracle Corporation

PURPOSE
Promotion

SIZE
24" x 32"
(61cm x 81.3cm)

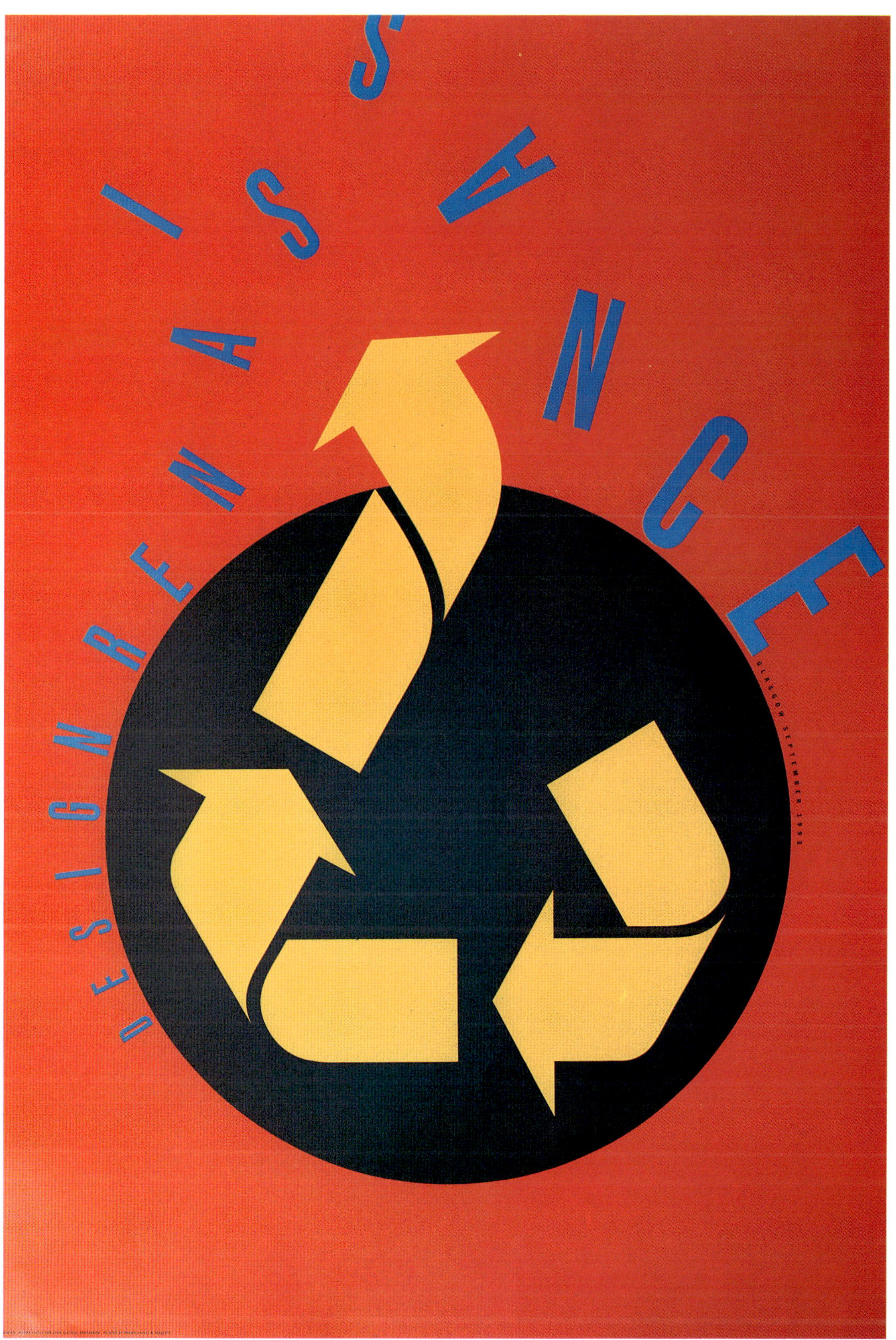

DESIGN FIRM
Pentagram Design

ART DIRECTOR
Woody Pirtle

DESIGNERS
**Woody Pirtle,
John Klotnia**

CLIENT
Ico Grada

PURPOSE
International Design Renaissance Congress promotion

SIZE
**23" x 33"
(58.4cm x 83.8cm)**

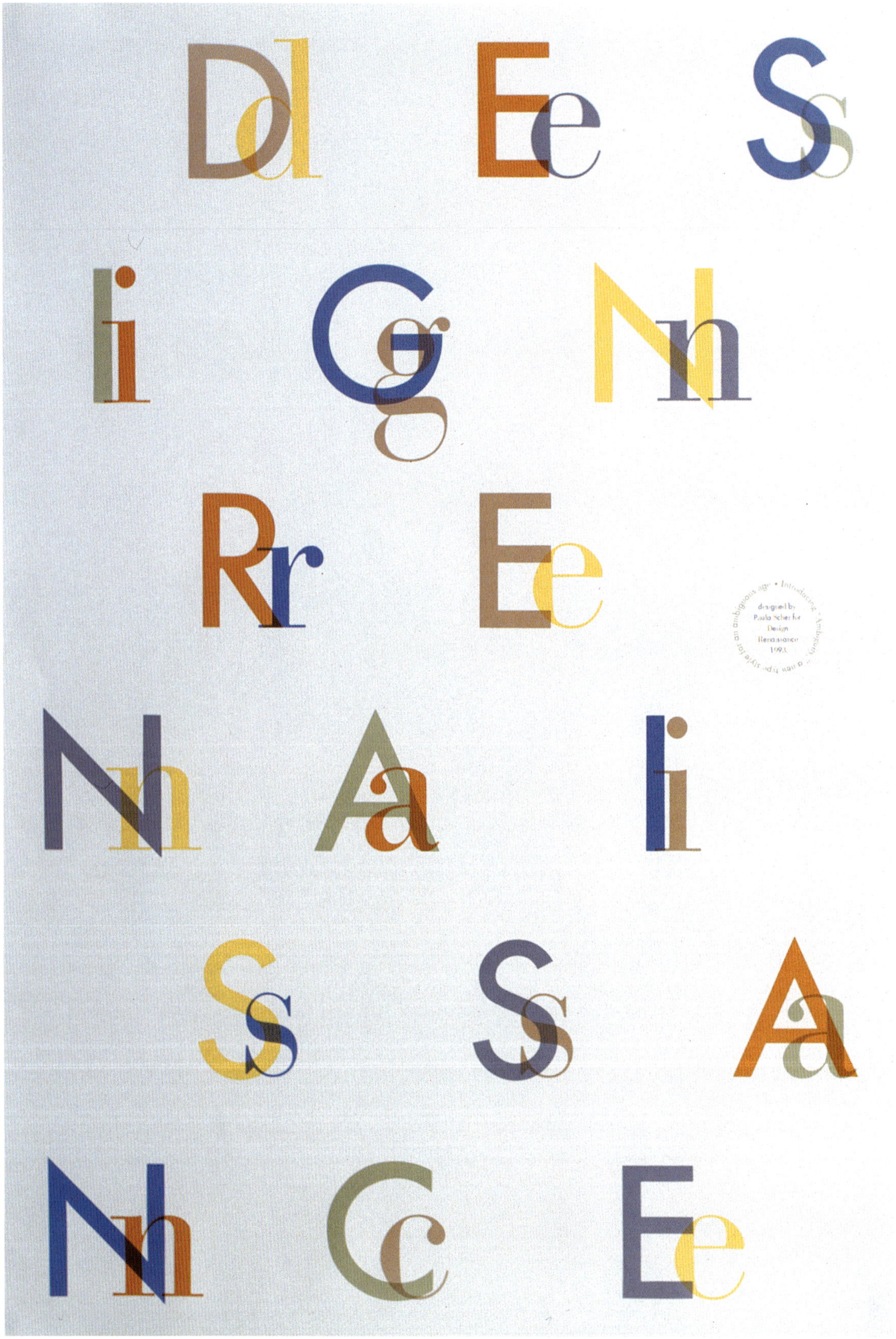

DESIGN FIRM
Pentagram Design

ART DIRECTOR
Paula Scher

DESIGNER
Paula Scher

CLIENT
Ico Grada

PURPOSE
International Design Renaissance Congress promotion

SIZE
23" x 33"
(58.4cm x 83.8cm)

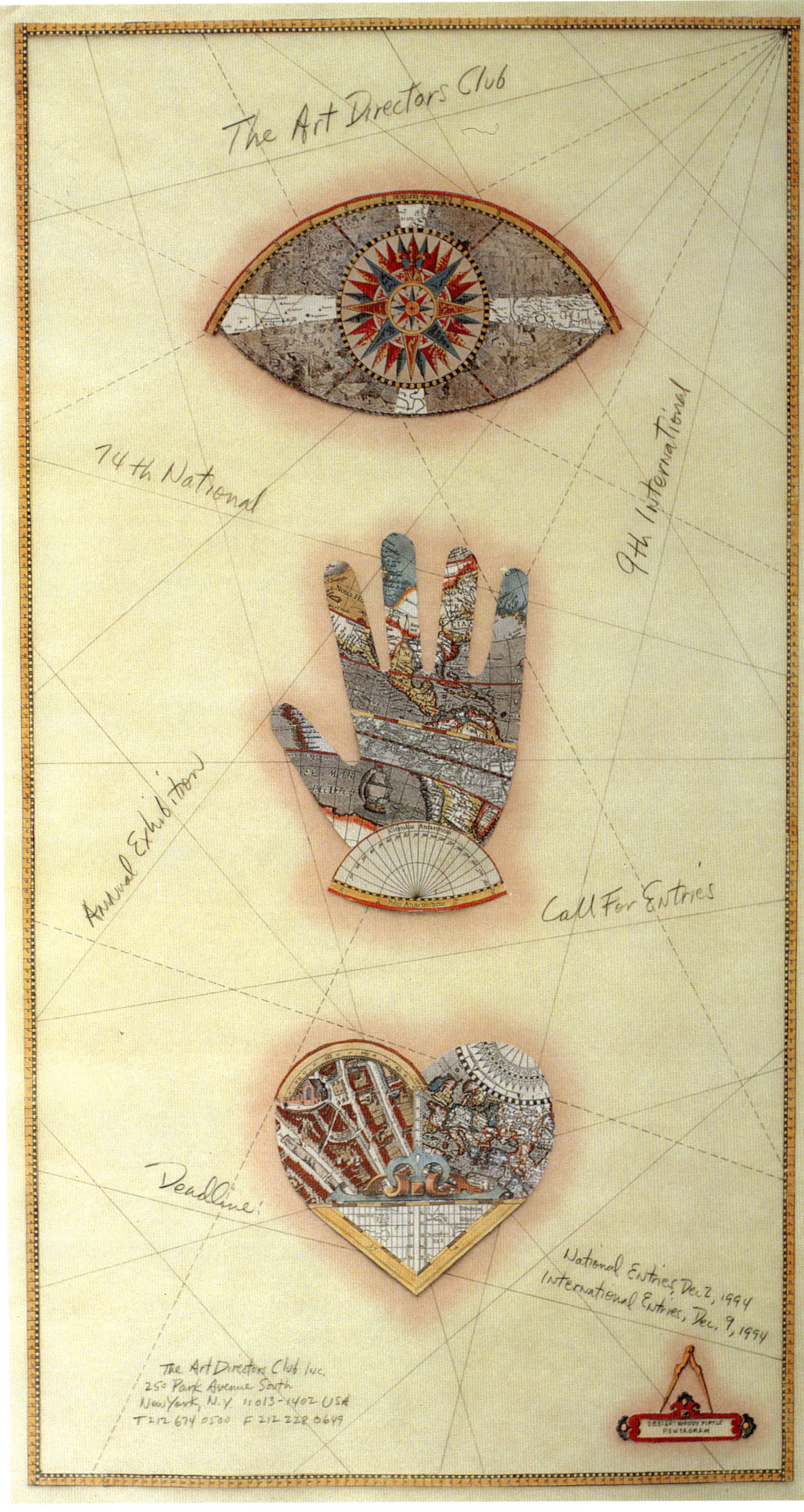

DESIGN FIRM
Pentagram Design

ALL DESIGN
Woody Pirtle

CLIENT
Art Directors Club, NYC

PURPOSE
Call for entries

SIZE
20" x 36"
(50.8cm x 91.4cm)

DESIGN FIRM
Pentagram Design

ALL DESIGN
Woody Pirtle

CLIENT
Art Directors Club of Cincinnati

PURPOSE
Lecture promotion

SIZE
24" x 36" (61cm x 91.4cm)

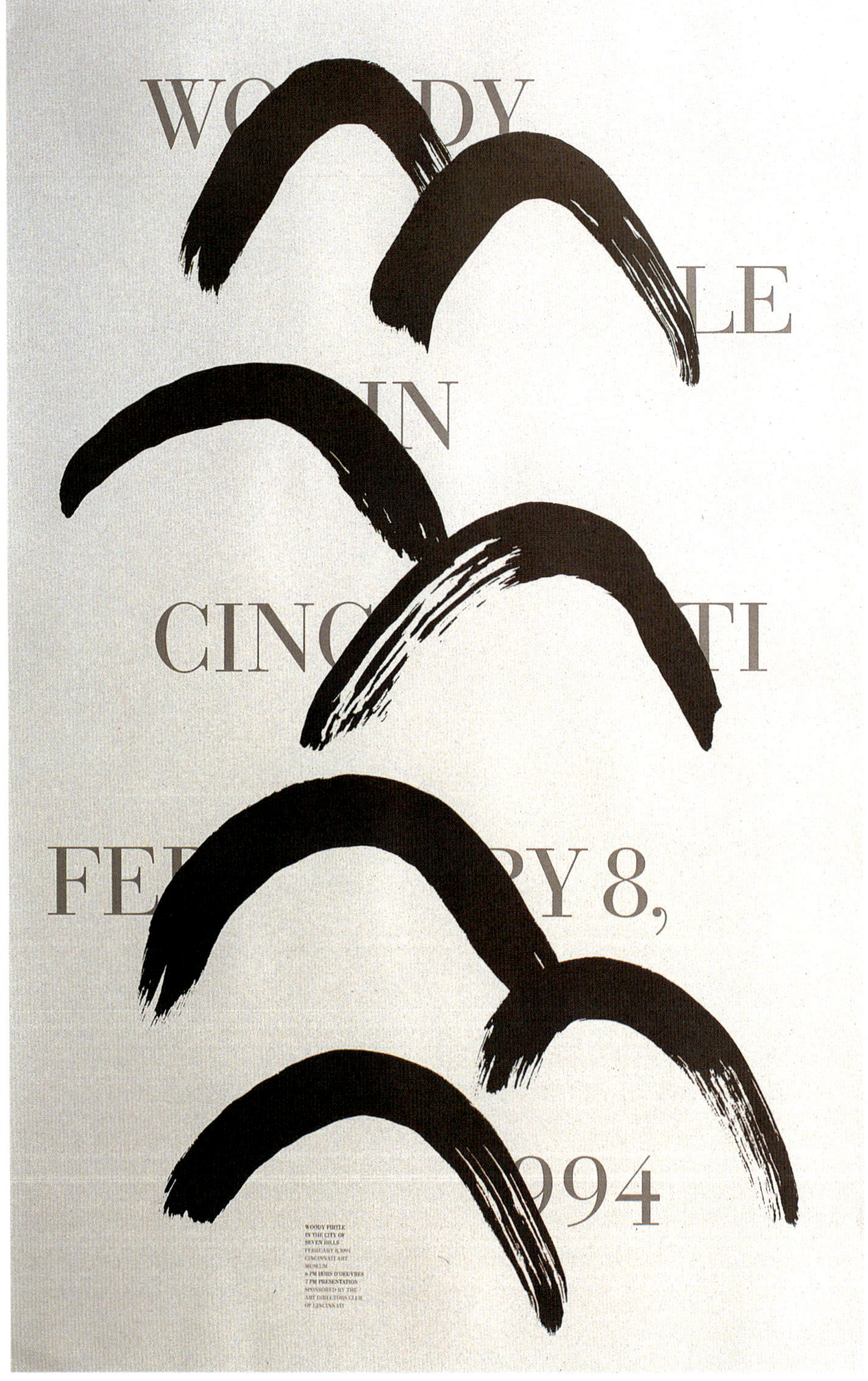

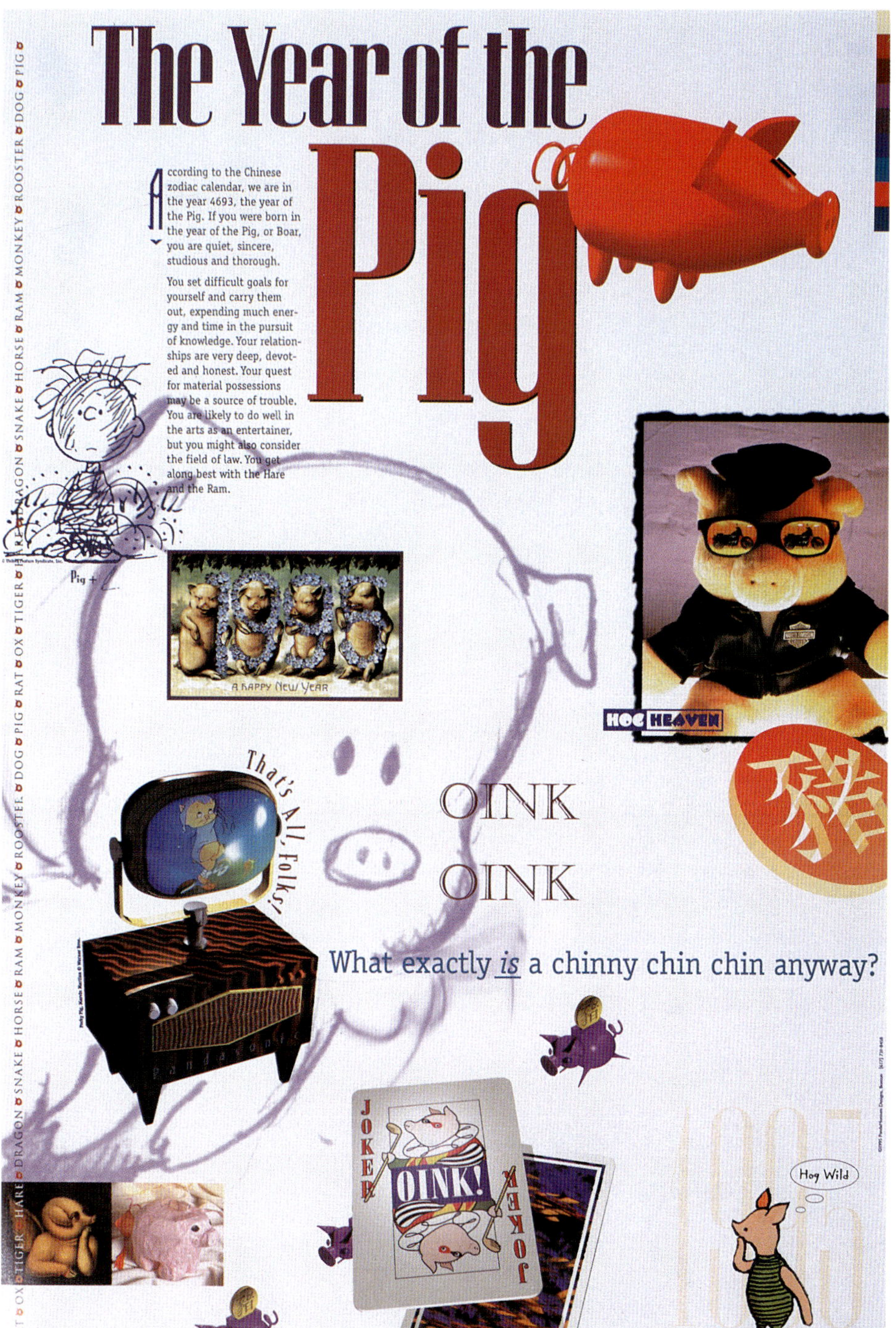

DESIGN FIRM
PandaMonium Designs

ART DIRECTOR
Raymond Yu

DESIGNERS
Raymond Yu, Steven Lee

ILLUSTRATORS
Raymond Yu, Steven Lee, Sue-Ann Tsan

PHOTOGRAPHER
Steven Lee

CLIENT
PandaMonium Designs

PURPOSE
Self-promotion

SIZE
12" x 18.75" (30.5cm x 47.6cm)

The entire poster, with all of its artwork, was created via Adobe Photoshop, Ray Dream Designer, Aldus FreeHand, Adobe Illustrator, and a Photo-CD, and was assembled in QuarkXPress. The electronic document was rasterized and imaged directly by lasers onto the rollers of the Heidelberg GTO-DI. This direct-to-press process accommodates a short-run 4-color process and eliminates film work.

DESIGN FIRM
Design Ahead

ALL DESIGN
Vocker Feddeck

CLIENT
Design Ahead

PURPOSE
Self-promotion

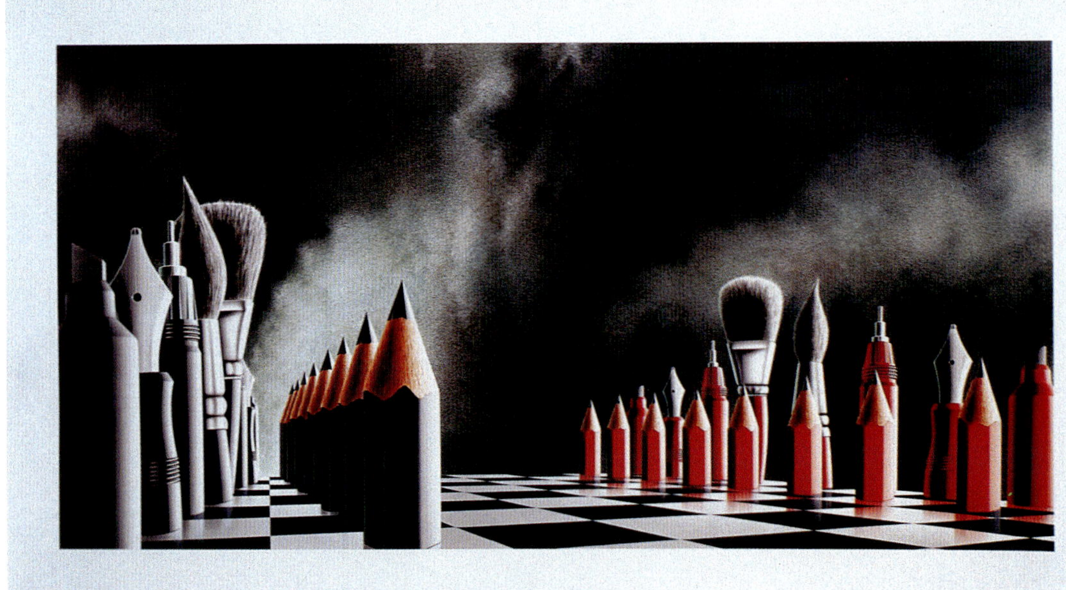

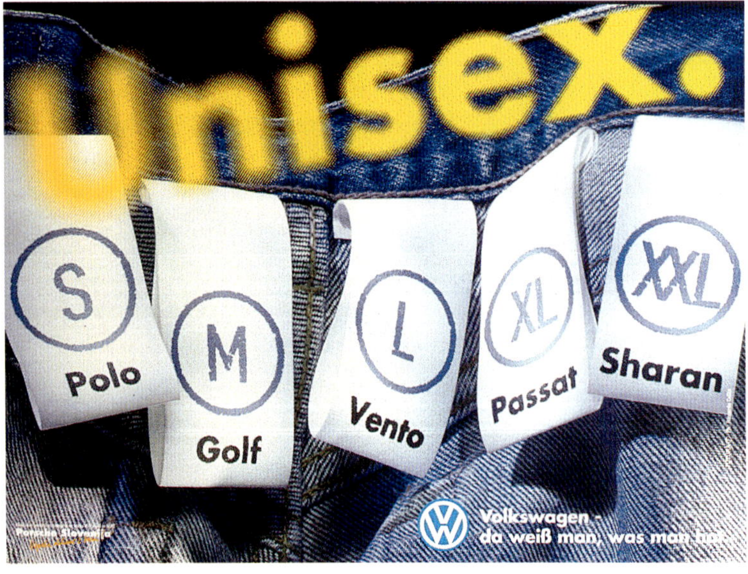

DESIGN FIRM
Futura

ART DIRECTOR
Vital Verlic

DESIGNER
Vital Verlic

PHOTOGRAPHER
Riccardo Callin

CLIENT
Porsche
Slovenia - Volkswagen

PURPOSE
Billboard campaign

SIZE
157.5" x 118"
(400cm x 300cm)

DESIGN FIRM
Mike Salisbury
Communications, Inc.

ALL DESIGN
Mike Salisbury

CLIENT
Tavarua Island
Surf Company

PURPOSE
Travel promotion

SIZE
20" x 30"
(50.8cm x 76.2cm)

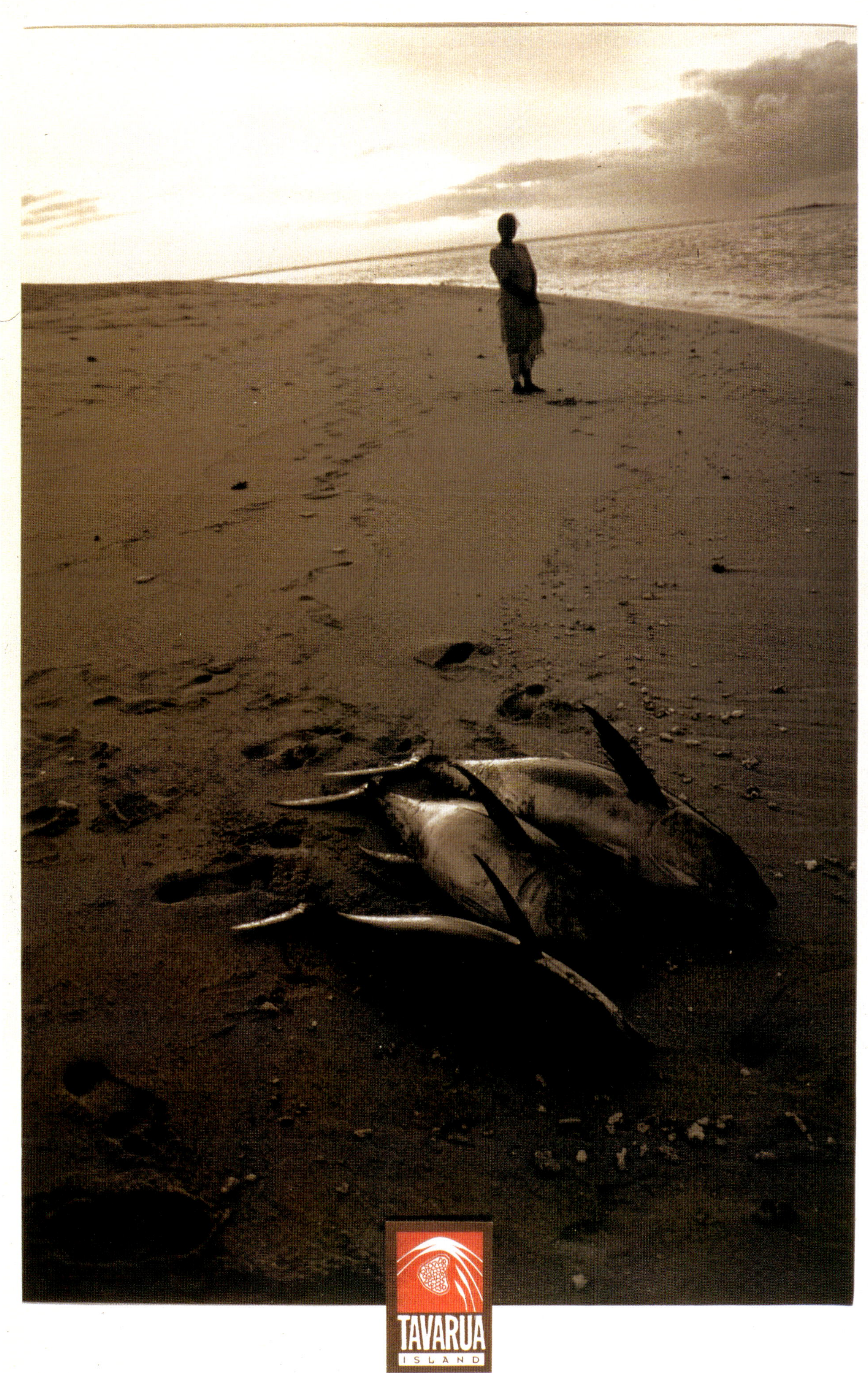
TAVARUA
ISLAND

DESIGN FIRM
Matsumoto Incorporated

ALL DESIGN
Takaaki Matsumoto

CLIENT
David A. Hanks & Associates/ Montreal Museum of Decorative Arts

PURPOSE
Exhibition announcement

Image was printed using four match colors.

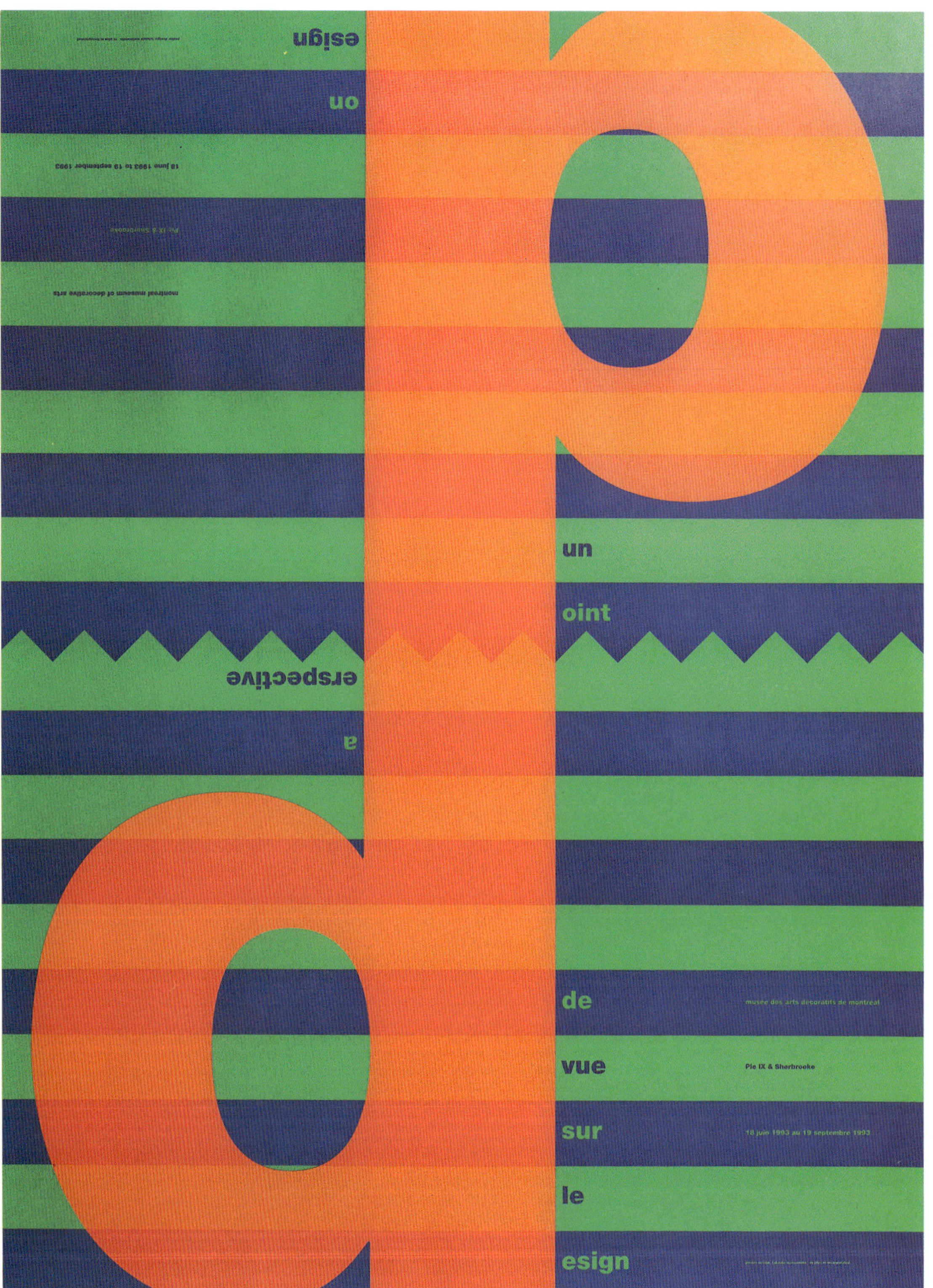

DESIGN FIRM
Kan Tai-keung Design & Associates Ltd.

ART DIRECTOR
Eddy Yu Chi Kong

DESIGNER
Eddy Yu Chi Kong

CLIENT
Kan Tai-keung Design & Associates Ltd.

PURPOSE
Self-promotion

[facing page]
The design is based on the Chinese names of the fifteen participants of the exhibition. By organizing them into a star shape, which represents China, it immediately brings out the message of the exhibition.

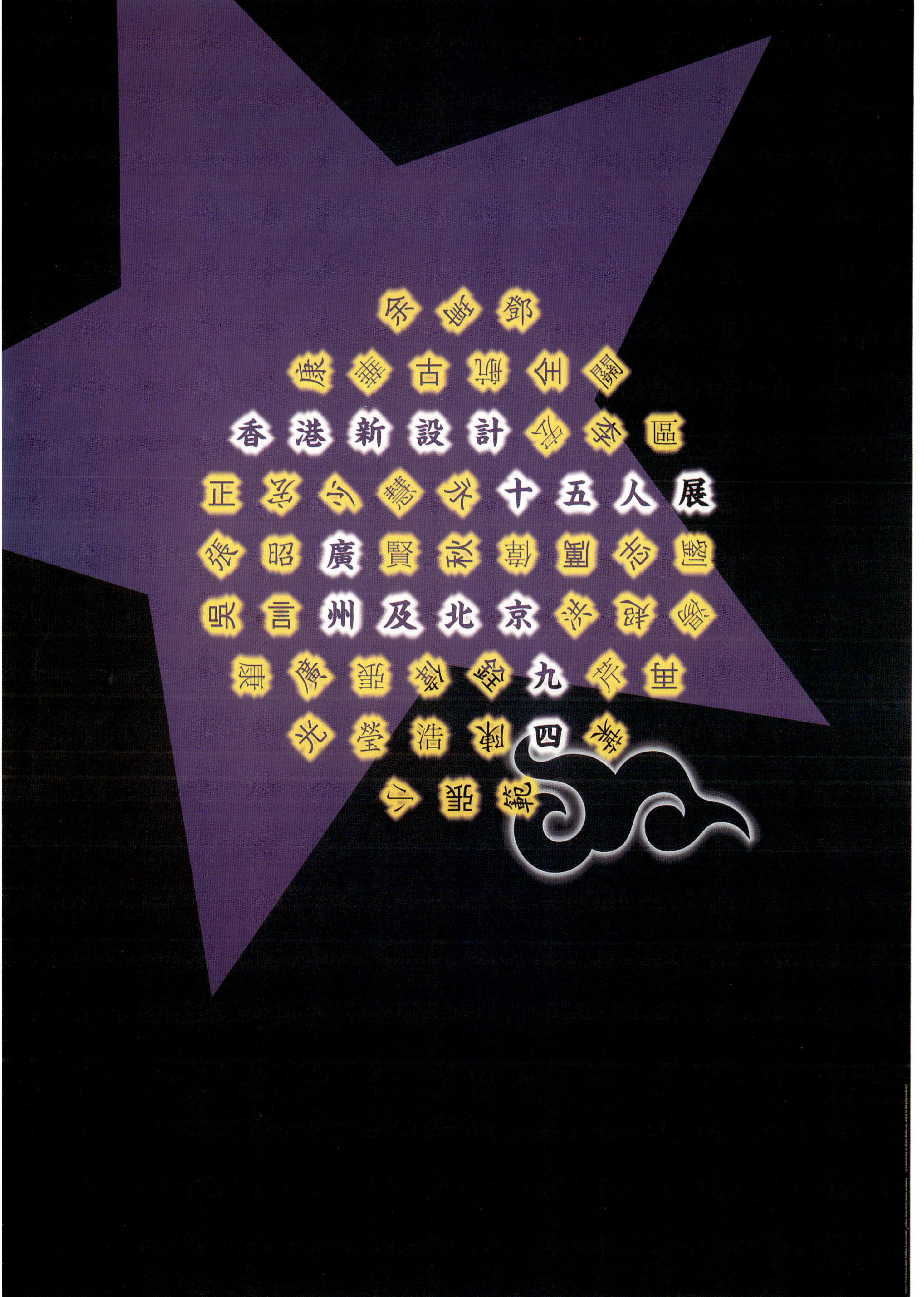
香港新設計
十五人展
廣州及北京
九四

Conserve Nature

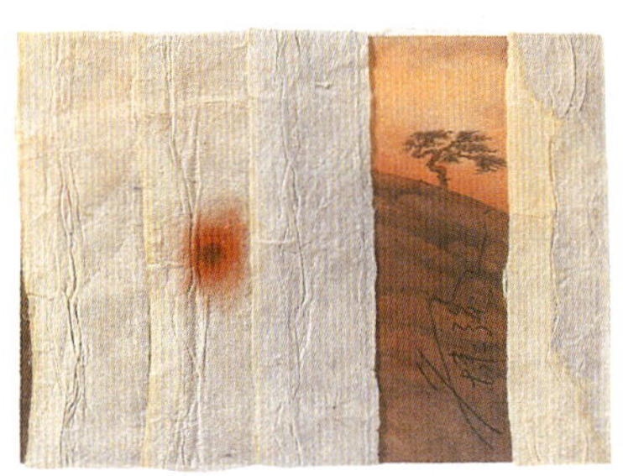

DESIGN AND ILLUSTRATION BY KAN TAI-KEUNG

愛

PRINTING BY YU LUEN OFFSET ON GRAPHIKA VELLUM COOL PCW WHITE 176GSM

護

PAPER SPONSORSHIP BY QUALITY PAPER SPECIALIST LIMITED.

自

JAMES RIVER FINE PAPERS LIMITED & THE OKAMOTO COMPANY LIMITED

然

DESIGN FIRM
Kan Tai-keung Design
& Associates Ltd.

ART DIRECTOR
Kan Tai-keung

DESIGNERS
Kan Tai-keung,
Benjamin Wong Wai Bun

ILLUSTRATOR
Kan Tai-keung

PHOTOGRAPHER
C K Wong

CLIENT
Kan Tai-keung Design
& Associates Ltd.

PURPOSE
Nature conservation promotion

SIZE
24" x 36"
(61cm x 91.4cm)

This poster series was created by adding various black color images. Even though they differ, the posters all aim to protest against the harm that man has done to nature.

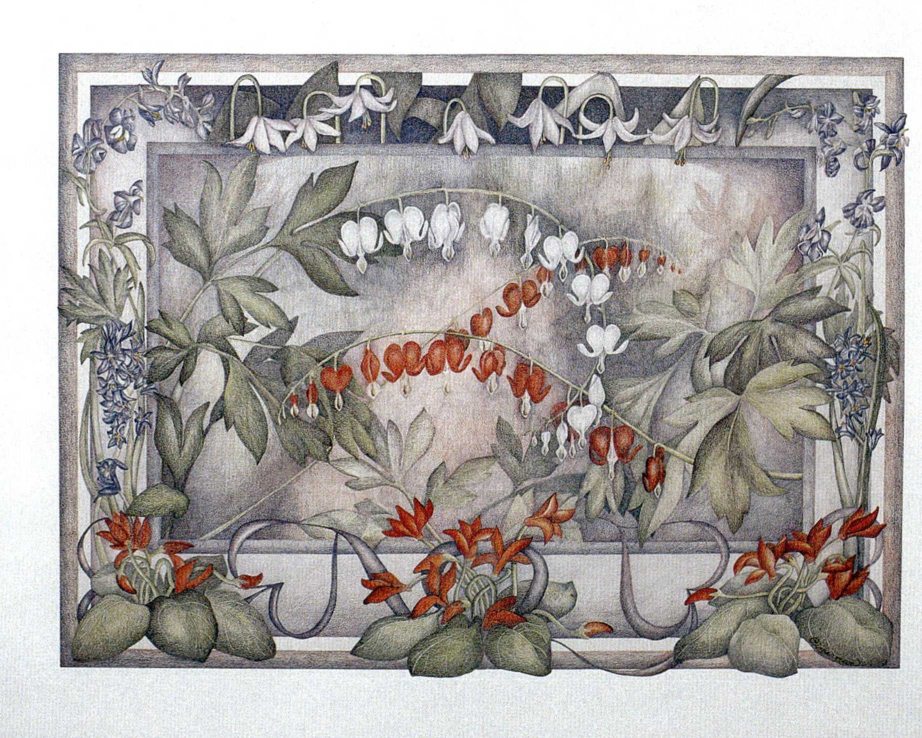

DESIGNER
Jan Rimerman

ILLUSTRATOR
Jan Rimerman

PHOTOGRAPHER
Color Services, Portland, OR.

CLIENT
Hazelbrook Middle School

PURPOSE
Art department fund-raiser

SIZE
32" x 28" (81.2cm x 71.1cm)

The original design was done in colored pencil and was designed from live models. The sale of the poster helped to support the art department when state and federal funding of elective classes was halted.

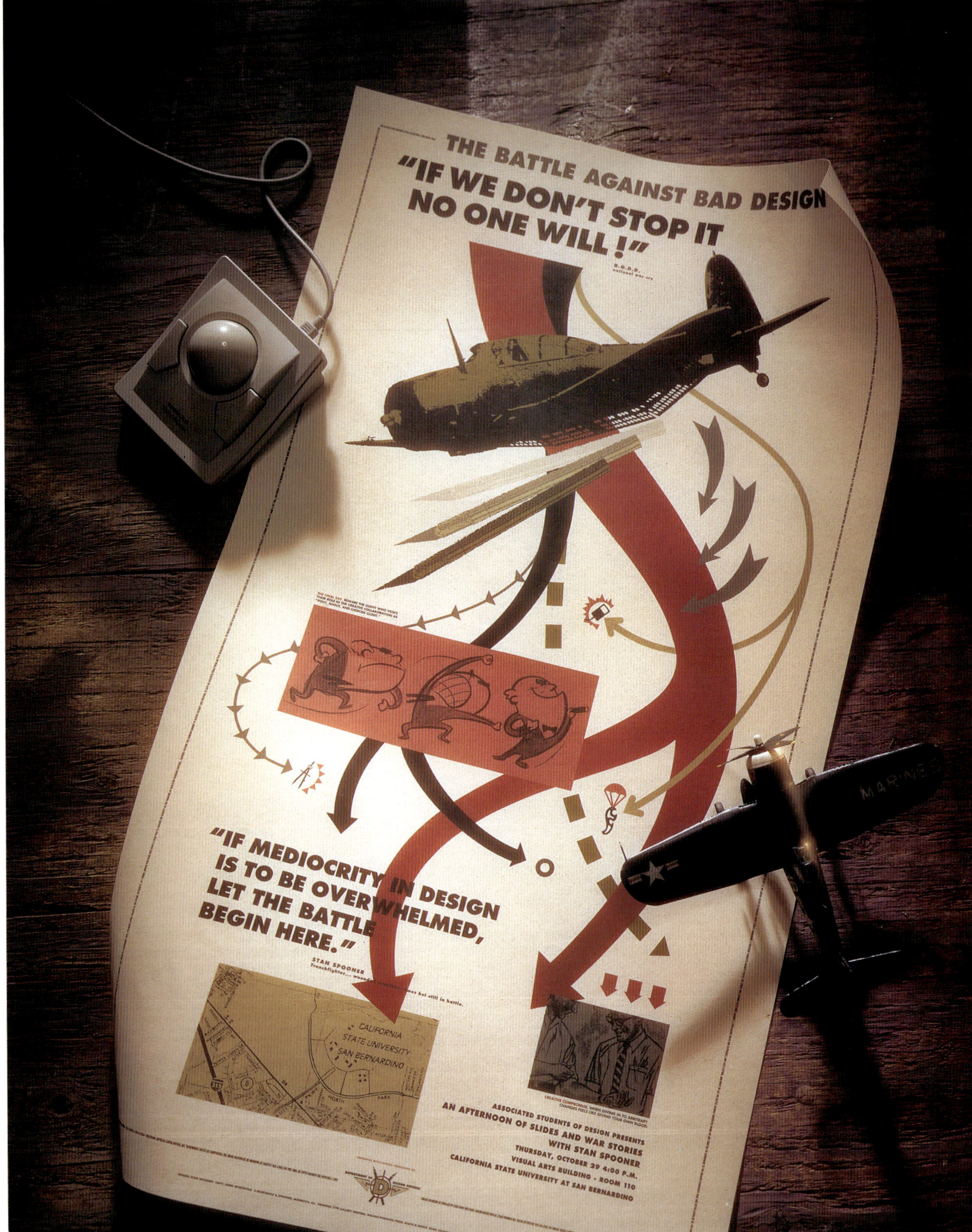

DESIGN FIRM
McMonigle & Spooner

ART DIRECTOR
Stan Spooner

COPYWRITER
Jamie McMonigle

CLIENT
California State University

PURPOSE
Speaking engagement promotion

SIZE
20" x 34" (50.8cm x 86.4cm)

Adobe Illustrator, Adobe Streamline, and Aldus PageMaker were used for this image.

DESIGN FIRM
Kan Tai-keung Design & Associates Ltd.

ART DIRECTOR
Kan Tai-keung

DESIGNERS
Kan Tai-keung, Veronica Cheung Lai Sheung

PHOTOGRAPHER
C K Wong

CLIENT
Kan Tai-keung Design & Associates Ltd.

PURPOSE
Self-promotion

[facing page] One from a set of four posters specially designed for an invitational show using Chinese calligraphy and traditional stationery to show the artistic and sentimental side of Chinese characters.

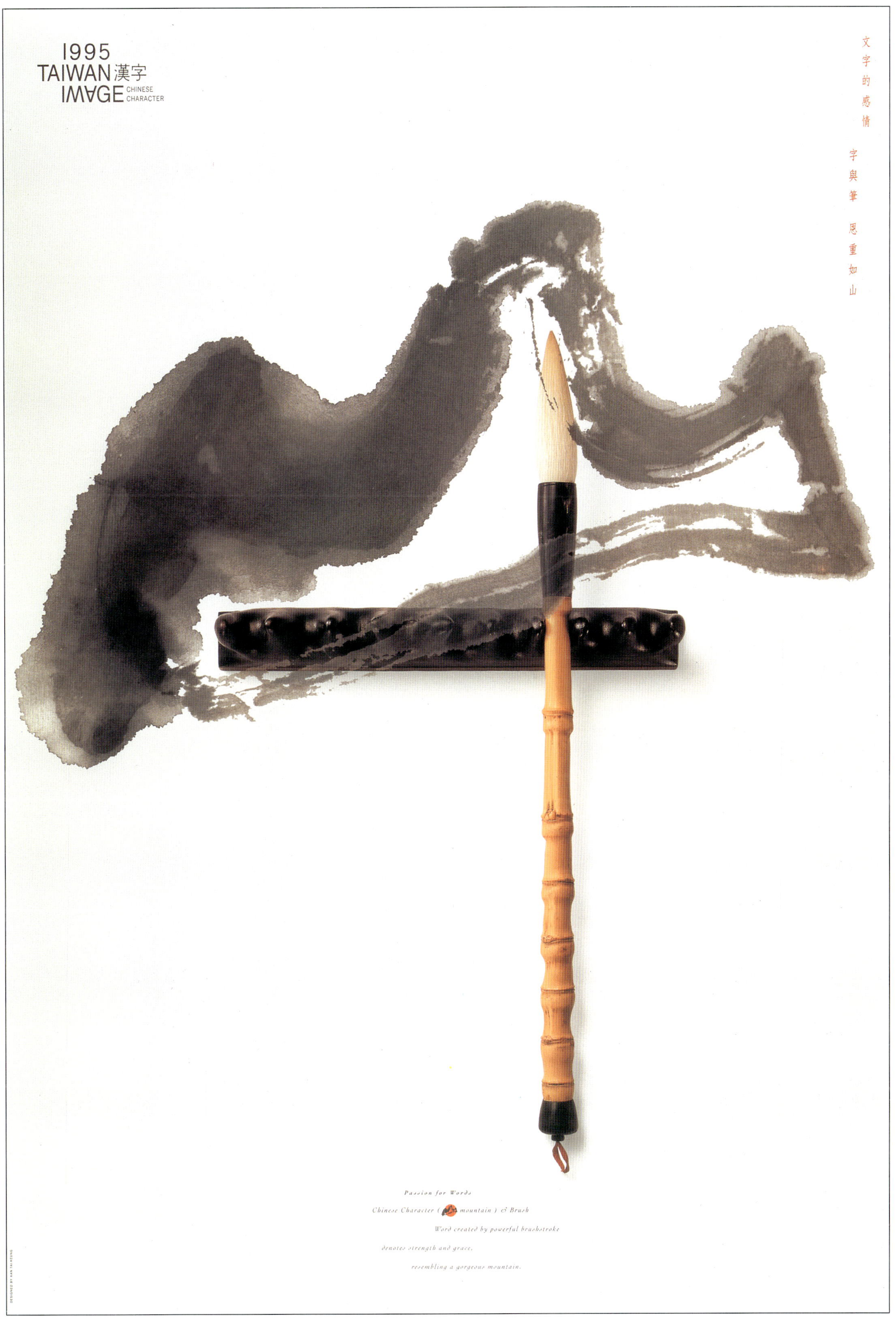
1995
TAIWAN 漢字
IMAGE CHINESE CHARACTER
文字的感情
字與筆 恩重如山
Passion for Words
Chinese Character (mountain) & Brush
Word created by powerful brushstroke
denotes strength and grace,
resembling a gorgeous mountain.

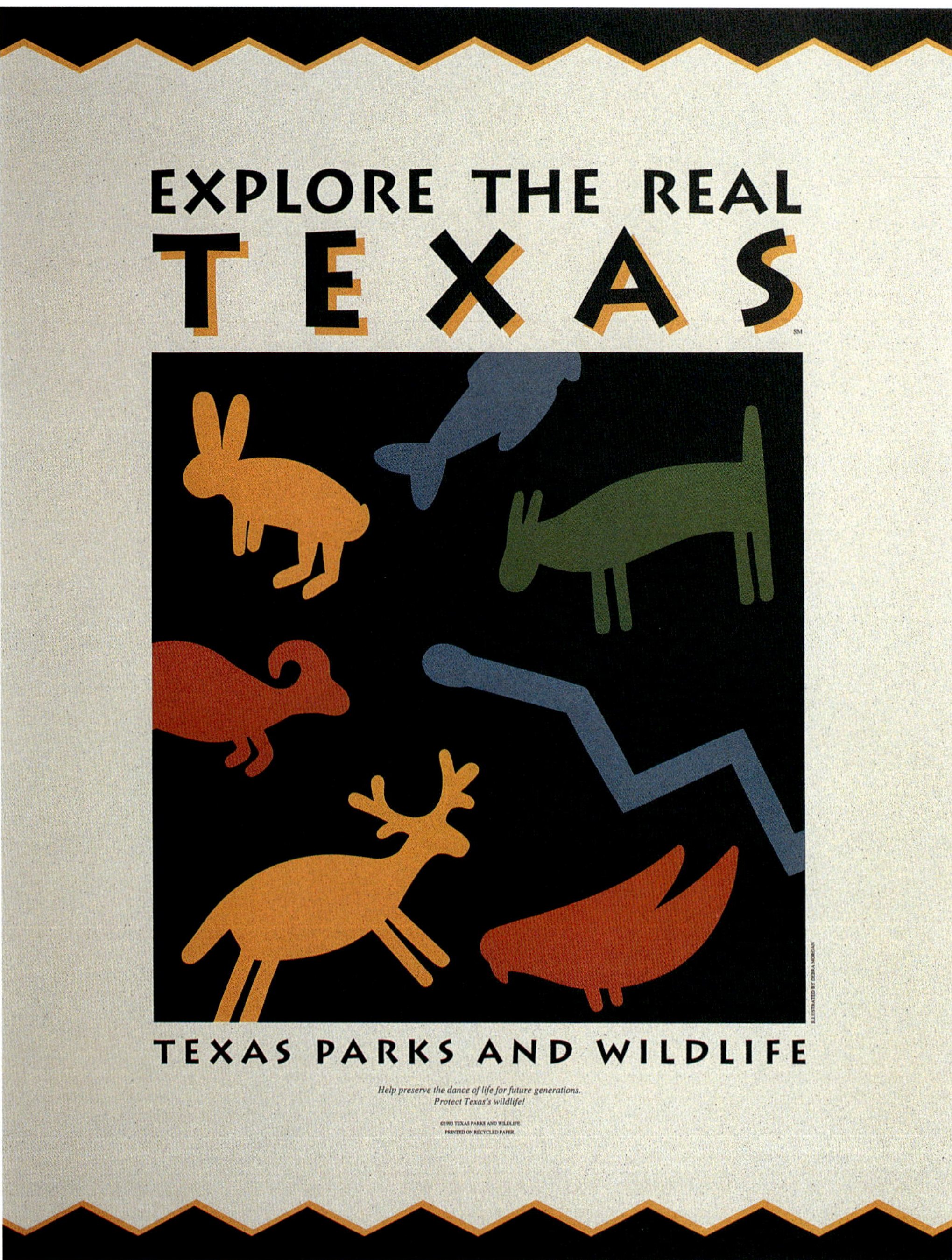

DESIGN FIRM
Texas Parks and Wildlife Department

ART DIRECTOR
Linda Adkins

DESIGNER
Debra Morgan

ILLUSTRATOR
Debra Morgan

CLIENT
Texas Parks and Wildlife Catalogue

PURPOSE
Species protection and bio-diversity preservation

SIZE
17" x 22" (43.2cm x 55.9cm)

Design used line art with PMS colors, along with type set on Aldus PageMaker.

DESIGN FIRM
Planet Design Co.

ART DIRECTORS
Dana Lytle, Kevin Wade

DESIGNER
Dana Lytle

ILLUSTRATOR
Dana Lytle

PHOTOGRAPHERS
Jodi Hougard, Jayme Schlepp

CLIENT
Montana State University School of Art

PURPOSE
MSU Art Department promotion

SIZE
26" x 36" (66cm x 91.4cm)

[facing page]
This design came together with the use of a Macintosh Quadra 700, Aldus FreeHand, and Adobe Photoshop.

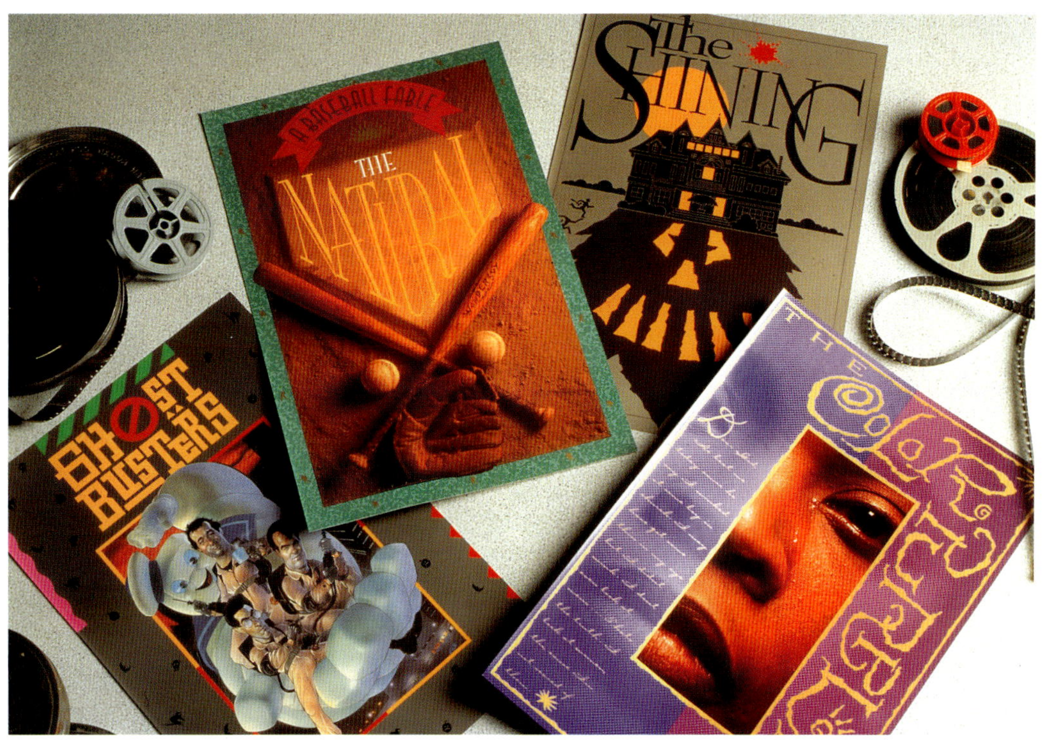

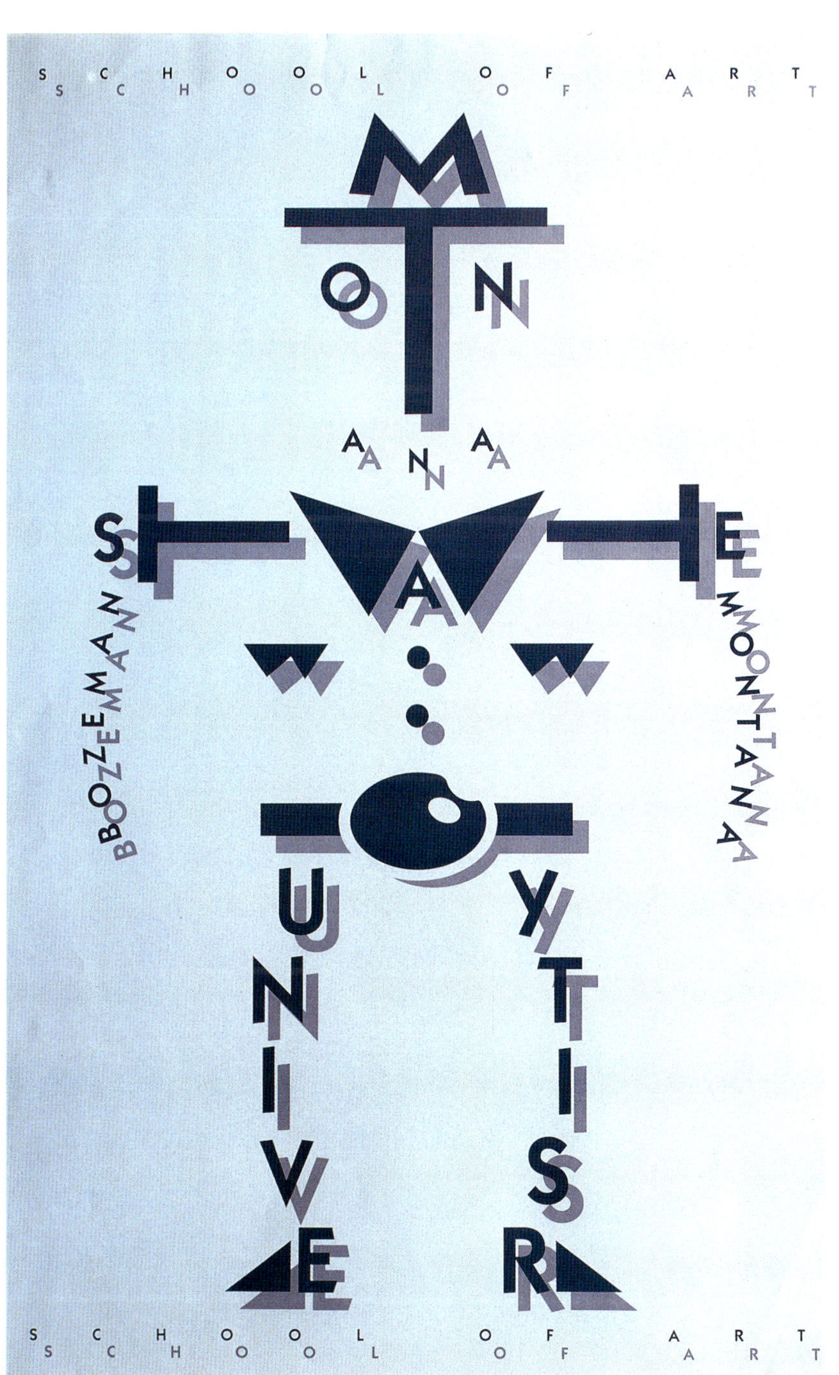

DESIGN FIRM
Rickabaugh Graphics

ART DIRECTOR
Eric Rickabaugh

DESIGNER
Eric Rickabaugh

ILLUSTRATORS
Eric Rickabaugh,
Michael Smith, Fred Warter

PHOTOGRAPHER
Paul Popus

CLIENT
Byrum Litho Graphics

PURPOSE
Printing promotion

SIZE
12" x 18" (30.5cm x 45.7cm)

This movie poster was part of an oversized brochure that compared movie making and printing as two very similar crafts.

DESIGN FIRM
Plant Design Co.

ART DIRECTORS
Dana Lytle, Kevin Wade

DESIGNER
Martha Graettinger

CLIENT
Milwaukee Ballet

PURPOSE
Announcement

SIZE
13.5" x 24"

Digital collage of type and images were completed in two colors. Adobe Photoshop and Aldus FreeHand were used to finish the project.

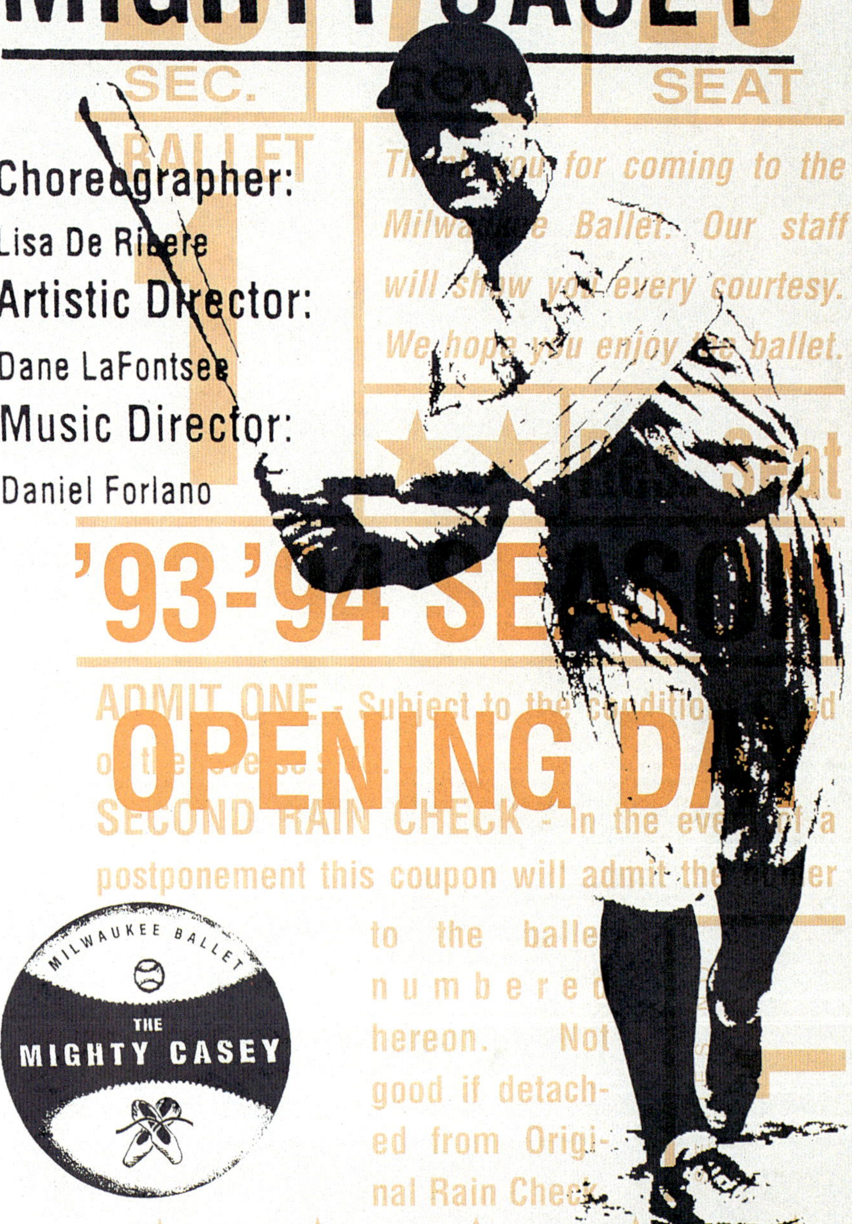

DESIGN FIRM

Hesse Designagentur GmbH

ALL DESIGN

Klaus Hesse

CLIENT

Fachhochschule Dortmund

PURPOSE

Competition, workshop, and exhibition promotion

SIZE

33" x 23.5" (84cm x 60cm)

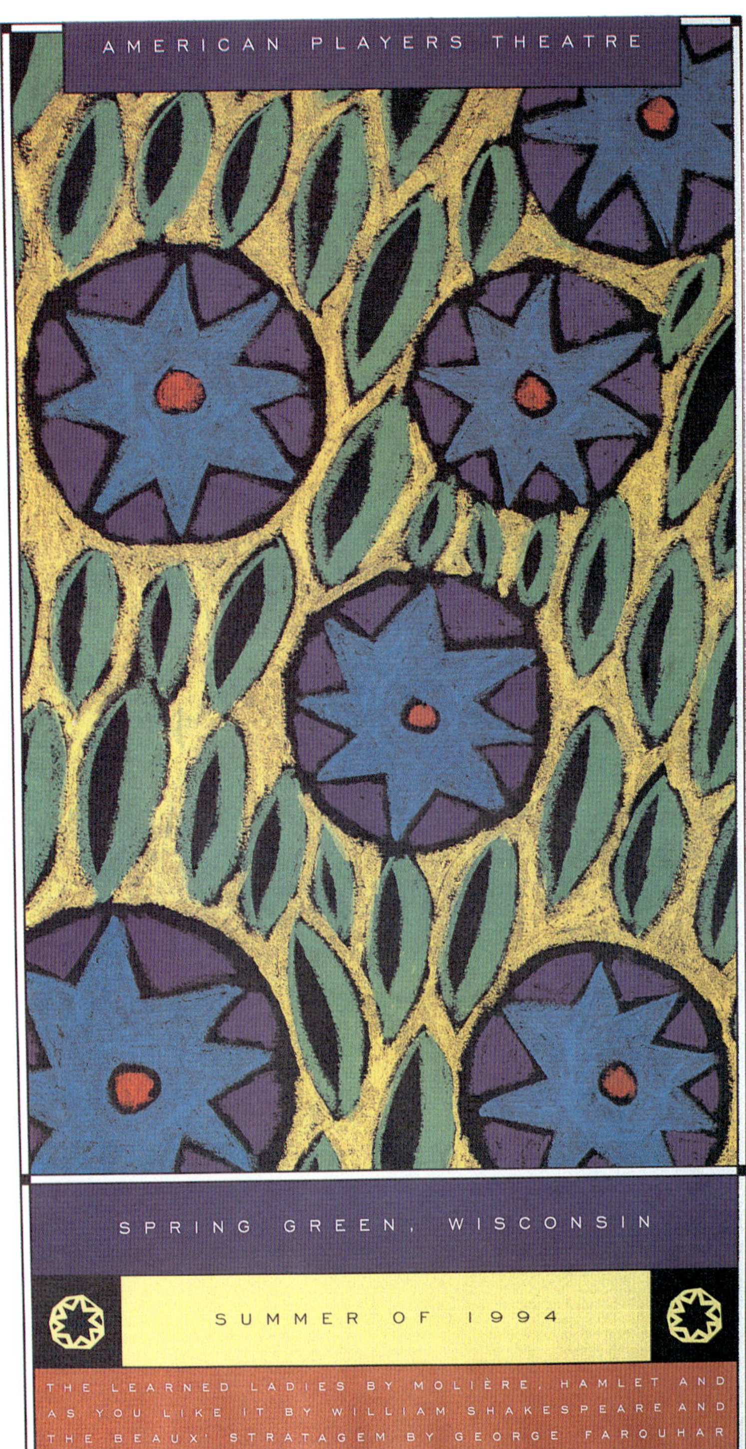
AMERICAN PLAYERS THEATRE
SPRING GREEN, WISCONSIN
SUMMER OF 1994
THE LEARNED LADIES BY MOLIÈRE, HAMLET AND AS YOU LIKE IT BY WILLIAM SHAKESPEARE AND THE BEAUX' STRATAGEM BY GEORGE FARQUHAR

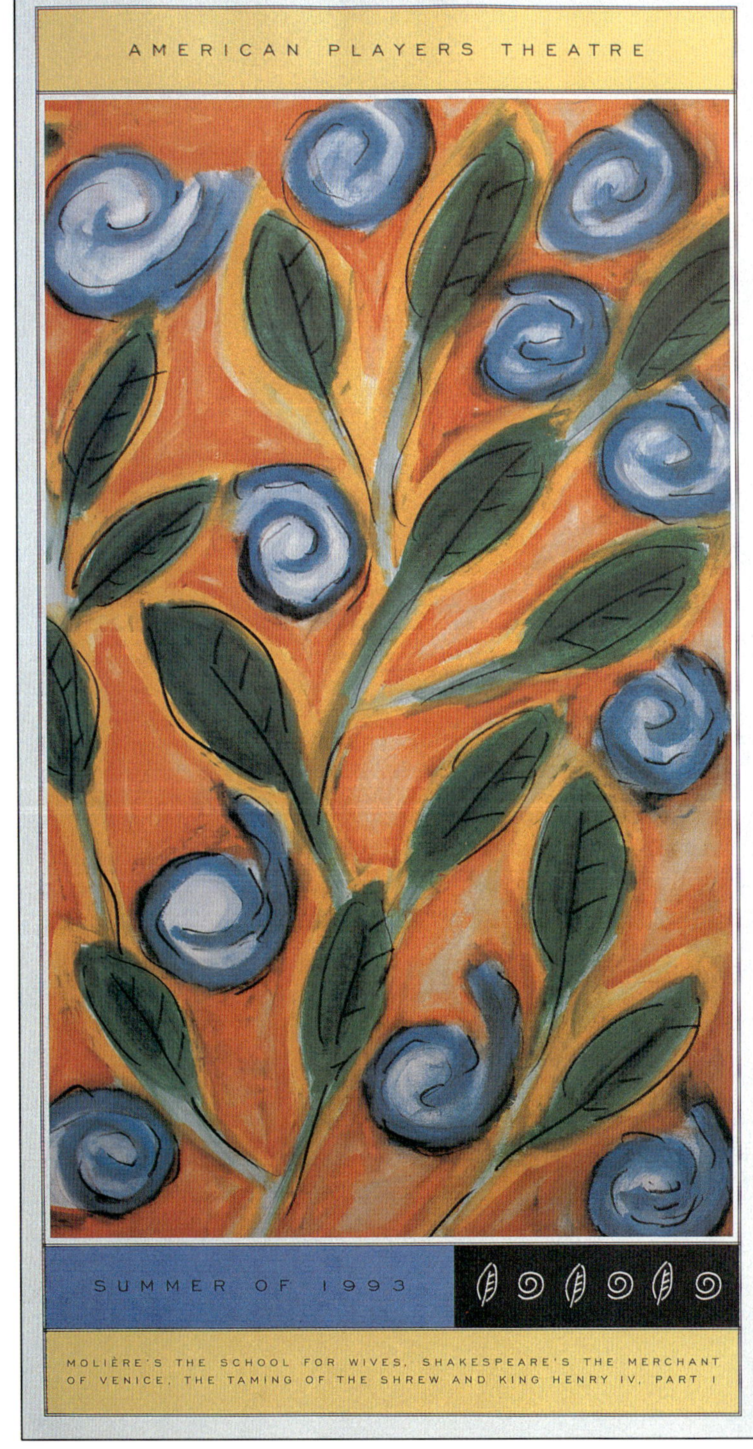
AMERICAN PLAYERS THEATRE
SUMMER OF 1993
MOLIÈRE'S THE SCHOOL FOR WIVES, SHAKESPEARE'S THE MERCHANT OF VENICE, THE TAMING OF THE SHREW AND KING HENRY IV, PART I

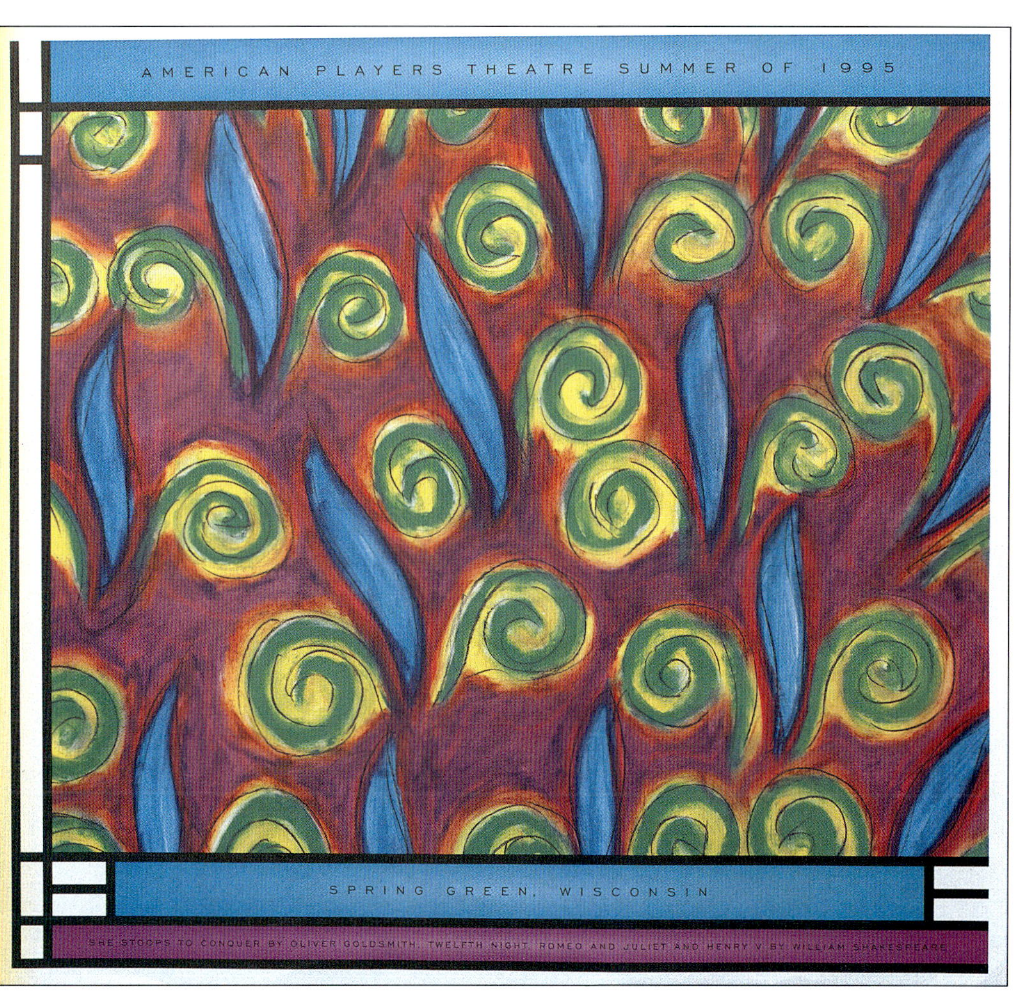

DESIGN FIRM

Planet Design Co.

ART DIRECTORS

Dana Lytle, Kevin Wade

DESIGNERS

[this page]

Dana Lytle, Raelene Mercer

[facing page]

Dana Lytle, Martha Ghraettinger

ILLUSTRATOR

Dana Lytle

CLIENT

American Players Theatre

PURPOSE

Theatre season promotion

SIZE

[this page]

26" x 24"

[facing page]

19" x 35.5"

Illustration done using cattle markers, oil pastels, and charcoal. Designer also used QuarkXPress on a Macintosh Quadra 700 for the design of this series of three posters.

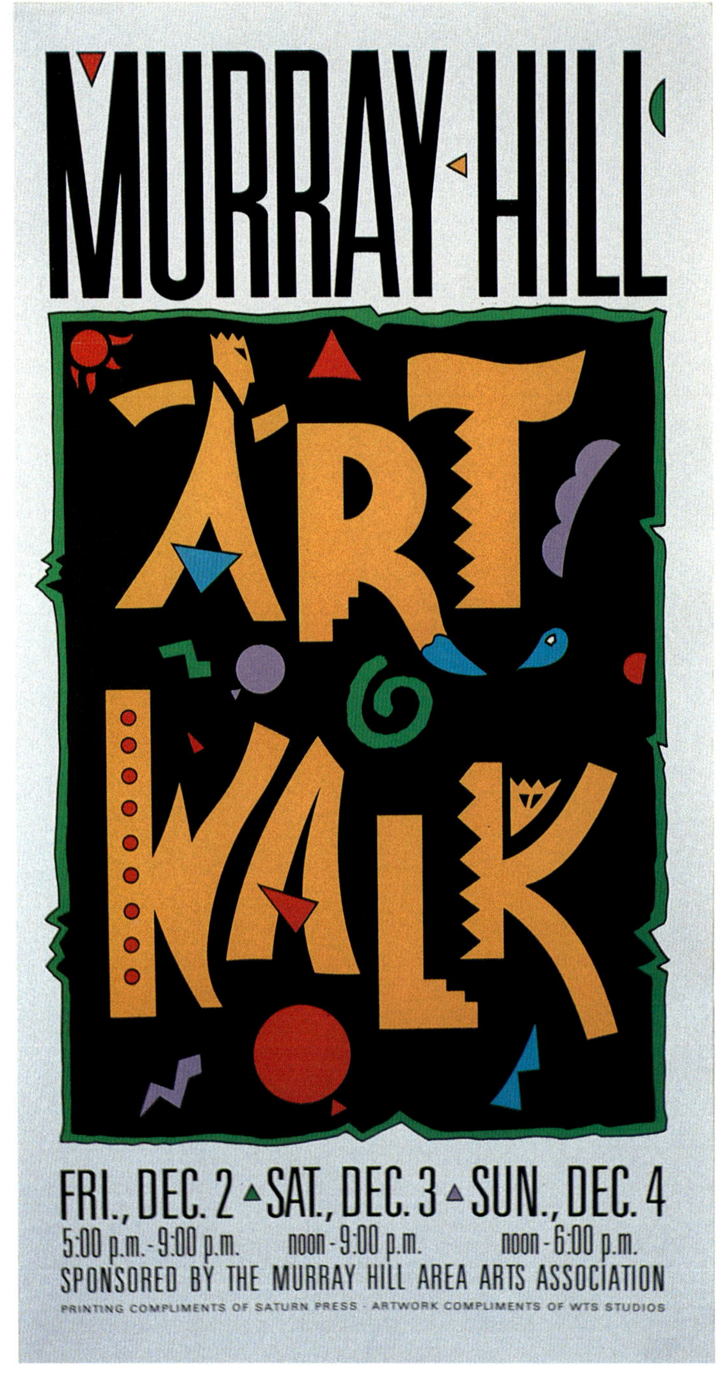

DESIGN FIRM
WTS Studios

ART DIRECTOR
Fanoula Sevastos
Public Relations

DESIGNER
William Silvers

ILLUSTRATOR
William Silvers

CLIENT
Murray Hill Area Arts Association

PURPOSE
Art Walk advertisement

SIZE
11" x 21" (27.9cm x 53.3cm)

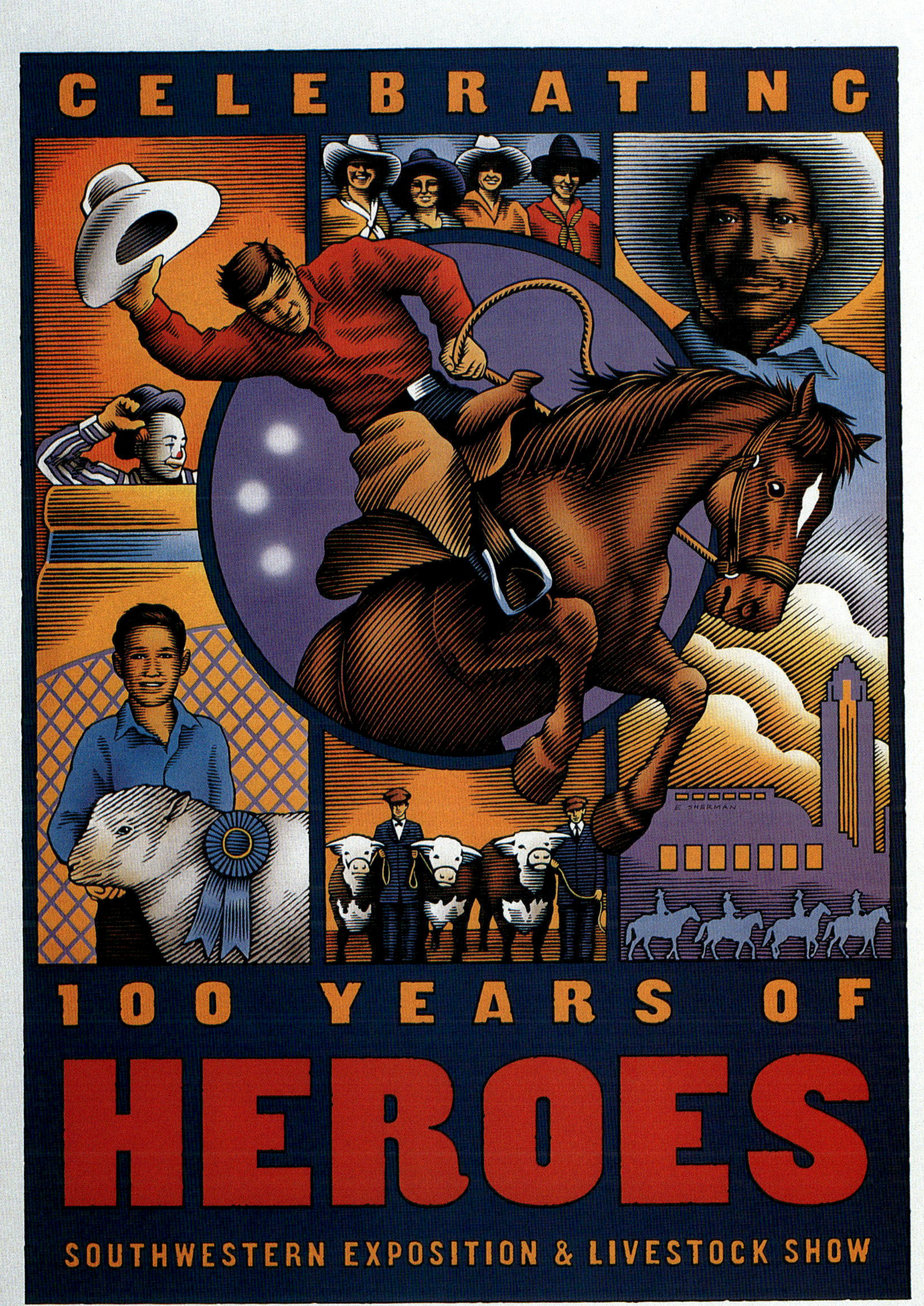

DESIGN FIRM
Witherspoon Advertising

ART DIRECTOR
Kyle Mize

DESIGNER
Kyle Mize

ILLUSTRATOR
Erwin Sherman

CLIENT
Southwestern Exposition
& Livestock Show

PURPOSE
100 Years of Heroes

SIZE
16" x 21.5"
(40.7cm x 54.2cm)

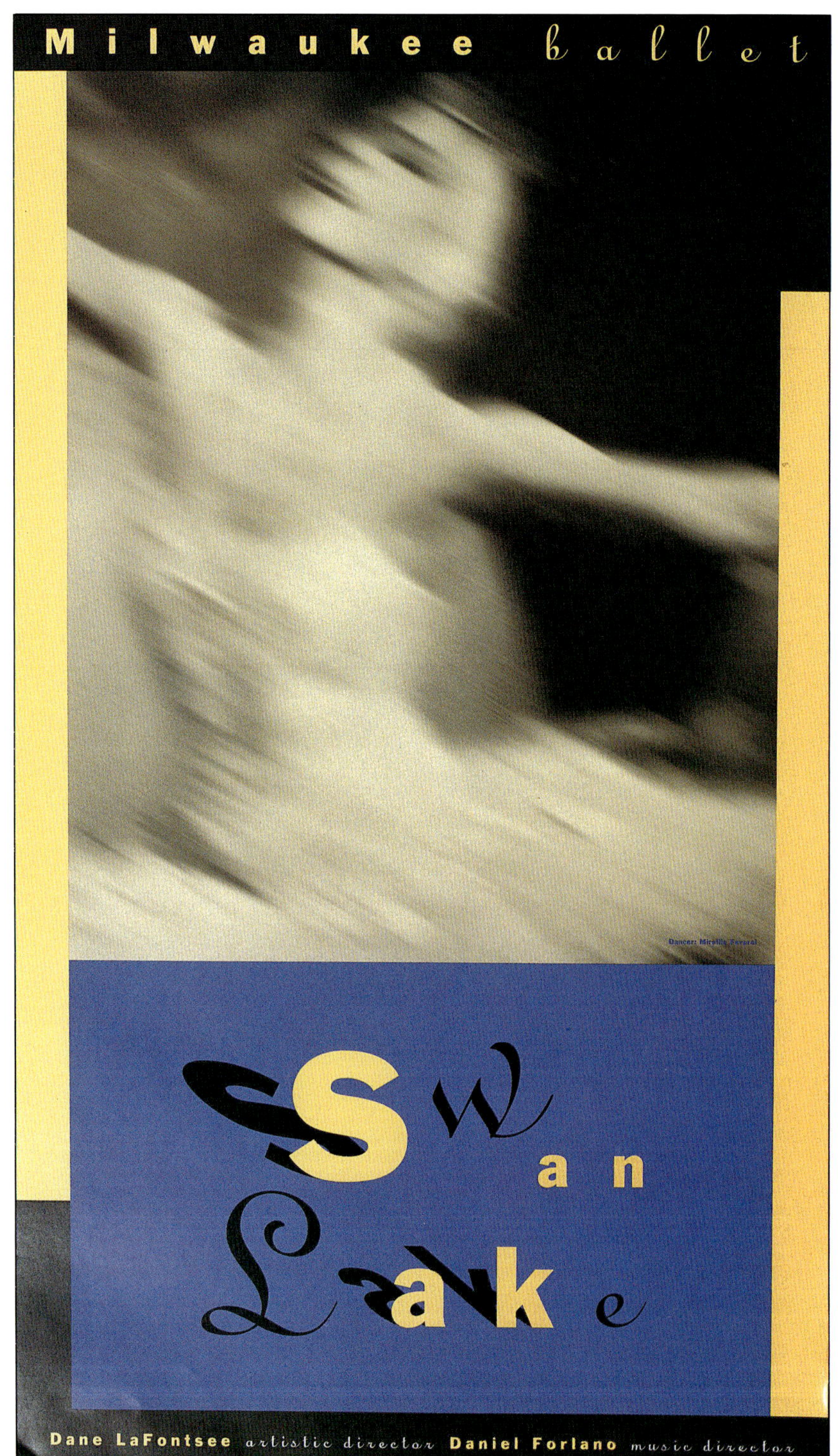

DESIGN FIRM

Planet Design Co.

ART DIRECTORS

Dana Lytle, Kevin Wade

DESIGNERS

Dana Lytle, Martha Graettinger

CLIENT

Milwaukee Ballet

PURPOSE

Season announcement

SIZE

14" x 24"

(35.6cm x 70cm)

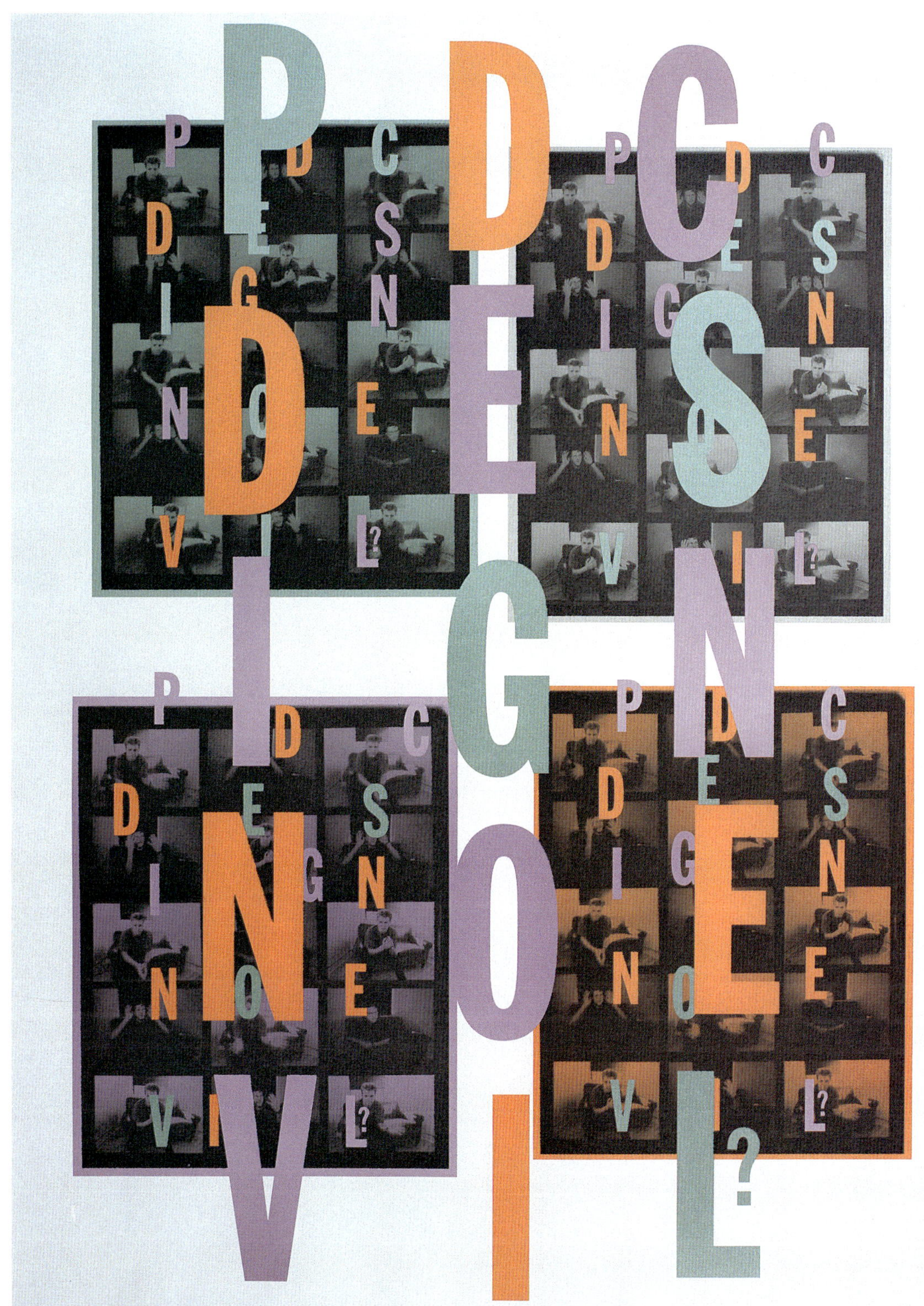

DESIGN FIRM
Planet Design Co.

ART DIRECTORS
Dana Lytle, Kevin Wade

DESIGNER
Kevin Wade

PHOTOGRAPHER
Leslie Barton

CLIENT
Visual Arts Alliance

PURPOSE
Speaking engagement announcement

SIZE
19" x 25"
(48.3cm x 63.5cm)

DESIGN FIRM

Antero Ferreira Design

ART DIRECTOR

Antero Ferreira

DESIGNERS

Antero Ferreira,
Eduardo Sotto Mayor

ILLUSTRATOR

Eduardo Sotto Mayor

PURPOSE

Clothing promotion

SIZE

26.8" x 18.9" (68cm x 48cm)

Design was completed on an Apple Macintosh with Aldus FreeHand and Adobe Photoshop software.

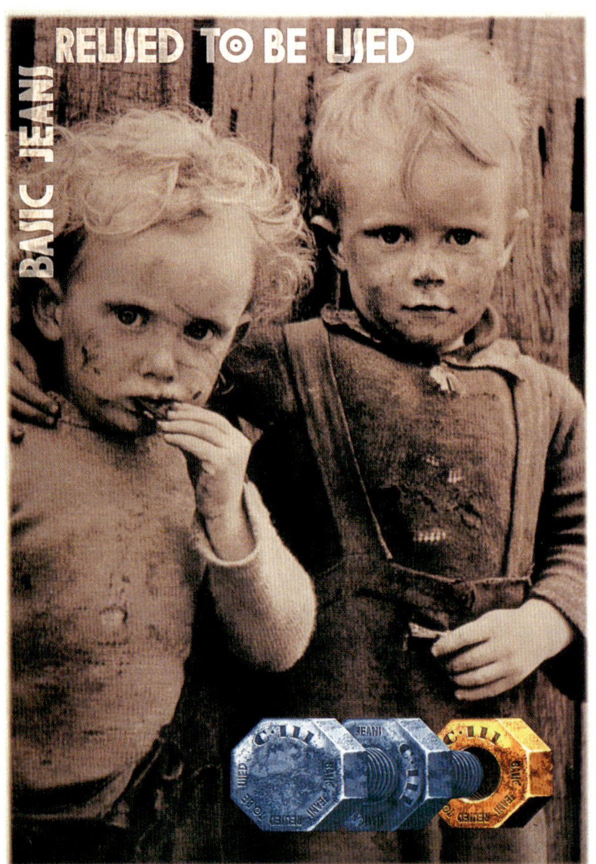

DESIGN FIRM

Antero Ferreira Design

ART DIRECTOR

Antero Ferreira

DESIGNER

Antero Ferreira

ILLUSTRATORS

Sofia Assalino,
Joana Alves

PHOTOGRAPHER

Oscar De Almeida

CLIENT

A.C. Pimenta

PURPOSE

Pimentinha Winter Collection promotion

SIZE

18" x 9" (46cm x 22cm)

Design was completed using 3-D illustration, photographs, and Aldus FreeHand and Adobe Photoshop software.

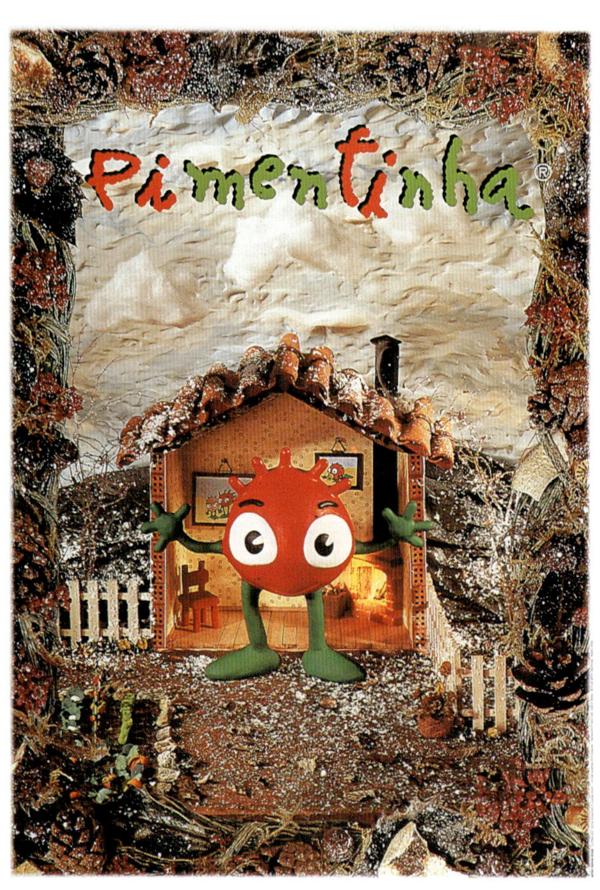

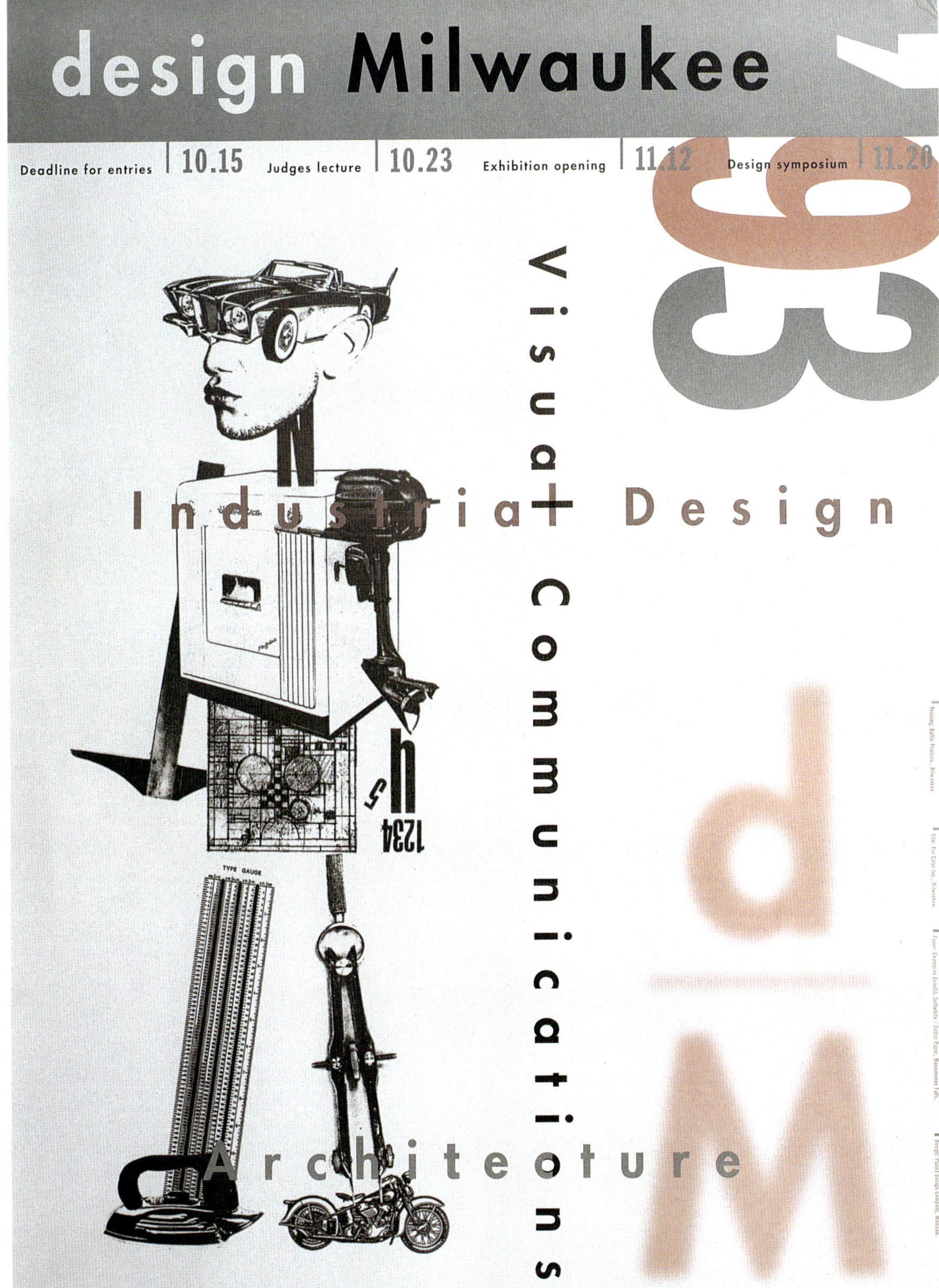

DESIGN FIRM
Planet Design Co.

ART DIRECTORS
Dana Lytle, Kevin Wade

DESIGNER
Kevin Wade

ILLUSTRATOR
Kevin Wade

CLIENT
Design Milwaukee

PURPOSE
Call for entries

SIZE
19" x 25"
(48.3cm x 63.5cm)

For this piece, a hand-built collage was scanned into Adobe Photoshop for adjustment. Type and layout were finished in Aldus FreeHand and QuarkXPress.

D E S I G N   F I R M

Watt, Roop & Co.

A R T   D I R E C T O R

Gregory Oznowich

D E S I G N E R S

Gregory Oznowich,
Kurt Roscoe

C L I E N T

Cleveland Music
School Settlement

P U R P O S E

Event promotion
and souvenir

S I Z E

24" x 36"
(61cm x 91.4cm)

This poster was produced in Aldus PageMaker 5.0. The illustration was originally a piece of clip art. To maintain its rough edges, designers sized the drawing up using a conventional stat camera. They then scanned the photo stat as a low-resolution file for position only, and later supplied the same stat to the printer as original art to be dropped in at high resolution.

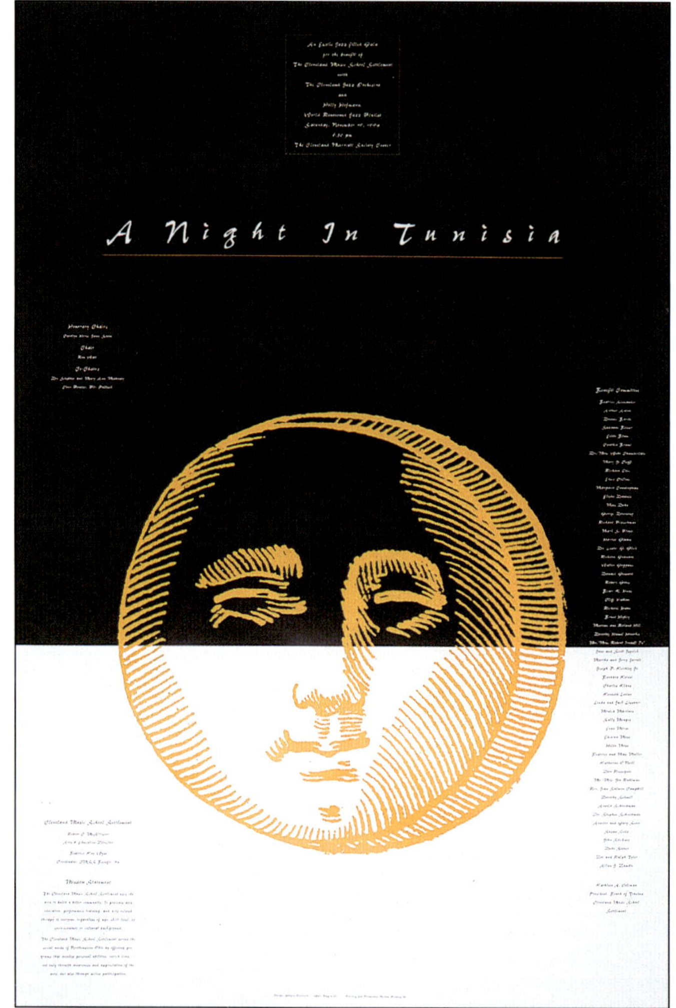

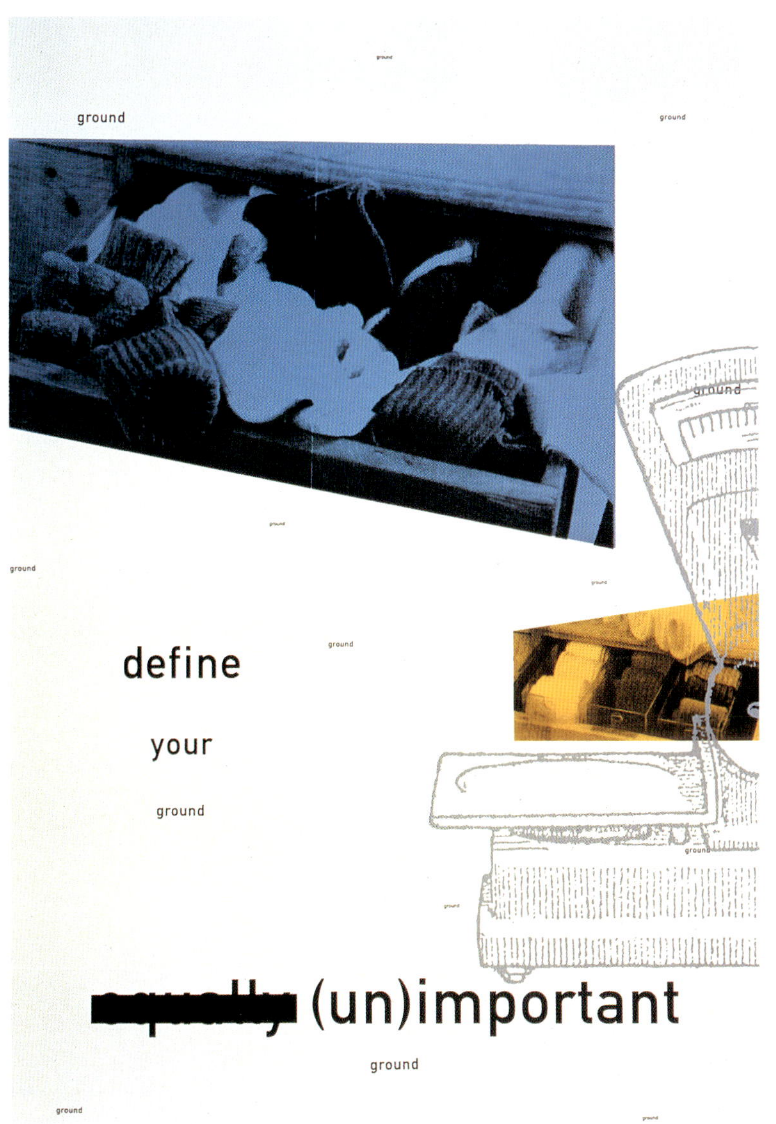

DESIGN FIRM
Cranbrook Academy of Art

ALL DESIGN
Jeremy F. Mende,
Carolyn Steinbeck

CLIENT
Self-published

PURPOSE
Promotion

SIZE
28" x 40"
(71.1cm x 101.6cm)

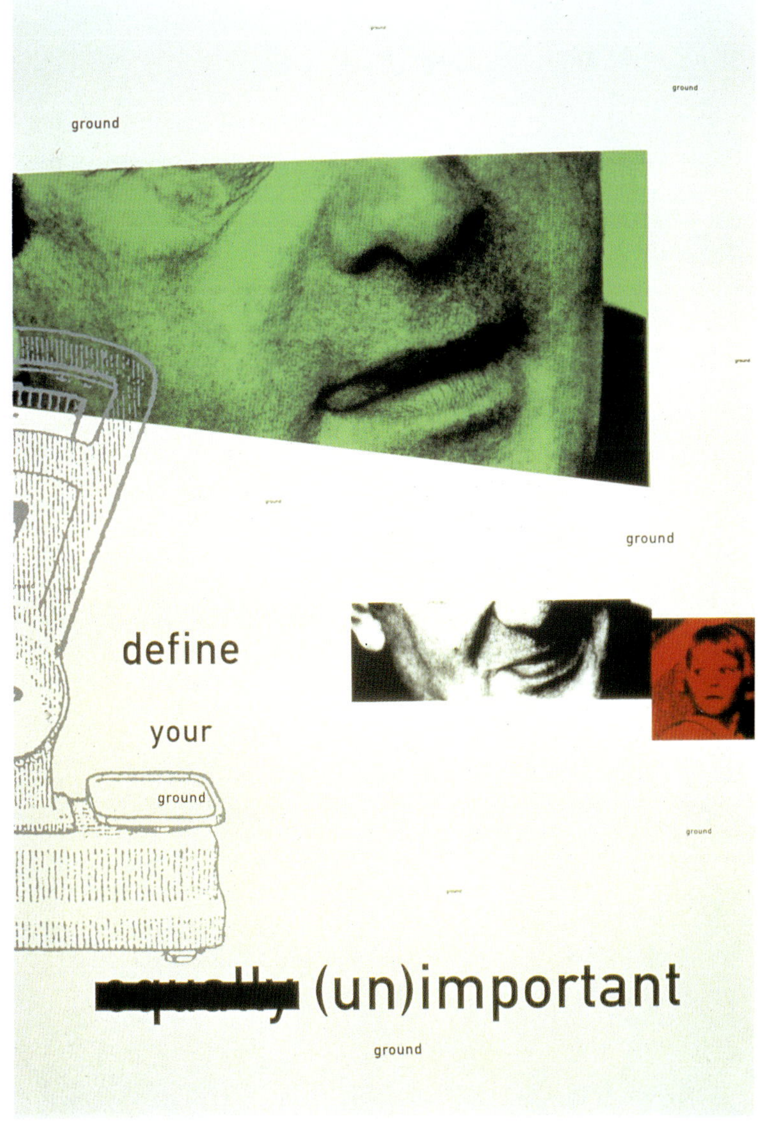

DESIGN FIRM
Leslie Chan Design Co., Ltd.

ALL DESIGN
Chan Wing Kei, Leslie

PHOTOGRAPHER
Outstanding Studio

CLIENT
Taiwan Image Poster
Design Association

PURPOSE
Self-promotion

SIZE
23" x 33.5" (60cm x 85cm)

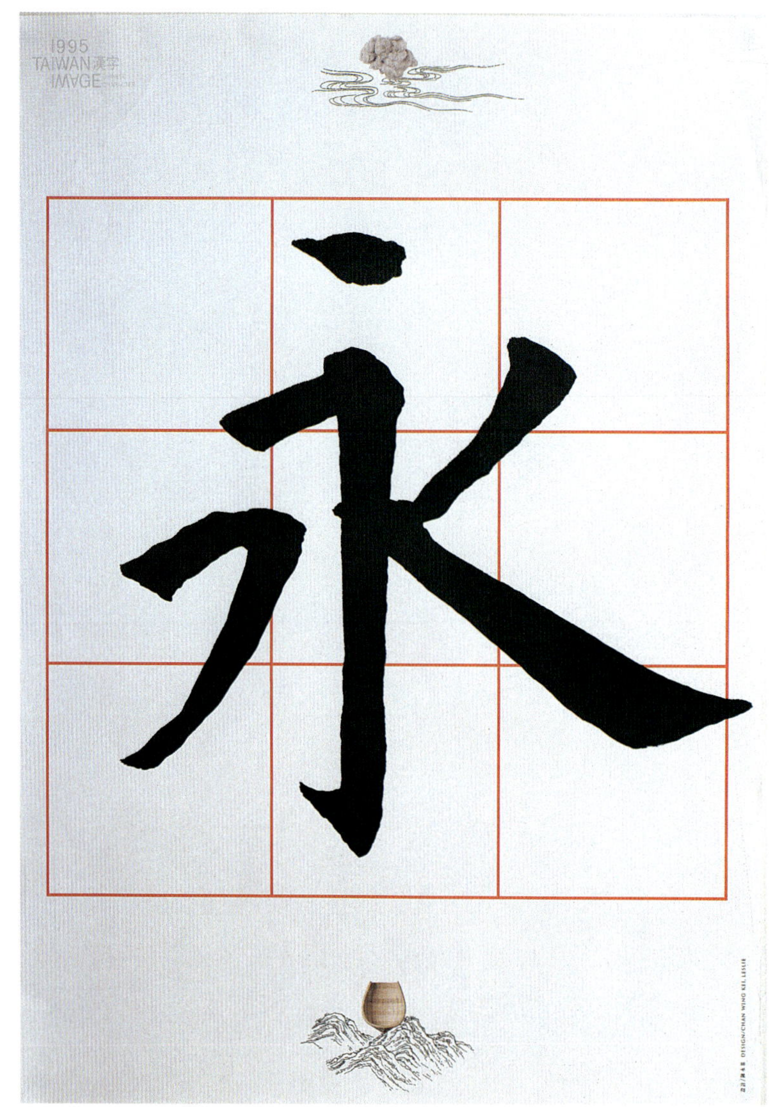

DESIGN FIRM
Leslie Chan Design Co., Ltd.

ALL DESIGN
Chan Wing Kei, Leslie

PHOTOGRAPHER
Yu Jung Chin

CLIENT
Poster Design Association

PURPOSE
Political awareness

SIZE
23" x 33.5" (60cm x 85cm)

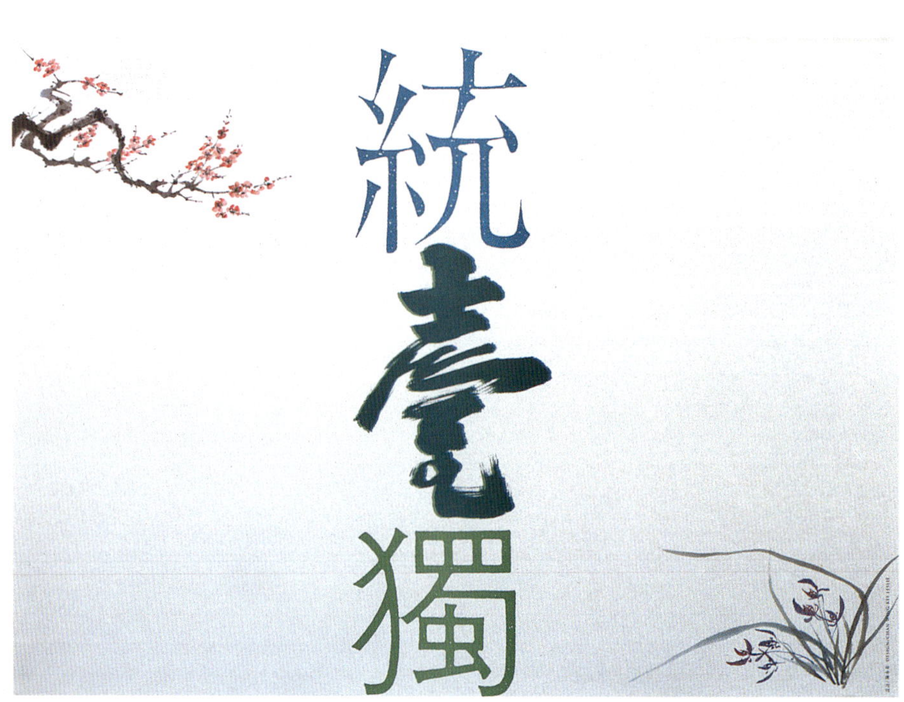

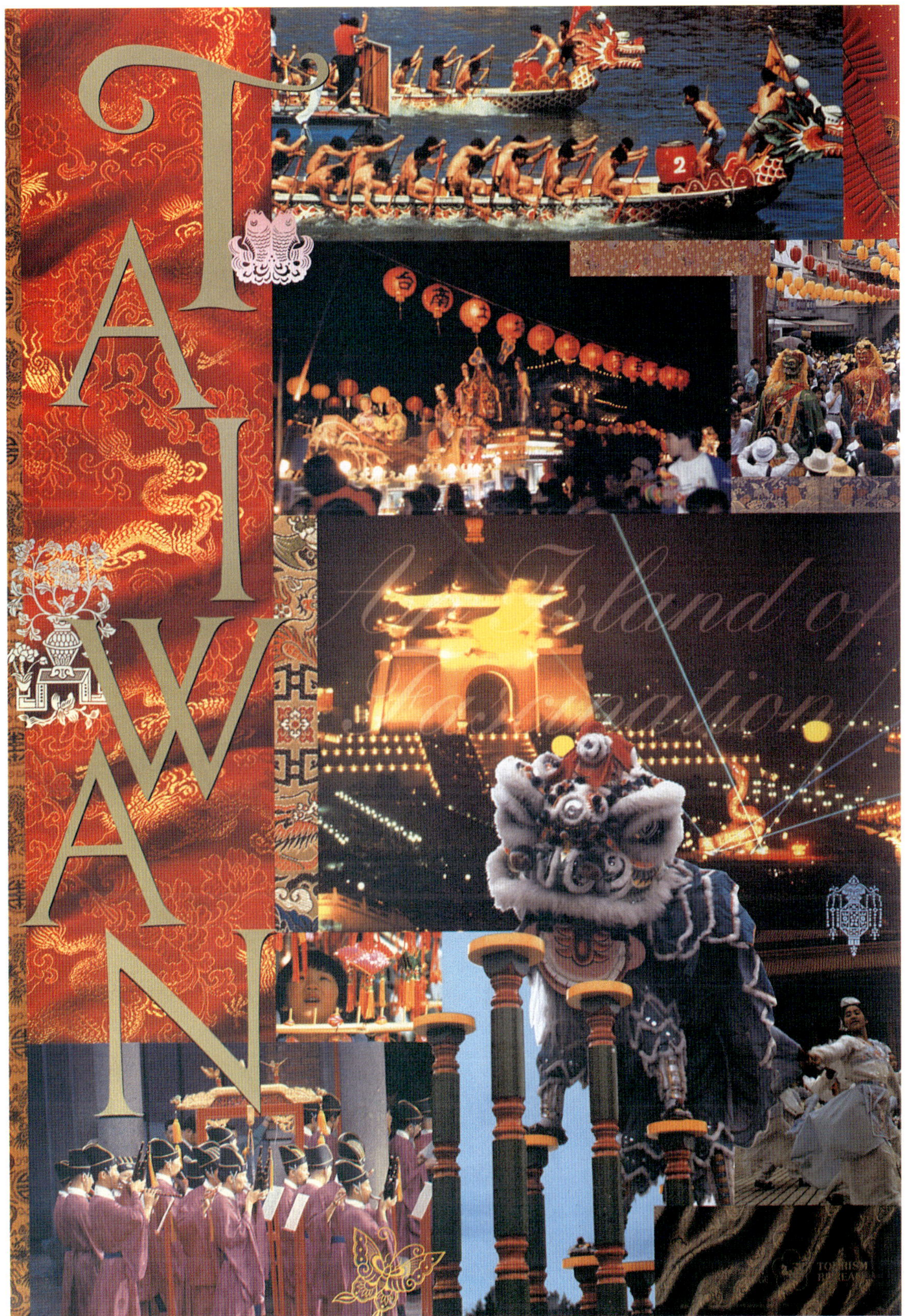

DESIGN FIRM
Leslie Chan Design Co., Ltd.

ALL DESIGN
Chan Wing Kei, Leslie

PHOTOGRAPHER
Yu Jung Chin

CLIENT
Bureau Republic of China

PURPOSE
Tourism promotion

SIZE
23" x 33.5" (60cm x 85cm)

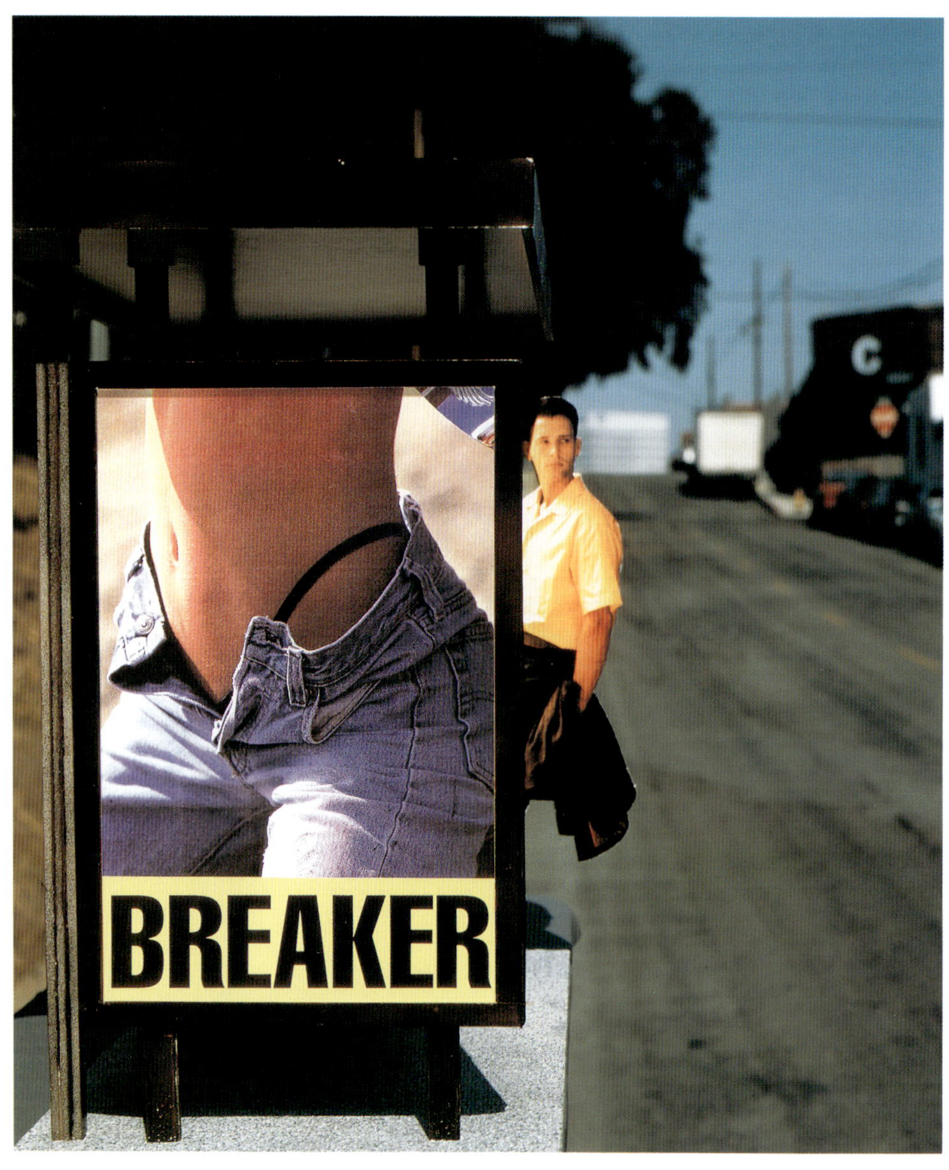

DESIGN FIRM
Mike Salisbury Communications, Inc.

ALL DESIGN
Mike Salisbury

CLIENT
Breaker Jeans

PURPOSE
Jeans advertisement

SIZE
25" x 40" (63.5cm x 101.6cm)

DESIGN FIRM
Mike Salisbury Communications, Inc.

ART DIRECTOR
Mike Salisbury

DESIGNERS
Terry Lamb, Dat Linso

ILLUSTRATORS
Wit Vinson, Brian Sisson

CLIENT
American Cinemtheque

PURPOSE
New facility announcement

SIZE
25" x 40" (63.5cm x 101.6cm)

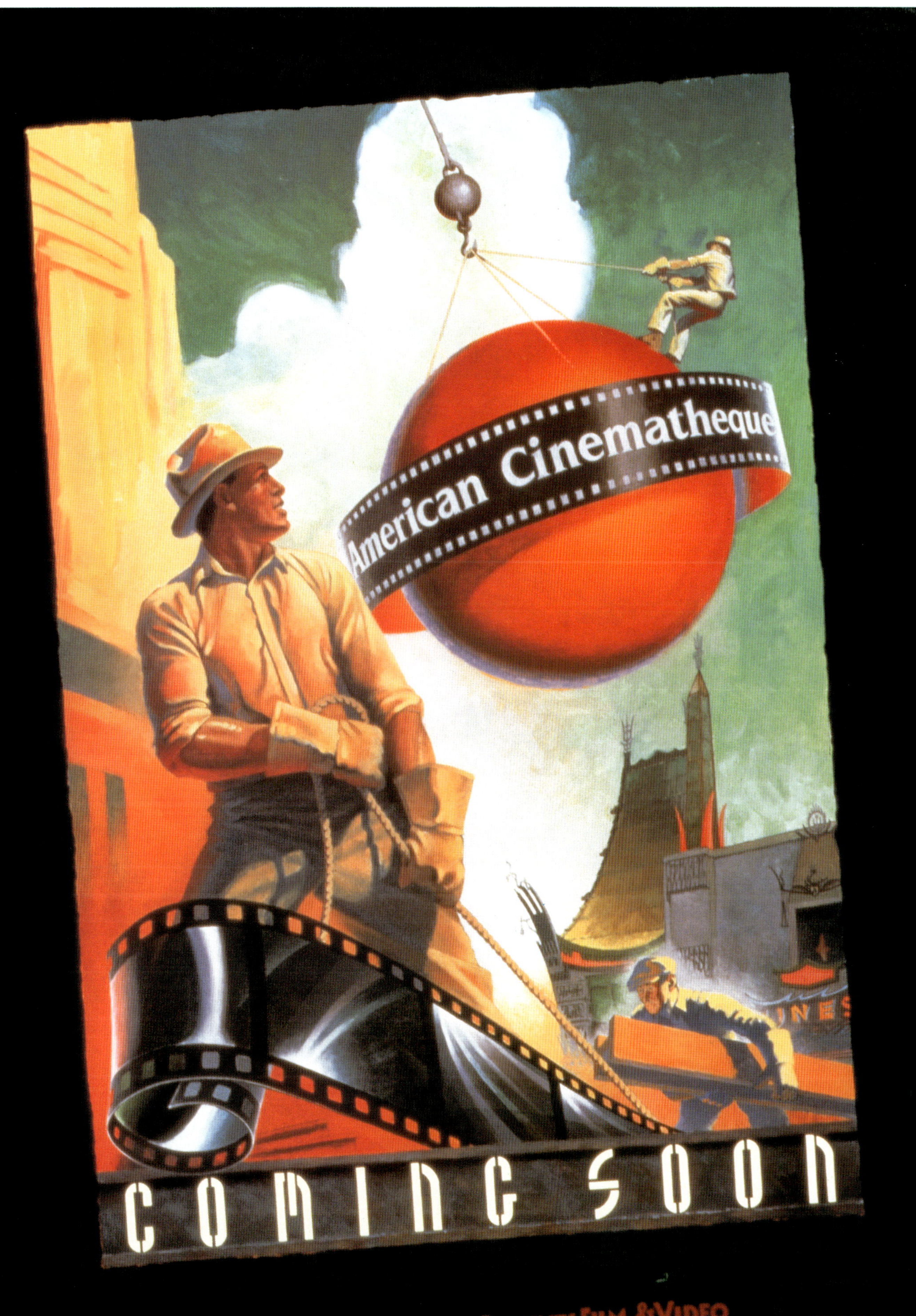
American Cinematheque
COMING SOON
MEANWHILE ... THE TEMPORARY CINEMATHEQUE PRESENTS FILM & VIDEO PROGRAMS ON THE SECOND WEEKEND of EACH MONTH AT THE DIRECTORS GUILD THEATER COMPLEX IN HOLLYWOOD
Mike Salisbury
PRINTING · CALIFORNIA LITHO ARTS

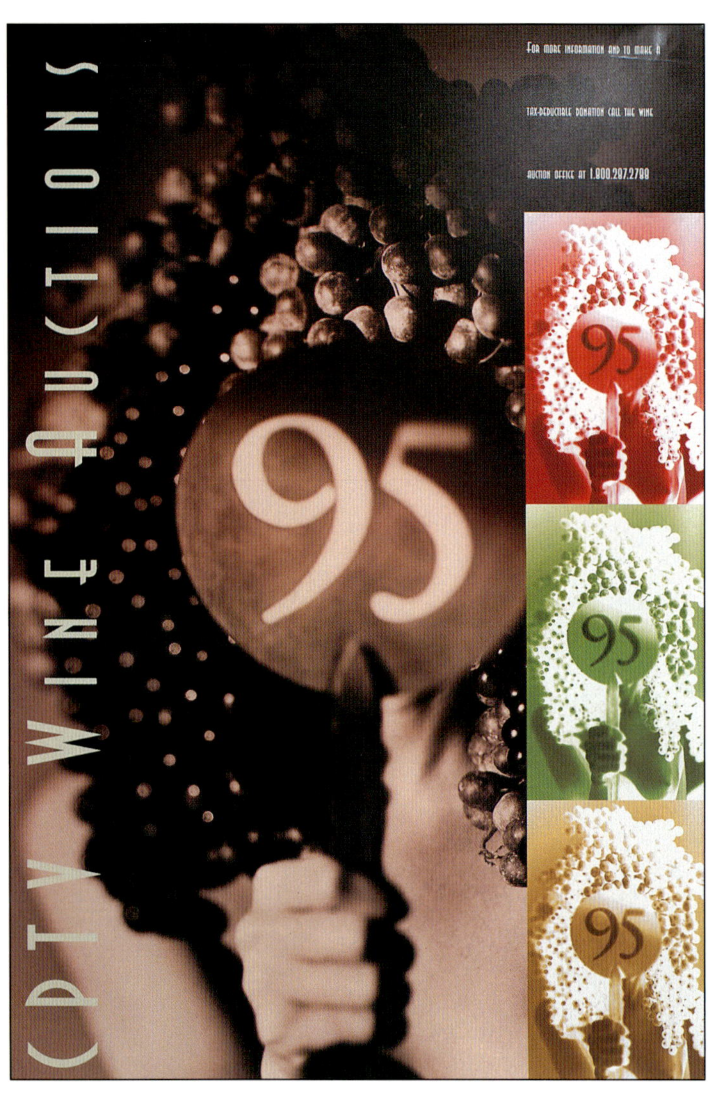

DESIGN FIRM
Keiler Design Group

ART DIRECTOR
Mike Scricco

DESIGNER
Jeff Lin

PHOTOGRAPHER
Frank Marchese

CLIENT
Connecticut Public Television

PURPOSE
Wine auction promotion

SIZE
34" x 24" (86.4cm x 61.0cm)

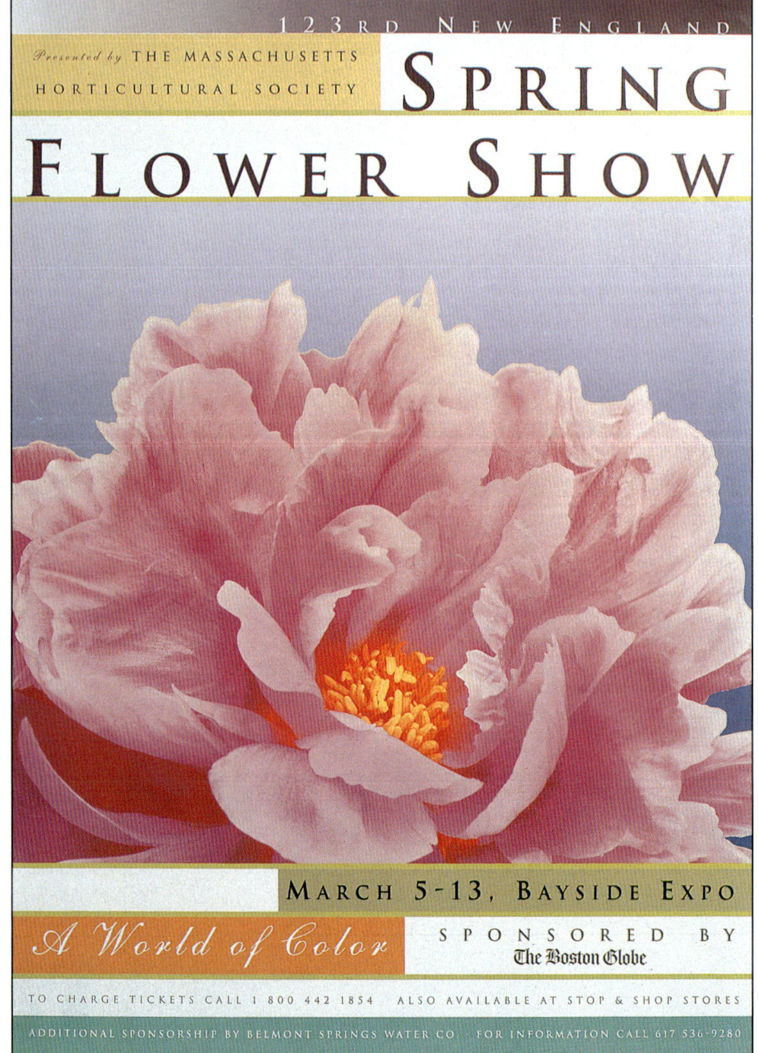

DESIGN FIRM
Clifford Selbert Design Collaborative

ART DIRECTOR
Melanie Lowe

DESIGNER
Melanie Lowe

ILLUSTRATOR
Marco Ventura

CLIENT
Massachusetts Horticultural Society

PURPOSE
Flower show promotion

SIZE
23" x 16" (58.4cm x 40.6cm)

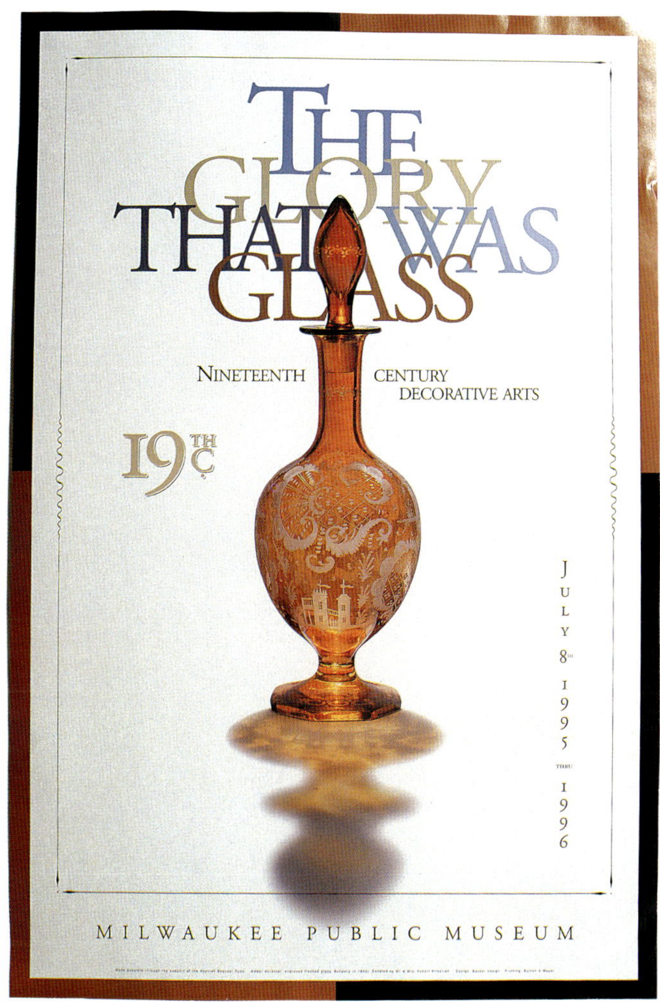

DESIGN FIRM
Becker Design

ART DIRECTOR
Neil Becker

DESIGNER
Neil Becker

PHOTOGRAPHER
Joanne Peterson

CLIENT
Milwaukee Public Museum

PURPOSE
Glass exhibit promotion

SIZE
24" x 36" (61cm x 91.4cm)

This piece features a work that is classic in form while having a good amount of detail etched into the glass. The etched images on the piece illustrate a story. These images, although actually very subtle, become quite an impact when light passes through and casts a rich golden shadow. It was important that the typography complement the glass piece. The subtle use of color and overlapping type resemble what might happen if the type were glass.

DESIGN FIRM
Plaid Cat Design

ALL DESIGN
Eric Scott Stevens

CLIENT
Winthrop University Theatre

PURPOSE
"Lettice & Lovage" play promotion

SIZE
11" x 17" (27.9cm x 43.2cm)

The illustrations on the poster were done by hand and the rough texture of the illustrations were created by drawing on watercolor paper with crayon. All of the copy, except the title of the play, is original hand-lettering.

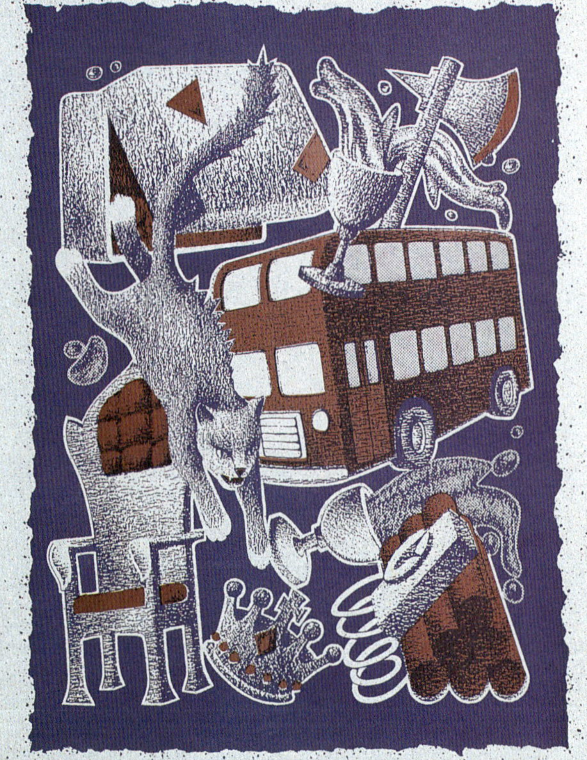

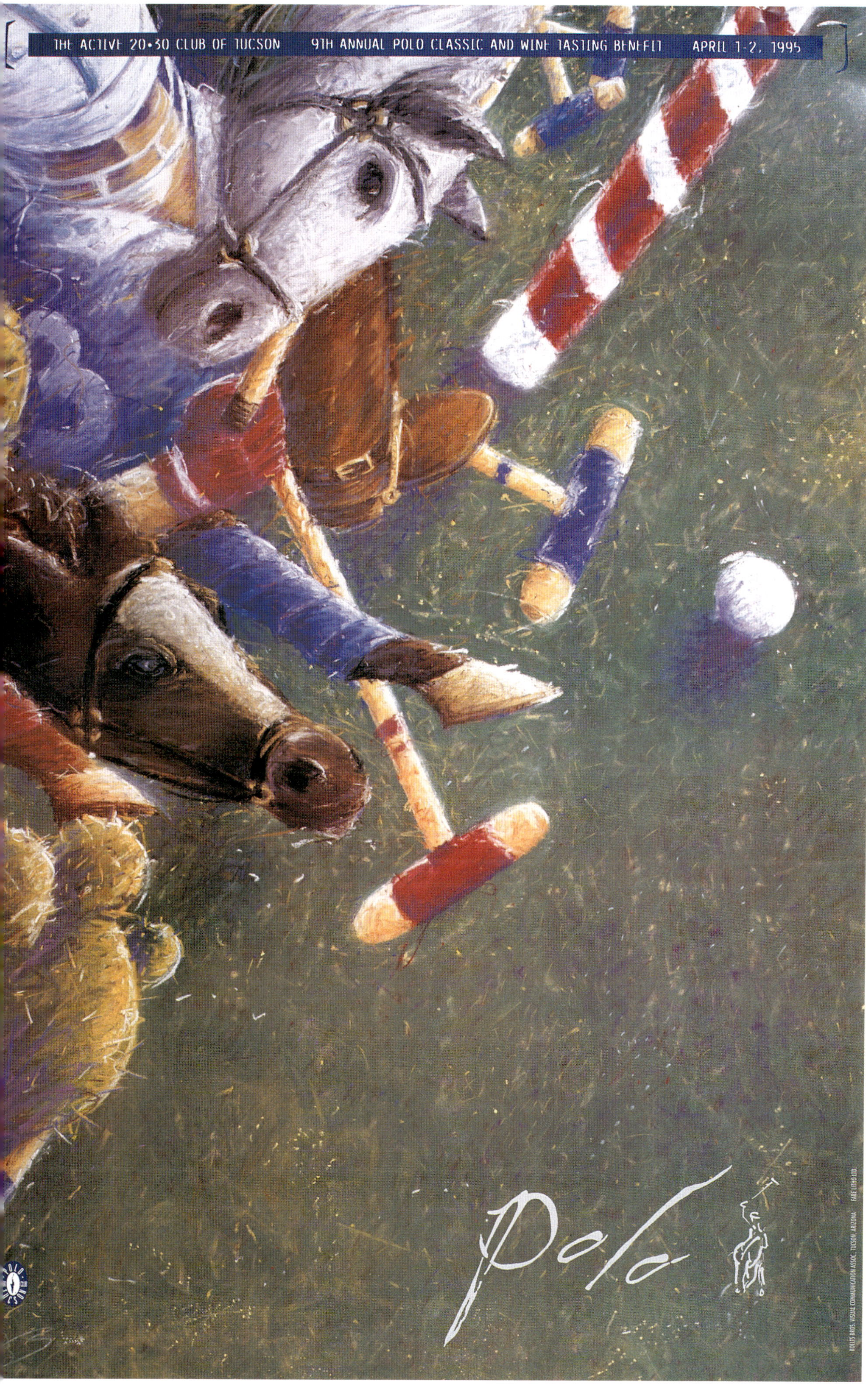

DESIGN FIRM
Boelts Bros. Visual Communication Assoc.

ART DIRECTOR
Jackson Boelts, Eric Boelts

DESIGNER
Jackson Boelts, Eric Boelts

ILLUSTRATOR
Eric Boelts

PHOTOGRAPHER

CLIENT
20.30 Club of Tucson

PURPOSE
Polo Tournament/ Fund-raiser promotion

SIZE
20" x 30" (50.8cm x 76.2cm)

Design completed with pastel illustration.

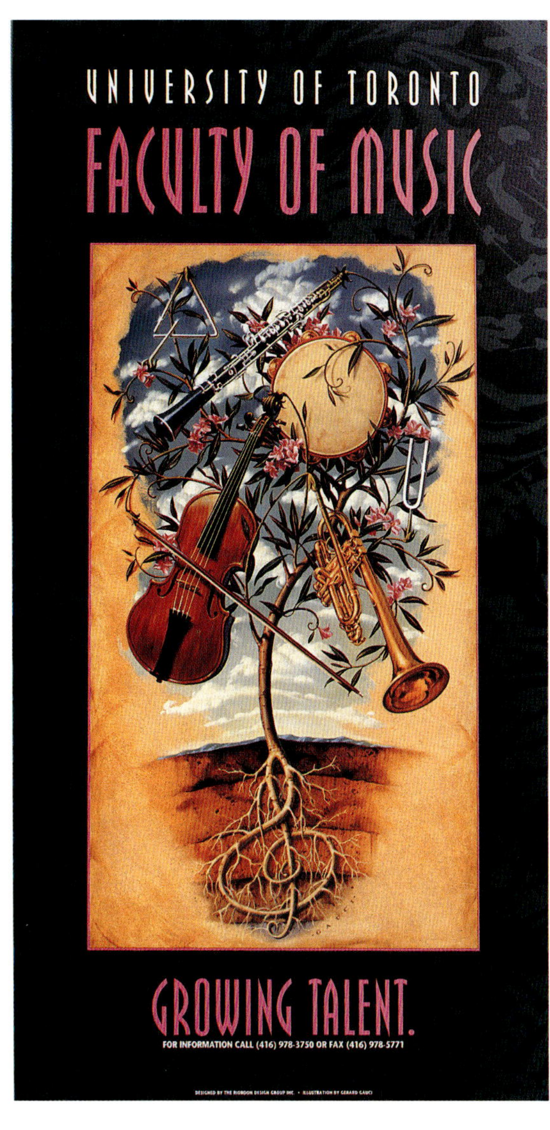

DESIGN FIRM
The Riordon Design Group Inc.

ART DIRECTOR
Ric Riordon

DESIGNERS
Shirley Riordon, Dan Wheaton

ILLUSTRATOR
Gerard Gauci

CLIENT
The University of Toronto

PURPOSE
Profile

SIZE
9.25" x 18"
(23.5cm x 45.7cm)

DESIGN FIRM
Eskind Waddell

ART DIRECTOR
Roslyn Eskind

DESIGNER
Donna Gedeon

CLIENT
McMaster University

PURPOSE
Lecture series announcement

SIZE
11" x 15" (27.9cm x 38.1cm)

The challenge was to create a generic format to be used year after year. The client simply updates the text changes and colors.

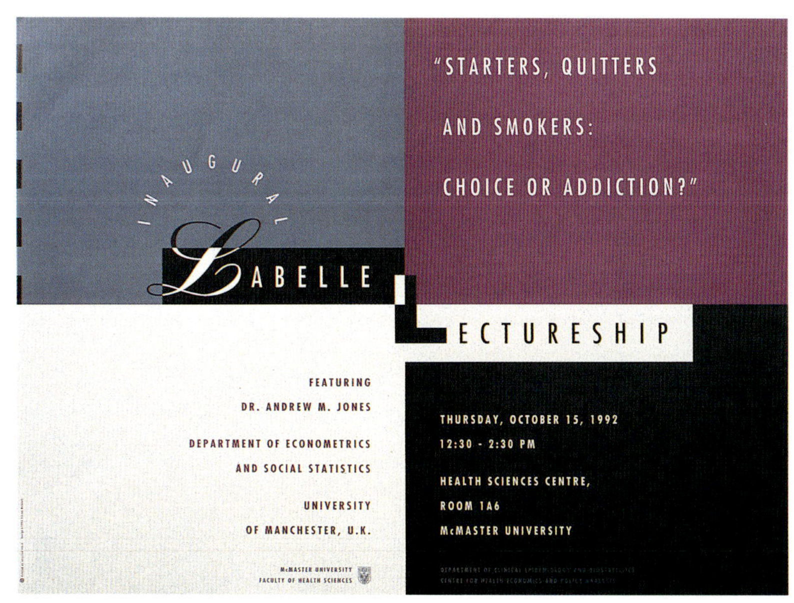

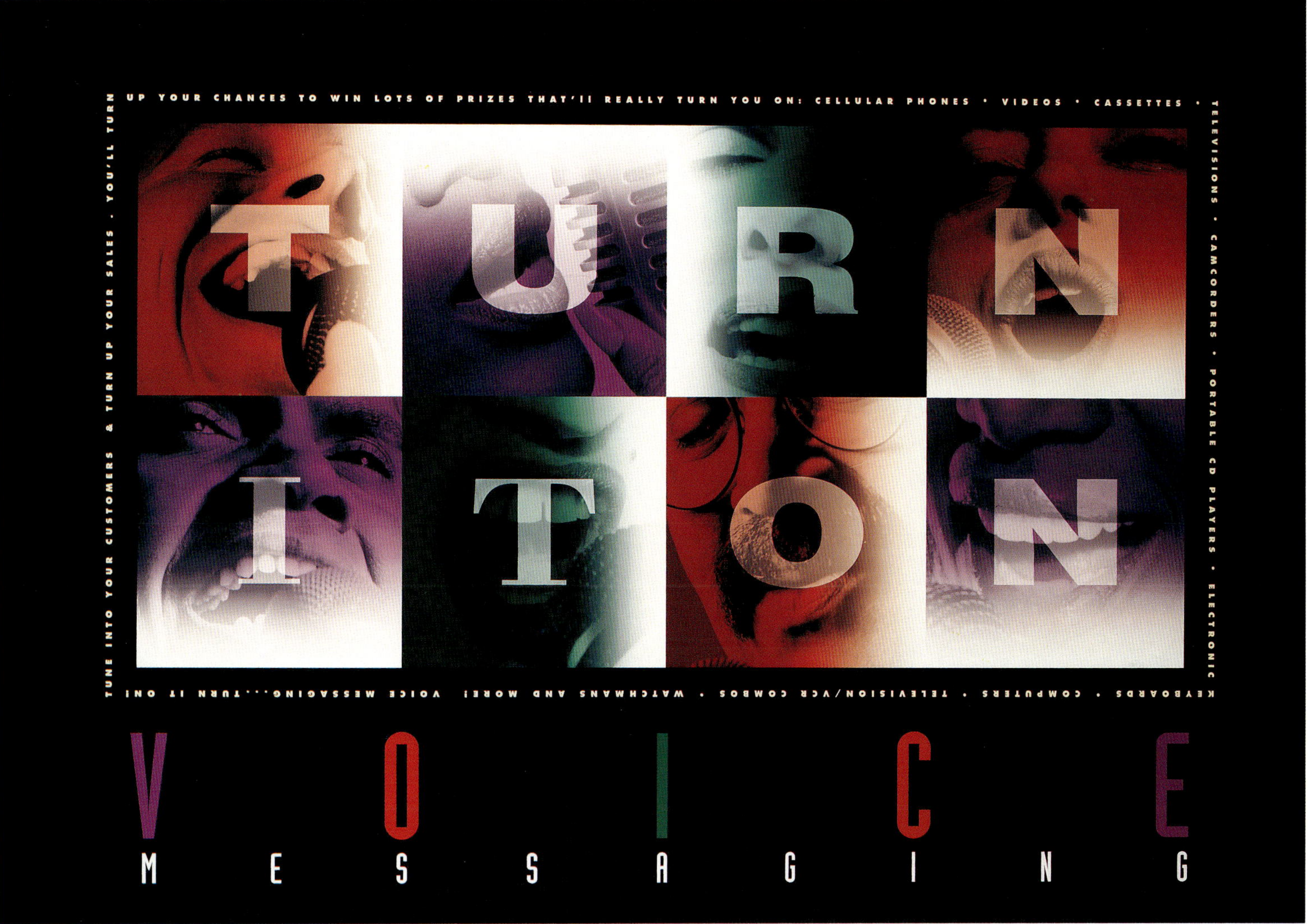

DESIGN FIRM
Vaughn Wedeen Creative, Inc.

ART DIRECTOR
Rick Vaughn

DESIGNER
Rick Vaughn

ILLUSTRATOR
Rich Vaughn

PHOTOGRAPHER
Valerie Satagto

CLIENT
US West Foundation

PURPOSE
Internal sales promotion

SIZE
24" x 36" (61cm x 91.4cm)

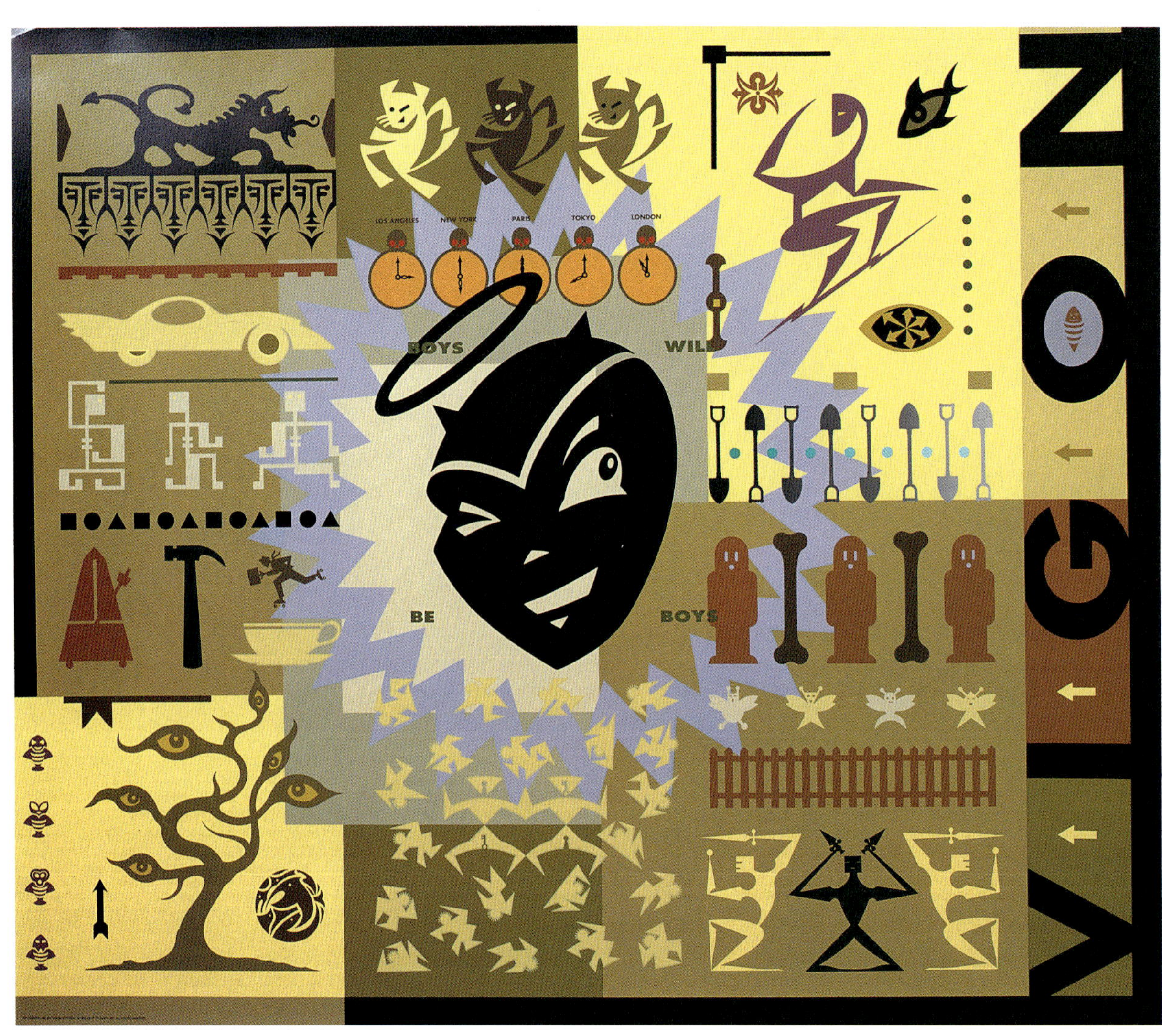

DESIGN FIRM

Jay Vigon Studio

ALL DESIGN

Jay Vigon

PURPOSE

Self-promotion

SIZE

30" x 25"
(76.2cm x 63.5cm)

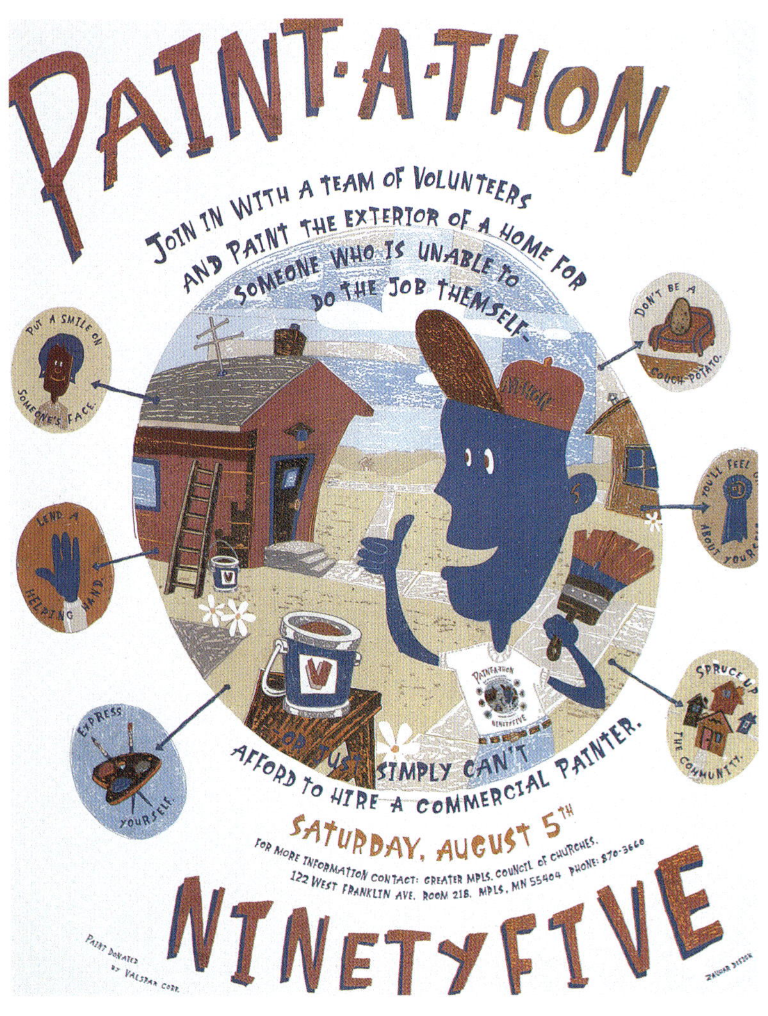

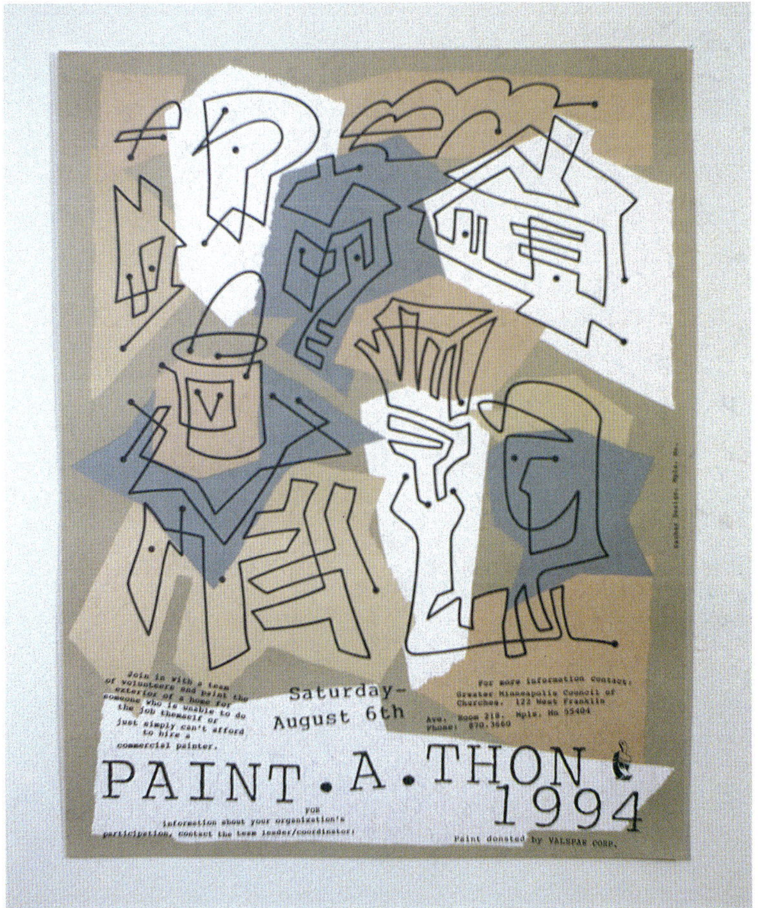

DESIGN FIRM
Zauhar Design

ALL DESIGN
David Zauher

CLIENT
Greater Minneapolis Council of Churches

PURPOSE
Paint-A-Thon announcement

SIZE
11" x 14" (27.9cm x 35.6cm)

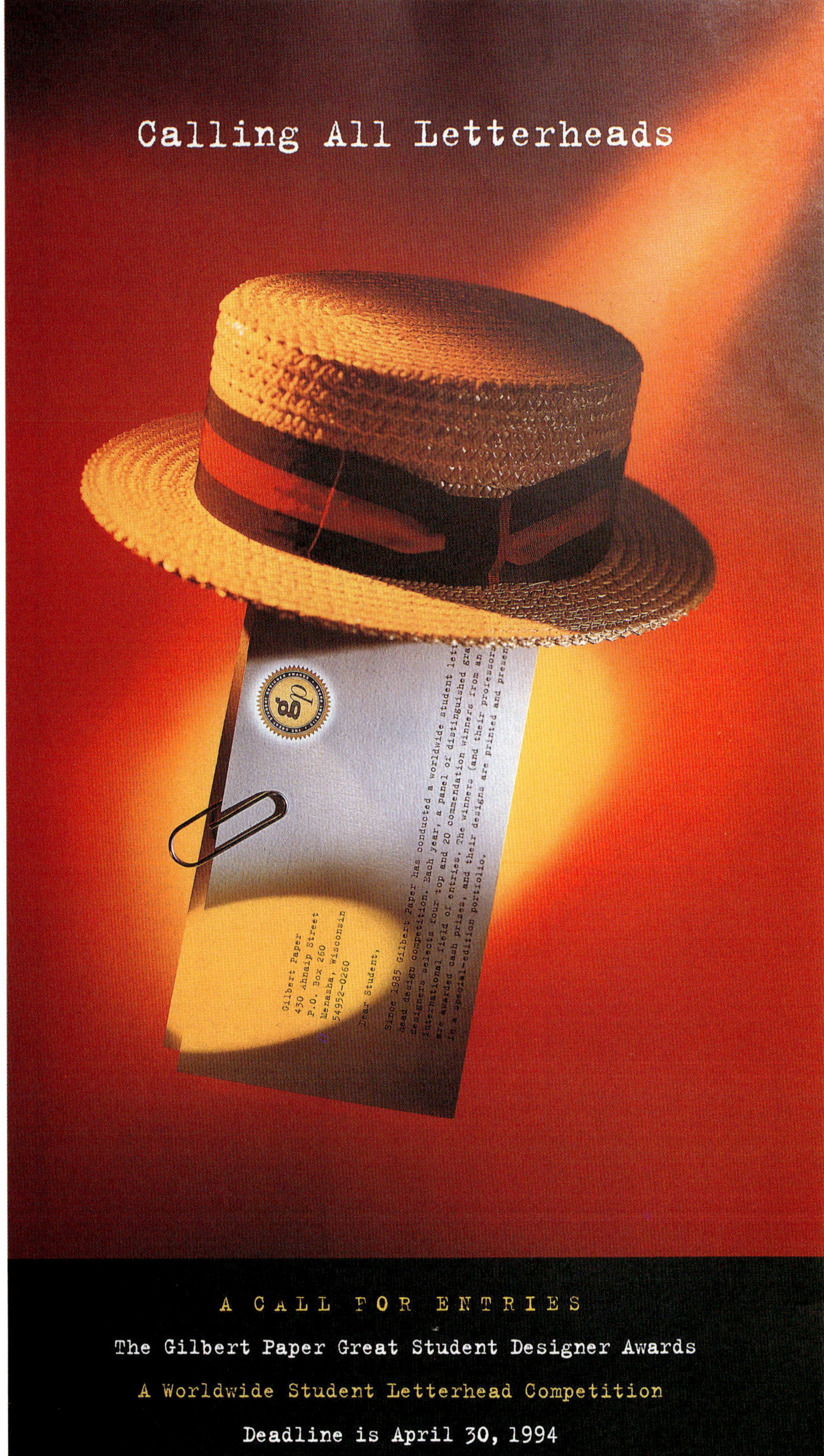

DESIGN FIRM
Alexander Isley Design

ART DIRECTOR
Alexander Isley

DESIGNER
Philip Bratter

PHOTOGRAPHER
Geoff Spear

CLIENT
Gilbert Paper

PURPOSE
Student letterhead competition promotion

SIZE
38.25" x 23" (97.2cm x 58.4cm)

D E S I G N   F I R M

Alexander Isley Design

A L L   D E S I G N

Alexander Isley

C L I E N T

Columbia Communications
Arts Society

P U R P O S E

Lecture promotion

S I Z E

22" x 34"
(55.9cm x 86.4cm)

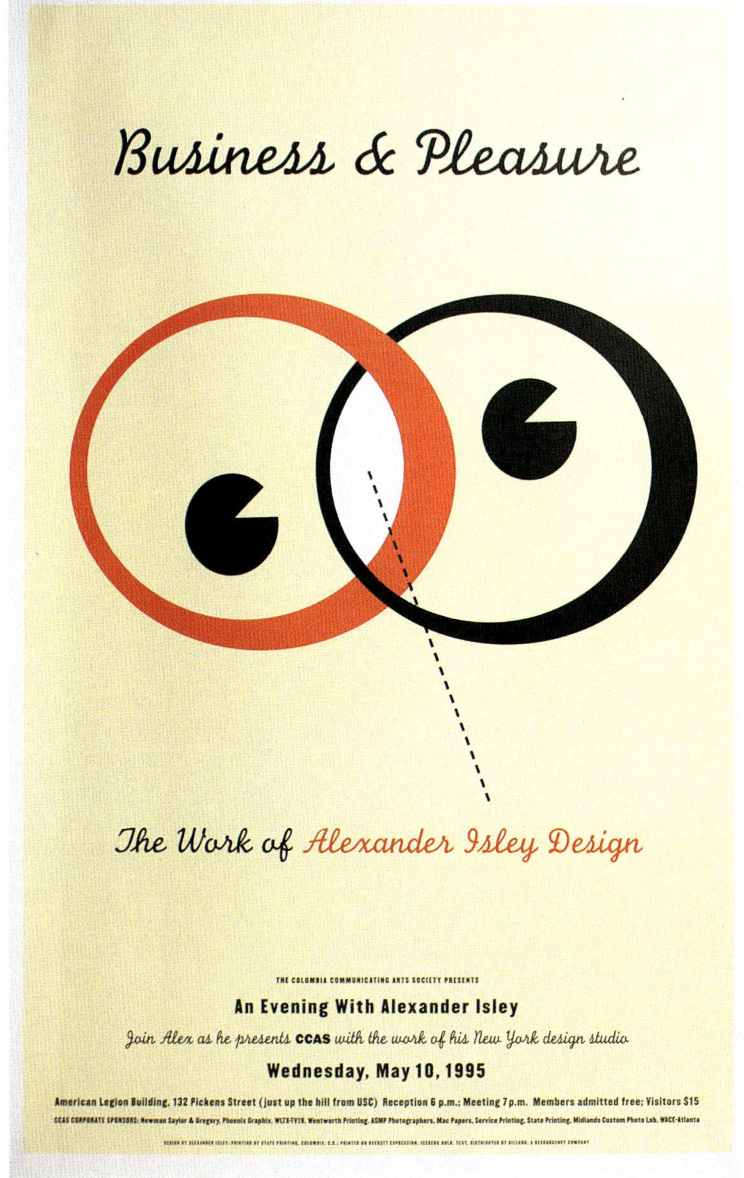

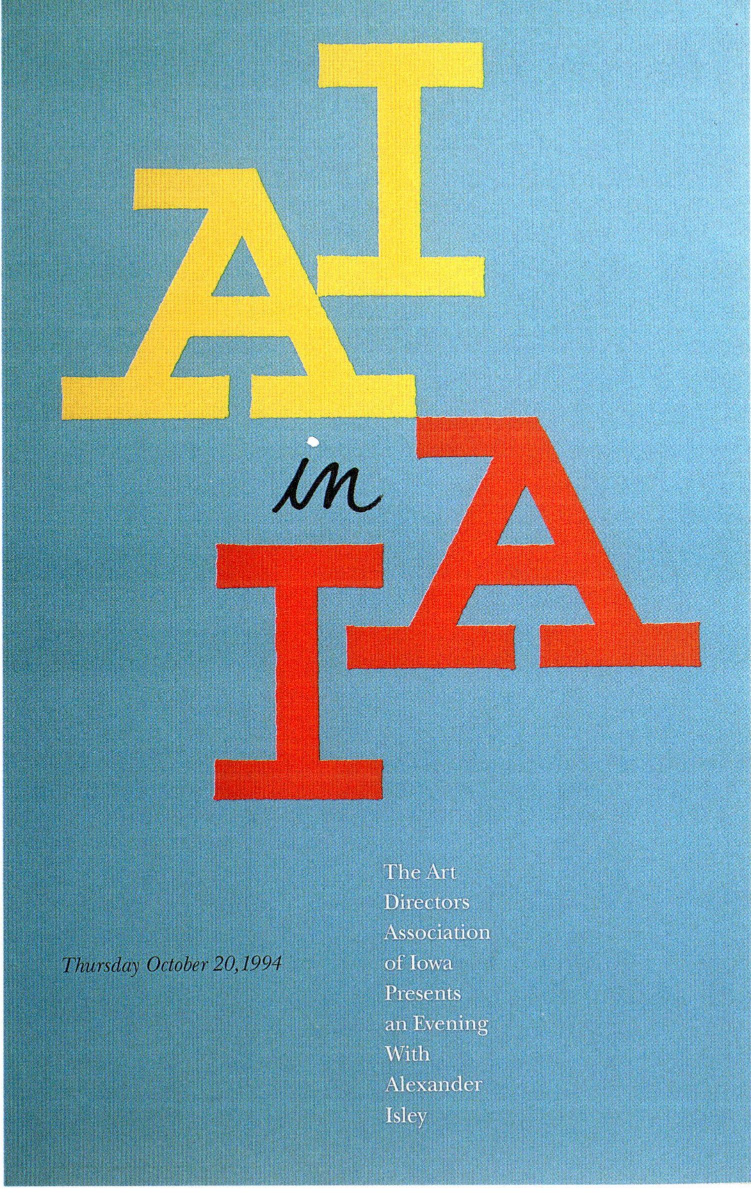

D E S I G N   F I R M

Alexander Isley Design

A L L   D E S I G N

Alexander Isley

C L I E N T

Art Directors Association
of Iowa

P U R P O S E

Lecture promotion

S I Z E

22" x 34"
(55.9cm x 86.4cm)

DESIGN FIRM

Tracy Sabin Graphic Design

ART DIRECTOR

Tanya Sterling

DESIGNER

Tracy Sabin

ILLUSTRATOR

Tracy Sabin

CLIENT

Village Millerest

PURPOSE

Entertainment schedule for a shopping center

SIZE

22" x 28" (55.9 cm x 71.1 cm)

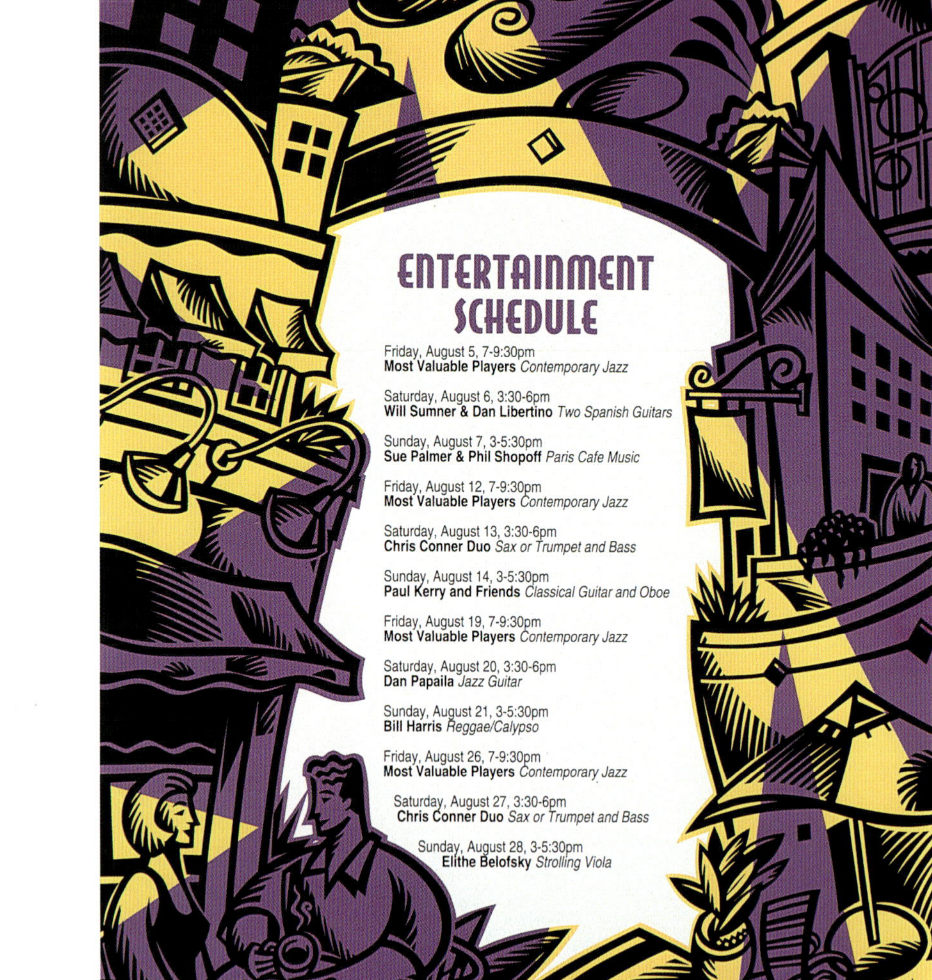

DESIGN FIRM

Bōwker Design

ART DIRECTOR

Scott Bowker

DESIGNER

Scott Bowker

ILLUSTRATOR

Scott Bowker

CLIENT

Bōwker Design

PURPOSE

Self promotion

SIZE

18" x 24" (45.7cm x 61.0cm)

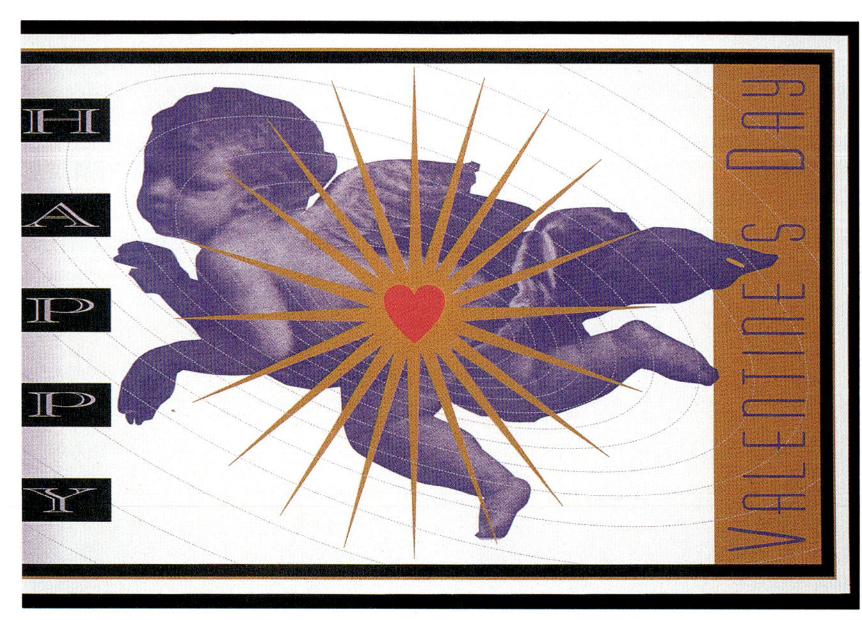

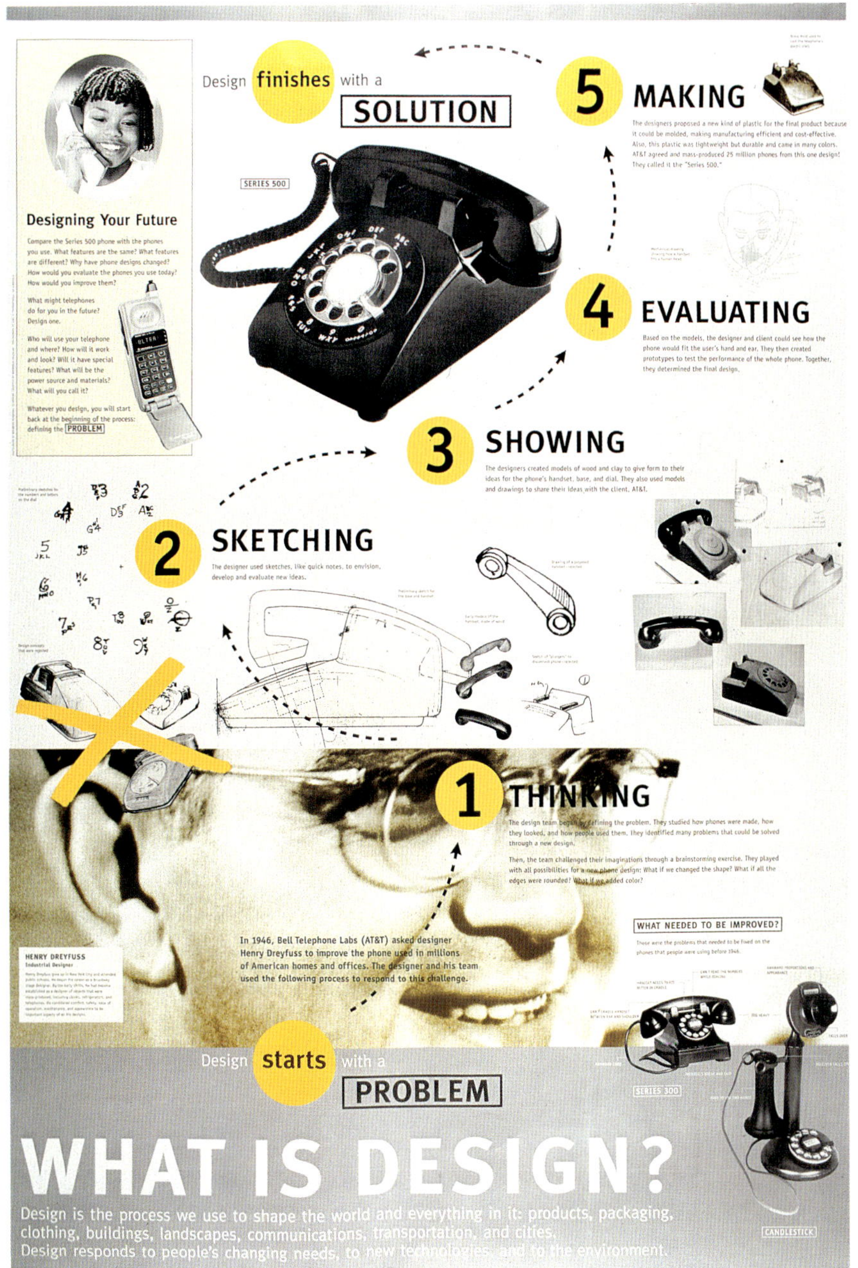

DESIGN FIRM
Alexander Isley Design

ART DIRECTOR
Alexander Isley

DESIGNER
Betty Lin

WRITER
Dorothy Dunn

CLIENT
The Cooper Hewitt National Design Museum and The National Endowment for the Arts

PURPOSE
To explain the concept of design to school children

SIZE
30" x 43"
(76.2cm x 109.2cm)

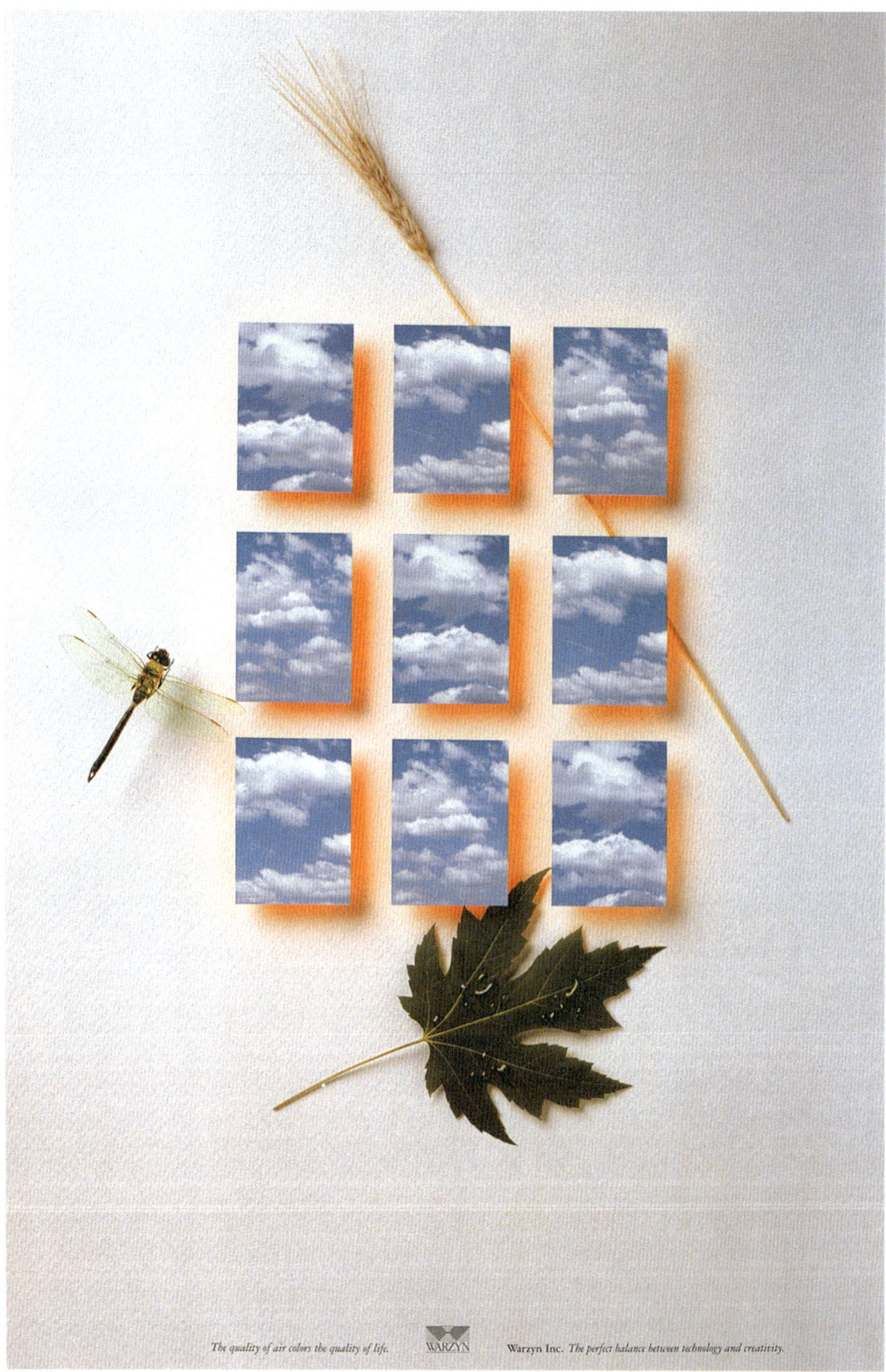

DESIGN FIRM
Hafeman Design Group

DESIGNERS
Bill Hafeman,
Gabrielle Schubart

PHOTOGRAPHER
Art Wise

CLIENT
Warzyn

PURPOSE
New service and capability advertisement

SIZE
22.5" x 34"
(57.1cm x 86.4cm)

lead with your heart

give to the united way

DESIGN FIRM

Peterson & Company

ALL DESIGN

Dave Eliason

CLIENT

Texas Instruments

PURPOSE

United Way fund-raiser

SIZE

23" x 32"

(58.4cm x 81.2cm)

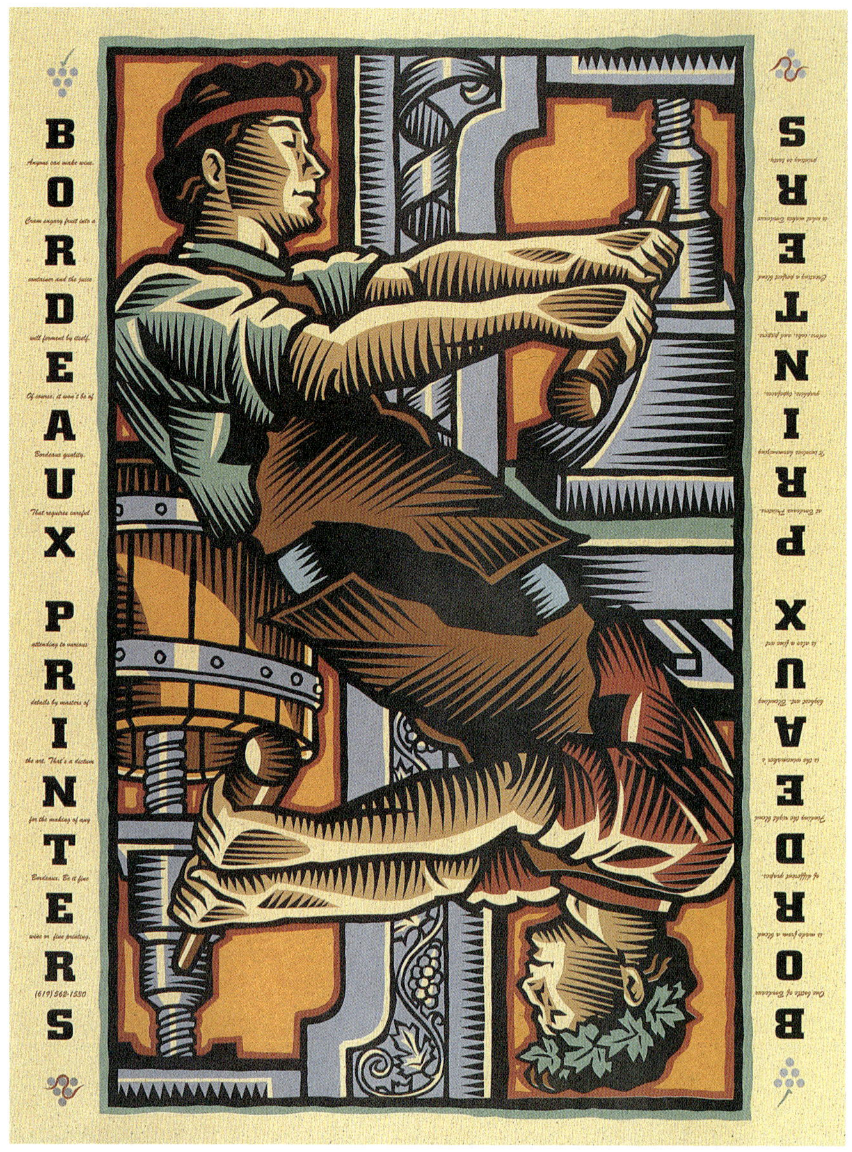

DESIGN FIRM
Tracy Sabin Graphic Design

ART DIRECTOR
José Serrano

DESIGNER
José Serrano

ILLUSTRATOR
Tracy Sabin

CLIENT
Bordeaux Printers

Purpose
Offset printer
self-promotion

SIZE
18" x 24" (45.7cm x 61cm)

DESIGN FIRM
NBA Properties, Inc.

ART DIRECTOR
Tom O'Grady

DESIGNER
Suzanne Gulbin

ILLUSTRATOR
Diane Borowski

CLIENT
NBA Properties, Inc

PURPOSE
NBA All-Star Weekend promotion

SIZE
18" x 36"
(45.7cm x 91.4cm)

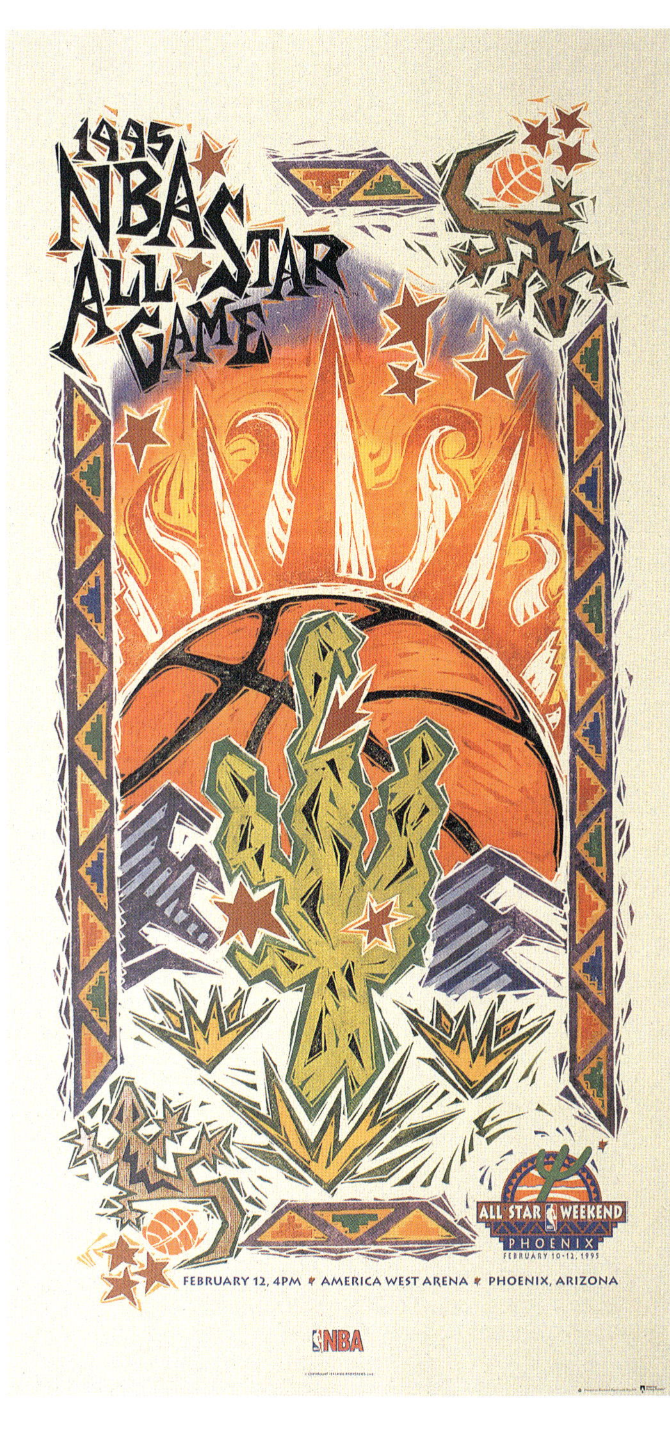

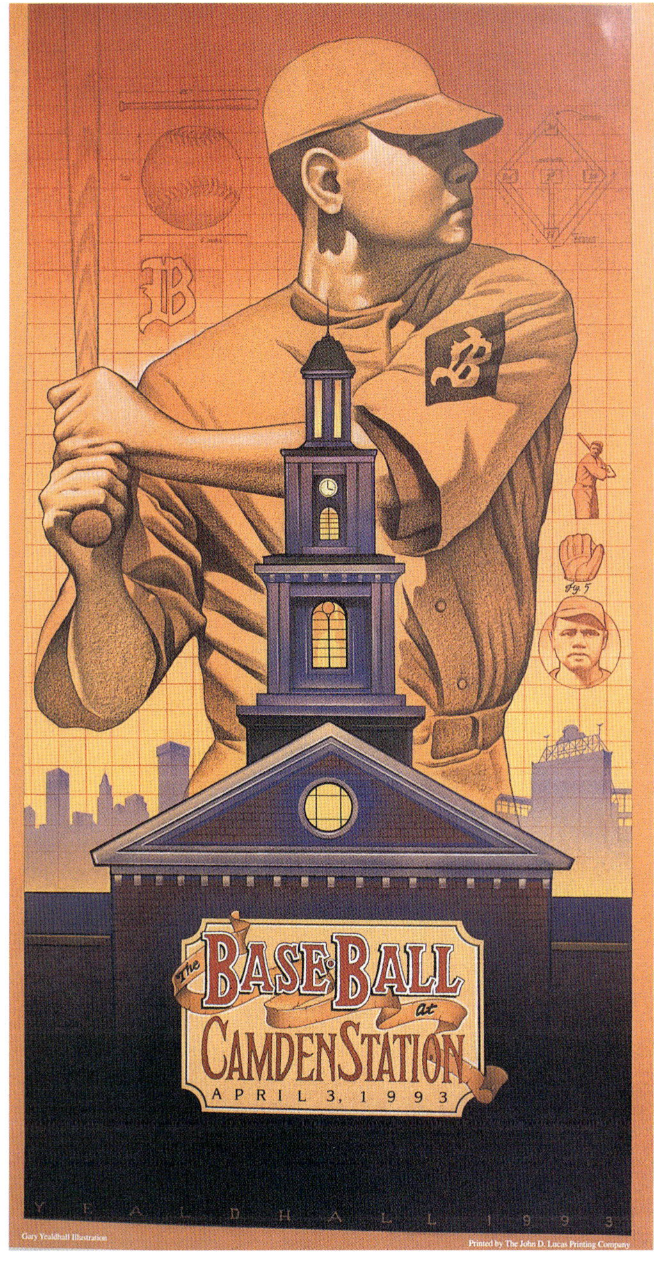

DESIGN FIRM
TBC Design

ART DIRECTOR
Lenny Rosenthal

ILLUSTRATOR
Gary Yealdhall

CLIENT
Babe Ruth Museum

PURPOSE
Babe Ruth Museum opening promotion

SIZE
16" x 30"
(40.6cm x 76.2cm)

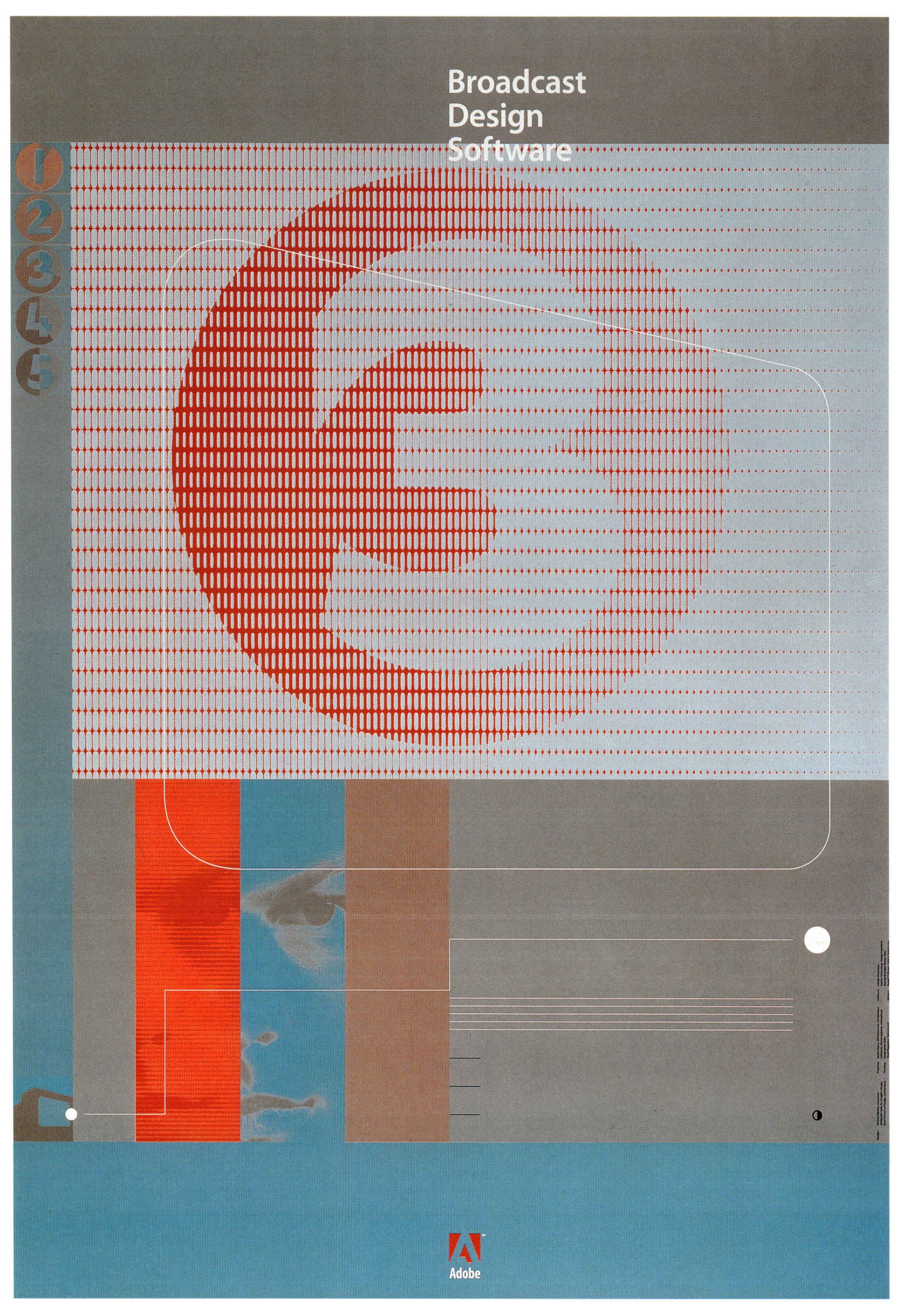
Broadcast
Design
Software
1
2
3
4
5
Adobe

DESIGN FIRM

Basel School of Design

ART DIRECTOR

Michael Renner

DESIGNER

Michael Renner

ILLUSTRATOR

Michael Renner

CLIENT

Adobe Systems Inc.,

Mountain View, CA

PURPOSE

Promotion

SIZE

35.5" x 50"

(90.5cm x 128cm)

DESIGN FIRM

Basel School of Design

ART DIRECTOR

Michael Renner

DESIGNER

Rick Mallarky

ILLUSTRATOR

Rick Mallarky

CLIENT

Adobe Systems Inc.,

Mountain View, CA

PURPOSE

Promotion

SIZE

35.5" x 50"

(90.5cm x 128cm)

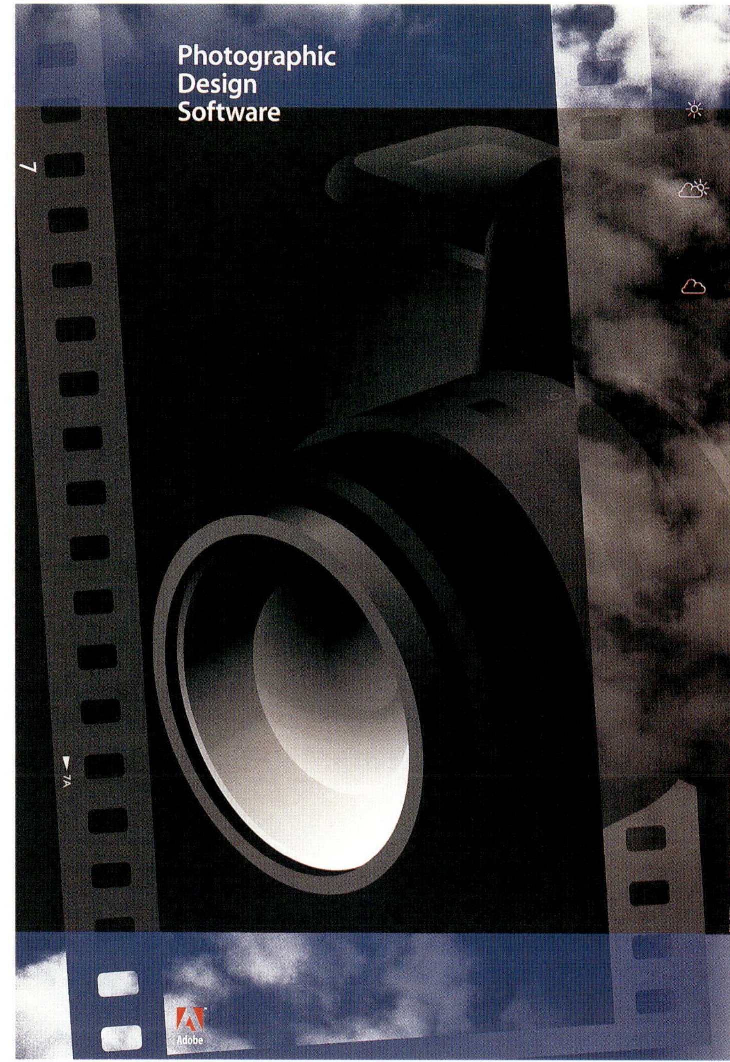

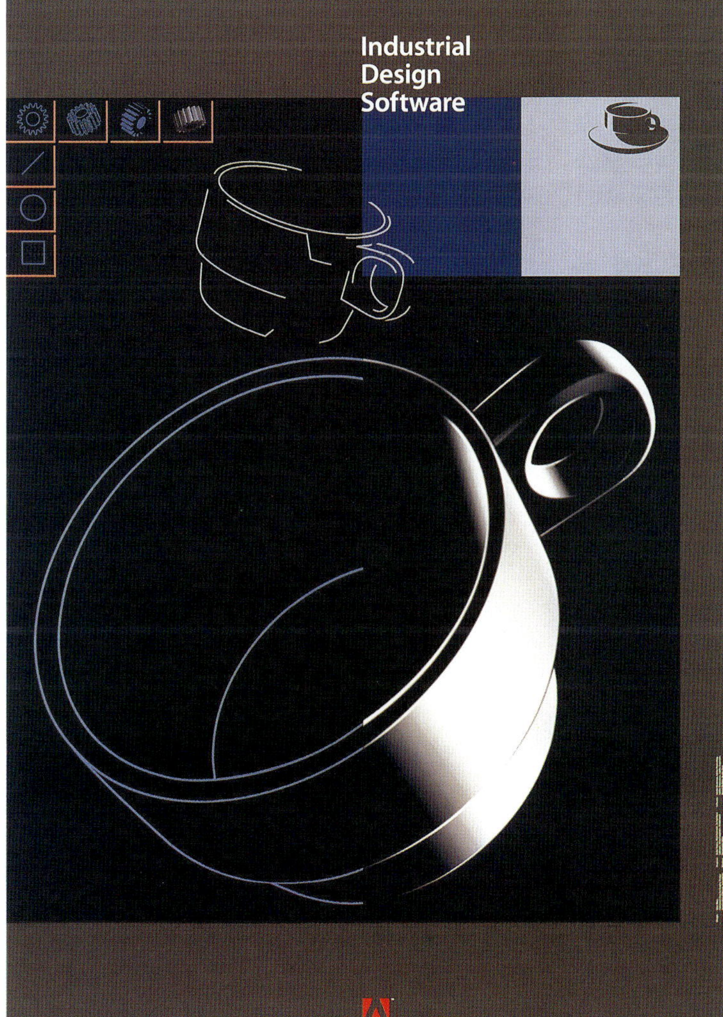

DESIGN FIRM

Basel School of Design

ART DIRECTOR

Michael Renner

DESIGNER

Gary Moss

ILLUSTRATOR

Gary Moss

CLIENT

Adobe Systems Inc.,

Mountain View, CA

PURPOSE

Promotion

SIZE

35.5" x 50"

(90.5cm x 128cm)

[facing page and this page]
All posters were designed and produced with Adobe software: Illustrator, Photoshop, Dimensions, Separator, and the font, Myriad. Films were produced with Agfa Select Set 7000.

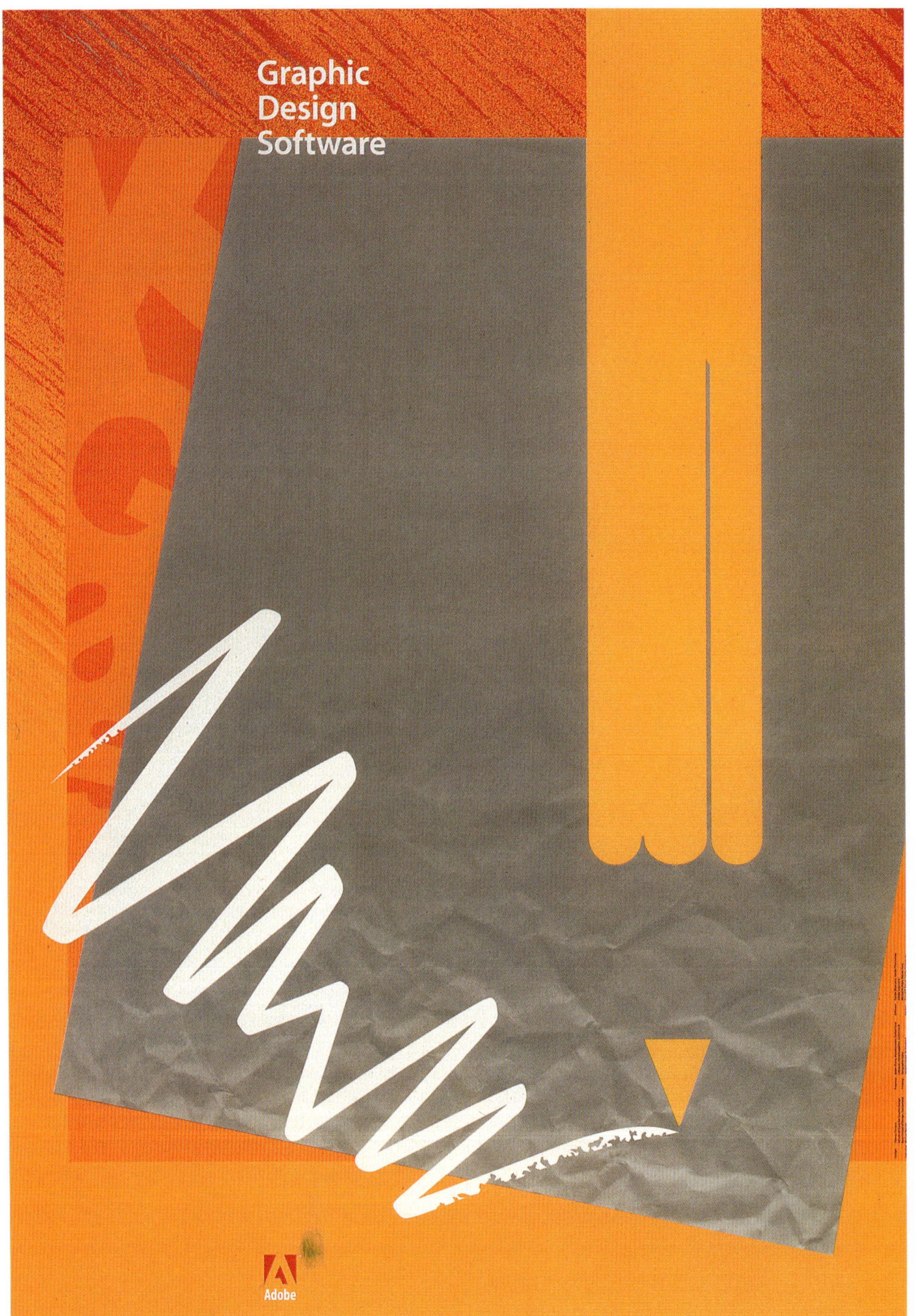

DESIGN FIRM
Basel School of Design

ART DIRECTOR
Michael Renner

DESIGNER
Thomas Ferraro

ILLUSTRATOR
Thomas Ferraro

CLIENT
Adobe Systems, Inc.
Mountain View, CA

PURPOSE
Promotion

SIZE
35.5" x 50"
(90.5cm x 128cm)

Poster was designed and produced with Adobe software: Illustrator, Photoshop, Dimensions, Separator, and the font, Myriad. Films were produced with Agfa Select Set 7000.

DESIGN FIRM
Jon Wells Associates

ART DIRECTOR
Jon Wells

DESIGNER
Jon Wells

ILLUSTRATOR
Dick Cole

CLIENT
New Century Chamber Orchestra

PURPOSE
Chamber orchestra promotion

SIZE
24" x 18" (61cm x 45.7cm)

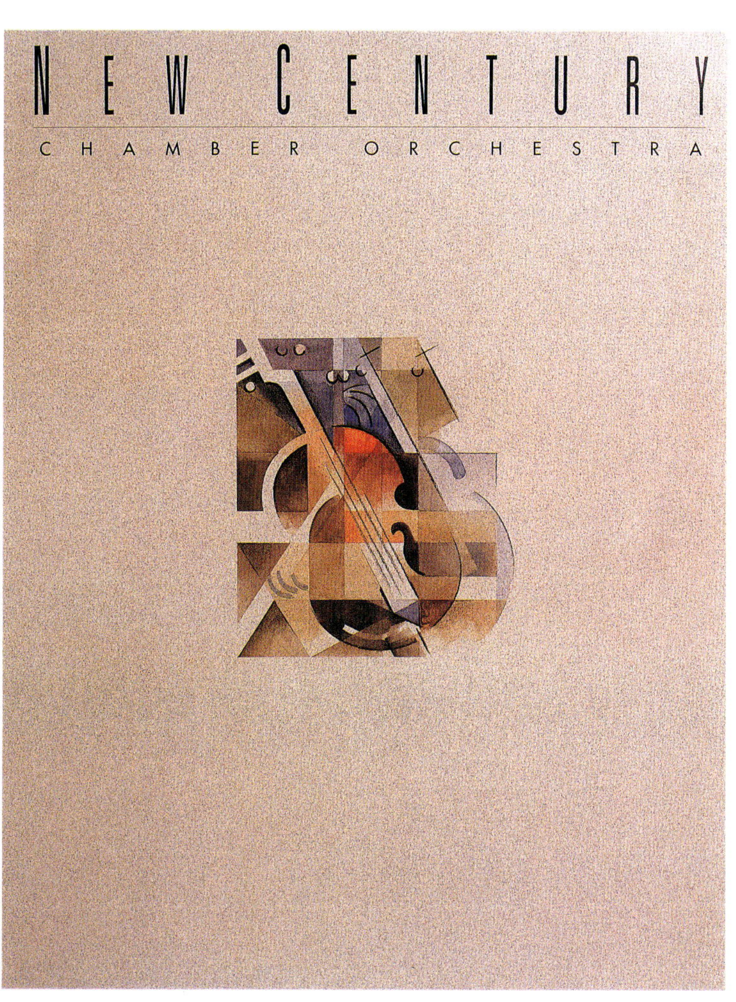

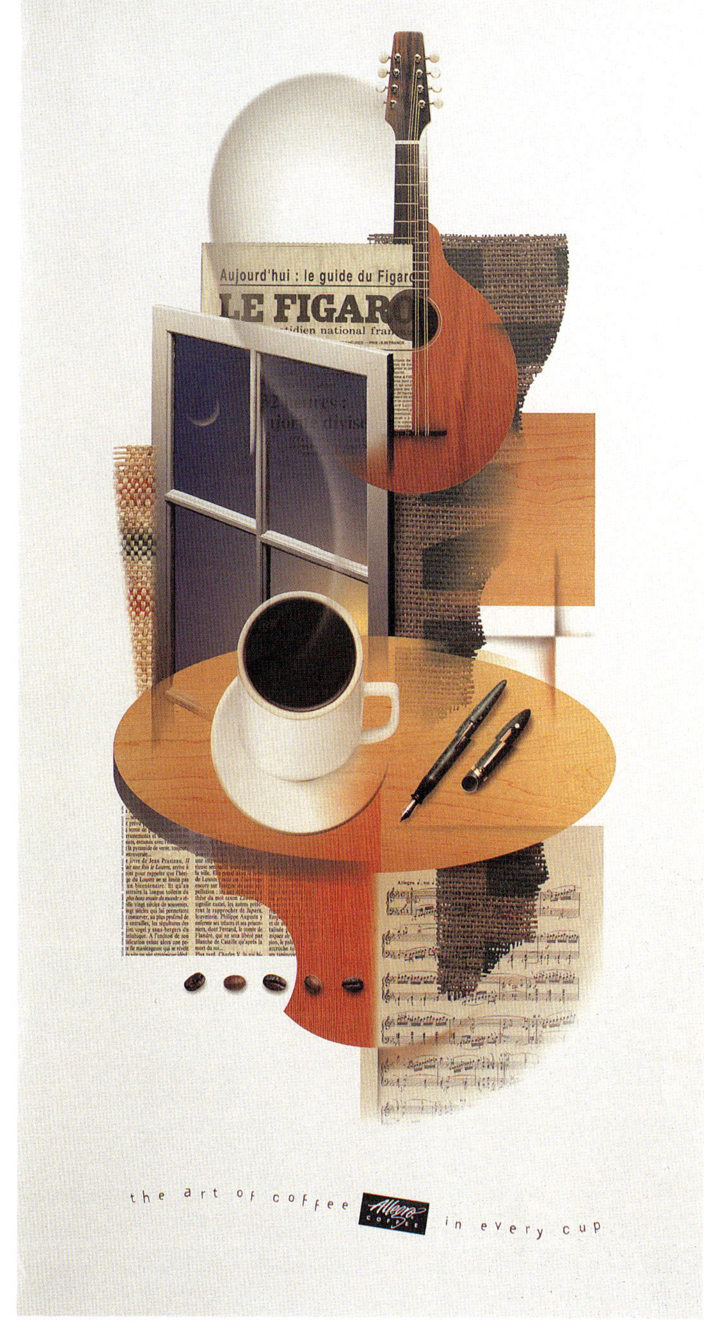

DESIGN FIRM
Vermilion Design

ART DIRECTOR
Robert J. Morehouse

DESIGNER
Janet Vogel

ILLUSTRATOR
James Vogel

PHOTOGRAPHER
Brian Mark

CLIENT
Allegro Coffee Company

PURPOSE
Sales support

SIZE
30" x 16"
(76.2cm x 40.6cm)

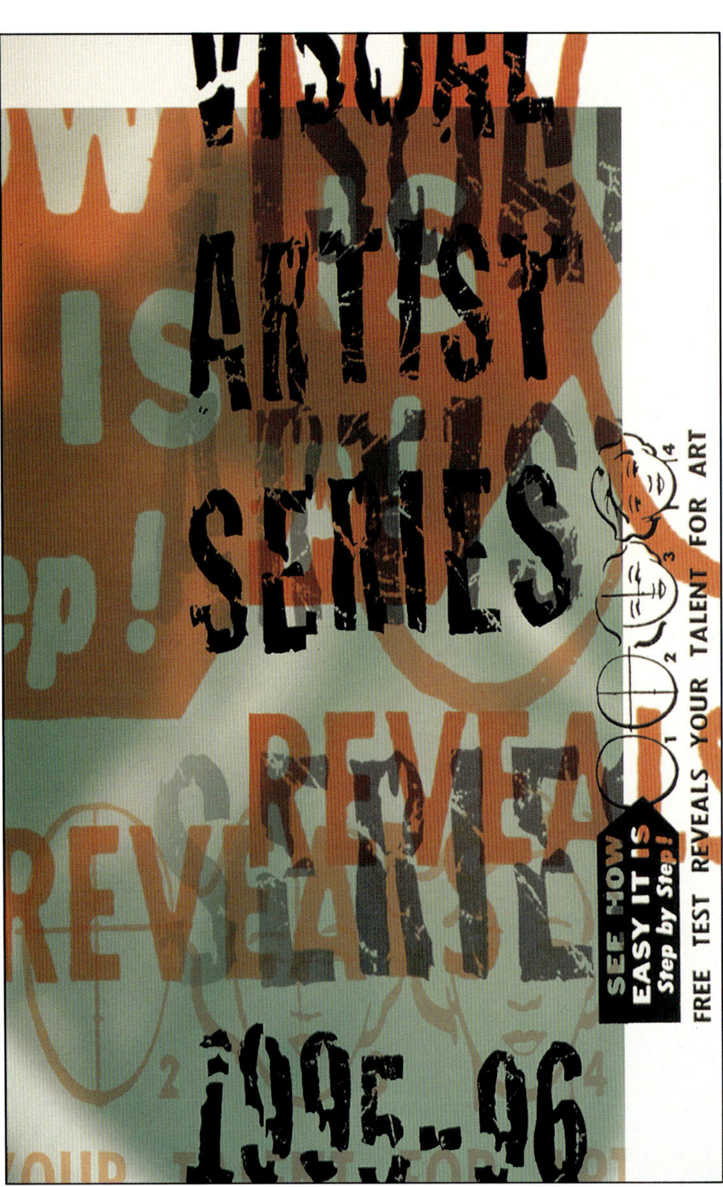

DESIGN FIRM
Design/Art, Inc.

ALL DESIGN
Norman Moore

CLIENT
Mark Spector Management/ Vanguard Records

PURPOSE
Record promotion

SIZE
24" x 36" (61cm x 91.4cm)

[facing page]
Still life of a photo collection and flowers was shot through a diffused lens and combined with art paper in QuarkXPress.

DESIGN FIRM
re: salzman design

ALL DESIGN
Rick Salzman

CLIENT
SUNY Plattsburgh

PURPOSE
Symposium promotion

SIZE
17" x 22" (43.2cm x 55.9cm)

[above and right]
The designer used Aldus FreeHand and Adobe Photoshop. These posters were output directly to film at actual size.

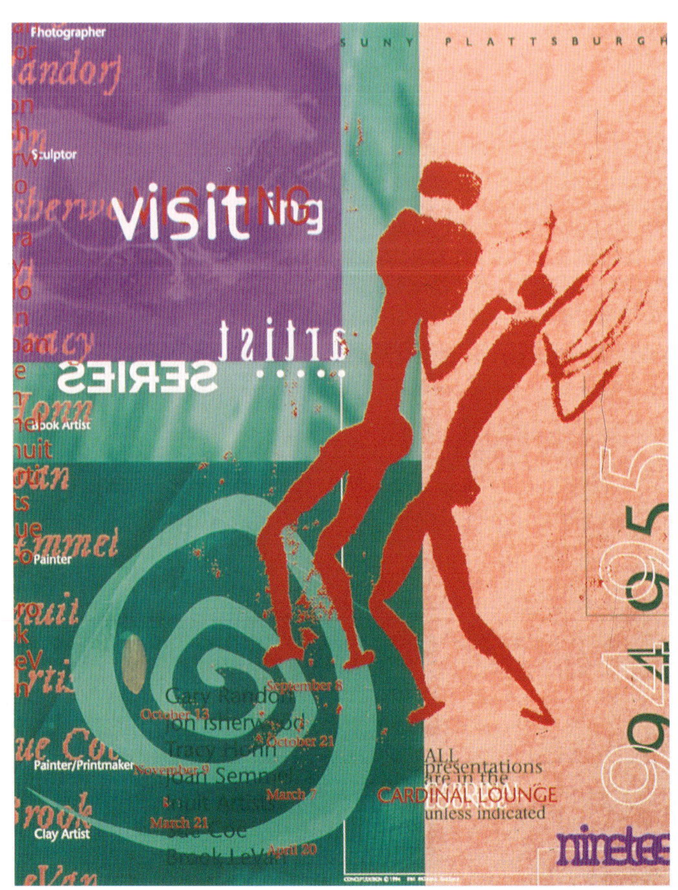

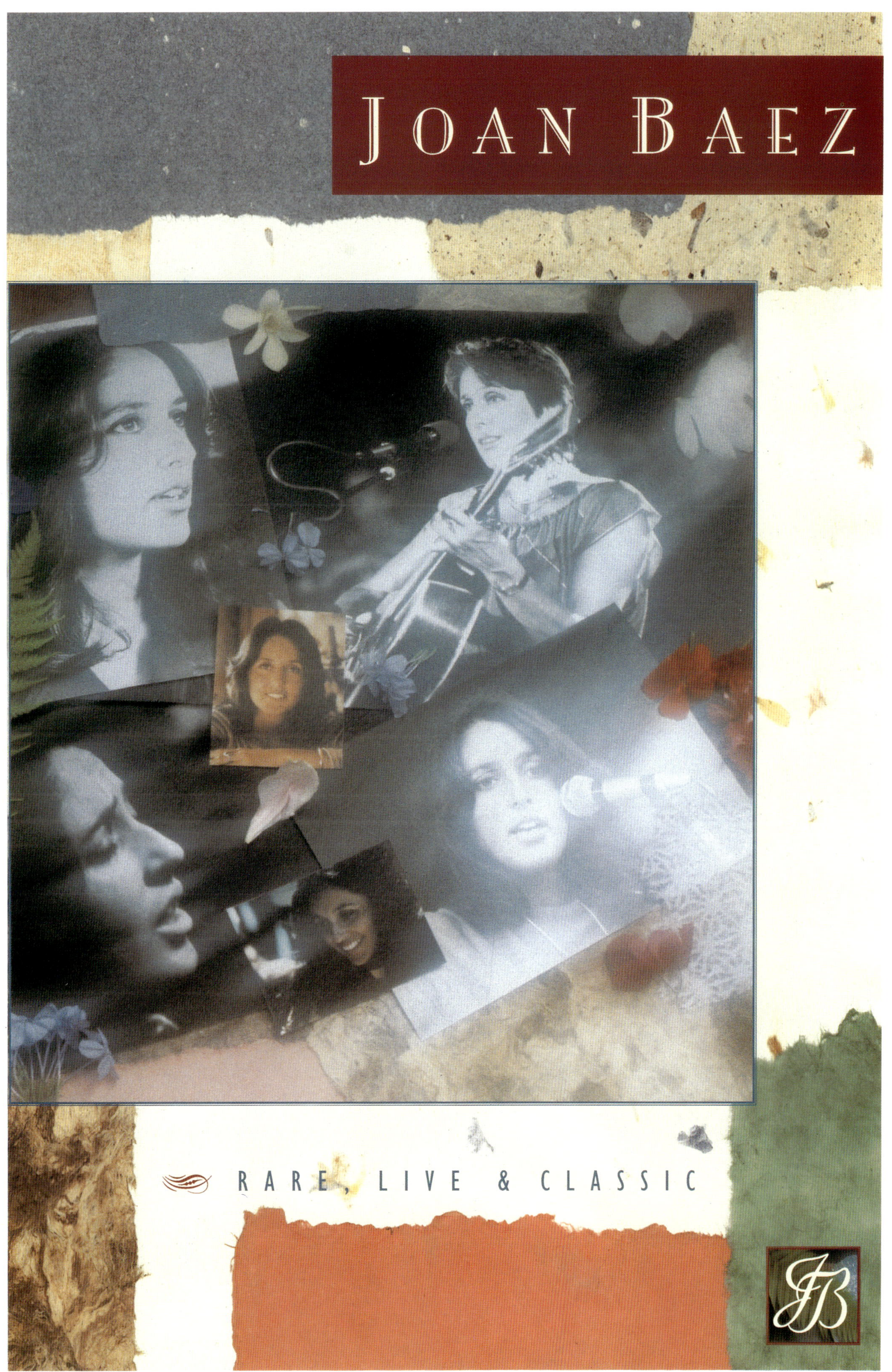
JOAN BAEZ
RARE, LIVE & CLASSIC
JB

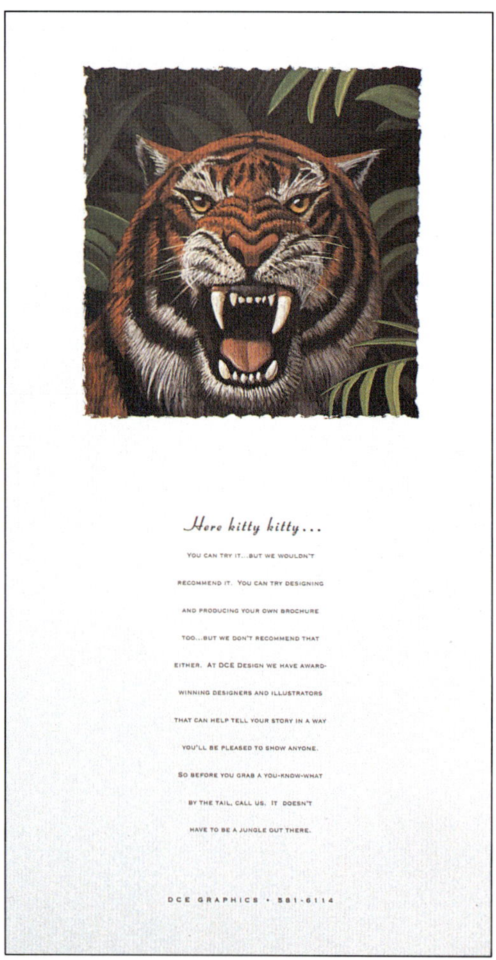

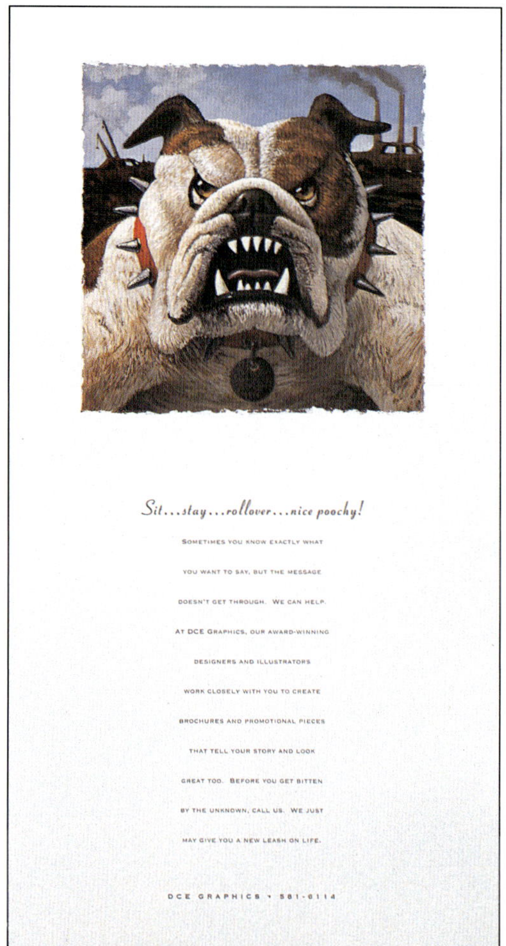

DESIGN FIRM
DCE Design

ART DIRECTOR
Scott Greer

DESIGNER
David Meikle

ILLUSTRATOR
David Meikle

CLIENT
DCE Marketing/Design

PURPOSE
Self Promotion

SIZE
9" X 16.5"
(22.86 cm x 42 cm)

The illustration for this poster was created by hand, using acrylic on gessoed etching paper.

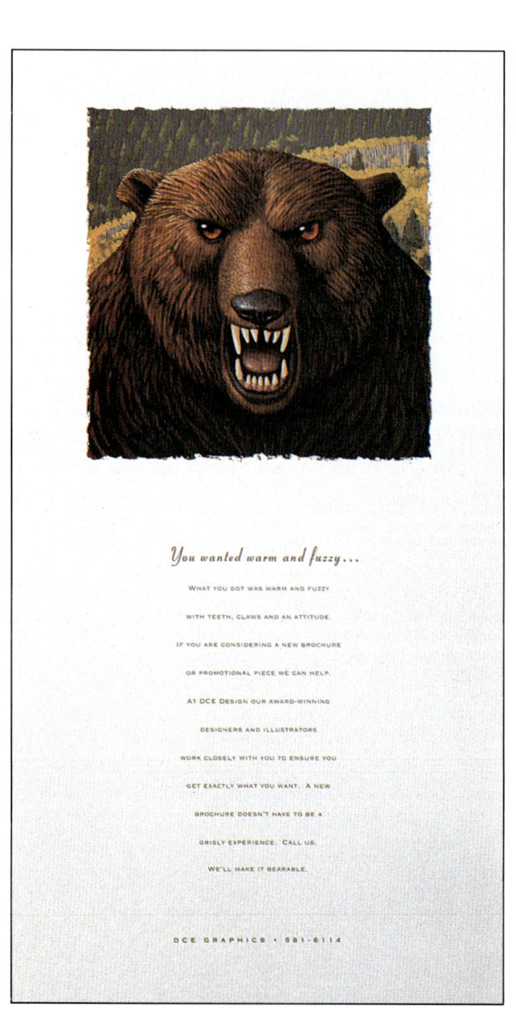

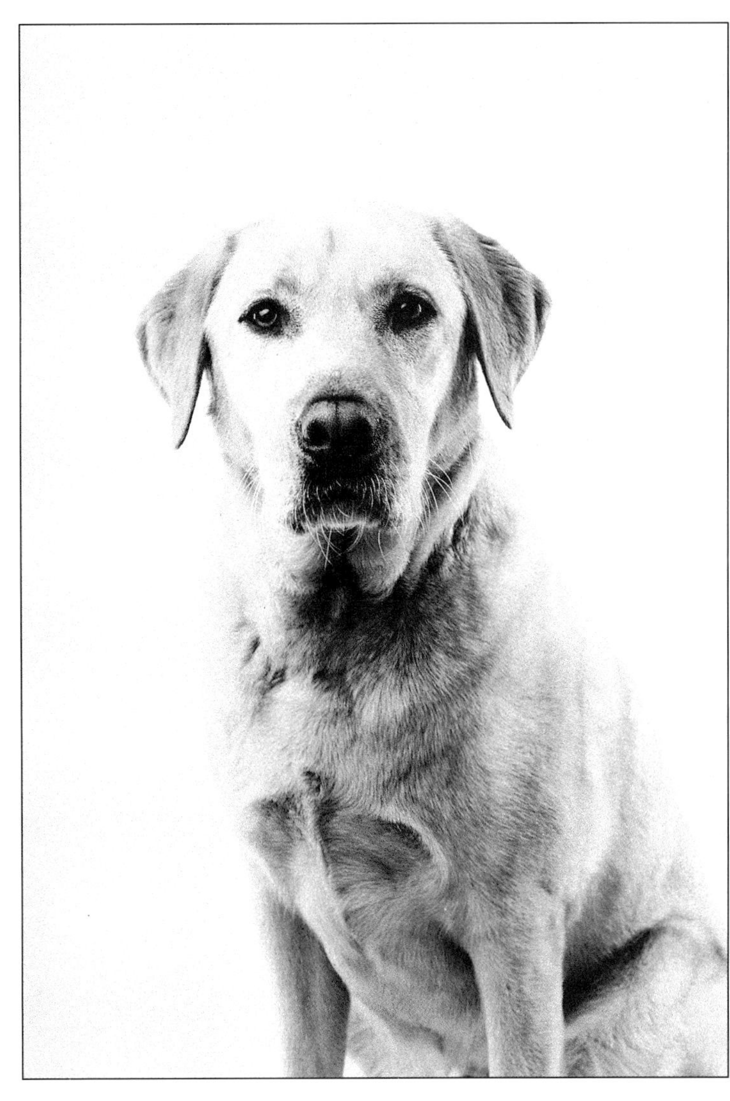

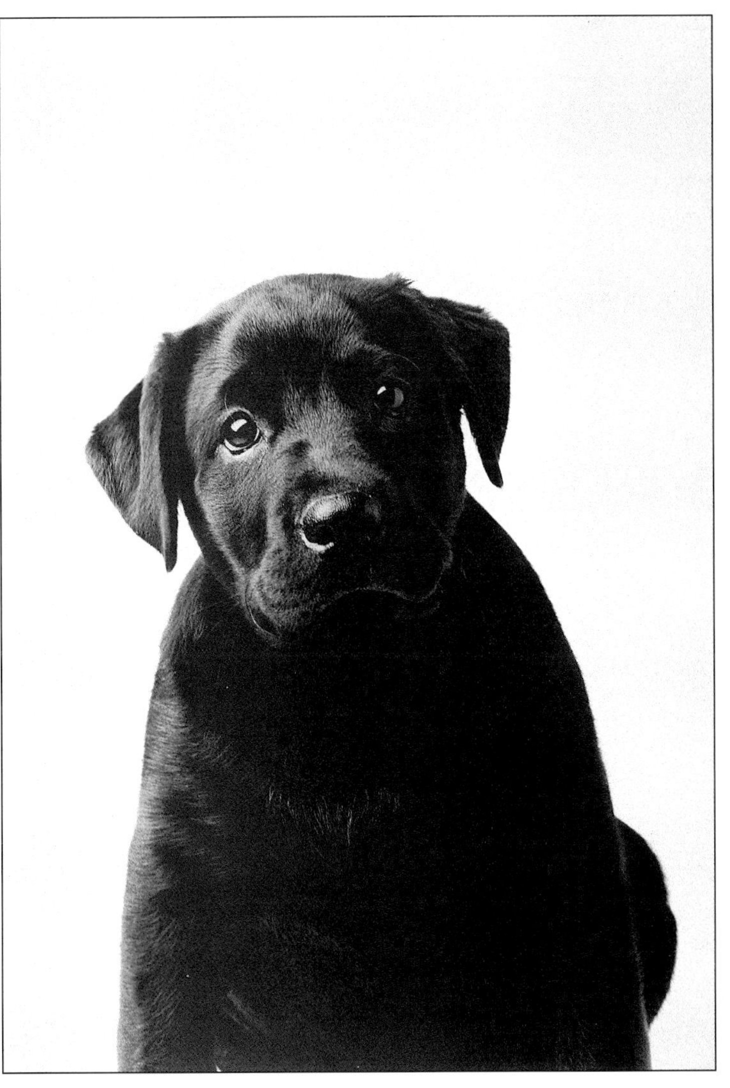

D E S I G N   F I R M

Raymond Bennett Design

A R T   D I R E C T O R

Ray Bennett

D E S I G N E R

Gina Batsakis

P H O T O G R A P H E R

Mark Llewellynn

C L I E N T

Guide Dog Association

P U R P O S E

Public relations

S I Z E

14" x 20"

(35.5 cm x 50.8 cm)

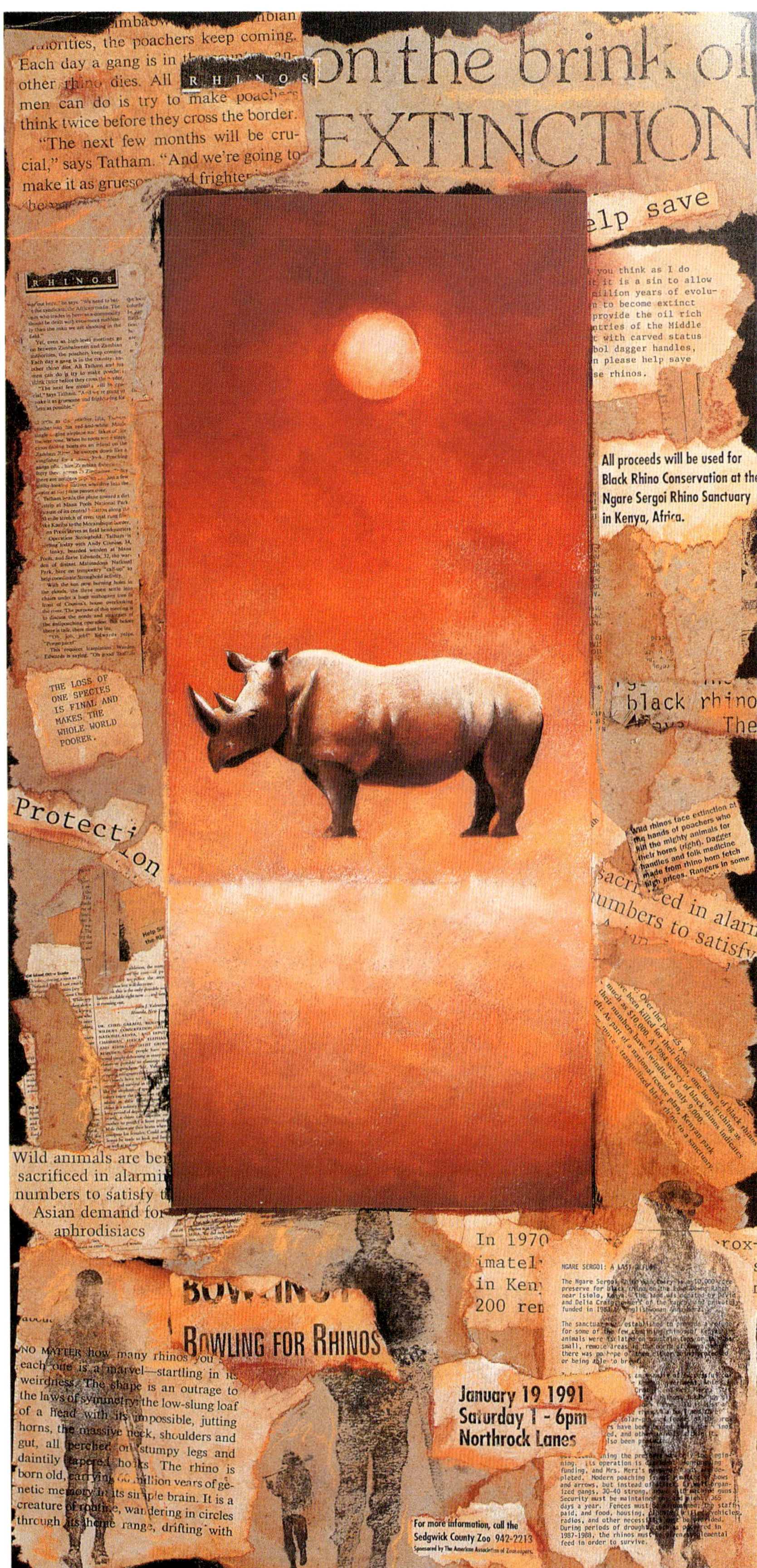

DESIGN FIRM
Greteman Group

ART DIRECTOR
Sonia Greteman

DESIGNER
Sonia Greteman

ILLUSTRATOR
Sonia Greteman

CLIENT
John Coultis

PURPOSE
Christmas Poster

SIZE
12" x 20"
30.5 cm x 50.8 cm)

DESIGN FIRM
Marla Murphy/LA

DESIGNER
Marla Murphy

ILLUSTRATOR
Marla Murphy

CLIENT
ESU Reptile,
Energy Savers Unlimited, Inc.

PURPOSE
Introduce reptile line
to pet industry

SIZE
22.875" x 29.125"
(58.1cm x 74cm)

Illustration is a soft pastel drawing. First in a series for the client, two more posters are planned for new products.

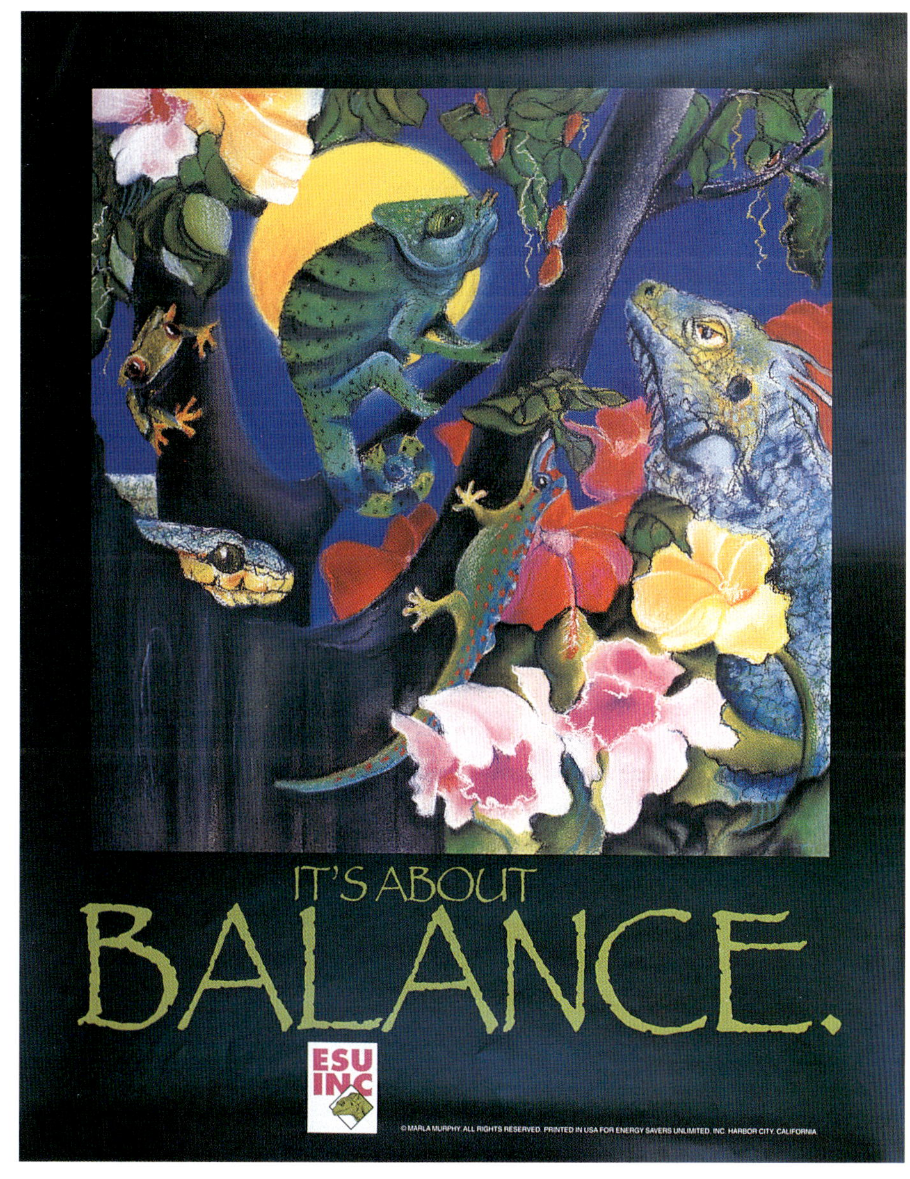

DESIGN FIRM
Sackett Design Associates

ART DIRECTOR
Mark Sackett

DESIGNERS
Mark Sackett, Wayne Sakamoto,
James Sakamoto, Mirjam Patscheider,
Tamar Kondy, Chandra Crissman

CLIENT
Brainfood Creative Programs

PURPOSE
Promotion

SIZE
5" x 30" (12.7cm x 76.2cm)

Found images of antique dolls and labels were scanned in and arranged into a background collage. The poster demonstrates how diverse one's research can be when looking for creative inspiration.

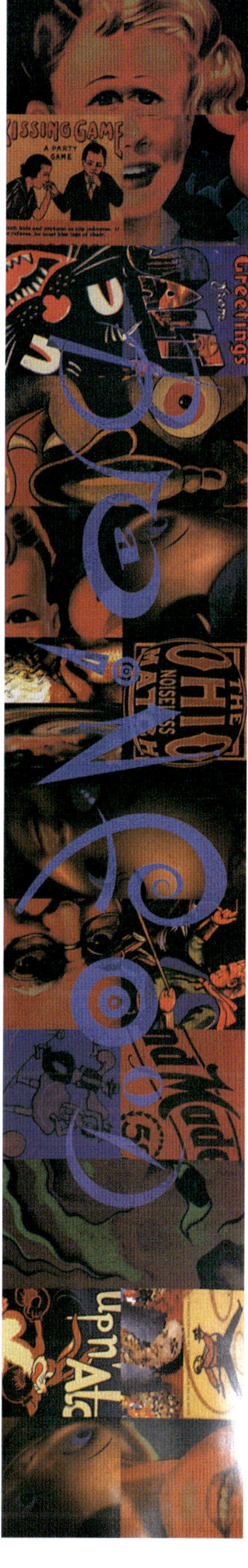

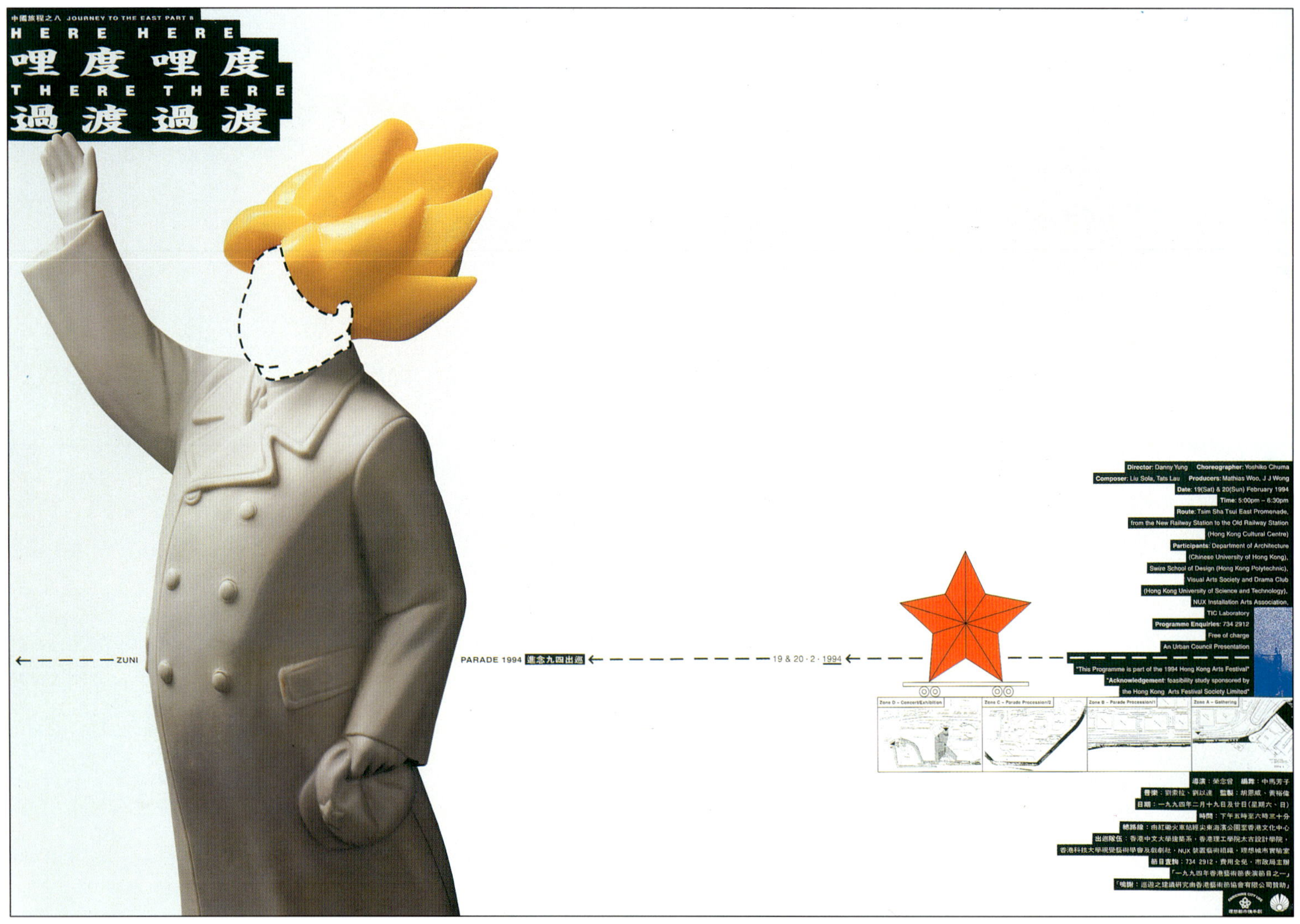

DESIGN FIRM
Kan Tai-keung Design & Associates Ltd.

ART DIRECTOR
Freeman Lau Siu Hong

DESIGNERS
Freeman Lau Siu Hong, Veronica Cheung Lai Sheung

PHOTOGRAPHER
C K Wong

CLIENT
Zuni Icosahedron

PURPOSE
Drama promotion

SIZE
28" x 39" (71.1cm x 99.1cm)

In this poster, the images of Mao and a red star are used to express the strong influence China has over the political situation in Hong Kong. However Hong Kong is in many ways also affected by popular culture. Therefore the hair of the Mao's statue appearing on the poster in fact belonged to a character in a very popular Japanese cartoon - Dragon Ball.

DESIGN FIRM
Art Chantry Design

ALL DESIGN
Art Chantry

CLIENT
Belltown P-Patch

PURPOSE
Grand opening concert promotion

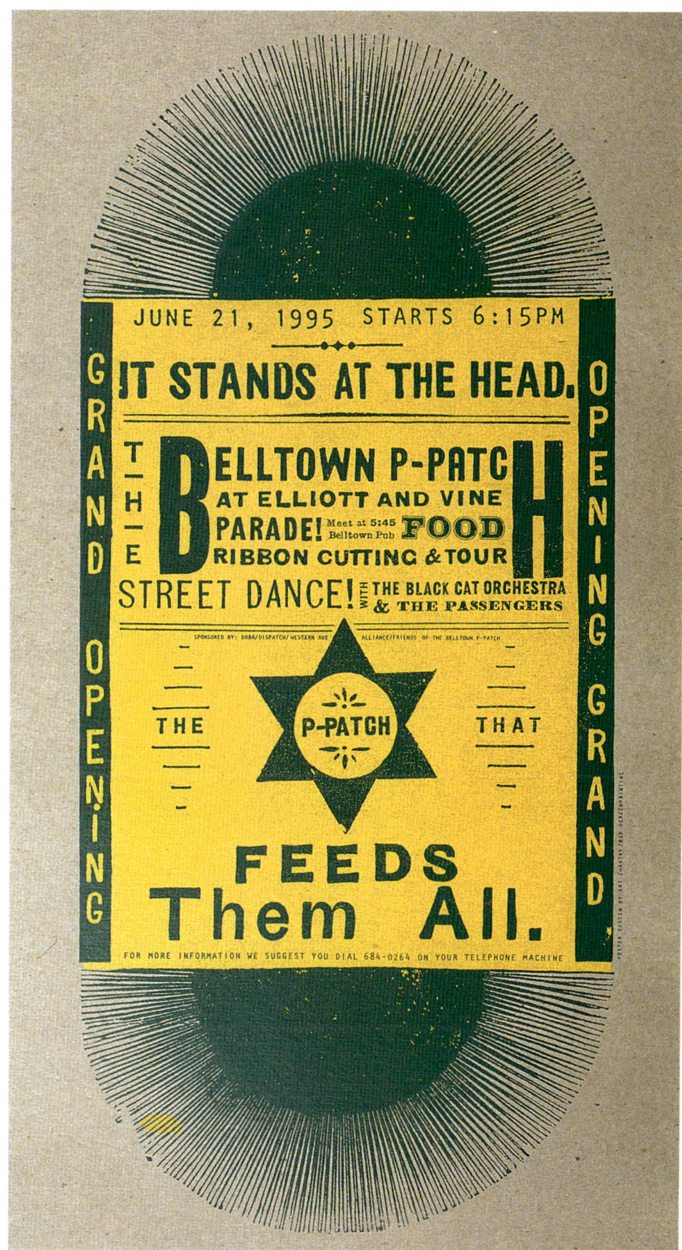

DESIGN FIRM
Luis Fitch Design Lab

ALL DESIGN
Luis Fitch

PHOTOGRAPHER
Paul Brown

CLIENT
Luis Fitch Design Lab

PURPOSE
Self-promotion

SIZE
24" x 36" (61cm x 91.4cm)

Luis Fitch's motto is, "Necessity is the mother of creativity." When he wanted to do a poster promoting his illustration style and studio but didn't have the money to go all-out he came up with a low-budget solution that did the trick. For the poster, 500 emulsions were generated on ASA Premium Opaque Diazo paper at minimal cost.

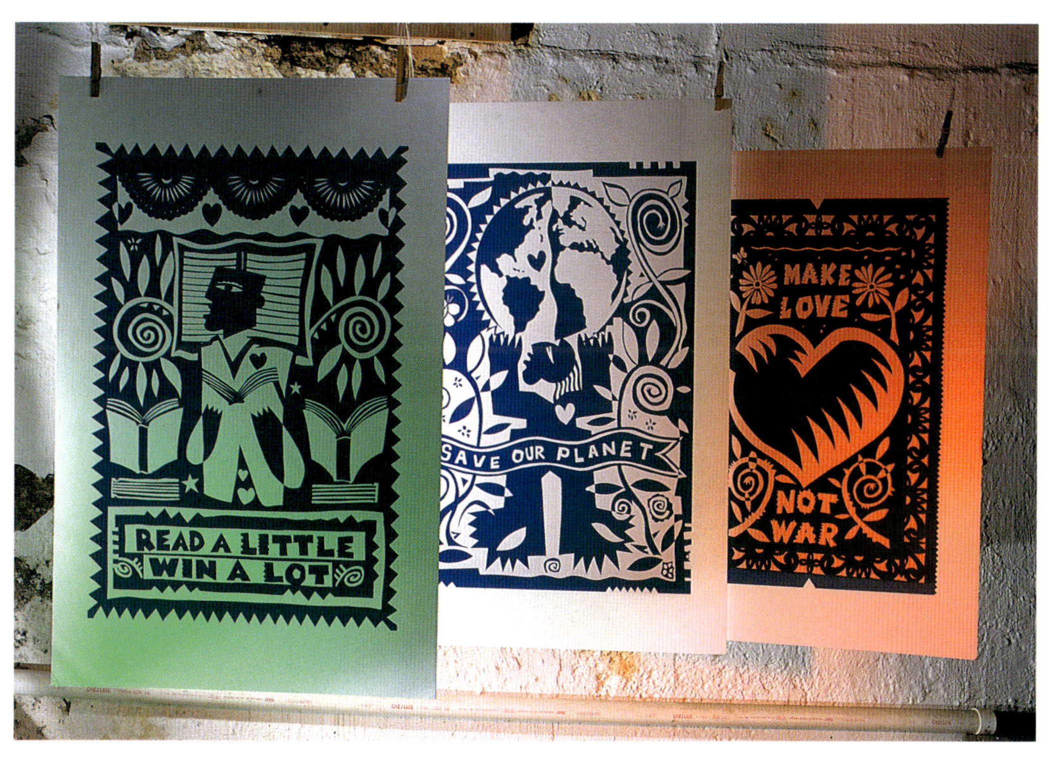

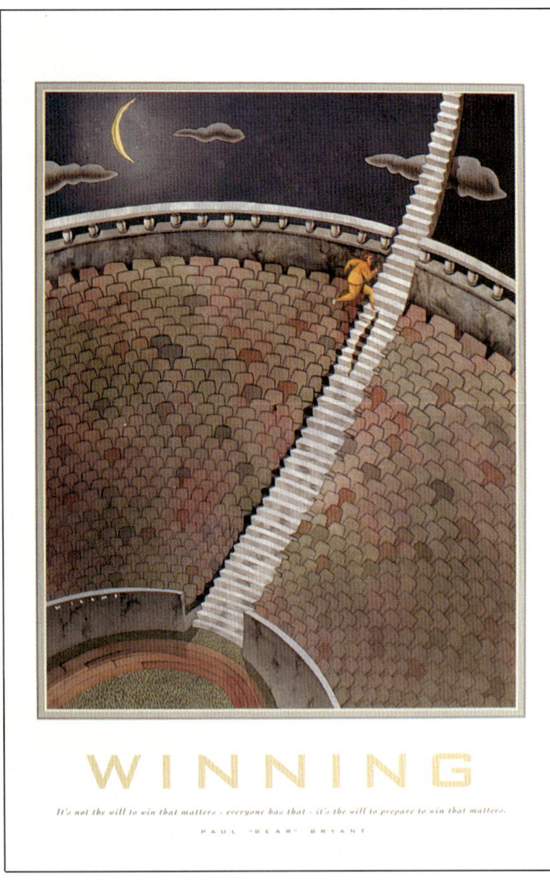

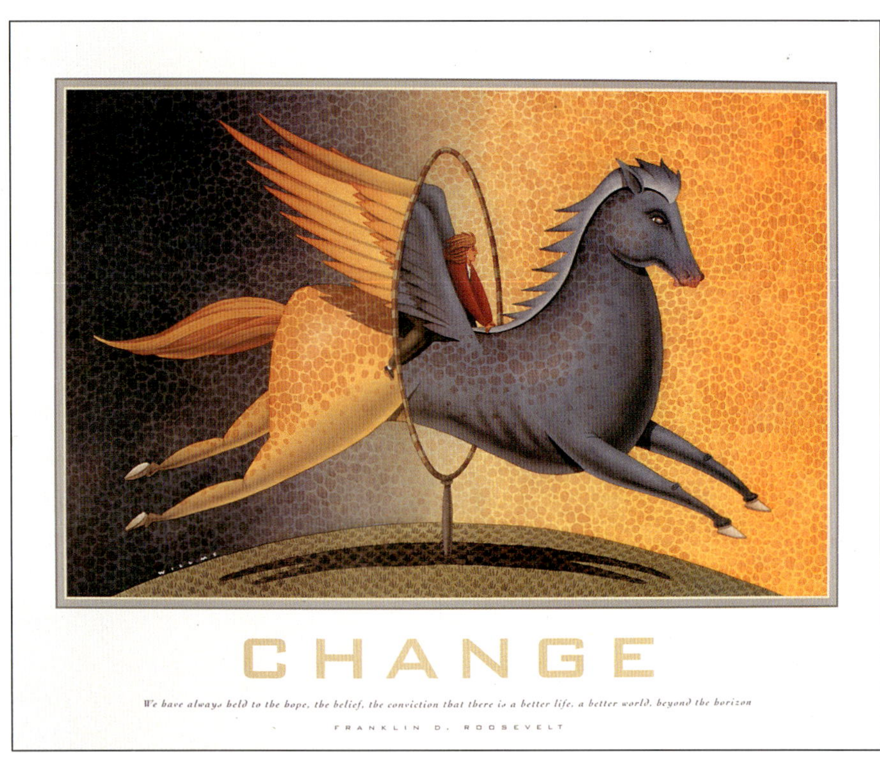

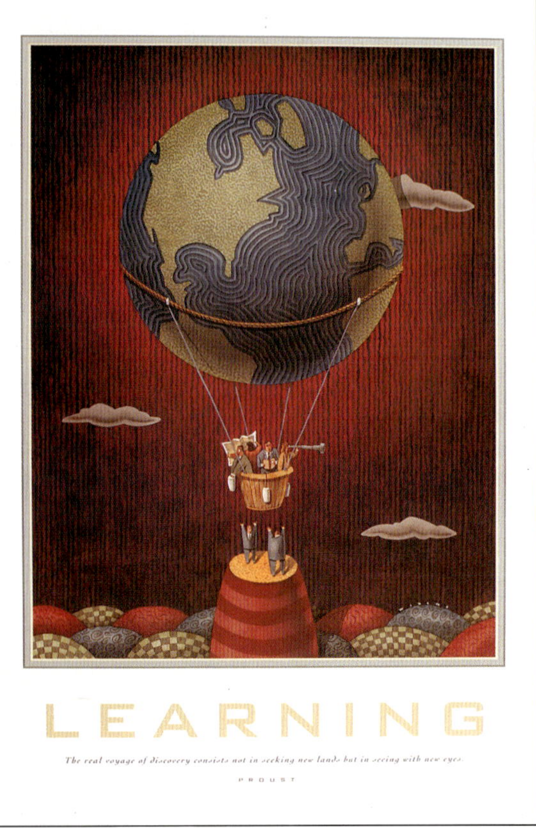

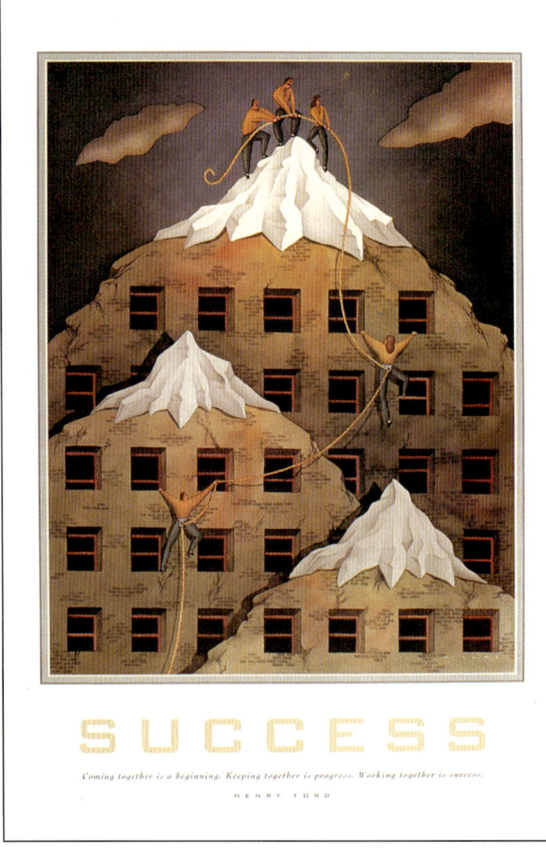

DESIGN FIRM
Suburbia Studios

ALL DESIGN
Russ Willms

CLIENT
Priority Management
(Series - 4)

PURPOSE
Retail

SIZE
18" x 24"
(45.7cm x 61cm)

DESIGN FIRM
Keiler Design Group

ART DIRECTOR
Christopher Passehl

DESIGNER
Christopher Passehl

PHOTOGRAPHER
Woodruff/Brown

CLIENT
Hartford Stage

PURPOSE
Play announcement

SIZE
20.5" x 34"
(52.1cm x 86.4cm)

directory

Alexander Isley Design
361 Broadway
New York, NY 10012

Antero Ferreira Design
Rua De Roriz 203
P-4100 Porto
PORTUGAL

Art Chantry Design
P.O. Box 4069
Seattle, WA 98104

Basel School of Design
Vogelsangstrasse 15
CH-4058 Basel
SWITZERLAND

Becker Design
225 East Saint Paul Avenue
Suite 300
Milwaukee, WI 53202

Boelts Brothers Visual
Communication Association
345 East University
Tucson, AZ 85705

Bōwker Design
120 Elm Street
Apartment SH30
Beverly, NJ 08010

Buttgereit & Heindenreich
Kommunikationsdesign
Recklinghäuser Strasse 2
D-45721 Haltern am See
GERMANY

BYU Graphics
527 N 2400 West
Provo, UT 84601

Clifford Selbert Design Collaborative
2067 Massachusetts Avenue
Cambridge, MA 02140

Cranbrook Academy of Art
Box 801
Bloomfield Hills, MI 48013

DCE Design
University of Utah
1157 Annex
Salt Lake City, UT 84112

Design Ahead
Kirchfeldstrasse 16
45219 Essen-Kettwig

Design/Art, Inc.
6311 Romaine Street
Los Angeles, CA 90038

Duncan Day Advertising
14850 Monfort, 131
Dallas, TX 75240

Dyer Mutchnick Group, Inc.
8360 Melrose Avenue
3rd Floor
Los Angeles, CA 90069

Emerson, Wajdowicz Studios, Inc.
1123 Broadway
New York, NY 10010

Eskind Waddell
471 Richmond Street West
Toronto, Ontario M5V 1X9
CANADA

Frank Heymann
AM Hoptengarten 4
D-30165 Hannover
GERMANY

Frazier Design
600 Townsend Street, #412 W
San Francisco, CA 94103

FUSE
420 Armour Circle NE
Atlanta, GA 30324

Futura
Livarska 12, Ljubljana
SLOVENIA

Grand Design Company
Room 1901, Valley Centre
80 Morrison Hill Road
HONG KONG

Greteman Group
142 North Mosley Street 3A
Wichita, KS 67202

Grouplzl
855 Boylston Street
Boston, MA 02116-2668

Gruppe Gut
222 West 14th Street, #15A
New York, NY 10011

Hafeman Design Group
935 West Chestnut, Suite 203
Chicago, IL 60622

Heins Creative, Inc.
1242 North 28th Street, Suite 4A
Billings, MT 59101

Hesse Designagentur GmbH
Rosmarinstrasse 12 k
D-40235, Düsseldorf
GERMANY

HMM Communications
57 Hope Street
2nd Floor
Brooklyn, NY 11211

Hornall Anderson Design Works, Inc.
1008 Western Avenue
Suite 600
Seattle, WA 98104

Images
Walter McCord Graphic Design
2014 Cherokee Parkway
Louisville, KY 40204

Jan Rimerman
P.O. Box 1350
Lake Oswego, OR 97035

Jay Vigon Studio
11833 Brookdale Lane
Studio City, CA 91604

Jon Wells Associates
407 Jackson Street, #206
San Francisco, CA 94111

Joseph Rattan Design
5924 Pebblestone Lane
Plano, TX 75093

Jowaisas Design
4 Oxbow Road
Cazenovia, NY 13035

Kaiserdicken
149 Cherry Street
Burlington, VT 05401

Kan Tai-keung Design & Associates
Ltd.
28/F Great Smart Tower
230 Wenchai Road
HONG KONG

Keiler Design Group
304 Main Street
Farmington, CT 06032

Larry Grossman
5309 Cold Water Canyon
Sherman Oaks, CA 91401

Leslie Chan Design Company, Ltd.
4F, 115 Nanking E. Road. Section 4
Taipei
TAIWAN

Louise Fili Ltd.
71 5th Avenue
New York, NY 10003

Luis Fitch Design Lab
1171 Neal Avenue
Columbus, OH 43201

Margo Chase Design
2255 Bancroft Avenue
Los Angeles, CA 90039

Marla Murphy/LA
2317 Edgewater Terrace
Los Angeles, CA 90039

Masterline Communications, Ltd.
Room 1902, Valley Centre
80 Morrison Hill Road
HONG KONG

Matsumoto Incorporated
17 Cornelia Street
New York, NY 10014

Maximum Marketing
430 West Erie Street
Suite 406
Chicago, IL 60610

McMonigle & Spooner
818 East Foothill Boulevard
Monrovia, CA 91016

Mike Salisbury Communications, Inc.
2200 Amapola Court
Torrance, CA 90501

Mink Design
537 N 2400 West
Provo, UT 84601

Mires Design, Inc.
2345 Kettner Boulevard
San Diego, CA 92101

Morla Design
463 Brynat Street
San Francisco, CA 94107

Muller + Company
4739 Belleview
Kansas City, MO 64112

NBA Properties, Inc.
450 Harmon Meadow Boulevard
Secaucus, NJ 07094

Nippon Design Center, Inc.
1-13-13 Ginza, Chuo-ku
Tokyo 104
JAPAN

Noonan Media
410 NW 18th Avenue
Suite 402
Portland, OR 97209

Oakley Design Studios
519 SW Park Avenue, #521
Portland, OR 97205

Ostro Design
147 Fern Street
Hartford, CT 06105

PandaMonium Designs
14 Mount Hood Road
Boston, MA 02135

Paul Kaza Associates
1233 Shelburne Road, C-3
South Burlington, VT 05403

Pentagram Design
204 Fifth Avenue
New York, NY 10010

Peterson & Company
2200 North Lamar, 310
Dallas, TX 75202

Plaid Cat Design
147 East Chestnut Street
Apartment 6
Asheville, NC 28801

Planet Design Company
229 State Street
Madison, WI 53703

Primo Angeli, Inc.
590 Folsom Street
San Francisco, CA 94105

Ramona Hutko Design
9607 Bulls Run Parkway
Bethesda, MD 20817

Raymond Bennett Design
202/349 Pacific Highway
Crows Nest, NSW
AUSTRALIA

Richards & Swenson, Inc.
350 South 400 East
Suite 300
Salt Lake City, UT 84111

Rickabaugh Graphics
384 West Johnstown Road
Gahana, OH 43230

The Riordon Design Group Inc.
131 George Street
Oakville, Ontario L6J-3B9
CANADA

Ron Kellum, Inc.
151 First Avenue PH-1
New York, NY 10003

Sackett Design Associates
2103 Scott Street
San Francisco, CA 94115-2120

re: salzman designs
293 Rabideau Street
Cadyville, NY 12918

Sea Dog Press
17 Bay Street
Watertown, MA 02172

Segura Inc.
361 West Chestnut Street
1st Floor
Chicago, IL 60610

Sharon Baden
12943 Clifton Boulevard, #206
Cleveland, OH 44107-1519

Sibley/Peteet Design
965 Slocum
Dallas, TX 75207

Stephen Peringer Illustration
17808 184th Avenue NE
Woodinville, WA 98072

Steve Lundgren Graphic
Design/Spangler Design Team
6524 Walker Street, #205
Minneapolis, MN 55426

Studio M D
1512 Alaskan Way
Seattle, WA 98101

Suburbia Studios
53 Tovey Crescent
Victoria, British Columbia V9B 1A4
CANADA

SullivanPerkins
2811 McKinney
Suite 320
LB111
Dallas, TX 75204

TBC Design
138 West 25th Street
Baltimore, MD 21218

Texas Parks and Wildlife Department
Graphics Department
4200 Smith School Road
Austin, TX 78744

Tom Fowler, Inc.
9 Webbs Hill Road
Stamford, CT 06903

Towers Perrin
200 West Madison
Suite 3100
Chicago, IL 60606

Tracy Sabin Graphic Design
13476 Ridley Road
San Diego, CA 92129

Trend Design Ltd.
1119 Hing Wai Centre
No. 7 Tin Wan Praya Road
Aberdeen
HONG KONG

Vaughn Weeden Creative, Inc.
407 Rio Grande NW
Albuquerque, NM 87104

Vermilion Design
2595 Canyon Boulevard
Boulder, CO 80302

Walcott-Ayers Group
1230 Preservation Road
Oakland, CA 94612

Watt, Roop & Co.
1100 Superior Avenue
Cleveland, OH 44114

Watts Graphic Design
79 Palmerston Crescent South
Melbourne, Victoria 3205
AUSTRALIA

Witherspoon Advertising
1000 West Weatherford
Fort Worth, TX 76102

WTS Studios
1300 Bobby Lane #305
Westlake, OH 44145

Yamamoto Moss
252 First Avenue North
Minneapolis, MN 55401

Yellow M
The Arch, Hawthorn House
Forth Banks
Newcastle upon Tyne
ENGLAND, NE1 3SG

Zauhar Design
510 First Avenue North #405
Minneapolis, MN 55403

index

Alexander Isley Design 136, 137, 139

Antero Ferreira Design 120

Art Chantry Design 155

Basel School of Design 144, 145, 146

Becker Design 129

Boelts Brothers Visual Communication Associates 131

Bōwker Design 138

Buttgereit & Heindenreich 30

BYU Graphics 87

Clifford Selbert Design Collaborative 128

Cranbrook Academy of Art 123

David Schultz 45

DCE Design 150

Design Ahead 102

Design/Art, Inc. 49, 50, 51, 52, 53, 149

Duncan Day Advertising 58, 59

Dyer Mutchnick Group 65, 66, 67, 68, 69, 70

Emerson, Wajdowicz Studios, Inc. 28

Eskind Waddell 132

Frank Heymann 48

Frazier Design 96

FUSE 13

Futura 102

Grand Design Co. 46, 47

Greteman Group 85, 152

Grouplzl 41

Gruppe Gut 26

Hafeman Design Group 95, 140

Heins Creative, Inc. 62, 63, 64

Hesse Designagentur GmbH 113

HMM Communications 6

Hornall Anderson Design Works, Inc. 84

Images 29

Jan Rimerman 107

Jay Vigon Studio 134

Jon Wells Associates 147

Joseph Rattan Design 88

Jowaisas Design 57

Kaiserdicken 22

Kan Tai-keung Design & Associates Ltd. 12, 14, 15, 16, 17, 18, 19, 20, 21, 105, 106, 109, 154

Keiler Design Group 40, 128, 157

Larry Grossman 56

Leslie Chan Design Co., Ltd. 124, 125

Louise Fili Ltd. 88, 89

Luis Fitch Design Lab 155

Margo Chase Design 6, 7

Marla Murphy/LA 153

Masterline Communications, Ltd. 46

Matsumoto Incorporated 104

Maxim Marketing 27

McMonigle & Spooner 108

Mike Salisbury Communications, Inc. 103, 126, 127

Mink Design 86

Mires Design, Inc. 73, 75, 78, 90, 91

Morla Design 93

Muller + Company 42

NBA Properties, Inc. 143

Nippon Design Center, Inc. 24, 25

Noonan Media 76

Oakley Design Studios 81

Ostro Design 87

PandaMonium Designs 101

Paul Kaza Associates 92

Pentagram Design 97, 98, 99, 100

Peterson & Company 80, 81, 82, 83, 141

Plaid Cat Design 130

Planet Design Co. 111, 112, 114, 115, 118, 119, 121

Primo Angeli, Inc. 54, 55

Ramona Hutko Design 94

Raymond Bennett Design 151

Richards & Swensen, Inc. 74

Rickabaugh Graphics 111

The Riordan Design Group Inc. 132

Ron Kellum, Inc. 28

Sackett Design Associates 55, 153

re: salzman designs 148

Sea Dog Press 23

Segura Inc. 74

Sharon Baden 79

Sibley/Peteet Design 32, 33

Stephen Peringer Illustration 71

Steve Lundgren Graphic Design/ Spangler Design Team 44

Studio Dunbar 8

Studio M D 35

Suburbia Studios 72, 156

SullivanPerkins 10, 11, 33

TBC Design 143

Texas Parks and Wildlife Department 110

Tom Fowler, Inc. 76, 77

Towers Perrin 43

Tracy Sabin Graphic Design 60, 61, 138, 142

Trend Design Ltd. 34

Vaughn Weeden Creative, Inc. 36, 37, 133

Vermilion Design 147

Walcott-Ayers Group 79

Watt, Roop & Co. 9, 122

Watts Graphic Design 31

Witherspoon Advertising 117

WTS Studios 116

Yamamoto Moss 61

Yellow M 38, 39

Zauhar Design 135